THE JOHN HARVARD LIBRARY

Bernard Bailyn
Editor-in-Chief

ROUTE FROM LIVERPOOL
TO
GREAT SALT LAKE VALLEY

By

FREDERICK HAWKINS PIERCY

Edited by Fawn M. Brodie

THE BELKNAP PRESS OF
HARVARD UNIVERSITY PRESS
Cambridge, Massachusetts
1962

CONTENTS

ROUTE FROM LIVERPOOL
TO
GREAT SALT LAKE VALLEY

CONTENTS

Chapter VI.

Chapter XIX.

Chapter XX.

Chapter XXI.

ILLUSTRATIONS

[following page 112]

STEEL ENGRAVINGS

[plates]

WOOD CUTS

[figures]

Introduction

Few painters of the American West have had their pictures reproduced as often as Frederick Hawkins Piercy. One sees portraits and
landscapes taken from his *Route from Liverpool to Great Salt Lake
Valley* (Liverpool, 1855) in anthologies of the gold rush, in general
histories of the area, and in countless books on Mormonism. The
original volume, however, with its gentle, factual narrative of a voyage with a group of Mormon converts sailing from Liverpool to New
Orleans, a steamboat ride up the Mississippi, and an overland journey by wagon to the Mormon Zion, has become rare.

Piercy himself has remained obscure, and data concerning his editor, James Linforth, whose voluminous notes elaborated the artist's
journal into a veritable emigrant's guide, have remained scattered
and thin. Yet the book is remarkable on several counts besides the
pictures, one of them being the fact that Piercy wrote the journal
and illustrated it when he was only twenty-three. He was one of the
earliest professional painters to make the overland voyage with the
express purpose of recording his impressions, and one of the best.
At a time when lurid exposés of Mormon polygamy were being
sought after by enterprising publishers he wrote without a whisper
of criticism for Mormon theology or behavior. His tenderness of
Mormon sensibilities might indicate that he may at the time have
been a potential convert—certain of his relatives had become Mormons and emigrated to Salt Lake City—and one should not forget
that his trip was arranged by Mormons in Liverpool, who edited
and published his book.

Piercy did not, however, become a Mormon, and his narrative
maintains throughout a quiet detachment that is reminiscent of the
tone of Captain Howard Stansbury and Captain John W. Gunnison,
both of whom by 1853 had written solid, useful accounts of Mormon
society without any hysterical denunciation.[1] The notes by Linforth

1 Howard Stansbury, *Exploration and Survey of the Valley of the Great Salt Lake
of Utah* (Philadelphia, 1852), and John W. Gunnison, *The Mormons or Latter-Day
Saints* (Philadelphia, 1852).

were placed strategically so as to give the reader an almost encyclo-
pedic commentary on every area through which Piercy passed. The
Mormon history and propaganda included in these notes were written with fervor and bias, but were nevertheless remarkably free of
cant, and the amount of factual information packed into the lines
of fine print is a tribute to the industry and intelligence of the editor.
In addition to the notes, most of which came from published sources,
there was a short history of the Mormon emigration movement with
wholly original material, as well as fresh, up-to-date information on
the new Mormon colonies extending outward from Great Salt Lake
City.

Frederick Piercy was born in Portsmouth, England, on January
27, 1830. By 1848, at eighteen, he was a talented artist with sufficient
professional attainment to have a portrait exhibited at the Royal
Academy of Arts in London. Between 1848 and 1880 he exhibited
in the Royal Academy altogether eleven times. The majority were
portraits, but there were several landscapes and one piece of sculpture,
the bust of "a gentleman." The portraits include one of a navy captain, R. N. Denman, and one of J. Risdon Bennett, President of the
Royal College of Physicians. It is to be presumed that he made portraits of similarly distinguished citizens of which there is no record,
but his reputation in England seems to have been limited. The
Royal Academy reports that his London address shifted frequently;
there are on file eight different addresses, which suggests restlessness
or poverty or both.[2]

In 1873, when he was forty-three, he published an eight-page illustrated pamphlet, *A Crucial Test in Cases of Disputed Identity*. Unfortunately, the only copy of this to reach the British Museum was
destroyed during an air raid in 1941. The Library of Congress has
no copy. In 1881 Piercy was stricken with paralysis. He lingered for
ten years, dying in London on June 10, 1891, at the age of sixty-one.[3]
It seems unlikely that he was able to continue painting through
these years, for 1880 was the last year he exhibited at the Royal
Academy.

[2] For a complete listing of Piercy's Royal Academy pictures see Algernon Graves,
*The Royal Academy of Arts, a complete dictionary of contributors and their work
from its foundation in 1769 to 1904* (London, 1906), Vol. VI.

[3] Information about his paralysis and death was furnished Robert Taft by the General Register Office, Somerset House, London, Certificate DA 093867. See Taft's *Artists
and Illustrators of the Old West, 1850–1900* (New York, 1953), p. 285.

Piercy's fame rests on the single volume resulting from his visit to America as a young man of twenty-three. This was a matter partly of talent, partly of timing. The book was published when there was an explosion of settlements in the West. Emigrants had been streaming to Oregon since 1842; Mormon converts were converging on Salt Lake City from every portion of the United States and several European countries, and a sizeable fraction of the nation's youth was en route to the California goldfields. Guides, maps, and journals were devoured by a public passionate to go west; they were read with an eye to utility, not historical perspective. Every exploring expedition had at least one naturalist, an artist if he could be found, and, after 1850, a photographer. Men handy with a pencil were common; good artists were rare.

Moreover, the Mormons encouraged Piercy's trip at a crucial period in their own history. In 1852, the year before his departure from Liverpool, Mormon officials for the first time had publicly acknowledged that they had been practising polygamy for almost a decade, and the whole church was awaiting with some trepidation the expected onslaught in the press and the adverse reaction in Congress. More important, the Mormon leaders wanted a detailed emigrant's guide sympathetic toward their own people, something written from the British point of view and aimed specifically at the thousands of Mormon converts in the British Isles. They wanted a book that would not deny polygamy but that would treat the explosive issue with dignity and extreme brevity.

In 1853 the Mormon missionary system in Great Britain was an astonishing force. Sixteen years earlier, when the Latter-day Saints consisted of little more than an obscure pocket of converts in Kirtland, Ohio, and a secondary pocket in Independence, Missouri, Joseph Smith ordered three of his ablest men, Heber C. Kimball, Orson Hyde, and Willard Richards, to organize a mission in England. Their success was immediate. In 1839, when the Mormons were expelled from Missouri with great brutality and migrated to Nauvoo, Illinois, Brigham Young and other of Joseph Smith's "apostles" left their newly constructed cabins and crossed the sea to continue the proselyting work in England. They were able men, blessed with organizing talent and fired with millennial zeal.

Many of these missionaries had lost everything in the Panic of 1837 and had tasted the fury of the anti-Mormon persecutions in

Missouri. They had a first-hand acquaintance with want and were travelling and preaching "without purse or scrip." Nevertheless, the poverty, unemployment, and wretched housing they found in the British cities appalled them. Thousands of workers were crowded into squat tenements, built without water or sewers, and almost without windows. Sporadic strikes were suppressed with cruelty, and the reform movement known as Chartism was looked upon as the dread specter of revolution. The hated Corn Laws were then in force, stifling trade and doubling the cost of bread. George A. Smith wrote back to Nauvoo: "I have seen more beggars here in one day than I saw in all my life in America."[4]

The Mormon elders were soon preaching the glory of America along with the glory of the new religion, and Brigham Young was specifically advocating emigration as the solution for the European problem of overpopulation. The *Millennial Star,* published by the missionaries in Liverpool, pointed out on February 1, 1842, that living in America was about one-eighth of what it cost in England. For the new convert, it said, "millions on millions of acres of land lie before them unoccupied, with a soil as rich as Eden, and a surface as smooth, clear and ready for the plough as the park scenery of England. Instead of a lonely swamp or dense forest filled with savages, wild beasts and serpents, large cities and villages are springing up in their midst, with schools, colleges, and temples . . . there being abundant room for more than a hundred millions of inhabitants."

The murder of Joseph Smith and the subsequent expulsion of the Mormons from Illinois in 1846 brought a two-year cessation in the emigration. It was not resumed until five months after Brigham Young and the first contingent of Mormon emigrants arrived in the valley of the Great Salt Lake. Then the word went back: "To the Saints in England, Scotland, Ireland, Wales, and adjacent islands and countries, we say, emigrate as speedily as possible to this vicinity. . . . come immediately and prepare to go West—bringing with you all kinds of choice seeds, of grain, vegetables, fruit, shrubbery, trees, and vines—everything that will please the eye, gladden the heart, or cheer the soul of man, that grows upon the face of the whole earth; also the best stock of beast, bird, and fowl of every kind; also, the best tools of every description, and machinery for spinning, or weaving, and

---

[4] Published in the *Times and Seasons,* Nauvoo, Illinois, I, 223 (November 15, 1840).

dressing cotton, wool, flax, and silk. &c., &c., or models and descriptions of the same, by which they can construct them. . . ."

There was a subtle change in tone here from the promise of millions and millions of acres of "soil rich as Eden." Between the lines one can sense the barrenness of the desert, the remoteness and isolation. Nor was the letter without an ominous piece of advice: "The Brethren must recollect that from this point they pass through a savage country, and their safety depends on good fire arms and plenty of ammunition. . . ."

Emigration from Great Britain was officially resumed February 1, 1848, and hailed in Orson Spencer's flowing millennial prose: "The long-wished for time of gathering has come. Good tidings from Mount Zion! The resting place of Israel, for the last days, has been discovered. Beautiful for situation, and the ultimate joy of the whole earth, is the stake of Zion established in the mountains. In the elevated valley of the Salt and Utah Lakes, with the beautiful river Jordan running through it, from south to north, is the newly established stake of Zion."[5]

Between February 1848 and February 1851, 5,369 British "Saints" left for America. By the end of 1855, when Piercy's book was published, the total of Mormon emigrants, including more than a thousand from Scandinavia and Germany, reached 21,911, and the number of converts who had not yet booked passage to Zion swelled to almost 33,000. The *London Times,* which gave the Mormons steady publicity in this period, on September 4, 1855, estimated the total number of Mormons in Great Britain at 30,000 to 40,000, adding, ". . . its combination of Judaism, Mohammedanism, socialism, despotism, and the grossest superstition, with much practical good sense, combine to make it the most singular phenomenon of modern times."

A Mormon shipping agency in Liverpool chartered vessels and insured adequate supplies of food and medicine, insisting on the strictest cleanliness and discipline, and maintaining a morale that astonished observers used to the squalor and suffering on the average emigrant ship. Classes were set up for the children; a regular time was set apart for community prayers, and lectures were organized for adults. A committee of the House of Commons, ordered to ex-

[5] Editor James Linforth included these dispatches in his notes accompanying the Piercy journal.

amine the conditions aboard emigrant ships in 1854, reported more comfort and security aboard the chartered Mormon ships than any others. "The Mormon ship is a Family under strong and accepted discipline," the report said, "with every provision for comfort, decorum, and internal peace."[6]

Charles Dickens in 1863 visited the London docks specifically to see what had become by then a well-known curiosity. He went aboard the *Amazon* on a hot June morning and talked to the captain, who reported that the 800 Mormons "established their own police, made their own regulations, and set their own watches at all the hatchways," making the ship "as orderly and quiet as a man-of-war," and all within two hours of their arrival on board. Dickens noted "great steadiness of purpose and much undemonstrative self-respect," and expressed astonishment at the "universal cheerfulness." He looked hard at "some single women of from thirty to forty . . . obviously going out in quest of husbands, as finer ladies go to India." "That they had any distinct notions of a plurality of husbands or wives, I do not believe," he wrote.[7]

Although the average expense from Liverpool to Council Bluffs, where the covered wagon trains were fitted out, was estimated at £10, this was only part of the total cost. Wagons, horses, mules, and oxen were at a premium in Nebraska Territory, and sharpers duped the innocent, selling inferior teams and equipment, with resulting tragedy in the mountain areas. To spare their own people, Mormons took over the responsibility of outfitting the immigrants and organized them into companies led by experienced men. The rules for Mormon behavior were strict; profanity was no more allowed than whiskey. "It was a discipline to which the Oregon and California immigrants would never have submitted," Dale L. Morgan has written, "and for the lack of which they paid a corresponding penalty in hardship and waste effort—a discipline possible only because it was backed up by an authority founded in God."[8]

To aid the needy convert, who was no less worthy in the eyes of Brigham Young than the man with means, a "Perpetual Emigration

---

[6] As reported by Lord Houghton in the *Edinburgh Review* for January 1862. See also William Mulder and A. Russell Mortensen: *Among the Mormons: Historic Accounts by Contemporary Observers* (New York, 1958), p. 334.

[7] Dickens' sketch, "Bound for the Great Salt Lake," is reprinted from *The Uncommercial Traveller* in William Mulder and A. Russell Mortensen: *Among the Mormons*, pp. 335–344.

[8] Dale L. Morgan, *The Great Salt Lake* (New York, 1947), p. 189.

Fund" was established as early as September 1849. Voluntary donations amounting to $5,000 were contributed the first year. Converts
could draw upon this fund by way of loans, which they repaid in
labor, livestock, or goods, after arriving in Great Salt Lake City.
"The funds are appropriated in the form of a loan, rather than a
gift," wrote Brigham Young on October 16, 1849, "and this will
make the honest in heart rejoice, for they love to labor, and be independent by their labor, and not live on the charity of their friends,
while the lazy idlers, if any such there be, will find fault, and want
every luxury furnished them for their journey, and in the end pay
nothing. The Perpetual Fund will help no such idlers; we have no
use for them in the Valley. . . . these funds are designed to increase
until Israel is gathered from all nations, and the poor can sit under
their own vine, and inhabit their own house, and worship God in
Zion." Within a decade the Perpetual Emigration Fund had on
deposit in Liverpool and London the sum of £30,000, roughly
$150,000.

When the first company of British Mormons to take advantage of
this fund arrived in Salt Lake City September 3, 1850, Brigham
Young and other leaders greeted them at the mouth of Emigration
Canyon. There were wagons loaded with cakes and melons, a brass
band, and artillery salutes which, as the *Deseret News* put it, "made
the everlasting hills to shake their sides with joy."

"You are in the midst of plenty," Brigham Young told them with
cheerful tact. "No person here is under the necessity of begging his
bread, except the natives; and they beg more than they care for, or
can use. . . . As for the poor, there are none here, neither are there
any who may be called rich, but all obtain the essential comforts of
life. Let not your eyes be greedy. When I met you this afternoon, I
felt to say, *this is the company that I belong to*—the 'Poor company,'
as it is called, and I always expect to belong to it, until I am crowned
with eternal riches in the celestial kingdom. In this world I possess
nothing, only what the Lord has given to me, and it is devoted to the
building up of His kingdom."[9]

Frederick Piercy set sail on the *Jersey*, February 5, 1853, with a
company of 313 Mormons, half of them English, the others Welsh.
The price of steerage passage to New Orleans ranged from £3 10s to

---

[9] Seeing the value of this story and these speeches by Brigham Young for the British
convert, James Linforth did not fail to include them among his notes.

£5 for adults. Except for a brief period of terror when fire broke out on deck, the voyage was uneventful and pleasant. "Merry groups assembled on the deck," he wrote, "and, sitting in the sunshine, told stories, sang songs, and cracked jokes by the hour together, and generally with a propriety most unexceptionable."

The ship docked at New Orleans on March 21, having been a little over six weeks en route. The Mormons were permitted to sample the French cooking, eating in restaurants where the total cost of a meal was five cents, and then embarked on the steamboat *John Simonds* for Council Bluffs. Piercy, however, made his way up the river separately, sketching the leading towns along the way. He took a lively interest in the American Negroes, noting their "keen sense of the ridiculous" and ready wit. "I certainly saw no evidence of constitutional inferiority in them, either mentally or physically," he wrote. "Indeed, the wonder is, considering their degraded state, that they are found so intelligent."

He made a special trip to Nauvoo, where he sketched the gutted shell of the Mormon temple, once an imposing edifice dedicated specifically to secret rituals, including baptism for the dead. The temple had been fired by an arsonist November 10, 1848, and the deed had shocked even the hostile Gentiles who had moved into Nauvoo. "To destroy a work of art," said the *Nauvoo Patriot*, "at once the most elegant in its construction and the most renowned in its celebrity of any in the whole west, would, we should think, require a mind of more than ordinary depravity; and we feel assured that no one in this community could have been so lost to every sense of justice, and every consideration of interest, as to become the author of the deed. Admit that it was a monument of folly and evil, yet it was, to say the least of it, a splendid and harmless one."[10]

Brigham Young had sold the ruin to a colony of French Icarians who had settled in Nauvoo and who hoped to remodel the remains of the temple into a school. A capricious tornado on May 27, 1850, had blown down the north wall and so weakened the remainder that the Icarians had been forced for safety's sake to pull down the east and southern walls. Only the west wall was left for Piercy to sketch, but the resulting picture proved to be the most valuable of all his landscapes, for shortly afterward the whole ruin was leveled.

---

[10] As reprinted in the *Millennial Star*, XI, 46 (February 1, 1849).

One can see clearly in his sketch the extraordinary capstones that, legend has it, were modeled after a face the Mormon prophet saw in a vision.

Piercy stayed overnight at the Mansion House, which had been Joseph Smith's home in Nauvoo, and which was then being occupied by his mother, Lucy Mack Smith, his widow Emma Smith, and her sons. Emma Smith defiantly held that her husband had never practised polygamy, despite painful evidence to the contrary, and had refused to follow Brigham Young west. Unfortunately, Piercy did not sketch her portrait—perhaps he was not permitted—but he did make a drawing of the mother of the Mormon prophet, the oldest son, Joseph Smith, Jr., and the youngest son, David, who had been born five months after the assassination of his father. These three portraits are a notable addition to the pictorial history of the Latter-day Saints. The fact that the faces of the sons were included in the volume suggests that the schism between the family and Brigham Young was not yet final, as it became later when Joseph Smith, Jr., became the leader of a splinter sect calling itself the Reorganized Church of Jesus Christ of Latter-day Saints, which bitterly opposed polygamy.

Of Joseph Smith's mother Piercy wrote: "Considering her age [seventy-seven] and afflictions, she, at that time, retained her faculties to a remarkable degree. She spoke very freely of her sons, and, with tears in her eyes, and every other symptom of earnestness, vindicated their reputations for virtue and truth."

From Nauvoo Piercy went on to Carthage, Illinois, where he made sketches of the jail in which Joseph Smith and his brother Hyrum had been murdered. He was shown the bullet holes in the walls and door and told that there were bloodstains on the floorboards under the carpet. "Having seen the place and made my sketches, I was glad to leave," he wrote. "Two lives unatoned for, and 'blood crying from the ground,' made the spot hateful." Unlike the Nauvoo Temple, Carthage jail was never torn down, and is today a Latter-day Saint shrine. Modern photographs convey very little, however, of its original dramatic character, whereas the bleak Piercy drawings are wholly appropriate to the site.

Piercy's visit to Nauvoo and Carthage gave the editor, Linforth, an opportunity to insert in the footnotes a compact retelling of the whole of Joseph Smith's history, summarized for the most part from the prophet's official history, which first appeared in the *Times and Seasons* in Nauvoo and later in the *Millennial Star* in Liverpool.

At Kanesville, better known as Council Bluffs, Piercy began the overland journey by covered wagon and continued up the well-beaten road along the Platte River. Although thousands of gold-hunters were deepening the ruts along the way, the trip was arduous and lonely, as well as potentially disastrous for the man who packed his wagon badly, who had green timber in the axles, or who started too late in the summer. Marauding Indians were always a danger. Piercy conversed with one Englishman bound for California and promised to take back messages to his family. Some time later he passed the man's grave; he had been slain while on night watch.

The British converts knew nothing about handling an ox team or about coaxing cattle to ford treacherous rivers, and like almost all emigrants they brought along too much, only to discard it along the journey. Although the young artist started out as green as any of his countrymen, before the trip was over he had learned how to drive the stubbornest mule, he had stood knee-deep in mud, pushing the wagons of his company through a slough, and though without any medical training he had set the broken leg of a friend so skillfully it had mended without complications.

When he came to write his own narrative, he drew freely upon his diary, but also added much sage advice for the benefit of the London tailor "whose knowledge of animals does not extend beyond his own goose." Warning of unscrupulous traders who "get prices the reverse of their consciences," he recommended tasting hams, crackers, and flour before buying, as well as milking the cows and trying out the oxen. Among his other recommendations were shorter skirts for the women and beards for the men. "Lock up your razors," he wrote, "and try to believe that you cannot improve God's greatest work."

In Salt Lake City Piercy painted a portrait of Brigham Young. This is the most disappointing in the book. It lacked the massive strength and vigor that inevitably came through in the photographs. Even the glowing Mormon review of the Piercy book which appeared in the *Millennial Star* April 5, 1856, called the portrait "deficient."

One feels keenly, too, the lack of any comment whatsoever about the Mormon leader. Piercy's narrative virtually ends with his arrival in Great Salt Lake, and he seems deliberately to have avoided discussing the Mormon society he found there. He made no mention of polygamy, an omission which is not surprising when one considers the restraint even his editors were under on this subject. Linforth devoted only two lines to polygamy in all his notes, writing that on July 12, 1843, "the Prophet Joseph received from the Lord the great Revelation on 'Plurality of Wives,' and the true order of the marriage covenant, but it was not published to the world until 1852," and adding in another note that the newly passed Kansas-Nebraska Act, which held that Congress had no right to regulate slavery in the territories, could apply equally to "plurality of wives."

This brevity was in line with the accepted missionary practice of saying little or nothing on the subject. Another British visitor to Great Salt Lake, William Chandless, noted in 1855: "I do not think that polygamy is held out as an inducement; but rather kept back from the generality, lest they should be scandalised: 'milk for babes, strong meat for men.' It might be an inducement to emigrate to Utah, but not to become Mormons; and the sacrifices to be made, and the hardships to be overcome before practicing it, are such that no sensualist would be much tempted."[11]

Foreign visitors like Chandless, and later the French botanist Jules Rémy, and the British scholar Richard Burton, took a detached, tolerant, and frequently amused attitude toward Mormon polygamy, noting with surprise the apparent lack of sensuality and the rigorous Puritanical aspects. Chandless wrote, ". . . they are not a specially sensual people," and "the wretchedness of wives in Utah has been greatly exaggerated." Rémy stated, perhaps with some disappointment, "The Mormons appeared to us less licentious than we were naturally inclined to suppose."[12]

American visitors, however, were much more likely to express indignation. The young Jewish artist from Baltimore, Solomon Carvalho, who was also painting Mormon portraits in Salt Lake City in 1853, counted polygamy "a false and vicious system . . . destructive to morality, female delicacy, and the sanctity of marriage." He insisted further that it went hand in hand with "ennervation" and

11 *A Visit to Salt Lake; being a journey across the plains and a residence in the Mormon settlements at Utah* (London, 1857), p. 175.
12 William Chandless, *A Visit to Salt Lake,* pp. 191–192; Jules Rémy and Julius Brenchley, *A Journey to Great Salt Lake City,* 2 vols. (London, 1861), II, 156, first published as the two-volume *Voyage au Pays des Mormons* (Paris, 1860), with only Rémy's name listed as author.

"effeminacy of character"—curious words, surely, for a man who had painted two portraits of Brigham Young. Still, Carvalho was not without a bit of humor on the subject. "Let them give a rib," he said, "for every additional wife."[13]

Chandless, Rémy, and Brenchley were all in Salt Lake City in 1855 when Piercy's book was published. Chandless seems to have missed seeing it altogether, which is not surprising, since it appeared late in the year. When he published his own perceptive and friendly account in 1857, he stated: "No English traveller, so far as I am aware, has written about Salt Lake." Rémy, however, purchased Piercy's book and wrote his name in it. This copy years later found its way into the Rare Book Room of the Library of Congress.

The *London Times* did not review the Piercy volume, though it was giving the Mormons considerable coverage through 1855 and 1856, with frequent dispatches from "our correspondent, New York" and an occasional extract from a speech by Brigham Young. Although it reprinted hostile articles on the Mormons from the *New York Herald*—including one on August 14, 1855, which called Mormondom "a living stigma and reproach . . . squatter sovereignty carried to licentiousness"—the *Times* for the most part maintained a dignified detachment. In reviewing, on September 4, 1855, the sensational *Female Life Among the Mormons, a narrative of many years personal experience. By the wife of a Mormon Elder recently from Utah,* the editor rightly detected the book to be "altogether apocryphal" and "the latest Yankee hoax."

Compared with rubbish of this sort, the Piercy book stands out as a document of high quality indeed. It should not, on the other hand, be judged by measuring it against the scholarship of Rémy and Brenchley, who were not only conscientious observers but also speculative moralists. Their joint work, though marred by errors of fact and judgment, remains one of the two best studies of Mormonism in the nineteenth century, the other being *The City of the Saints* (London, 1861), by the great British orientalist and explorer, Richard Burton. Piercy's work was not social documentation. It stands as a unique collaboration between Mormon and non-Mormon, a charmingly written descriptive journal, and a superb collection of pictures of the West.

[13] *Incidents of Travel and Adventure in the Far West* (New York, 1858), preface, and pp. 151–152.

The value of Piercy's pictures as historical documents becomes increasingly evident if one looks at what else was painted on the American frontier at the same time. Thanks in part to accident and loss, the surviving collections are surprisingly sparse. George Catlin (1796–1872), the great pioneer ethnologist and painter of the western Indian, had made a trip to the upper Missouri as early as 1832. The resulting *Letters and Notes on the Manners, Customs, and Conditions of the North American Indians* (with 400 illustrations) had been immensely popular. It would see twenty editions between 1841 and 1860, many of them in European countries.

There was the talented landscape artist, Alfred Jacob Miller (1810–1874), who had sketched widely in the Indian country and Rocky Mountains in 1837. His patron was Sir William Drummond Stewart, a Scottish nobleman who was enamored of the American West, and who hired Miller to make a pictorial record of his expedition. Stewart then persuaded the artist to accompany him to Scotland and had him cover the walls of Murthly Castle with pictures representing aboriginal Indian life and the glory of the mountains. But his work remained virtually unknown in America till the Baltimore museum displayed a collection of water-color reproductions.[14]

John James Audubon made an extensive trip up the Missouri to the Yellowstone River area in 1843, gathering material to finish *The Viviparous Quadrupeds of North America* (1842–1846). But he counted himself a naturalist and only incidentally an artist, and it is worth noting that he took along a young painter, Isaac Sprague of Massachusetts, for the express purpose of drawing plants and views for backgrounds.[15]

John M. Stanley, who had a more intimate and comprehensive knowledge of the West than any other artist of the time, had begun exploring the area in 1842. His great collection of Indian paintings was exhibited in the Smithsonian Institution in 1852, and there was much agitation to persuade Congress to purchase it for a permanent

[14] Clyde and Mae Reed Porter came into possession of one hundred of his water color sketches in 1939. See *Matthew C. Field, Prairie and Mountain Sketches, collected by Clyde and Mae Reed Porter,* edited by Kate L. Gregg and John Francis McDermott (University of Oklahoma Press, 1957). Several of the superb Alfred Jacob Miller pictures are reproduced in this book.

[15] See *Up the Missouri with Audubon, the Journal of Edward Harris,* edited and annotated by John Francis McDermott (University of Oklahoma Press, 1951), p. 8.

exhibit. The bill failed several times to pass the House, however, and a fire in the Smithsonian in 1865 destroyed all but five of his 200 paintings. "Not only did Stanley suffer a heart-breaking loss," as Robert Taft has written, "but the nation suffered an irreparable loss in its historical portraiture."[16]

The year 1853, which saw Frederick Piercy crossing the plains to Salt Lake City, was a memorable one for artists of the West. This was the year in which Congress, after much bitter debate, appropriated $150,000 for surveys of a route for a railroad to the Pacific. These were conducted by the United States Army Corps of Topographical Engineers. All the expeditions, six of which were active in 1853–54, employed artists and illustrators. The surveys would be published in thirteen volumes, with superb illustrations.[17]

Along with scientific exploration and adventure there were, however, hardship, suffering, and loss. One artist, young Richard H. Kern, was ambushed and slain by Ute Indians, along with Captain John W. Gunnison in 1853. The talented portrait painter, Solomon Nunes Carvalho (1815–1897), who went west with John C. Frémont's 1853 expedition, loaded with oils, canvas, and daguerreotype equipment, had to abandon Frémont in central Utah and recover his health among the Mormons. Suffering from frostbite and scurvy, and having lost forty-four pounds, he made his way to Salt Lake City, where he was feted by the church leaders. He left several portraits of leading Mormons.

The ownership of Carvalho's expedition pictures, however, remained with Frémont, who expected to use them as illustrations for his own report of the trip. Frémont became so absorbed in politics and in his presidential campaign of 1856, that he had no leisure to write the story. When Carvalho was persuaded to publish his own valuable *Incidents of Travel and Adventure in the Far West* in 1856, he had no access to his own pictures. He painted two new ones, but

---

[16] *Artists and Illustrators of the Old West, 1850–1900*, p. 13.

[17] See *Reports of Explorations and Surveys to Ascertain the Most Practicable and Economical Route for a Railroad from the Missouri River to the Pacific Ocean.* The first ten volumes were published in 1855 as United States Congress, 33rd Congress, 2nd Session, Senate Executive Document No. 78. A supplementary volume was published in 1859 as United States Congress, 35th Congress, 2nd Session, Senate Executive Document No. 46. In 1860 two more volumes were ordered published by the 36th Congress, 1st session. Robert Taft, in his excellent survey of artists of the West, described in detail the life, the work, and the ultimate fate of the pictures of several of the artists accompanying these expeditions, and has furnished data on all the others.

the remainder were sketches by another artist. Then a disastrous warehouse fire destroyed all Frémont's notes, and most, if not all, of the Carvalho collection.[18] This was another loss to American art, as well as to the history of the West, and the only function the fire served was to make Piercy's pictures of the period even more valuable for their rarity.

Fortunately, thirteen of Piercy's original drawings were preserved and presented in recent years to the Missouri Historical Society. Four of these—St. Louis, Loup Fork Ferry, Camp at Wood River, and Chimney Rock, had been reproduced as engravings in the book. Mary M. Powell, writing a description of the drawings in the *Missouri Historical Society Bulletin* for October 1948, discusses some of his techniques, pointing out how cleverly he used Chinese white to brighten the sides of bare cliffs and eroded river banks and to show the intense light of the western country. He used a sepia wash for his more important sketches, which are singularly good at suggesting the open reaches of sky and earth.

Carvalho, Miller, Piercy, and Stanley all sketched and painted in a style characteristic of the mid-century; it differed markedly from that of artists of the West who came a generation later—Charles Russell, William R. Leigh, and Frederick Remington.[19] There is nothing of the flamboyant romanticism of the men who were to paint the vanishing frontier, with its glorification of the cowboy and the cult of the bronco. In the 1850's and 1860's the frontier was a formidable barrier between the Mississippi River and California, and the artists who painted it sketched what they could manage: familiar landmarks—Chimney Rock, Scott's Bluffs, Independence Rock—Shoshone faces, buffalo drinking in the Platte River, the impressive face of Brigham Young. Their style is stiff, almost primitive, but unmistakably authentic.

18 See the introduction by Bertram Wallace Korn in the centenary edition of Carvalho's *Incidents of Travel and Adventure in the Far West, 1853–1854: Including Three Months Residence in Utah and a Perilous Trip Across the Great American Desert to the Pacific,* published by the Jewish Publication Society of America (Philadelphia, 1954). Korn states that some of the Carvalho prints had been developed by Mathew Brady before the fire and may have been retained in his collection. If so, they are still unknown and unmarked in the National Archives in Washington, D.C. This centenary edition reproduces a number of Carvalho's portraits, but none that he made in Utah.

19 The illustrations in Robert Taft's *Artists and Illustrators of the Old West* show the gradually evolving style. For a representative collection of paintings made late in the century, see *Gallery of Western Paintings,* edited by Raymond Carlson, 1951.

Little can be unearthed about James Linforth, Piercy's editor, except for the brief period when he was active in the Mormon Church in Liverpool. He was born September 1, 1827, in Birmingham, England, the son of Edward H. and Caroline S. Linforth, and was baptized a member of the church November 15, 1842, at the age of fifteen. At twenty-three he published a long article in the *Millennial Star* called "Baptismal Regeneration or the Controversy in the Church of England," which showed marked familiarity with the theological disputes of the time.[20]

Early in 1851 he published an eight-page pamphlet, *The Reverend C. W. Laurence, "Few Words from a Pastor to his People on the Subject of the Latter-day Saints," replied to and refuted by James Linforth* (Liverpool, J. Sadler, 1851), an extract of which appeared in the *Millennial Star* of June 15, 1851. In 1852 he edited *The Government of God, by John Taylor, one of the Twelve Apostles of the Church of Jesus Christ of Latter-day Saints* (S. W. Richards: Liverpool, Latter-day Saints book depot, 1852).

His work on the Piercy volume was prodigious, and the accuracy and timeliness of the details he accumulated to describe an immense area he had never visited are evidence of devoted patience and intellectual acumen. For Mormon historical material he drew from the *Times and Seasons* and the *Millennial Star;* for up-to-date information from Utah he used extracts from the *Deseret News,* Captain Howard Stansbury's *Exploration and Survey of the Valley of the Great Salt Lake* (Philadelphia, 1852), and John W. Gunnison's *The Mormons, or Latter-day Saints* (Philadelphia, 1852). He consulted the United States census reports for 1850 and drew heavily upon James D. B. DeBow: *The Industrial Resources of the Southern and Western States* (New Orleans, 1852–3), one of the many editions of George Conclin's *New River Guide,* and John Mason Peck's *New Guide to the West* (Cincinnati, 1848). He also quoted from or cited books by David Turnbull, Henry Rowe Schoolcraft, Sir Charles Lyell, Emma Hart Willard, and Richard Robert Madden.

Linforth was one of the most steadfast and generous contributors to the Mormon Church in Liverpool. His name appears in almost every *Millennial Star* "List of Contributors" from September 1850 to January 1856. Each month he donated something between £10

---

[20] This ran serially in the *Millennial Star* from September 15 through December 1, 1850 (XII, 277 ff).

and £25. In 1856 he joined the stream of British emigrants to Utah, taking his wife and children. He wrote a letter to the *Millennial Star* from Florence, Nebraska Territory, September 1, 1856, indicating that he expected to begin the overland journey on September 3.

There was no hint of anxiety at starting so late in the season. "I had my first lesson, practically, at 'geeing and hawing' in driving one of the two teams," he wrote, ". . . I may tell you that I have drawn water, chopped wood, and done sundry other things incidental to camp life, and all with as good grace as I could. I hope soon to be sufficiently familiar with all these things to do away with my present awkwardness."

The *Millennial Star* published a brief extract from another letter "five miles west of Fort Laramie."[21] Regrettably, this letter was not published in full, for Linforth no doubt had much to tell, having picked the most hazardous autumn in a decade to travel west. He was caught in the same storms and freezing weather that paralyzed the celebrated fourth and fifth Mormon handcart companies, the last of five groups which crossed the plains without wagons, their belongings piled into simple, crudely constructed carts. The James G. Willie handcart company had started from Florence August 19 with 400; the Edward Martin company followed on August 25 with 580. Linforth and his family, travelling in a wagon in Captain Hunt's company, must certainly have caught up with the second group, and probably with the first. Before reaching Salt Lake City on November 9, 1856, the Willie company saw 70 die; the Martin company buried 145 before reaching Salt Lake City on November 30.[22]

Certainly it must have shaken the young British editor, when faced with the horrors of these disasters, to remember the cheerful expectation and glowing hope implicit in his recently published emigrant's guide. Back in Florence, Nebraska, he had watched the departure of the Martin company, which included several of his friends. "Most of the company were in good health, and few were sick," he had reported in his letter to the *Millennial Star,* "but all seemed in good spirits and lively faith concerning their journey." In departing "they made the air ring with a good hurrah! three times repeated." One can only guess at his subsequent feelings of disillusionment and personal guilt.

It is worth noting that despite his obvious literary talents Linforth did no writing and editing for the church in Utah. Eventually he moved to San Francisco, in these years an almost certain sign of apostasy or near-apostasy. However, when he died January 16, 1899, at the age of seventy-one, he was favored with a brief obituary notice[23] in the *Deseret News* in Salt Lake City:

JAMES LINFORTH DEAD

The relatives of James Linforth are grieved to learn of his death, by paralysis, at San Francisco, on Monday January 16, at 11:30 PM. The deceased was formerly well known in connection with the Latter-day Saints in England, and also as a resident in Utah. From here he moved to California and engaged in merchandising.

One must regret that James Linforth stopped writing, that he did not, at the least, do one more book, his own *Route from Liverpool to Great Salt Lake Valley*.

FAWN M. BRODIE

January 1962.

[23] I am indebted to Mrs. Louise M. Card, of Salt Lake City, for this obituary notice, and also for the information concerning Linforth's birth, baptism, and death, which is on file in the archives of the Church of Jesus Christ of Latter-Day Saints.

NOTE ON THE TEXT

The fact that Frederick Piercy's volume has become so rare is partly the result of the peculiar processing of the original publication. The prospectus, published in the *Millennial Star* (XVI:330), May 27, 1854, stated in part: "This work will be published at this office in 14 monthly parts, Superroyal 4 to, 1s each. Part 1 to be ready July 1st. Subscribers who emigrate to Utah before the work is completed, can, by paying at this office before their departure, obtain the remaining parts in Great Salt Lake City."

According to the prospectus, the steel engravings were made by Charles Sims. Actually he made none of them. Most of the engraving work was done by Charles Fenn, with Edwin Roffe and W. H. Gibbs assisting. All of the landscapes and five of the portraits were made from original Piercy sketches. The pictures of several Mormon leaders were hastily assembled at the last moment from other sources, and the joint portrait of two Ute Indian chiefs, Joseph Walker (or Wakara), and Arapeen, was made from an original drawing by W. W. Major.

The book was at first issued in fifteen separately stitched parts, in separate wrappers, continuing from July 1854 to September 1855. The title page and contents were stitched in the back of part fifteen. As a result, obviously, many copies were never even properly bound. Others bound and shipped from England were accidentally ruined on the way. Robert Ernest Cowan, bibliographer and expert on Americana, attached a note to the frontispiece of his own copy (now in the Rare Book Collection of the University of California at Los Angeles), which said: "It is doubtful if any very good copy of Linforth's work is in existence. In the transit from St. Louis to Salt Lake, it suffered greatly from water, and many copies were entirely lost. The work was of peculiar interest to the Mormon people, and the few extant copies were thoroughly (and most carelessly used,) and all are in very indifferent condition."

A facsimile reprint, made by Bookcraft in Salt Lake City, appeared in 1959, but copies are no longer available.

In editing this volume I have corrected the errata listed by James Linforth and additional printer's errors, including the incorrect numbering of the chapters. I have not, however, modified antique spellings, such as Washita (for Ouachita), Wahsatch (for Wasatch), Kanyon (for canyon), and San Pete (for Sanpete). For the convenience of the modern reader excessive punctuation of the period has been reduced to conform more nearly to current usage, and a few minor corrections of place names have been made.

Where the editor omitted first names I have, whenever possible, either inserted them in brackets in the text or identified the persons fully in footnotes. Since Linforth was often careless about quotation marks, it was not always easy to know whom he was quoting, or whether he was quoting or paraphrasing. I have been able to identify most of his original sources, and wherever possible have listed authors and titles in footnotes.

The awkwardness of printing Linforth's lengthy, parenthetically numbered footnotes immediately below Piercy's text, as they appeared in the original edition, has been overcome by placing them together in Appendix II. My additions to them and to other original notes in earlier chapters appear in brackets. All other notes are my own.

No attempt has been made to point out or correct the errors of omission or emphasis in Linforth's long sections on Mormon history, which were written with the ardor of a devout convert. The student who cares to examine modern scholarly studies which cover the same period of Mormon history might consult Ray B. West: *Kingdom of the Saints; the Story of Brigham Young and the Mormons* (New York, 1957), Thomas O'Dea: *The Mormons* (University of Chicago Press, 1957), and Fawn M. Brodie: *No Man Knows My History, the Life of Joseph Smith the Mormon Prophet* (New York, 1945).

I am grateful to librarians at the British Museum, the Royal Academy of Arts in London, the Library of Congress, the Utah Historical Society, and the University of California at Los Angeles. Mr. Russell A. Mortensen, director of the University of Utah Press, was extremely helpful, as were Dale L. Morgan of the Bancroft Library, and Mrs. Louise M. Card of Salt Lake City.

F. M. B.

Route from Liverpool
to Great Salt Lake Valley

ROUTE FROM LIVERPOOL

TO

Great Salt Lake Valley

ILLUSTRATED

WITH STEEL ENGRAVINGS AND WOOD CUTS FROM SKETCHES MADE BY

FREDERICK PIERCY,

INCLUDING

Views of Nauvoo and the Ruins of the Temple, with a historical account of the City; Views of Carthage Jail; and Portraits and Memoirs of Joseph and Hyrum Smith; their Mother, Lucy Smith; Joseph and David Smith, Sons of the Prophet Joseph; President Brigham Young; Heber C. Kimball; Willard Richards; Jedediah M. Grant; John Taylor; the late Chief Patriarch, Father John Smith; and the present Chief Patriarch, John Smith, Son of Hyrum.

TOGETHER WITH

A Geographical and Historical Description of Utah, and a Map of the Overland Routes to that Territory from the Missouri River.

ALSO,

AN AUTHENTIC HISTORY OF THE LATTER-DAY SAINTS' EMIGRATION FROM EUROPE FROM THE COMMENCEMENT UP TO THE CLOSE OF 1855, WITH STATISTICS.

EDITED BY JAMES LINFORTH.

Liverpool:
PUBLISHED BY FRANKLIN D. RICHARDS, 36, ISLINGTON.
London:
LATTER-DAY SAINTS' BOOK DEPOT, 35, JEWIN STREET, CITY
MDCCCLV.

[*The original title page*]

[Detail of the original map]

PREFACE

The following Work was originated in 1853, by a desire on the part of many of the Latter-day Saints to possess a collection of engravings of the most notable places on the Route between Liverpool and Great Salt Lake City.

To gratify this desire, Mr. Piercy and Elder S. W. Richards, then the publisher of the L. D. Saints' Works in this country, entered into arrangements for the publication of such a collection, and the former made a journey to G. S. L. City and back to obtain original sketches. The Artist could not pass within so short a distance of Nauvoo and Carthage, places of undying interest, and not visit them. Hence we have the views and portraits taken there. These necessitated the introduction of the portraits of Willard Richards and John Taylor, and on arriving in G. S. L. City, the Artist was kindly favoured by President Young with his portrait for publication also.

On Mr. Piercy's return to England, the collection made had far exceeded the original design, but it then seemed imperfect without the portraits of President [Heber C.] Kimball and the Patriarch, Father John Smith, both of which were obtained. After the demise of President W. Richards and Father John Smith, portraits of their successors, Jedediah M. Grant and John Smith, were procured from G. S. L. City.

Having obtained the sketches, it was determined to publish them with the Artist's narrative of the journey, and entitle the Work "Route from Liverpool to Great Salt Lake Valley." At this stage it was placed in our hands to edit, and in order to render it not only ornamental and interesting, but really useful, it was arranged that notes should be written upon the respective States and Territories through which the Route lay, and upon the Cities and points of greatest attraction touched at, and be introduced with the narrative; also, that a Map showing the overland portion of the Route, with Utah Territory, should be constructed and accompany the Work. The Artist's visit to Nauvoo and Carthage likewise enabled us to introduce a historical account of the former, refer to the tragedies which have disgraced the latter, and insert memoirs of the Prophets Joseph and Hyrum Smith, their mother, two of the sons of Joseph, and Willard Richards and John Taylor.

The nature of the Work being so intimately connected with the L. D. Saints' Emigration, the idea was suggested at the commencement to give a review of the same, with statistics down to the latest time. Nothing of the kind had previously appeared, and many particulars were fast fading from existence, which rendered it a most onerous undertaking. We, however, succeeded in compiling the history which precedes the Work, and resumed the subject with the last Part, bringing it down to the close of 1855.

The versatility of the subjects embraced in the following pages, and the historical and statistical information embodied therein having to be drawn from sources far and wide, some of them very imperfect at the best, we have experienced considerable difficulty in the compilation. Where it was possible to collate information on any of the subjects, we have done so, in order to give the facts as correctly as they might be, and throughout, have striven to prevent errors creeping in. With all our vigilance, however, some items have escaped us, or we were at the time unable to detect them, but a perusal of the Errata[1] will prevent any wrong impression from being imbibed.

In the course of the Work we have received valuable assistance from numerous Elders whose position, or personal acquaintance with many things alluded to, has given us access to documents and information otherwise unattainable. To name any, unless all, would be invidious, we therefore refrain from particularizing, but assure each of our gratitude, and trust that our joint labours will be appreciated.

JAMES LINFORTH.

Liverpool, December, 1855.

[1] In this edition the errata have been corrected.

CHAPTER I

[James Linforth Introduces the Journey]*

Commencement of The Latter-day Saints' Emigration— History Until the Suspension in 1846

BEFORE commencing our interesting journey to the Valley of the Great Salt Lake, we will take a retrospective view of the emigration of the Latter-day Saints from Europe, and after reviewing its history to 1854, we shall introduce tables, showing, as near as possible, the departures of the respective ships, the number of passengers carried by each, and the arrangements under which they emigrated. Information upon this subject has been much sought after, not only by the Latter-day Saints themselves, but by many well-meaning authors and journalists who have written upon the subject for the benefit of the public. Owing, however, to the absence of any complete statement emanating from the Latter-day Saints, their emigration has been variously estimated, some persons keeping within the facts, and others going much beyond them. The history which we shall give of the past emigration will be complete in every particular, as far as it can be ascertained. The early part of the subject is a little obscure, and reference cannot now be made to the books of some of the persons who conducted it, but so far as we have the privilege of referring to documents and our own personal experience for the past five years will assist us, accuracy may be relied upon.

The first regularly organized company of emigrants, numbering about 200, appear to have sailed from Liverpool for New York, on the 7th of August, 1840, in the ship *North America,* under the presidency of Elder Theodore Turley, a returning missionary, and Elder William Clayton,[1] one of the earliest English converts, although some

* Frederick Piercy's narrative begins at Chapter X.

[1] William Clayton (1814–1879), one of the earliest British converts, conducted a company of Latter-day Saints from England to Nauvoo in 1840, and became one of the trusted secretaries of Joseph Smith. Brigham Young appointed him historian of the first expedition to Great Salt Lake. See his much used *Latter-day Saints Emigrants' Guide* (St. Louis, Mo., 1848).

few families had sailed at intervals in the early part of the year. Owing to the expensiveness of the route *via* New York, many of this company fell short of means to complete the journey to Nauvoo, formerly Commerce, Illinois, they therefore divided at Buffalo, New York, a part going to settle in Kirtland and other settlements of the Saints in Ohio, and the balance to Nauvoo, to which place Joseph Smith states he had the pleasure of welcoming about one hundred of them in the fall of the year. The second vessel was the *Sheffield,* which sailed in February, 1841. About the time of the departure of the *Sheffield,* a company, gathered from Herefordshire and the neighbouring counties, sailed from Bristol. Since that time the main emigration has been direct from Liverpool to New Orleans, but numerous individuals have sailed between the seasons to New York, Philadelphia, Boston, and other American ports.

Few particulars can be gleaned respecting the vessels in which the earliest companies embarked, but Elder P. P. Pratt stated in June, 1841, that about 1000 persons had then emigrated.

In an Epistle of the Twelve Apostles, dated Manchester (Eng.) April 15, 1841, and signed by eight members of that body, Elder Amos Fielding was appointed an agent of the Church, to superintend the fitting out of the companies of emigrants from Liverpool, and to protect them from being victimized while waiting in port to sail. Elder Fielding being a man of much experience and good judgment, no doubt performed with every satisfaction the duties assigned to him. He acted in concert with Elder P. P. Pratt, until the departure of the latter from this country, October 29, 1842, when the business was conducted by himself and Hyrum Clark, who left Nauvoo for that purpose, on the 23rd of June, 1842, under instructions from the Church authorities. We believe the details of the emigration effected by the last two agencies are nearly complete.

The next person who had the charge of the emigration was Elder Reuben Hedlock, who was appointed in Nauvoo, by the Quorum of the Twelve Apostles, on the 23rd of May, 1843. The details during his agency are not complete, but again we are fortunate in having a statement made by himself, in February, 1846, to the effect that he had shipped 990 persons, 113 of whom were allowed to pay their passage in Nauvoo, the amount of which was £466 12s. He does not appear to have shipped more, unless it was a few to the Eastern States.

Up to the time of Elder Hedlock's agency, and during a part of it, nearly the whole tide of emigration poured into Nauvoo, but still some of the emigrants settled in other towns and villages of Illinois and in the then territory of Iowa, the south-west corner of which had been very favourably reported upon in July, 1840, by George Miller and John A. Mikesell, a Committee appointed to examine it and report its advantages and the facilities it offered for settlers. The main object, however—that of building up Nauvoo—was never lost sight of, and the authorities, Joseph Smith and the Twelve Apostles, constantly exhorted the immigrating Saints who had capital to establish manufactories in that city, that employment might be given to the labouring classes as they arrived, and the interests of all be enhanced; but the continued law-suits which the Saints in Nauvoo were engaged in to defend the Prophet Joseph and the effects of speculation in land by some monied men from without, who bought lands at a low rate and sold them again at enormous prices, exhausted the pockets of the Saints, crippled all manufacturing interests, and left the city, after the Prophet's assassination, in an almost helpless condition, in a pecuniary point of view. The Twelve Apostles, nevertheless, still desired that Nauvoo should be built up and that employment should be given within the city to artizans, and recommended that every lawful means be used to bring it about; but in the meantime, the Saints emigrating from Great Britain, who were wholly dependent upon their labour for support, were advised to emigrate to New York, Philadelphia, Pittsburg, Salem, Boston, and other large towns in the eastern states, where branches of the Church existed, and where employment could be procured, which would give the emigrants the means to go west when the way should open.

In February, 1846, the exodus of the Saints from Nauvoo commenced, and as they had no permanent location until their arrival at Council Bluffs in the June following, the emigration from Great Britain was suspended. The ultimate destination of the exterminated Saints was from the first intended to be beyond the Rocky Mountains, and, in the meantime, the Saints from Great Britain were directed to make for the bay or port of San Francisco. Elder Hedlock, in an address in February, 1846, intimated that a company would leave in the following September for California; and in another address in April stated that, following the instructions given by Elder Woodruff previous to his departure, and the voice of the General Conference, held in Manchester, he should submit to the next

General Conference the formation of the first company of emigrants, that all things might be prepared to send out a vessel on the 10th of September. These arrangements, however, were never carried into effect; but on the arrival of Elders O. Hyde and John Taylor, on the 3rd of October, and P. P. Pratt, on the 14th, the emigration was further suspended. Having been appointed to come to England, these three Apostles left Council Bluffs in the previous summer, and on their arrival took charge of the British Mission.

CHAPTER II

Memorial to the Queen—Re-opening of the Emigration—History Until 1851

OWING to the suspension of emigration, to the headquarters of the Church, and the great amount of distress prevailing at that time, in the British Islands, the Latter-day Saints here, under the advice of Elders Hyde, Pratt, and Taylor, presented in February, 1847, a Memorial to the Queen, setting forth the distress existent among a large portion of her Majesty's subjects, and proposing a plan for emigration to Oregon or Vancouver Island. Although the document is lengthy we give it in full, as it shows the spirit of the time and forms an interesting link in the history of the emigration.

Memorial to the Queen, for the relief, by Emigration, of a portion of her Poor Subjects.

TO THE QUEEN'S MOST EXCELLENT MAJESTY.

May it please your Majesty:

We, the undersigned, men and women of the United Kingdom of Great Britain, approach your Majesty with every sentiment of loyal and affectionate devotion to your person, and with sincere respect for the Patriotic Virtues by which your Reign has been so eminently distinguished. We feel the strongest confidence in your Majesty's deep and earnest desire for the happiness and prosperity of your people. We know, from your Majesty's own assurance, that the privations and sorrows of the unemployed and destitute portions of the community, have not in vain appealed for sympathy and compassion to your heart. We, therefore, anticipate for this, our respectful memorial, a gracious and considerate reception.

Your memorialists are moved to address your Majesty by the unexampled amount of abject, helpless, and unmerited misery which at present prevails among the labouring classes of this country. By all your memorialists this wretchedness has, to some extent, been witnessed; by all it has been deplored; and by many among them it has been bitterly felt. The sufferings and destitution of these portions of your Majesty's subjects have, in the judgment of your memorialists, reached a point at which it has become the duty of both sexes, and of all ranks, to use every constitutional means for their relief and remedy.

Your memorialists are daily the witnesses of a frightful increase of poverty and pauperism: while those who are at present in circumstances above the reach of absolute want, are constantly becoming less able to sustain the burden of supporting the poor.

Your memorialists beg your Majesty to believe that in bringing these painful facts under your Majesty's notice, and in pointing to what, to your memorialists, appears a just and necessary measure of relief, they are impelled by an overwhelming sense of moral obligation and Christian duty, and that no less a motive would have induced them to appear thus prominently in public affairs.

Your memorialists, without attempting to enumerate the many alleged causes of the present national distress and suffering, feel convinced that Emigration to some portion of your Majesty's vacant territories is the only permanent means of relief left to a rapidly increasing population, which, if retained here, must swell the aggregate amount of misery, wretchedness and want.

Your memorialists believe that, if a part of the poor and destitute portion of your Majesty's loyal subjects were sent to the Island of Vancouver, or to the great territory of Oregon, through your Majesty's gracious interference and Royal aid, they might there find a field of labour and industry, in which, after a short period, they could not only benefit themselves, but open an effectual door for the interchange of commodities with the home country, having brought into cultivation the soil that now lies untenanted, and thus indirectly raise a revenue that would more than balance the expenditures of the present emigration.

It is now fully settled and determined, that Vancouver's Island, with a large portion of the Oregon territory, on the Great Pacific coast, belongs to your Majesty's Empire.* Their fine and extensive fisheries, their safe

* OREGON.—During the time the difference between Mexico and the United States was pending, "a difficulty arose between the latter and England respecting the northern boundary of Oregon; both nations claiming the extensive portion of that country north of the Columbia river to the Russian settlements [54° 40']. The full statement of the claims on either side is long and intricate; but there is no contradition made to the facts that the Columbia river, and its vicinity, belong to the Americans, by right of the discovery made in 1792, by Captain Grey, of Boston, and by the exploration of Lewis and Clark, in the employ of the American Government, made in the years 1804–5. John Jacob Astor, of New York, founded Astoria at the mouth of the Columbia, in 1811. The first house on its waters was, however, established on Lewis river, by the Missouri Fur Company in 1808." (Willard's History of the United States, p. 403.) [This is Emma Hart Willard, one of the great educators of her day, and champion of education for women. Her History of the United States or Republic of America was first published in 1828.] After this time expeditions by fur traders were frequent, and these with the British Hudson Bay Co. held joint possession of the country. But jealousies and rivalries led to bloody contests, and in consequence of complaints made by American settlers, Congress passed an Act, on the 16th of April, 1846, declaring that a joint occupation of the disputed territory, formerly agreed to in the conventions of 1818 and 1827, must after a year cease. This step on the part of the United States government led almost to war with England, but, happily, a compromise was effected by a treaty negotiated at Washington, on the 18th of June, 1846, between Mr. Packenham, the British Minister, and Mr. Buchanan, the American Secretary. By this treaty all below 49° N. Lat. was given to the United States, and the

and commodious natural harbours for ships, the salubrity of their climate, and their remarkable similarity to the climate of the south of England— all, in the opinion of your memorialists, offer strong inducements to the surplus population of England to make that delightful section their future home.

Your memorialists believe that your Majesty cherishes the wish, and they pray your Majesty to exert all that constitutional influence and power which will effectually accomplish their removal to the distant shores of a country, the natural resources of which are waiting to be developed, to reward the hand of industry, and to fill with plenty thousands that wander here at present without employment, and, consequently, without bread.

Your memorialists are no less aware than your Majesty, that the government of the United States is doing much to favour the settlement of its territories on the Western Coast, and even to settle territory now in dispute between it and the Republic of Mexico. While, therefore, the United States do manifest such a strong inclination not only to extend and enlarge their possessions in the West, but also to people them, will not your Majesty look well to British interests in those regions, and adopt timely and precautionary measures to maintain a balance of power in that quarter—which, in the opinion of your memorialists, is destined, at no very distant period, to participate largely in the China trade?

Your memorialists, therefore, humbly but earnestly supplicate your Majesty to take the present afflicting condition of your subjects into your prompt and gracious consideration, and to interpose your Royal aid, as far as it may be constitutionally rendered, to provide means for the immigration of your memorialists who are not able to provide for themselves —to give them employment in improving the harbours of those countries, or in erecting posts of defence; or if this be inexpedient, to furnish them provisions and means of subsistence until they can produce them from the soil.

Your memorialists further ask your Majesty to consider the propriety of sending out a small military force for the protection of emigrants against savage invaders upon that coast. And again, your memorialists ask your Majesty to favourably consider the propriety of allowing to each male emigrant, who is more than twenty-one years old, who may become an actual settler, a grant of land corresponding in extent to grants proposed by the United States' Government to its subjects, who become actual settlers in its extreme Western territories, namely, from three hundred and twenty to six hundred and forty acres.

---

island of Vancouver, with rights to the joint navigation of the Columbia river, was given to the British.

VANCOUVER, called also QUADRA and VANCOUVER.—This island is 300 miles long and 75 broad and is estimated to have 16,000 square miles. The surface is mountainous and rich in wood. Fort Vancouver is the principal settlement of the Hudson Bay Company. The population of the island is now about 12,000, and the inhabitants live principally by fishing and hunting.

Your memorialists are mostly anxious to avail themselves of the earliest opportunity to sail to the place of their future desired home, where they may begin to convert "the wilderness and the solitary place into fruitful fields," hoping, that under the blessing of Heaven, and under the gracious protection and fostering care of their Sovereign, they may soon close their eyes upon the stern and angry frowns of poverty and want, and open them to greet the smiles of peace and plenty.

Finally the prayer which your memorialists offer at the footstool of HIM by whom Kings reign and Princes decree justice is, that your Majesty's reign may be protracted and peaceful in the midst of a devoted and prosperous people; that the choicest of heavenly blessings may descend upon your Majesty's person, upon your Royal Consort, and upon your illustrious offspring; and that, after a long and righteous administration, you may be able to say, "When the ear heard me, then it blessed me; and when the eye saw me, it gave witness to me, because I delivered the poor that cried, the fatherless, and him that had none to help him. The blessing of him that was ready to perish came upon me, and I caused the widow's heart to sing for joy. I put on righteousness and it clothed me; my judgment was a robe and a diadem."—And thus, your memorialists will ever pray.

This instrument measured 168 feet in length and contained nearly 13,000 names. A copy of the Memorial was forwarded to each member of Parliament and other distinguished individuals. The following diagram and explanation were attached —

1	2	3	4	5	6	7
8	9	10	11	12	13	14
15	16	17	18	19	20	21
22	23	24	25	26	27	28
29	30	31	32	33	34	35
36	37	38	39	40	41	42
43	44	45	46	47	48	49

DIAGRAM AND EXPLANATION

The squares represent each a section, or six hundred and forty acres. Should it please her Majesty to grant the Petition of her Memorialists, the even numbers might be given to emigrants and the odd numbers retained, so that in future years the improvements made upon the property of the settlers, or even numbers, would greatly enhance the value of that retained by her Majesty and that ere long, as those districts became more densely populated, a price might be obtained for the sections represented by the odd numbers, that would go far to recompense the British Government for their present expenditure. This, not to speak of relief from starvation to many thousands of her Majesty's subjects here, should induce you to forward the desires of the industrious poor. In most schemes by emigration hitherto approved and aided by Government, great difficulty has been found to induce the people of this country to leave their native isle; but we are prepared, and shall guarantee, to send twenty thousand people of all trades, and from most districts in Scotland, England and Wales, at once, or as soon as vessels can be found to convey them.

The Memorial induced the following correspondence—

FROM DR. BOWRING, M.P.

House of Commons, February 8th, 1847.

Dear Sir—I should be glad to see emigration called in to aid in the reduction of our existing embarrassment; but emigration to Western America is emigration of the most costly character; and how do you propose to find the funds?

I am yours,

JOHN BOWRING.[1]

Thomas D. Brown, Esq., Liverpool.

FROM LORD JOHN RUSSELL, PRIME MINISTER

Downing Street, February 9th, 1847.

Sir—Lord John Russell has desired me to acknowledge the receipt of your letter of the 5th instant, transmitting the printed copy of a Memorial to the Queen, for the relief of the poor by emigration.

I am, Sir, your obedient servant,

GEORGE KEPPEL.[2]

Mr. Thomas D. Brown.

COPY OF REPLY SENT TO DR. BOWRING.

6, Goree. Liverpool, February 11th, 1847.

Dear Sir—To your favour of the 8th, on the subject of emigration to the Western Coast of America, and how we propose to find the funds, &c., I now reply.

We shall send a mixture of men, who have some means, with the multitudes who have none; "To take charge of them at the port of disembarkation, to remove them to the fields of employment," and *direct their energies when there:*—men who CAN govern, and in whom the people have the utmost confidence. But first, we want *grants of land*—as you will see from the printed copy of the Memorial I sent you—to be subsequently paid for by the sale of intermixed and reserved lands, which they will

---

[1] John Bowring (1792–1872) was an English linguist, translator, and political scientist, literary executor of the works of Jeremy Bentham. He was a member of Parliament from 1841 to 1849.

[2] George Thomas Keppel (1799–1891), secretary to Lord John Russell in 1847, was later the sixth Earl of Albemarle.

improve by their presence (see Diagram and Explanation on printed Memorial.) And we further desire, that all who cannot pay for their own passage to Western America, should be provided with *a free passage,* or its equivalent, Ten Pounds, for each grown up person, to be repaid within six years. The locality selected is Vancouver's island and Oregon; we have landed one ship's cargo in the bay of St. Francisco already, containing two hundred and thirty-four souls, bearing seeds and implements with them, &c., at their own cost; and we have many more ready to go, but those already there want labourers, mechanics, &c., who will require the above assistance to carry them thither; and we have nearly twenty thousand able and intelligent people ready and willing to depart now, chiefly from Scotland, England, and Wales. Our friends who have landed there, are at present in a disputed territory, under the American flag, and are solicited to remain. The Americans offer many inducements to settlers in California, but our friends would prefer the protection of the British nation.

Allow me here, dear Doctor, to make a remark on the present popular scheme now before your honourable House. It is proposed to borrow Sixteen Millions from the nation's fund, for twenty-two years, to make railways in Ireland, and thus, for a time only, give employment to the starving poor. This surely should draw forth the approbation of Irish landlords in your honourable House, for their property will thus become more valuable, by British capital, and the sinews of the Irish labourers, but these have no inheritance there, thus permanently improved. What is their condition when the railways are made? Not permanently better. Whereas, with one sixty-fourth part of this amount, and that too, only as a loan, to be repaid within six years, we immediately and *permanently* benefit twenty-five thousand people, and give a large inheritance to them, which may descend to their children's children; or with the same sum, now proposed to be lent to the Irish landlords, or expended on railways, ostensibly for the good of the poor, but really for the benefit of the soil, and of the already wealthy owners thereof, we could liberate, enrich, and elevate sixteen hundred thousand souls, in Western America, and extensively benefit the manufactures and commerce of Great Britain; and their very presence in these wilds would so enhance the value of the lands retained as security for the loan, that the prices paid by future settlers for this land, thus improved, would in a few years immeasurably exceed the first outlay or loan for removing them thither, and even the present cost of all the lands we respectfully request Her Majesty and Government to grant.

I have the honour to subscribe myself, dear Doctor,

Yours, most respectfully,

THOMAS D. BROWN.

John Bowring, LL.D., M.P.

P.S.—Allow me to call your attention to two articles in a little periodical I send you this day—No. 4, Vol. 9, of the *Millennial Star;* one is,

"American Project for Irish Emigration," the other, on "The State of Ireland."

London, 13th February, 1847.

Dear Sir—I do not know any resources from which the government would be disposed to vote public money for emigration to North Western America. The Railway Scheme in Ireland must be considered as rejected —but still the enormous demand upon the treasury will, I fear, exhaust its coffers—and you must be aware that it does not suffer to pay the amount of transport alone, for pauper emigrants. There must be provision made for their existence, and that is an expensive matter. Voluntary and self-supported emigration I should be glad to see encouraged towards Oregon and Vancouver's Island, and I would expect such emigrants as had pecuniary resources at their disposal would meet with encouragement from the government.

Yours very truly,

JOHN BOWRING.

Thos. D. Brown, Esq., Liverpool."

Just previous to the Memorial being despatched to the Queen, Lord John Russell, then Prime Minister, made a speech in the House of Commons, upon the subject of emigration, in which he disapproved of the removal of the poor to the United States and the Colonies. It is not our intention to discuss the arguments adduced by the Minister, in support of his position, it will be sufficient to say, that the Memorial was heard of no more.

Oregon and Vancouver, however, were not lost sight of, but on the 1st of April, Elder O. Spencer, then presiding over the Latter-day Saints in Great Britain and Ireland, issued the following notice—

"Emigration of the Saints from Islands to Island, and the opening up of their way from the four quarters of the earth to the final place of their destination." From this extract of President Young's letter, it will be perceived, that Vancouver Island is the gathering point of the Saints from the islands and distant portions of the earth. To this point the Saints of England should steadily direct their attention in all their arrangements for emigration. Any other arrangements, such as going in the company of Elder ———, through the States, or to some point east of the Rocky Mountains, must not be made upon our responsibility, or upon that of the Presidency in America. No companies are counselled by competent authority to go to any other parts of America than Vancouver Island. . . . We are perfectly aware that many have little or no employment, and some are anxious to emigrate before their means are too much exhausted. Perhaps some of the followers of Moses at the Red Sea, when they were hemmed in by surrounding difficulties, thought it better to press through the lesser difficulties of mountains or enemies, than to wait patiently for the word of the Lord by the mouth of their leader; but the Lord's way proved, in that instance, two things; first, the patience and faith of the people: second, their perfect deliverance by his hand. The poor Saints that were left in Nauvoo, through want of means to carry them all at once to the wilderness, were in constant jeopardy of their lives and property from blood-thirsty men. They were told that the way would open for them all to re-unite with their brethren in the wilderness, if they would abide faithful. This was the best instruction that the Council could give to their afflicted brethren that remained ungathered to the wilderness; and what was the result? They had eaten their last meal and meat, and sickness, fatigue, and the inhuman imprecations of violent and bloody men were upon them, but in the midst of it all, God also was there; he hearkened and heard their cry, mingled with the profanation of his holy name, by ungodly men; his eye pitied, and his arm brought salvation; he inspired the quails to come and offer themselves a willing sacrifice to the destitute and needy. The Saints partook thereof and were satisfied; God supplied their empty table. Oh ye beloved and afflicted Saints of England, fear not, but trust in the living God. You shall yet see the rod of the oppressor broken; and the inspiration of the Almighty that moved the fish to bring tribute money in his throat purse to Jesus, and the raven to minister to the prophet, shall uphold you in the day of great distress, if your faith fail not.

Notwithstanding the Saints had this permission to emigrate in the meantime to Vancouver, they did not avail themselves of it, but remained in constant expectation of counsel from the Twelve Apostles, which should point out the course to be taken in future by the emigrants. At length the Pioneers, who left Winter Quarters, Omaha Nation, west bank of the Missouri River, on the 14th of April, 1847, in search of a location beyond the Rocky Mountains, for the Saints to gather to, returned on the 31st of October, having fixed upon the Great Salt Lake Valley as the most suitable spot. The Twelve issued on the 23rd of December an Epistle to the Saints throughout the earth, in which the long wished for word to re-open the emigration from Great Britain and Ireland was given, which we quote.

To the Saints in England, Scotland, Ireland, Wales, and adjacent islands and countries, we say, emigrate as speedily as possible to this vicinity, looking to and following the counsel of the Presidency at Liverpool; shipping to New Orleans, and from thence direct to Council Bluffs, which will save much expense. Those who have but little means, and little or no labour, will soon exhaust that means if they remain where they are, therefore, it is wisdom that they remove without delay; for here is land on which, by their labour, they can speedily better their condition for their further journey. And to all Saints in any country bordering upon the Atlantic, we would say, pursue the same course: come immediately and prepare to go West—bringing with you all kinds of choice seeds, of grain, vegetables, fruit, shrubbery, trees, and vines—every thing that will please the eye, gladden the heart, or cheer the soul of man, that grows upon the face of the whole earth; also, the best stock of beast, bird, and fowl of every kind; also, the best tools of every description, and machinery for spinning, or weaving, and dressing cotton, wool, flax, and silk, &c., &c., or models and descriptions of the same, by which they can construct them; and the same in relation to all kinds of farming utensils and husbandry, such as corn shellers, grain threshers and cleaners, smut machines, mills, and every implement and article within their knowledge that shall tend to promote the comfort, health, happiness, or prosperity of any people. So far as it can be consistently done, bring models and drafts, and let the machinery be built where it is used, which will save great expense in transportation, particularly in heavy machinery, and tools and implements generally.

The Brethren must recollect that from this point they pass through a savage country, and their safety depends on good fire arms and plenty of ammunition;—and then, they may have their teams run off in open daylight, as we have had, unless they shall watch closely and continually.

This news was gladly received by tens of thousands who had been anxiously desiring for a long time to join the main body of the Church. It is true that many would have set out in search of it while it was wandering in the Indian territory and in the wilds of Iowa— but then very recently settled, and in which hundreds of Indians still roamed, not having been removed by the United States. The far-seeing prudence of the leaders, both in America and England, however, prevented such a step, until some permanent abiding place could be found.

On receiving the foregoing information, Elder Orson Spencer, issued instructions under date of February 1, 1848, to the following effect—

EMIGRATION.—The channel of Saints' emigration to the land of Zion, is now opened. The long-wished for time of gathering has come. Good tidings from Mount Zion! The resting place of Israel, for the last days, has been discovered. Beautiful for situation, and the ultimate joy of the whole earth, is the stake of Zion established in the mountains. In the elevated valley of the Salt and Utah Lakes, with the beautiful river Jordan running through it, from south to north, is the newly established stake of Zion.

It is now designed to fit out a ship's company of emigrants as soon as practicable. It is not well to embark from Liverpool later than about the first of March, until the warm season is past. In September, again, it may do to commence sending companies as far as Council Bluffs, from whence they can remove over the mountains in the following spring. The first company this winter ought to be embarked from Liverpool, as early as the 9th of February. The Presidents of Conferences are requested to forward to us the number of those who are prepared to emigrate by the 9th of February, and also the number that will be ready by the 23rd of February. The persons who wish their names registered to go in the first vessel that sails, are requested to forward their names with an advanced payment of £1, as deposit moneys. With this sum we shall secure the passages of those whose names and moneys are forwarded. The utmost economy, cheapness, and comfort will be studiously sought out for the passengers. We have no means of certifying definitely the price of passage to Council Bluffs or St. Louis. It would be well to calculate upon £7 passage-money to St. Louis; children under 12 years half price, including provisions and stores. The distance from St. Louis to the Bluffs, by the river, may be about 800 miles. The whole expense from Liverpool to the Bluffs, for one person, may be £10. Emigrants going beyond St. Louis, by the Missouri River, should be ready to go up that river early enough in the Spring to have the benefit of high water, as boats do not often pass as far as the Bluffs in the summer. Those also who intend to cross the mountains will find it desirable to leave Council Bluffs before the summer begins. Those who have adequate means for passing the mountains this season, it is thought, will be advised to do so, whilst others may tarry at the Bluffs until they can furnish the necessary means for pursuing their journey to Salt Lake. Some others may be advised, for want of adequate means, to tarry at St. Louis, until sufficient can be earned to carry them forward. The poor, and those who have not adequate means, will be assisted as far as practicable, obligating themselves to make remuneration when it is in their power. Our hopes, in regard to the deliverance of the poor, are firm and bright; never have they been more so than at the present moment. Let them wait their day, and watch their opportunity, keeping the commandments with all diligence, and they shall find deliverance sooner and more perfectly than the sceptical apprehend.

On the 20th of February, 1848, the *Carnatic*, Captain McKenzie, re-opened the emigration after a suspension of two years, and conveyed 120 passengers to New Orleans, under the presidency of Elder Franklin D. Richards,[3] assisted by Elders C. H. Wheelock and Andrew Cahoon, all three returning missionaries. This company was rapidly made up and sailed under the most pleasing anticipations. Nearly one hundred of the company were adults.

[3] For an account of the missionary work and later life of Franklin D. Richards see Franklin L. West: *Life of Franklin D. Richards* (Deseret News Press, Salt Lake, 1924).

On the 22nd of April, 1848, Elder Orson Pratt, one of the Twelve Apostles, was appointed at Winter Quarters to come to England, to superintend all the affairs of the Church in this and adjacent countries, and arrived on the 26th of July. On the 15th of August, in an Epistle to the Saints, Elder Pratt announced that he should conduct the emigration, and that the season for operation would be from the early part of September of one year until March of the next. Council Bluffs was still the intermediate station between Great Britain and Great Salt Lake Valley, and the emigration during this agency began to extend amazingly. It was thought by many of the Saints that none would be counselled to emigrate who were unable to go direct through to the Valley, but this impression being removed by the following explanation, which we extract from Elder Pratt's Epistle of September 15, 1849, some thousands emigrated during his agency who otherwise might have remained a longer time—

There has been much inquiry amongst the Saints of late, whether it is their privilege to go from this country unless they have means sufficient to carry them through to the Salt Lake Valley. We answer, that if none were to go only such as have sufficient funds to perform the whole journey, there would not be much gathering from this Island. We should hardly judge that there were a hundred families among the Saints in Great Britain who are able to go direct from this to the Salt Lake Basin. If there were mechanics here who had money to perform the whole journey without stopping, it would be wisdom to organize themselves into a company, and go directly to the Valley, according to the late Epistle of the Twelve, published in the 16th number of the present volume of the STAR. But the circumstances of the mechanics and agriculturists are such, that almost every one will be under the necessity of stopping in the States to procure something to bear their expenses still further. This extreme poverty will, for the present, we are sorry to say, prevent mechanics from following out the good and wise suggestions relative to organization. We are in hopes that the time will soon come when there will be capital sufficient to enable the Saints to pass on to the place of their destination without any delay.

As many of the Saints as can, should continue to gather up to Council Bluffs, where they will be far better situated than in any place abroad. We are certain that any healthy, able bodied person can, with one half the labour performed in this country, procure a good comfortable living from the soil. But let no one gather to the Pottawattomie country, with an expectation of being helped after they get there; for the Saints who are there are poor, having been several times, in years past, robbed of all their property. Let the Saints go with an expectation of helping themselves, without throwing a heavier burden upon the American Brethren.

After arriving at the Bluffs, diligence and patience will, within a few years, enable you to perform the balance of the journey.

Three of the Twelve Apostles, O. Hyde, G. A. Smith, and E. T. Benson, had been stationed at Council Bluffs by the Presidency of the Church, to receive the emigrants from abroad, and to promote their speedy removal to the Valley, as well as the removal of those Saints who had concentrated there after their exodus from Nauvoo and had not already taken their departure. Thus, many hundreds who left England with scarcely enough money to get to that point found upon their arrival many facilities for obtaining a fit-out for the balance of the journey, and at the present time few Saints indeed reside in that vicinity.

Elder O. Pratt's agency extended to Feb., 1851, and comprised twenty-one vessels carrying 5369 souls.

CHAPTER III

History of the Perpetual Emigrating Fund—Act of Incorporation by the General Assembly of Deseret

PREVIOUS to leaving Nauvoo, the Latter-day Saints entered into a solemn covenant in the Temple, that they would not cease their exertions until every individual of them who desired, and was unable to gather to the Valley by his own means, was brought to that place. This engagement was not forgotten, but as soon as the Saints in the Valley began to reap the rewards of their toil, and stock and the produce of the earth accumulated in their hands, the pledge was sacredly redeemed. The subject was introduced at the October Conference in 1849 by President H. C. Kimball, and a unanimous vote was there and then taken, to raise a fund for the fulfilment of the promise. A Committee, consisting of Willard Snow, John S. Fullmer, Lorenzo Snow, John D. Lee,[1] and Franklin D. Richards, was appointed to raise the money, and Bishop Edward Hunter was appointed to carry it to the States, to purchase wagons and cattle and to bring the poor Saints from the Pottawattomie lands. About 5000 dollars were raised this season. It was resolved at the same Conference that Elders A. Lyman and C. C. Rich be appointed agents to gather up means for the Fund in California; also that the Perpetual Emigrating Fund for the poor be under the direction of the First Presidency of the Church.

The objects of this Fund are set forth at length in the following extracts of letters, from President B. Young, to Orson Hyde, and Orson Pratt—

Great Salt Lake City, Oct. 16, 1849.

President Orson Hyde: Beloved Brother—We write to you more particularly at this time, concerning the gathering, and the mission of our general agent, for the PERPETUAL EMIGRATING FUND, for the coming year, Bishop Edward Hunter, who will soon be with you, bearing the funds

[1] John D. Lee later became notorious for his participation in the Mountain Meadow Massacre. For an excellent biography see Juanita Brooks: *John D. Lee* (Arthur H. Clark: Glendale, California, 1961).

already raised in this place; and we will here state our instructions to Bishop Hunter, so that you may fully comprehend our designs.

In the first place, this Fund has been raised by voluntary donations, and is to be continued by the same process, and by so managing as to preserve the same, and cause them to multiply.

Bishop Hunter is instructed to go direct to Kanesville, and confer with the general authorities of the Church at that place, and by all means within his reach, procure every information, so as to make the most judicious application of the funds in the purchase of young oxen and cows, that can be worked in effectually to the Valley, and that will be capable of improving and selling after their arrival, so as to continue the Fund the following year.

We will give early information, to those whom we have directed to be helped, and such others as he shall deem wisdom, being aided in his judgment by the authorities among you, so that they may be preparing their wagons, &c., for the journey.

Wagons are so plenty here, that it is very desirable not to purchase with the Perpetual Fund; but let those to be assisted make wagons of wood, when they cannot get iron, such as will be strong and safe to bring them here, so that all the funds may be appropriated to the purchase of such things as will improve in value, by being transferred to this place.

The poor can live without the luxuries of life, on the road and in the Valley, as well as in Pottawattomie and other places; and those who have means to purchase luxuries have moneys to procure an outfit of their own, and need no help, therefore let such as are helped, receive as little assistance in food and clothing, wagons, &c., as can possibly make them comfortable to this place, and when they arrive, they can go to work and get their outfit, of all things necessary for comfort and convenience, better than where they are, and even luxuries.

As early in the spring as it will possibly do, on account of feed for cattle, Brother Hunter will gather all his company, organize them in the usual order, and preside over the camp, travelling with the same to this place; having previously procured the best teamsters possible, such as are accustomed to driving, and will be gentle, kind and attentive to their teams.

When the Saints thus helped arrive here, they will give their obligations to the Church to refund to the amount of what they have received, as soon as circumstances will permit; and labor will be furnished, to such as wish, on the public works, and good pay; and as fast as they can procure the necessaries of life, and a surplus, that surplus will be applied to liquidating their debt, and thereby increasing the Perpetual Fund.

By this it will readily be discovered, that the funds are to be appropriated in the form of a loan, rather than a gift; and this will make the honest in heart rejoice, for they love to labor, and be independent by their labor, and not live on the charity of their friends, while the lazy idlers, if any such there be, will find fault, and want every luxury furnished them for their journey, and in the end pay nothing. The Perpetual

Fund will help no such idlers; we have no use for them in the Valley, they had better stay where they are, and if they think they can devise a better way of appropriating the emigrating funds, than we propose, let them go to work, get the funds, make the appropriation, set us a better pattern, and we will follow it; and by that time we are confident they will have means of their own, and will need no help.

Brother Hunter will return all the funds to this place next season, when the most judicious course will be pursued to convert all the cattle and means into cash, that the same may be sent abroad as speedily as possible on another mission, together with all that we can raise besides to add to it; and we anticipate the Saints at Pottawattomie and in the States, will increase the funds by all possible means the coming winter, so that our agents may return with a large company.

The few thousands we send out by our agent, at this time is like a grain of mustard seed in the earth; we send it forth into the world, and among the Saints, a good soil, and we expect it will grow and flourish, and spread abroad in a few weeks so that it will cover England, cast its shadow on Europe, and in process of time compass the whole earth: that is to say, these funds are designed to increase until Israel is gathered from all nations, and the poor can sit under their own vine, and inhabit their own house, and worship God in Zion.

If from any cause, there should be a surplus of funds in the hands of our agent, when he leaves the States with a company, he will deposit the same with some good house, subject to our order, or bring it with him as wisdom dictates.

We remain your Brethren in the Gospel,
BRIGHAM YOUNG,
HEBER C. KIMBALL,
WILLARD RICHARDS.

Great Salt Lake City, October 14, 1849.

To Elder Orson Pratt: Dear Brother—You will learn from our General Epistle, the principal events occurring with us, but we have thought proper to write you, more particularly in relation to some matters of general interest, in an especial manner, the Perpetual Emigration Fund for the poor Saints. This Fund, we wish all to understand, is *perpetual,* and in order to be kept good, will need constant accessions. To further this end, we expect all who are benefited by its operations, will be willing to reimburse that amount as soon as they are able, facilities for which will, very soon after their arrival here, present themselves in the shape of public works. Donations will also continue to be taken from all parts of the world, and expended for the gathering of the poor Saints. This is no Joint Stock Company arrangement, but free donations. Your office in Liverpool is the place of deposit for all funds received either for this, or the tithing funds, for all Europe, and you will not pay out only upon our order, and to such persons as we shall direct.

BRIGHAM YOUNG.

On the 29th of March, 1850, Elder Franklin D. Richards, one of the Twelve Apostles, arrived in England, having been appointed at Great Salt Lake City, on the 6th of October, 1849, to co-operate with Elder Orson Pratt, who was then presiding here, and immediately introduced the subject of the Perpetual Emigrating Fund to the British Churches. Donations were made straightway, and the first received was 2s. 6d., from Mark and Charlotte Shelly of Woolwich, on the 19th of April, 1850. The next was £1 from Geo. P. Waugh of Edinburgh on the 19th of June. This Fund during the second year of its existence was increased in value in Utah to about 20,000 dollars, and at a General Conference in Great Salt Lake City, on the 7th of September, 1850, a Committee of three, consisting of Willard Snow, Edward Hunter, and Daniel Spencer, was appointed to take care of and transact the business of the Poor Fund. It was also agreed to organize the Committee into a Company and get it chartered by the State.

In the same month the General Assembly of the Provisional State of Deseret passed an Ordinance incorporating the Perpetual Emigrating Fund Company which we give below—

Ordinance incorporating the Perpetual Emigrating Company.

Sec. 1.   Be it ordained by the General Assembly of the State of Deseret, that the General, or a Special Conference of the Church of Jesus Christ of Latter-day Saints, to be called at such time and place as the First Presidency of said Church shall appoint—is hereby authorized to elect, by a majority, a company of not less than *thirteen* men, one of whom shall be designated as their President, and the others Assistants.

Sec. 2.   This Company is hereby made and constituted a body corporate, under the name and style of the Perpetual Emigrating Company; and shall have perpetual succession, and may have and use a common seal, which they may alter at pleasure.

Sec. 3.   This Company, under the name and style aforesaid, shall have power to sue, and be sued, plead, and be impleaded, defend, and be defended, in all Courts of law or equity, and in all actions whatsoever; to purchase, receive, and hold property, real and personal; to receive, either by donation, on deposit, or otherwise, money, gold dust, grain, horses, mules, cows, oxen, sheep, young stock of all kinds, as well as any and every kind of valuables, or property, whatsoever; to emit bills of credit and exchange; to sell, lease, convey, or dispose of property, real and personal; and finally to do and perform any and all such acts as shall be necessary and proper for the interest, protection, convenience, or benefit of said Company.

Sec. 4. A majority of said Company at Head Quarters shall form a quorum, to do business, and shall elect from their number a Secretary, Treasurer, and Recorder; and shall have power to select and appoint all other officers and agents necessary to transact the business of said Company.

Sec. 5. It shall be the duty of the President of the Company to superintend all the business of the Company: he shall also sign all certificates, bills, vouchers, as well as all other papers and documents pertaining to the general business of the Company, which shall be countersigned by the Secretary.

Sec. 6. It shall be the duty of the Recorder, to record in a fair and legible hand, all the general business transactions of the Company, in good and sufficient books suitable for the purpose, which he shall procure at the expense of the Company, and safely keep and preserve the same.

He shall also make a faithful and accurate record of all donations to the Fund, of the names of persons donating, the amount, kind of property, &c., in books separate and apart from any other entries, and safely keep and preserve all the books and papers of the Company, the said books being free to the inspection and examination of all persons interested.

Sec. 7. The President and Assistants shall individually give bond and security in a sum of not less than ten thousand dollars, to be approved by the First Presidency of said Church, and filed in the General Church Recorder's office.

Sec. 8. The Secretary, Treasurer, and Recorder, and all other officers or agents appointed by the Company, shall give bond and security to be approved by the President of the Company, and filed in the Company Recorder's office; and all the Company shall be responsible for the acts of all officers and agents so appointed.

Sec. 9. There shall be a general settlement of all the business transactions of the Company, so far as returns are received from abroad, as often as once in each year; and it shall be the duty of all the officers and agents, to make out correct returns of all their transactions, and deliver or transmit the same to the Secretary of said Company, on or before the first day of December in each year; and it shall be the duty of the President of the Company to produce or exhibit a manifest of the same, and file it in the Recorder's office; as also, a copy of the same in the General Church Recorder's office, as soon as practicable thereafter.

Sec. 10. It shall be the duty of the Treasurer to keep an accurate account of all money or property received and disbursed by him, and make returns as herein before directed.

Sec. 11. The Company being collectively responsible for their own officers and agents, shall have the power of substituting others in their places, or dismissing them or any of them from office, and it shall be the duty of all persons so superseded or dismissed, to pay over and to pass into the hands of their respective successors, or the Company, all moneys, property, books, papers, accounts, of every name and nature, belonging, or in any way pertaining to the business of said Company.

Sec. 12. It shall be the duty of the Company to appoint one or more of their number to travel on the business of the Company, to procure wagons, cattle, mules, horses, &c., as shall be necessary for the purpose of the Emigration of the Poor; who shall also have the general direction of all matters and things pertaining to said Emigration, while abroad; and he or they shall also make their annual returns, as herein before directed.

Sec. 13. The entire proceeds of the business of this Company shall inure to the Perpetual Emigrating Fund for the Poor; whether arising from donations, insurance, deposits, exchange, increased value of property, or in any other way or manner whatsoever. And the general business of the Company shall be devoted, under the direction and supervision of the First Presidency of said Church, to promote, facilitate, and accomplish the Emigration of the Poor.

Sec. 14. The members of this Company, shall hold their offices at the pleasure of the Conferences herein before mentioned; but the First Presidency of said Church shall have power to fill all vacancies that may occur by death, removal, or otherwise; and all such persons so appointed, shall qualify as herein before directed, and hold the offices until superseded by an election.

Sec. 15. No officer, agent, or member of the Company, shall be permitted to retain in his hands any portion of the funds of the Company, as compensation; but shall receive such remuneration as shall be awarded him or them upon settlement with the Board of President and Assistants.

Sec. 16. All persons receiving assistance from the Perpetual Emigrating Fund for the Poor, shall reimburse the same in labor or otherwise, as soon as their circumstances will admit.

Sec. 17. The Islands in the Great Salt Lake, known as Stansbury's Island and Antelope Island, are hereby reserved and appropriated for the exclusive use and benefit of said Company, for the keeping of stock, &c."

At a Special Conference of the Church, held on the 15th of the same month, Brigham Young was chosen President of the Company; and Heber C. Kimball, Willard Richards, Newel K. Whitney, Orson Hyde, George A. Smith, Ezra T. Benson, Jedediah M. Grant, Daniel H. Wells, Willard Snow, Edward Hunter, Daniel Spencer, Thomas Bullock, John Brown, William Crosby, Amasa Lyman, Charles C. Rich, Lorenzo D. Young, and Parley P. Pratt, assistants.

The organization was completed by electing Willard Richards, Secretary; Newel K. Whitney, Treasurer; and Thomas Bullock, Recorder. Newel K. Whitney died on the 23rd of the same month, and Daniel Spencer was elected Treasurer in his stead. Elders Orson Hyde, Orson Pratt, Franklin D. Richards, and John Brown were appointed Travelling Agents.

The Latter-day Saints in the British Isles have contributed nobly to this Fund ever since its existence among them. Donations as high as £400 have been made to it by single individuals, and the total amount contributed up to July, 1854, was £6832 19s. 11d. European missions and persons residing abroad, some of them actually residing at the foot of the Himalaya mountains, had, up to the same time, deposited with the British agency £280 0s. 9¼d., making a total of £7113 0s. 8¼d., in addition to the value of the Fund in Utah. One very important feature of the Fund is that it enables persons residing in Utah to send for their friends from the old countries or from wherever an agency is established. This object is effected by depositing with the P. E. Fund Company in the Valley the amount of the passage money, and they direct the agent abroad to send the parties out. By reference to the table it will be seen that up to April, 1854, 349 persons of this class had been sent out from the British Isles. As the number of immigrants increases in Utah, it is highly probable that this branch of the Company's operations will be proportionately extended.

The total number sent out by the British agency up to the close of the last season was 1724 and included 33 from the French mission, 12 from the Italian, and 3 from the Swiss. The Scandinavian agency appropriated in 1853, to the assistance of such emigrants, £136 15s. 6d., and in January, 1854, sent out two other persons.

In the selection of persons to be emigrated by these donations, regard is had, first, to integrity and moral worth; and secondly, to occupations. The selection, to a considerable extent, is intrusted to the Presidents of the Conferences and Branches of the Church, who, from their intercourse with the Saints, are undoubtedly the best able to judge of their respective claims upon the assistance of the Fund.

CHAPTER IV

History of the Emigration from 1851 to 1852—
Contemplated Routes *via* the Isthmus of Panama
and Cape Horn

ELDER Orson Pratt was succeeded by Elder Franklin D. Richards, in the emigrational department, in February, 1851. The first vessel despatched under this agency was the *Olympus,* which closed the business until January, 1852. In the meantime the Fifth General Epistle of the Presidency of the Church had been issued, and it was stated therein that Elders Amasa Lyman and Charles C. Rich, with a company occupying about 150 wagons, had been sent to form a settlement in the southern part of California, near the port of San Diego,* Williams' Ranche, and the Cajon pass, with a view to the forming of a line of settlements between the Pacific and Great Salt Lake City, a distance of about 800 miles, and passable in the winter.† In connexion with this, the English Saints were directed to cease emigrating by the usual route through the States, and up the Mississippi and Missouri rivers, and to remain where they were until they should hear again from the Presidency. It was designed to open up a way

---

* San Diego, on San Diego Bay, the capital of the county of San Diego, State of California, is about 470 miles in a straight line nearly S. E. from San Francisco, and on the main road from Sacramento city. Lat. 32° 44′ 41″ N., long. 117° 8′ W. It is a post-town and port of entry. The Bay is about 6 miles long, and from 1 to 2 wide, and the harbour is said to be the best on the coast after Acapulco. The foreign arrivals at this port for the year ending June 30th, 1852, were 29 (tons 19,016), 28 of which were American vessels. The clearances for foreign ports for the same period were 13 (tons 5169), 12 of which were American vessels.

† A settlement was made by this company at San Bernardino, on the San Diego and Salt Lake road. The valley in which it is situated is exceedingly beautiful, having great natural advantages, and is about 30 miles long, east and west, and 15 miles wide, north and south. On the east is the San Bernardino mountain rising almost to the region of perpetual snow. Besides having a multitude of springs, the valley is watered by the Santa Anna river. About 60 miles to the south-west is the coast—Los Angeles being 60 miles, San Pedro 75 miles, and San Diego 80 miles distant. San Bernardino has been constituted by the State of California, a separate county, and sends one representative to the Legislature. Before the settlement was a year old, roads were made, houses, flour and saw mills were built, and flour was sent to the San Francisco market, where the settlement also made large purchases of merchandise. The population is something over 1000. San Diego is intended to be the trading point.

via Panama, Tehuantepec, or around Cape Horn, and to land the passengers at San Diego, and thus save three thousand miles of inland travelling, mostly through a sickly climate. The Presidency in Liverpool were directed to make inquiry as to the expense and facilities of the various routes from Liverpool to San Diego, and to report at an early date to the First Presidency, that, if possible, arrangements might be made for emigration that way by the next fall. Inquiry was immediately instituted by Elder Richards for vessels that the Saints could be shipped in from this country by the above contemplated routes, so as to carry out the instructions of the epistle, but it was found that the expense and the difficulties attending these routes would at that time have precluded emigration from this country, and report was made accordingly. The result was the emigration was reopened by the Sixth General Epistle of the Presidency, on the old route, *but not upon the old plan*. Formerly all were counselled to emigrate who could reach Council Bluffs, but now, in consequence of the contemplated evacuation of that place by the Saints, and indeed of the whole territory of Iowa, none were advised to emigrate who could not accomplish the entire journey to Great Salt Lake Valley without detention. This required about £20 per head, and of course the emigration was considerably reduced under this agency, only two ships being sent out after the issue of the epistle; but at the same time it is quite probable that the number of emigrants that reached the Valley that year was larger than it would have been, if unrestricted emigration to Council Bluffs had been advised.

The interests of the P. E. Fund were well cared for and promoted under this agency, so much so, that up to January, 1852, £1410 had been donated, and in the two ships that sailed in January and February 251 persons were sent out, requiring above £1000 more than had then been donated. This extra outlay was supplied in the meantime by Elder Richards. This was the first operation, and it required much careful thought and wise deliberation to adopt plans that would carry this branch of the emigration properly through to the Valley. It was also the first time that arrangements had been made before leaving Liverpool for the passage through. It is presumed that such a journey as this was never before undertaken by so large a number of people and with such limited resources. An ocean had to be traversed, rivers ascended, and plains crossed, and the whole must be provided for before embarkation.

The subject was well canvassed, the plans were matured, and Elder Abraham O. Smoot, an American Elder, and a man of much experience, was selected to go forward with means to procure teams, flour, meat, and other necessary articles, and have them ready upon the frontiers of the plains by the time the company should arrive from England.

In addition to this charge he was instructed to continue with the company to the end of the journey, to superintend all its interests. It was also necessary that men of experience should be selected to accompany the emigrants to New Orleans, to pay their passage up the rivers, and deliver them into Elder Smoot's hands. This was intrusted to Elder John S. Higbee, who sailed with the *Kennebec,* and Elder Isaac C. Haight, who sailed with the *Ellen Maria.* The latter was specially instructed to assist Elder Smoot in fitting up the company for the plains, and then to return to England, which he did on the 27th of June of the same year.

In order to carry out the spirit and intent of the 16th section of the Ordinance, incorporating the Perpetual Emigrating Fund Company, which reads, "All persons receiving assistance from the Perpetual Emigrating Fund for the Poor, shall re-imburse the same in labour or otherwise, as soon as their circumstances will admit," the annexed engagement was entered into by the emigrants, and still is by all persons who leave the British Isles under the auspices of the Company—

-*Perpetual Emigrating Fund Company, organized at Great Salt Lake City,*

Deseret, U.S.A., October 6th, 1849.
————————————— Agent, Liverpool.

We, the undersigned, do hereby agree with and bind ourselves to the Perpetual Emigrating Fund Company, in the following conditions, viz.—

That, in consideration of the aforesaid Company emigrating or transporting us, and our necessary Luggage, from Great Britain to the Valley of the Great Salt Lake, according to the Rules of the Company, and the general instructions of their authorized Agents;

We do severally and jointly promise and bind ourselves to continue with, and obey the instructions of, the Agent appointed to superintend our passage thither: that we will receipt for our passages previous to arriving at the several ports of New Orleans, St. Louis, and Kanesville;

And that, on our arrival in the Great Salt Lake Valley, we will hold ourselves, our time, and our labour, subject to the appropriation of the Perpetual Emigrating Fund Company, until the full cost of our emigration is paid, with interest if required.

In the May following the departure of the P. E. Fund emigrants, the presidency of Elder F. D. Richards in the British Isles closed, and this gave him an opportunity of arriving in the Valley in time to join the convoy which welcomed the pilgrims into the city; and also the pleasure of seeing the final success of those plans which had, a few months previously, cost him so much anxious care, for it must be remembered that, after all, this first operation was only an experiment. We subjoin an interesting account from the *Deseret News* of the arrival of this company, with President Young's address to the emigrants—

*Report of the First Arrival from England by the
Perpetual Emigrating Fund*
ADDRESS TO THE EMIGRANTS, BY PRESIDENT B. YOUNG
Friday, Sept. 3, 4½ *p.m.*

Capt. A. O. Smoot's company, of thirty-one wagons, was escorted into this city, by the First Presidency of the Church, some of the Twelve Apostles, and many of the citizens on horseback and in carriages.

Capt. Pitt's band, in the President's spacious carriage, met the company at the mouth of Emigration kanyon, where the Saints of both sexes, of nearly 70 years of age, danced and sung for joy, and their hearts were made glad by a distribution of melons and cakes; after which the band came in the escort, and cheered the hearts of the weary travellers with their enlivening strains.

Next in the procession came a band of pilgrims—sisters and children, walking, sunburnt, and weather-beaten, but not forlorn; their hearts were light and buoyant, which was plainly manifest by their happy and joyful countenances.

Next followed the wagons. The good condition of the cattle, and the general appearance of the whole train, did credit to Bishop Smoot, as a wise and skilful manager,—who was seen on horse, in all the various departments of his company, during their egress from the kanyon to encampment.

As the escort and train passed the Temple Block, they were saluted with nine rounds of artillery, which made the everlasting hills to shake their sides with joy; while thousands of men, women, and children gathered from various parts of the city, to unite in the glorious and joyful welcome.

After coralling on Union Square, the emigrants were called together, and President Young addressed them as follows:—

"I have but a few words to say to the brethren and sisters, at the present time. First I will say, may the Lord God of Israel bless you, and comfort your hearts. (The company and bystanders responded AMEN.)

"We have prayed for you continually; thousands of prayers have been offered up for you, day by day, to Him who has commanded us to gather

Israel, save the children of men by the preaching of the Gospel, and prepare them for the coming of the Messiah. You have had a long, hard, and fatiguing journey across the great waters, and the scorched plains; but, by the distinguished favours of heaven, you are here in safety.

"We understand that the whole company that started under brother Smoot's guidance, are alive and well, with but a few exceptions. For this we are thankful to our Father in heaven; and our hearts are filled with joy, that you have had faith to surmount the difficulties that have lain in your path; that you have overcome sickness and death, and are now with us to enjoy the blessings of the people of God in these peaceful valleys. You are now in a land of plenty, where, by a reasonable amount of labour, you may realize a comfortable subsistence.

"You have had trials and sufferings in your journey, but your sufferings have been few compared with thousands of your brethren and sisters in these valleys. We have, a great many of us, been under the harrow for the space of 21 years. I trust you have enjoyed a good measure of the Spirit of the Lord in the midst of your toils; and now, as you have arrived here, let your feelings be mild, peaceable, and easy, not framing to yourselves any particular course that you will pursue, but be patient until the way opens before you.

"Be very cautious that you do not watch the failings of others, and by this means expose yourselves to be caught in the snares of the devil; for the people here have the failings natural to man, the same as you have; look well to yourselves, that the enemy does not get the advantage over you; see that your own hearts are pure, and filled with the spirit of the Lord, and you will be willing to overlook the faults of others, and endeavour to correct your own.

"With regard to your circumstances and connexions here, I am little acquainted; but this I can say, you are in the midst of plenty. No person here is under the necessity of begging his bread, except the natives; and they beg more than they care for, or can use. By your labour, you can obtain an abundance; the soil is rich and productive. We have the best of wheat, and the finest of flour; as good as was ever produced in any other country in the world. We have beets, carrots, turnips, cabbage, peas, beans, melons, and I may say, all kinds of garden vegetables, of the best quality.

"The prospects are cheering for fruits of different kinds. The grapes that we have raised this season, are, doubtless, as fine as were ever exhibited for sale in the London market. The peach, we expect, will do well also. We had but few last year; this season we have more. We are under the necessity of waiting a few years before we can have much fruit; but of the staple articles of food, we have a great abundance.

"With regard to your obtaining habitations to shelter you in the coming winter,—all of you will be able to obtain work, and by your industry, you can make yourselves tolerably comfortable in this respect, before the winter sets in. All the improvements that you see around you, have been

made in the short space of four years; four years ago this day, there was
not a rod of fence to be seen, nor a house, except the Old Fort, as we call
it, though it was then new. All this that you now see, has been accomplished by the industry of the people; and a great deal more that you do
not see, for our settlements extend 250 miles south, and almost 100 miles
north.

"We shall want some of the brethren to repair to some of the other
settlements, such as mechanics and farmers; no doubt they can provide
themselves with teams, &c., to bear them to their destinations. Those who
have acquaintances here, will all be able to obtain dwellings, until they
can make accommodations of their own.

"Again, with regard to labour,—don't imagine unto yourselves that
you are going to get rich, at once, by it. As for the poor, there are none
here, neither are there any who may be called rich, but all obtain the
essential comforts of life.

"Let not your eyes be greedy. When I met you this afternoon, I felt to
say, *this is the company that I belong to*—the 'Poor company,' as it is
called, and I always expect to belong to it, until I am crowned with
eternal riches in the celestial kingdom. In this world I possess nothing,
only what the Lord has given to me, and it is devoted to the building up
of His kingdom.

"Do not any of you suffer the thought to enter your minds, that you
must go to the gold mines, in search for riches. That is no place for the
Saints. Some have gone there, and returned; they keep coming and going,
but their garments are spotted, almost universally. It is scarcely possible
for a man to go there and come back to this place with his garments
pure. Don't any of you imagine to yourselves that you can go to the gold
mines to get anything to help yourselves with: you must live here; this
is the gathering place for the Saints. The man who is trying to gain to
himself the perishable treasures of this world, and suffers his affections to
be staid upon them, may despair of ever obtaining a crown of glory. This
world is only to be used as an apartment, in which the children of men
may be prepared for their eternal redemption and exaltation in the
presence of their Saviour; and we have but a short time allotted to us
here, to accomplish so great a work.

"I will say to this company, they have had the honour of being escorted
into the city by some of the most distinguished individuals of our society, and a band of music, accompanied with a salutation from the cannon. Other companies have not had this mark of respect shown to them;
they belong to the rich, and are able to help themselves. I rejoice that
you are here; and that you will find yourselves in the midst of abundance
of the common necessaries of life, a liberal supply of which you can easily
obtain by your labour. Here is the best quality of food; you are in the
best atmosphere that you ever breathed; and we have the best water that
you ever drank. Make yourselves happy, and do not let your eyes be like
the fool's eye, wandering after the things of this world; but inquire what

you can do that shall be for the best interest of the kingdom of God.

"No man or woman will be hurried away from the wagons; but you may have the privilege of living in them, until you get homes.

"I hope the brethren who live near by, or those who live at a distance, will send our brethren and sisters some potatoes and melons or any thing else they have, that they may not go hungry; and let them have them free of charge, that they may be blessed with us, as I exhorted the people last Sabbath.

"I have not anything more to say to you at this time, as my presence is wanted in another place. I pray the Lord God of Israel to bless you; and I bless you in the name of Jesus. Amen."[1]

[1] The French Botanist Jules Rémy and British naturalist Julius Brenchley heard Brigham Young say publicly in 1855, in discussing the Perpetual Emigration Fund: "The assistance given to the emigrants has brought the Church into debt to the amount of 70,000 dollars; now you must pay this sum, otherwise I will sell up your property; and if this is not enough, I will then sell your wives and children." Jules Rémy and Julius Brenchley: *A Journey to Great Salt Lake City*, II, 60.

CHAPTER V

History of the Emigration from 1852 to April, 1854~ Extensive Operations of the Perpetual Emigrating Fund Company

ON the 1st of May, 1852, Elder Samuel W. Richards came into charge of the British Mission, and under his agency the emigration attained to greater perfection and was opened up to a larger number of individuals, in the same amount of time, than at any previous period. The anxiety of thousands of the Saints to gather to Utah had become intense, so much so, that Elder Richards was frequently desired to organize companies who would walk the entire overland journey and assist to haul the provisions and luggage also. Much prudence and caution were now required to restrain the overflowing spirit which the Saints were giving way to, and at the same time to promote the emigration of as large a number as practicable in the approaching season. In the meantime the Seventh General Epistle of the First Presidency of the Church had been issued, and on the 17th of July was published to the British Churches. The Saints were, in this Epistle, exhorted to gather to Utah speedily, by tens of thousands. The language was—"Let all who can procure a loaf of bread, and one garment on their back, be assured there is water plenty and pure by the way, and doubt no longer, but come next year to the place of gathering, even in flocks, as doves fly to their windows before a storm." This needed no interpretation but was reiterated by hundreds of Elders throughout the country and gave fresh vigour to the desire already burning in the breasts of thousands to emigrate in the coming season. This anxious desire had to be met in some way or other, and after much deliberation it was determined to fit out companies of emigrants in 1853, for the entire journey, at £10 for each person over 1 year old, and £5 each for those under that age, and it was hoped that by sending efficient men in advance to procure the necessary supplies and teams, the emigrants might be got through upon those terms. As many as 957 persons availed themselves of this arrangement, but it was found necessary to procure a loan upon the teams to complete the journey.

Elder S. W. Richards was appointed, September 30th, 1852, an agent to the P. E. Fund Company, and during this season 400 persons were assisted out by the P. E. Fund, for whom similar arrangements were made to those for the £10 companies.

There were 955 emigrants, who either made their own arrangements for the overland journey, or procured their teams by sending money forward in advance of themselves by the agent charged with the superintendence of the P. E. Fund and the £10 emigration. The price of a team consisting of two pairs of oxen, two cows, and one wagon, was estimated at £40, and £2748 10s. was sent forward by this class. The emigration now consisted of four classes, first, the P. E. Fund emigrants ordered from the Valley; second, the P. E. Fund emigrants selected in the British Isles; third, the £10 emigrants; and fourth, the ordinary emigrants, embracing those who sent money forward to procure teams, and all the balance. The entire expense involved in this season's emigration could not have been less than £30,000. The agent intrusted with the overland part of the journey, for both the P. E. Fund and £10 emigration, was Elder Isaac C. Haight, who had in the previous year assisted Elder Smoot. The president of each ship's company, in which there were emigrants of these descriptions, had charge of them until their delivery to Elder Haight.

From the experience of 1853, and the increased prices of cattle, wagons, and provisions, occasioned by the great California and Oregon emigration, which has scoured the frontiers and many miles around for several years past, it was found necessary during the last season to charge £13 per head instead of £10, for those who went in companies similar to the £10 companies of 1853. This amount will possibly cover the expense. The growing interest of the P. E. Fund in the minds of the Saints, however, reduced this class to 86, by inducing those of the emigrants who were not ordered from the Valley by the P. E. Fund Company, nor selected here by its agent, or who did not provide their own outfit, to come under the auspices or arrangements of the P. E. Fund Company, and many of them donated to the Fund all the money they had, and signed the bond to pay in the Valley the whole cost of their passage money to that place. The amount thus donated was £1800 8s., and although the benefit of this was not felt last season, the Fund was actually enriched to that amount.

The ordinary emigration was not so large last season as it was in the previous season, but more money was sent forward for the purchase of teams, the amount being £3575. The price of a team was estimated at £45, but it appears from recent advices to be higher.

The P. E. F. Emigration of last season was very large, and the agent charged with the superintendence of the overland journey is Elder Wm. Empey, a man of experience in the customs and business of the United States, and in the purchase of the outfit. He has the assistance of Elder Dorr P. Curtis and of other Elders of experience *en route* for the Valley. It is fully anticipated that their joint labours will be abundantly sufficient to carry the emigration in a prosperous state into the Valley. The supervision of the emigrants from Liverpool until their delivery to Elder Empey was given to the Presidents of the respective ships, and they will aid, if directed, until the companies are through the Valley.

The total number of persons shipped under this agency was 4346, and it was expected that very few would fail of going through to the Great Salt Lake Valley. The emigration of this number would involve from first to last an expenditure of not less than £70,000.

CHAPTER VI

Foreign Emigration Passing Through Liverpool

AFTER the Latter-day Saints had established missions upon the continent, emigrants soon began to pass through Liverpool *en route* for Great Salt Lake Valley. The first company, numbering 28, was from the Scandinavian Mission and was re-shipped at Liverpool, on board the *Italy* for New Orleans, on the 11th of March, 1852, under the direction of Elder Erastus Snow, one of the Twelve Apostles, and founder of the Scandinavian mission. The next company was from the same mission and numbered 297, and was re-shipped at Liverpool on board the *Forest Monarch* for New Orleans, on the 16th of January, 1853, under the direction of Elder Willard Snow, President of the mission at that time.

Donations to the Perpetual Emigrating Fund having been commenced to be made in Scandinavia, particularly in Denmark, £136 15s. 6d. was appropriated during Elder Willard Snow's Presidency, to the assistance of a number of the persons that sailed in the *Forest Monarch*.

The next company from the continent was 17 persons from the German mission, who sailed from Liverpool in August or September, 1853.

In January, 1854, and under the Presidency of Elder John Van Cott, Scandinavia sent out two companies, numbering 678 persons, two of which were assisted by the P. E. Fund. Elders were sent in charge of the Saints and were to continue with them from Copenhagen to Great Salt Lake Valley, men who could speak both English and Danish and had travelled the whole route before. To accomplish the overland journey, £3667 was sent forward to Elder Empey, to procure the teams, provisions, &c. The point of embarkation from the Scandinavian mission is Copenhagen, and to this place the emigrants gather and form one company or more as the case may be. They are then conveyed from Copenhagen to Liverpool. The route taken in 1853 was across the Baltic to Kiel, from thence per railway to Altona, from thence across the North sea, to Hull, and then per railway to Liverpool. During the last season the route was a little difficult being from Kiel to Gluckstadt, instead of Altona. It will readily be conceived that the continental emigration is characterized by more vicissitudes than the British, and requires a proportionately greater amount of careful and prudent arrangement to preserve the lives of the people and guard their pockets. Under the wisest and most economical guidance, the removal of this 678 people from their homes in Frederickstadt, Osterzisöer, and Brevig in Norway; Schana, in Sweden; and Zealand, Jutland, Lalland, Falster, Möen and Fyen in Denmark, to Great Salt Lake Valley, will consume not less than £10,000.

In the first vessel occupied by the Scandinavian emigration in the last season were 33 persons from the German mission, shipped under the direction of Elder Daniel Carn, President of the mission at that time.

The emigration from the French, Swiss, and Italian missions has hitherto, upon arrival in Liverpool, joined the British, and has been shipped in the vessels sent out by the President of this mission as will be seen by referring to the table. Interpreters speaking French, Italian, and English have accompanied them.

CHAPTER VII

Statistics of The Latter-day Saints' Emigration from the British Isles

WE HERE introduce tables showing the statistics of the emigration from the British Isles and from Europe, for the commencement. They are deficient in some particulars; but are, no doubt, as complete and correct as it is possible now to make them.

Date of Sailing	Parley P. Pratt, Agent. *1840—1*				
	Vessel	Tons	Captain	President	No. of Souls
1840 Aug. 7	North America			Theodore Turley	200
1841 Feb.	Sheffield Echo Uleste			Hyrum Clark	235

A vessel sailed about February from Bristol.
Elder P. P. Pratt states that up to April, 1841, about 1000 had emigrated.
[For James Linforth's corrected account of the statistics of 1840–41, see p. 137].

	Parley P. Pratt and Amos Fielding, Agents. *1841—2*				
Sep. 21	Tyrean			Joseph Fielding	207
Nov. 8	Chaos			Peter Melling	170
1842 Jan. 12	Tremont				143
Feb. 5	Hope		Soule		270
" 20	John Cummins				200
Mar. 12	Hanover			Amos Fielding	200
Sep. 17	Sidney		Cowen	Levi Richards	180
Soon after the *Sidney*	Medford		Wilber	Orson Hyde	214
	Henry		Peirce	John Snider	157
Oct. 29	Emerald		Leighton	Parley P. Pratt	250
					1991

The number of passengers in the *John Cummins* and *Hanover* are approximate.

There is a discrepancy in the number of souls on the last vessel. Elder Hyrum Clark, who assisted to fit out the company, says she carried 314, but we have taken the number stated by Elder Pratt.

	Amos Fielding and Hyrum Clark, Agents. *1843*					
1843						
Jan. 17	Swanton	709	Davenport	Lorenzo Snow		212
Mar. 8	Yorkshire	808	Bache			80
″ 21	Claiborne	686	Burgess			106
Sep. 5	Metoka	944	M'Laren			280
Oct. 21	Champion	729	Cochrane			91
						769
	Reuben Hedlock, Agent. *1844—6*					
1844						
Jan. 23	Fanny	529	Patterson			210
Feb. 6	Isaac Allerton	594	Torney			60
″ 11	Swanton	677	Davenport			81
Mar. 5	Glasgow	594	Lambert			150
Sep. 19	Norfolk	661	Elliott			143
1845						
Jan. 17	Palmyra	691	Barstow	Amos Fielding		
Sep.	Oregon	650	Borland			
1846						
Jan. 16	Liverpool	600	Davenport	Hyrum Clark		45

The particulars during this agency are very deficient. Some vessels are altogether omitted, but Mr. Hedlock states that from the commencement of his agency up to February, 1846, he shipped 990 souls, 113 of whom agreed to pay their passage money, amounting to £466 12s., in Nauvoo. He does not appear to have shipped any L. D. Saints afterwards, though it is possible he did.

		Orson Spencer, Agent. 1848			
1848					
Feb. 20	Carnatic	654	M'Kenzie	F. D. Richards	120
Mar. 9	Sailor Prince	950	M'Kechnie	Moses Martin	80
					200
		Orson Pratt, Agent. 1848—51			
Sep. 7	Erin's Queen	821	Campbell	Simeon Carter	232
" 24	Sailor Prince	950	M'Kechnie	L. D. Butler	311
Nov.	Lord Sandon	678	Walsh		11
1849					
Jan. 29	Zetland	1283	Brown	Orson Spencer	358
Feb. 6	Ashland	422	Harding	John Johnson	187
" 7	Henry Ware	539	Nason	Robert Martin	225
" 25	Beuna Vista	547	Linnell	Dan Jones	249
Mar. 5	Hartley	466	Morrell	W. Hulme	220
" 12	Emblem	610	Cammett	Robert Deans	100
Sep. 2	James Pennell	570	Fullerton	Thomas Clark	236
" 5	Berlin	613	Smith	James G. Brown	253
Nov. 10	Zetland	1293	Brown	S. H. Hawkins	250
1850					
Jan. 10	Argo	999	Mills	Jeter Clinton	402
Feb. 18	Josiah Bradlee	649	Mansfield	Thomas Day	263
Mar. 2	Hartley	445	Morrell	David Cook	109
Sep. 4	North Atlantic	800	Cook	David Sudworth	357
Oct. 2	James Pennell	570	Fullerton		254
" 17	Joseph Badger	890	Schofield	John Morris	227
1851					
Jan. 6	Ellen	893	Phillips	J. W. Cummings	466
" 22	G. W. Bourne	663	Williams	William Gibson	281
Feb. 2	Ellen Maria	768	Whitmore	George D. Watt	378
					5369

Franklin D. Richards, Agent. 1851—2

Date of Sailing	Vessel	Tons	Captain	President	P. E. Fund			Ordinary	Total
					Ordered	Otherwise	Total		
1851 March 4	Olympus	744	Wilson	William Howell				245	245
1852									
Jan. 10	Kennebec	1070	Smith	John S. Higbee	27	42	69	264	333
Feb. 10	Ellen Maria	768	Whitmore	I. C. Haight	19	163	182	187	369
March 6	Rockaway							30	30
					46	205	251	726	977

Samuel W. Richards, Agent. 1853

Date of Sailing	Vessel	Tons	Captain	President	P. E. Fund			£10 Company	Ordinary	Total
					Ordered	Otherwise	Total			
1853 Jan. 17	Ellen Maria	768	Whitmore	Moses Clawson		13	13	189	130	332
„ 23	Golconda	1170	Kerr	Jacob Gates		24	24	128	169	321
Feb. 5	Jersey	954	Day	Geo. Halliday	9	33	42	178	94	314
„ 15	Elvira Owen	958	Owen	J. W. Young		11	11	154	180	345
„ 28	International	1100	Brown	Chris. Arthur				237	188	345
March 26	Falcon	900	Wade	Cor. Bagnall	70	165	235	35	54	425
April 6	Camillus	780	Day	C. E. Bolton	4	67	71	36	121	324
	(Miscellaneous)				4		4		19	228
					87	313	400	957	955	23
										2312

Samuel W. Richards, Agent. 1854

Date of Sailing	Vessel	Tons	Captain	President	P. E. Fund			£13 Company	Ordinary	Total
					Ordered	Otherwise	Total			
Jan. 22	Benjamin Adams	1457		H. P. Olsen	3	3	6		6	6
Feb. 4	Golconda	1170	Drummond	Dorr. P. Curtis	29	205	234	27	203	464
" 22	Windermere	1299	Kerr	Daniel Garn	55	207	262	26	189	477
March 5	Old England	1117	Fairfield	John O. Angus					45	45
" 12	John M. Wood	1146	Barstow	Rob. Campbell	34	205	239	21	133	393
April 4	Germanicus	1167	Hartley	Richard Cook	25	75	100	2	118	220
" 8	Marshfield	999	Fales	William Taylor	70	161	231	10	125	366
" 24	Clara Wheeler	995	Torrey						29	29
	(Miscellaneous)		Nelson			1	1		33	34
					216	857	1073	86	875	2034

The *John M. Wood* and *Marshfield* include in their total numbers 59 persons from the Swiss and Italian missions and 45 from the French mission.

Summary of the Emigration by the British Agency

Year	Agent	P. E. Fund			£10 Company	£13 Company	Ordinary	Total
		Ordered	Otherwise	Total				
1840–1841	Parley P. Pratt						1000	1000
1841–1842	Pratt & Fielding						1991	1991
1843	Fielding & Clark						769	769
1844–1846	Reuben Hedlock						990	990
1848	Orson Spencer						200	200
1848–1851	Orson Pratt						5369	5369
1851–1852	F. D. Richards	46	205	251			726	977
1853	S. W. Richards	87	313	400	957		955	2312
1854	Do.	216	857	1073		86	875	2034
Totals		349	1375	1724	957	86	12875	15642

Scandinavian Emigration Re-shipping at Liverpool

Date of Sailing from Liverpool	Vessel	Tons	Agent	Captain	President	P. E. Fund	Ordinary	Total
1852 March 11	Italy	749	Erastus Snow	Reid				28
1853 January 16	Forest Monarch	976	Willard Snow	Brewer	J. S. Forssgren			297
1854 January 3	Jesse Munn	895	John Van Cott	Duckett	B. C. Larsen			300
,, 22	Benjamin Adams	1457		Drummond	H. P. Olsen	2	376	378
								1003

A portion of the emigrants on board the *Forest Monarch*, received assistance in their emigration from the P. E. Fund, to the amount of £136 15s. 6d., but we cannot give the number so helped.

The countries from which this emigration was principally made up were Denmark, Norway, and Sweden.

German Emigration Re-shipping at Liverpool   Daniel Carn, Agent

Date of Sailing from Liverpool	Vessel	Tons	Captain	President	Total
1853 About Aug. 24	Jesse Munn	895	Duckett	B. C. Larsen	17
1854 January 3					33
					50

General Summary

British Agency	15,642
Scandinavian do	1,003
German do	50
	16,695
To this number may be safely added for persons who have emigrated between the seasons, or not through the established Agencies, &c.	500
Total	17,195

Commencing with the Company that sailed in the *Argo,* the professions and occupations of the emigrants through the British agency have been noted, and the following classification will show to what extent each trade or calling has been represented.

A

2 Artists, 1 Accountant.

B

2 Bookbinders, 1 Bootcloser, 47 Blacksmiths, 2 Butlers, 1 Boatbuilder, 4 Block printers, 4 Bleachers, 26 Bakers, 21 Butchers, 15 Brick makers, 96 Boot and Shoe makers, 6 Basket makers, 9 Builders, 23 Bricklayers, 4 Brass founders, 1 Barm dealer, 10 Boiler makers, 1 Britannia Metal smith, 1 Bookseller, 2 Ballers, 2 Brass tube makers, 1 Bobbin reeler, 2 Brush makers, 2 Brokers, 3 Boatmen, 1 Bobbin turner, 1 Brazier, 1 Brewer, 1 Blacking maker, 1 Blade forger.

C

3 Chemists, 12 Cabinet makers, 5 Coopers, 1 Calico dyer, 28 Clerks, 5 Cutlers, 55 Carpenters, 1 Carder, 7 Coach-makers, 4 Clothlappers, 4 Carriers, 1 Curry-comb maker, 6 Cotton spinners, 1 Cloth drawer, 3 Cutter men, 2 Cloth dressers, 1 Coach harness maker, 6 Calico printers, 2 Compositors, 6 Comb makers, 1 Carpet weaver, 1 Clogger, 1 Coke burner, 1 Coal merchant, 10 Cordwainers, 2 Chair makers, 2 Carters, 2 Coachmen, 1 Candle maker, 2 Carvers, 1 Commission merchant, 2 Clothiers, 2 Confectioners, 1 Cork-screw maker, 1 Cotton-wipe sizer, 1 Carding master, 2 Coach painters, 1 Chandler, 1 Currier, 1 Cloth tenter, 1 Copper and tin-plate worker, 1 Coachsmith, 1 Cattle dealer, 1 Crosshand.

D

11 Dyers, 6 Dealers, 3 Dressers, 7 Drapers, 1 Delver, 1 Designer, 1 Doll maker, 4 Druggists, 1 Dancing master, 1 Diesinker, 1 Dentist.

E

6 Engine fitters, 46 Engineers, 3 Engravers, 1 Edge-tool maker, 2 Excavators, 2 Enginesmiths.

F

1 Feltmonger, 20 Frame-work-knitters, 2 Fancy dyers, 120 Farmers, 2 Feeders, 4 Fitters, 5 Firemen, 1 Furnace man, 2 File cutters, 6 Flax dressers, 1 Fustian dresser, 2 File hardeners, 2 Fishermen, 1 Footman, 1 Fork grinder, 1 Fruiterer, 1 Framesmith, 1 Fender maker.

G

2 Gamekeepers, 43 Gardeners, 12 Grocers, 5 Gas fitters, 1 Gas-lamp maker, 1 Gas-tube maker, 2 Glass workers, 1 Glass stainer, 2 Glass cutters, 1 Gun-implement maker, 1 Gate-keeper, 1 Grinder, 1 Gas-meter maker, 1 Gun-lock maker, 2 Glaziers, 2 University Graduates, 1 Groom, 1 Gun finisher, 5 General dealers.

H

3 Hackle and gill-pin grinders, 3 Hosiers, 5 Hatters, 1 Hackle and gill-pin scourer, 6 Hair dressers, 5 Hawkers, 1 Horse-nail forger, 1 Harness

maker, 1 Hemp dresser, 1 Harness man, 1 Haberdasher, 1 House decorator.

I

2 Ironmongers, 2 Innkeepers, 1 Iron fitter, 3 Iron moulders, 1 Iron-bedstead fitter, 1 India-rubber maker, 3 Iron founders, 1 Iron-stone contractor.

J

38 Joiners, 1 Jobbing-smith, 1 Joiner and Cabinetmaker, 1 Jeweller, 1 Knife grinder.

L

457 Labourers of all kinds, 1 Linen weaver, 3 Lace makers, 1 Land agent, 1 Law stationer, 1 Lead miner, 1 Lime burner, 1 Lace-machine builder, 1 Lath maker, 2 Last makers, 1 Lamp maker, 1 Linen draper, 1 Lawyer.

M

6 Mechanics, 226 Miners, 15 Millers, 73 Masons, 35 Mariners, 5 Master mariners, 8 Moulders, 1 Mill man, 1 Milk dealer, 1 Maltster, 4 Machine makers, 4 Millwrights, 1 Manager, 1 Mill warper, 1 Musician.

N

1 Needle maker, 1 Naval officer, 1 Nailer, 1 Needle pointer.

O

3 Overlookers, 1 Omnibus conductor, 1 Oil refiner, 20 Oil makers, 1 Oil merchant.

P

7 Plumbers and Glaziers, 1 Print colourer, 15 Painters, 12 Potters, 2 Ploughmen, 8 Printers, 17 Plasterers, 2 Paviers, 1 Piano-forte maker, 1 Pitman, 8 Puddlers, 3 Paper makers, 7 Porters, 1 Pearl worker, 3 Piercers, 1 Perfumer, 2 Packers, 1 Pot-burner, 2 Pressers, 1 Points-man, 1 Penciller for engravers, 1 Pressman, 1 Pawnbroker, 1 Polisher, 2 Platelayers, 1 Pattern maker, 1 Plait dealer, 1 Pattern designer, 1 Pen-blade grinder, 1 Physician.

Q

3 Quarrymen.

R

6 Rope makers, 5 Ribbon weavers, 2 Reed makers, 1 Rope-yarn hackler, 3 Rollers, 2 Riggers, 1 Rule maker, 1 Railway goods manager.

S

4 Stewards, 1 Stay maker, 5 Schoolmasters, 5 Silk weavers, 1 Silk manufacturer, 22 Spinners, 1 Stationer, 10 Shepherds, 27 Smiths, 15 Servants, 3 Shovel makers, 30 Sawyers, 3 Slaters, 1 Scale maker, 12 Stone masons, 4 Shopkeepers, 1 Salesman, 3 Sailmakers, 1 Sweep, 1 Silversmith, 1 Shipbuilder, 2 Ship carpenters, 9 Shipwrights, 1 Stoker, 6 Soldiers, 1 Sailcloth weaver, 1 Shopman, 1 Sword maker, 1 Sizer, 1 Screw maker, 2 Stonecutters, 1 Storekeeper, 1 Sugar refiner, 1 Stone sawyer, 1 Strop-pecker maker, 1 Stone merchant, 1 Sugar boiler, 2 Stampers, 1 Surgical Instrument maker, 1 Saddler, 2 Sugar bakers, 1 Steel-pen maker.

T

74 Tailors, 6 Tinmen, 1 Typefounder, 2 Tea dealers, 3 Commercial travellers, 1 Thread maker, 1 Toll-gate keeper, 1 Teamster, 2 Tanners, 1 Tobacconist, 1 Twiner, 1 Tinner, 1 Throstle tenter, 1 Trimming maker, 1 Tape finisher, 1 Twist hand, 1 Table-knife hafter.

U

2 Upholsterers, 4 Umbrella makers.

V

1 Vellum binder, 2 Valets, 1 Vice maker, 1 Velvet weaver.

W

2 Warpers, 9 Weavers, 2 Watch-glass makers, 3 Watchmakers, 2 Wood turners, 7 Wool combers, 17 Wheelwrights, 2 Whitesmiths, 3 Warehousemen, 1 Wiredrawer, 1 Woodman, 2 Wool spinners, 4 Warp dressers, 1 Winder, 1 Watch and Clock maker.

Y

1 Yeoman.

450 not stated.[1]

[1] The listing of these professions and trades is a quiet reminder of the difficulties most of the emigrants would have in adjusting to life on the frontier. Here are a few definitions:

barm—a yeast formed on brewing liquors
cooper—a buyer or trader
clogger—a maker of clogs or wooden soles for clogs
chandler—a maker of candles
currier—a dresser of leather
delver—an excavater
hackle—a comb for dressing flax
hawker—a falconer
maltster—a maker of malt
puddler—one who converts cast iron into wrought iron by puddling
pointsman—switchman
rigger—one who fits the rigging of sailships
sawyer—one who saws timber into planks
slater—one who lays slates
throstle—a machine for spinning wool, cotton, etc.
whitesmith—one who works in tin or galvanized iron

CHAPTER VIII

Mode of Conducting the Emigration

THE object of the Latter-day Saints' emigration being not a speculation, but the fulfilment of a divine command, the spiritual and temporal comfort and happiness of the emigrants are the prominent aim on the part of those charged from time to time with the superintendence of the business. Consequently, from the first we find that arrangements have been made to assist the emigrants while in Liverpool, and experienced Elders have been sent with the vessels to superintend the voyage, in connexion with the masters. The time selected for embarkation has been from September until March or April, and latterly, from January to April, which enables the emigrants to arrive upon the U. S. frontiers between April and June, sufficiently early to cross the plains and the mountains before winter sets in and the mountain passes are partially filled with snow. While the emigration was only to Nauvoo or to Council Bluffs, these circumstances did not of course interfere, the only object then being to pass New Orleans before the summer and sickly season commenced. The duties and responsibilities of all charged with the oversight of any part of the business were proportionately less than they are now, yet they have always been sufficiently onerous and have exercised the best faculties of the Elders and others engaged.

Applications for passage are received by the agent, and when sufficient are on hand a vessel is chartered by him, and the passengers are notified by printed circulars containing instructions to them how to proceed, when to be in Liverpool to embark, also stating the price of passage, the amount of provisions allowed, &c. It is often the case that one Conference or district furnishes a ship load, or the greatest part of it. In such cases arrangements are made for them to embark together, and the President of the Conference or some other suitable person contracts with the Railway Company for their conveyance to Liverpool altogether, which saves much expense.

In contracting for the vessel, it is agreed that the passengers shall go on board either on the day of their arrival in Liverpool or the day following, and although this arrangement may be inconvenient to them, it saves the ruinous expense of lodging ashore and preserves many an inexperienced person from being robbed by sharpers, who make extensive experiments in this port upon the unwary. When the passengers are on board, the agent, who is always now the President of the Church in the British Islands, proceeds to organize a Committee, consisting of a President and two Counsellors, and, if possible, Elders are selected who have travelled the route before, or, at least, have been to sea. These men are received by the emigrants by vote, and implicit confidence is reposed in them. The Committee then proceed to divide the ship into wards or branches,[1] over each of which an Elder or Priest is placed, with his assistants, to preside. The President of the company than appoints from among the adult passengers, watchmen, who in rotation stand watch day and night over the ship until her departure, and after nightfall prevent any unauthorized person from descending the hatchways. When at sea the Presidents of the various wards see that passengers rise about 5 or 6 o'clock in the morning, cleanse their respective portions of the ship, and throw the rubbish overboard. This attended to, prayers are offered in every ward, and then the passengers prepare their breakfasts, and during the remainder of the day occupy themselves with various duties. At 8 or 9 o'clock at night, prayers are again offered, and all retire to their berths. Such regularity and cleanliness, with constant exercise on deck, are an excellent conservative of the general health of the passengers, a thing already proverbial of the Latter-day Saints' emigration. In addition to this daily routine, when the weather permits, meetings are held on Sundays, and twice or thrice in the week, at which the usual Church services are observed. Schools for children and adults are also frequently conducted. When Elders are on board who are either going or returning to the Valley, and have travelled in foreign countries, they interest the passengers by relating the history of their travels and describing the scenes they have witnessed and the vicissitudes through which they have passed. From the *John M. Wood* which sailed on the 12th of March, 1854, we have accounts that the Swiss and Italian emigrants studied the

---

[1] The "ward" is the unit in the Mormon Church which corresponds to a parish. "Branch" usually refers to the same kind of unit in an area where Mormon activities are governed by missionaries.

English language; and the English emigrants, the French and Italian languages. In this they were aided by several missionaries from Italy and Switzerland, conversant with those languages. Lectures on various subjects also were delivered. These agreeable exercises no doubt break the monotony of a long sea-voyage and improve the mental capacities of the passengers. The good order, cleanliness, regularity, and moral deportment of the passengers generally seldom fail to produce a good impression upon the Captain, crew, and any persons on board who are not Latter-day Saints. The result is they attend the religious meetings or exercises, and few ships now reach New Orleans without some conversions taking place. In the *Olympus* which sailed in March, 1851, fifty persons were added to the Church during the voyage, and in the *International* which sailed in February, 1853, forty-eight persons, including the Captain and other officers of the ship were added. Not the least good resulting from the excellent management of the companies is the relaxation of much rigidity necessarily belonging to Captains at sea, and the extension of many a favour to the passengers in times of sickness, and when they can well appreciate the kindness. Most of the vessels sent out have had humane and gentlemanly Captains, some of whom have been presented at New Orleans with testimonials from the passengers.

As an instance of the estimation in which the mode of conducting the L. D. Saints' emigration is held in high quarters, we quote from the *Morning Advertiser* of June 2. "On Tuesday, says the London correspondent of the *Cambridge Independent Press,* I heard a rather remarkable examination before a committee of the House of Commons. The witness was no other than the supreme authority in England of the Mormonites [Elder S. W. Richards] and the subject upon which he was giving information was the mode in which the Emigration to Utah, Great Salt Lake, is conducted. . . . He gave himself no airs but was so respectful in his demeanour, and ready in his answers, that, at the close of his examination he received the thanks of the committee in rather a marked manner. . . . There is one thing which, in the opinion of the Emigration Committee of the House of Commons, they [the L. D. Saints] can do, viz.—teach Christian shipowners how to send poor people decently, cheaply, and healthfully across the Atlantic."

On arriving at New Orleans, the emigrants are received by an agent of the Church stationed there for that purpose, and he procures suitable steamboats for them to proceed on to St. Louis without detention. Elder James Brown was the agent for the last season. It is the duty of this agent, furthermore, to report to the President here the condition in which the emigrants arrive and any important circumstances that may be beneficial to be known to him. At St. Louis another agent of the Church co-operates with the agent sent from England. From thence the emigrants are forwarded still by steamboat to the camping grounds, which were last year at Keokuk in Iowa, at the foot of the lower Rapids of the Mississippi, 205 miles from St. Louis, and this year at Kanzas, in Jackson County, Missouri, 14 miles west of Independence. Here the emigrants find the teams which the agent has prepared waiting to receive them and their luggage. Ten individuals are the number allotted to one wagon and one tent. The Perpetual Emigrating Fund Company this year allowed 100 lbs. of luggage, including beds and clothing, to all persons above eight years old; 50 lbs. to those between eight and four years old; none to those under four years. The wagons are procured to order in Cincinnati and St. Louis and are conveyed by steamboat to the camping grounds. The wagon-bed is about 12 feet long, 3 feet 4 inches wide, and 18 inches deep, and boxes should be made to fit to advantage.

The cattle are purchased of cattle dealers in the western settlements and are driven to the camping grounds. The full team consists of 1 wagon, 2 yoke of oxen, and 2 cows. The wagon-covers and tents are made of a very superior twilled cotton, procured in England for the emigration of 1853 and the present year. It is supplied to the emigrants before their departure, and they make the tents and covers on the voyage and thus save expense. A common field tent is generally used. The material is 27 inches wide, and 44 yards are used for a tent, and 26 for a wagon-cover. The two cost about two guineas. The poles and cord are procured by the agent in the United States.

Each wagon this year containing the £13 and P. E. Fund emigrants was supplied with 1000 lbs. of flour, 50 lbs. of sugar, 50 lbs. of bacon, 50 lbs. of rice, 30 lbs. of beans, 20 lbs. of dried apples and peaches, 5 lbs. of tea, 1 gallon of vinegar, 10 bars of soap, and 25 lbs. of salt. These articles, and the milk from the cows, the game caught on the plains, and the pure water from the streams, furnish to hundreds better diet, and more of it, than they enjoyed in their native lands, while toiling from 10 to 18 hours per day for their living. Other emigrants, who have means, of course, purchase what they please, such as dried herrings, pickles, molasses, and more dried fruit and sugar, all of which are very useful, and there is every facility for obtaining them from New Orleans to the edge of the plains.

As soon as a sufficient number of wagons can be got ready, and all things are prepared, the company or companies move off under their respective Captains. The agent remains on the frontiers until all the companies are started, and then he goes forward himself, passing the companies one by one, and arrives in the Valley first to receive them there and conduct them into Great Salt Lake City. We shall not detail further under this head as we shall have occasion to do it upon the route.

From the review we have taken of the modus operandi of the emigration, although we have merely glanced at the frame-work, it will be readily seen that it is of no ordinary magnitude, but brings into requisition directly and indirectly the labours of hundreds of individuals besides the emigrants themselves, and at the present time involves an outlay of not less than £40,000 to £50,000 each year, an amount nevertheless small, when the number of emigrants and the distance are considered. It is only by the most careful, prudent, and economical arrangements that such a number of persons could be transported from their various British and European homes across the Atlantic Ocean and three thousand miles into the interior of America with such a sum of money.

CHAPTER IX

Instructions to Emigrants

IN preparing to emigrate to Great Salt Lake Valley, the exercise of a little forethought will save much disappointment and probably expense. In the first place, an intending emigrant's means must be his guide. If he be a mechanic and have sufficient money to pay his passage and to procure suitable clothing, and have a few pounds in his pocket afterwards, he would do well to procure some of the best tools of his trade and useful books; if a professional man, a few of the most useful instruments and treatises pertaining to his profession, but all unnecessary things, especially weighty ones, should be left behind. The expense of transporting such goods—shipping and re-shipping, loading and unloading—is frequently more than they are worth, or the owner has money to pay, they are consequently left behind when too late, and where in many instances they will sell for nothing at all, or, at least, for little; the emigrant then discovers his miscalculation. It must also be remembered that many articles are now being made in Utah, and that there are large mercantile houses which are constantly trading between there and the States, supplying the inhabitants with an endless variety of goods, especially of the finer sorts. Substantial clothing, linen, flannels, cottons, tapes, thread, needles, pins, worsted, hooks and eyes, buttons of all descriptions, thimbles, combs, writing paper, pens and pencils, are very useful articles to take, and some of them occupy but little room, and are very light. All kinds of fineries, such as silks, satins, velvet, ribbons, &c., &c., can be obtained to a great extent of the merchants there and of the California emigrants, who are sometimes glad to exchange those articles in the Valley for its fresh produce. It is well to take good firearms, especially rifles, for use upon the plains and afterwards, but it should be remembered that no powder or other combustibles can be taken on board the ship; they can be procured in the United States. A general assortment of choice seeds of the hardier sorts should be taken, and should be hermetically sealed to prevent their being spoiled. Capitalists might take a great many other articles, and machinery to advantage, which are much required in Utah, but the bulk of the emigrants, having but limited means, should not encumber themselves, if they wish to get through the journey without partial or complete detention by the way. Indeed most of the emigrants have too much luggage, and it has been a great fault with some who have supposed that the shipping of their goods at Liverpool would be the last expense. If they would get through without hindrance, they should first make sure of their passage, then of some good warm clothing (for there are many chilling blasts between England and Utah) and afterwards, as circumstances will permit, of some or all of the articles named above, and they will find the benefit of such a course many times before the journey is completed.

The space allowed on ship-board for luggage is ten cubic feet, but it is better for the passengers to have as much as possible put into the hold, which will give them more room around their berths and a freer ventilation between decks. Clothes that would spoil by dampness and those wanted during the voyage should be kept up. Passengers should have among them a claw-hammer, a few tenpenny nails, and some cord, that they may make fast all their boxes which are kept up between decks, before going to sea and getting sick, when they are unable to do it. Much confusion is caused and damage done if boxes are left loose.

The price of steerage passage to New Orleans ranges from £3 10s. to £5 for adults, and from £3 to £4 10s. for children between 14 years and 1 year old; infants are free. The *Passengers' Act* of June, 1852, secs. xxvii and xxxii, requires the broker or agent to supply the passengers with 70 days' provisions, if the ship sails between the 16th of January and the 14th of October, and 80 days' if she sails between the 14th of October and the 16th of January, according to the following scale—

DIETARY SCALE

3 quarts water, daily
2½ lbs. Bread or Biscuit, not inferior in quality to Navy Biscuit
1 lb. Wheaten Flour
5 lbs. Oatmeal
2 lbs. Rice
½ lb. Sugar
2 oz. Tea
2 oz. Salt

} Weekly to each statute adult, and half the amount to children between 14 years and 1 year old.

The Act authorizes substitution as follows—

5 lbs. of good potatoes, or $\frac{1}{2}$ lb. of Beef or Pork exclusive of bone, or of Preserved meat, or $\frac{3}{4}$ lb. of dried Salt Fish, or 1 lb. of Bread or Biscuit, not inferior in quality to Navy Biscuit, or 1 lb. of best Wheaten Flour, or 1 lb. of Split Peas for $1\frac{1}{4}$ lb. of Oatmeal, or for 1 lb. of Rice; and $\frac{1}{4}$ lb. of Preserved Potatoes may be substituted for 1 lb. of Potatoes. Vessels clearing out from *Scotch* or *Irish* Ports may not issue less than $3\frac{1}{2}$ lbs. of Oatmeal for each statute adult weekly.

In addition to the above scale, the L. D. Saints are furnished for the voyage with $2\frac{1}{2}$ lbs. of sugar, 3 lbs. of butter, 2 lbs. of cheese, and 1 pint of vinegar for each statute adult, and half the amount to children between 14 years and 1 year old; 1 lb. of beef or pork weekly to each statute adult is substituted for its equivalence in oatmeal. This quantity of provisions enables many of the passengers to live during the voyage more bountifully than they were in the habit of living in this country, but we would still advise those who can do it to procure more flour and sugar and a few other articles such as we will enumerate:—potatoes, ham, dried salt fish, onions, pickled onions, preserves, cayenne pepper, baking powders, mustard, sherbet, carbonate of soda, lime juice, plums, and currants. Marine soap is very useful on ship-board.

Roasted potatoes can be eaten by most persons during sea sickness. Lime juice mixed with sugar and water is healthy, agreeable, and cheap. About two spoonfuls to half a pint of water, sweetened to taste, make a pleasant drink.

Such provisions as are unconsumed on arrival at New Orleans are given to the passengers, instead of being returned to this country, as is the case with other emigrant ships. If a vessel make a quick trip, there is a considerable amount left, which of course is a valuable assistance to poor passengers. The *John M. Wood* made a short trip, and the amount of provisions saved to the P. E. Fund Passengers was 150 lbs. of tea, 19 barrels of biscuit, 5 barrels of oatmeal, 4 barrels and 4 bags of rice, and 3 barrels of pork.

The first part of a sea voyage has often an astringent effect upon the bowels, and emigrants would do well to provide themselves with aperient medicines, if any. By regulating their diet and partaking, as far as possible, of such food as tends to relaxation instead of constipation, emigrants would very much escape sea-sickness and its attendant irregularities.

Passengers furnish their own beds and bedding, and likewise their cooking utensils, such as a boiler, saucepan, and frying-pan. They should also provide themselves with a tin porringer, tin plate, tin dish, knife and fork, spoon, and a tin vessel, or an earthen one encased in wickerwork, to hold three quarts of water for each person. A box or barrel for provisions, and small bags or boxes for tea, salt, &c., are required. A strong canvas bag to hold the biscuits is far preferable to putting them with other provisions, as it prevents the biscuits from acquiring a disagreeable taste. The cooking utensils and other articles named should be purchased, if possible, before the passengers leave home, as they can be procured of a better quality than those sold in Liverpool, which in many cases are unfit for use.

The ship provides the cooking apparatus and fuel, and the Passengers' Act requires that "every 'Passenger Ship' carrying as many as one hundred statute adults shall have on board a seafaring person, who shall be rated in the Ship's Articles as Passengers' Steward, and who shall be approved by the Emigration Officer at the Port of Clearance, and who shall be employed in messing and serving out the provisions to the passengers, and in assisting to maintain cleanliness, order, and good discipline among the passengers, and who shall not assist in any way in navigating or working the ship" (sec. xxxv). Likewise that "every 'Passenger Ship' carrying as many as one hundred statute adults shall also have on board a seafaring man, or if carrying more than four hundred statute adults, two seafaring men, to be rated and approved as in the case of Passengers' Stewards, who shall be employed in cooking the food of the passengers" (sec. xxxvi). When the number of passengers exceeds one hundred statute adults, and the space allotted to each on the passengers' deck is less than fourteen clear superficial feet, or when, whatever may be the space allotted to the passengers, the number of persons on board (including cabin passengers, officers, and crew) exceeds five hundred, the Act requires a duly qualified Medical Practitioner to be carried, and rated on the ship's articles.

The Act provides for the berthing of the passengers. It requires that the berths shall be six feet in length, and that eighteen inches in width shall be allowed to each statute adult. No two passengers, unless members of the same family, may be placed in the same berth, nor in any case may persons of different sexes, above the age of fourteen years, unless husband and wife, be placed in the same berth. All unmarried male passengers of the age of fourteen years and upwards are berthed in the fore part of the vessel and are separated from the rest of the passengers by a strong bulk head. The Government Emigration Officer at the port of embarkation, previous to the ship's departure, sees that all these regulations are carried out, and that the provisions and water are shipped of good quality, and in the proper quantity for the passengers on board. If that functionary properly fulfils his duty, it is almost impossible for an emigrant ship to proceed to sea under an infraction of any clause of the Passengers' Act. The details of this Act properly carried out, and the regulations established by the L. D. Saints, in all their ships, secure to the passengers an amount of comfort, security, and health, which other emigrants of the same class are strangers to.

In getting on board, a stated time for receiving the luggage having been advertized, and the adult male passengers being mostly at the ship at the same time, they assist each other, and save the expense of porters, and the liability of being robbed by a class of men who frequent all emigrant ships, ostensibly as porters, but really to pilfer from the passengers. If porters are engaged, it should be those who are licensed. They are designated by a badge worn on the arm, and if complaint is necessary, reference to the porter's number will aid the police to find him.

While in Liverpool, emigrants should not expose themselves to wet or cold, or weary themselves unnecessarily. They should be especially careful of their children. By going on ship-board in a good degree of health, passengers are much better able to withstand the effects of sea-sickness, and change of diet and habit.

The Parliamentary Committee on Emigrant ships before referred to have issued two Reports, wherein they make a number of recommendations, calculated to be of great benefit to emigrants generally, but especially to such as do not sail in the Latter-day Saints' ships. The excellent sanitary arrangements and good discipline which characterize all their ships have prevented that fearful mortality which has occurred on other emigrant ships, and aroused the very serious attention of the Governments of Great Britain and the United States, to the importance of providing further legislative enactments to check the growing evil.

The Committee recommended that an addition should be made to the Dietary Scale; that the water should be carried in metal casks;

that not less than 14 feet between decks should be allowed to each statute adult; that the practice of counting two children under 14 years old as only one adult, should be modified; that no ship should carry more than 500 passengers, except in special cases; that the number of passengers allowed to be carried without a surgeon should be reduced from 500 to 300; that power should be given to the Government to prevent emigrant ships from leaving any ports where cholera or other epidemics prevail, and should any exception be made, that the ship should carry a surgeon, though the number of passengers should be under 300; and that the detention money for the support of emigrants when the ship is delayed, should be raised from 1s. to 1s. 6d., per day, for each statute adult. The stowage of the cargo; the manning of the ship; the boats and other appliances for saving life; the compasses, and numerous other matters have received the attention of the Committee, and valuable suggestions are made thereon. The Committee also consider that vessels bringing emigrants across the Irish Channel for embarkation should be compelled to protect them from the weather, and thus prevent that sickness resulting from exposure which often lays the foundation for permanent disease. At present the cattle are better protected on those boats than the deck passengers. Lodging houses too, have been under consideration. Finally, it is urgently suggested by the Committee, that negotiations should be immediately opened with the Government at Washington for an effective co-operation in some system, for the mutual enforcement of regulations calculated to insure the advantages to emigrants now under contemplation. We are happy to see that several of the items referred to in the Report are such as Elder S. W. Richards, in his evidence before the Committee, made remarks upon.

On the 7th of December, 1853, the United States appointed a select Committee of the Senate, "to consider the causes and extent of sickness and mortality prevailing on board the emigrant ships in the voyage to America, and whether any and what legislation is needed for the better protection of the health of passengers on board such vessels." This Committee have made their Report, and we give the following extracts from a digest of it—

The First Section is devoted to securing a sufficient supply of pure air for the emigrants, by limiting the number of passengers to one, for every three tons in the Winter, and two for every five tons in the Summer, and requiring a clear space upon the upper deck, proportioned in size to the number of passengers, to be appropriated to their use as a promenade. It also requires a well provided medicine chest in each ship, and provides for a decent and wholesome arrangement of all private accommodations for the passengers.

The Second Section is penal, and fixes 100 dollars as the fine for each passenger above the legal number, and 500 dollars for the violation of any other provision of the First Section.

The Third Section requires that the provisions for the emigrants shall be cooked and distributed under the orders of the Captain, under a penalty of a fine of 1000 dollars, and imprisonment, and damages to the amount of 3 dollars per day to each passenger for neglect of any kind in the performance of this duty.

The Fourth Section is devoted to the enforcement of discipline, cleanliness, and order, and is one of the most important in its object and wise in its provisions which the Committee has reported.

Two infants under one year of age are to be counted as one passenger, and the Eighth Section provides that if deaths from any cause shall have occurred during a passage, the Captain of the vessel, within twenty-four hours after making his return to the collector of the port where he arrives, in which the fact of such death is of course stated, shall pay the passage money received from the passenger or passengers so dying into the hands of the collector, who shall pay it to the executors or administrators of the deceased, if it be applied for by them within twelve months, if not, to the Board or Commissioners of emigration appointed by the States, to the entire exclusion of national or religious protective societies. Death also determines the right to collect unpaid passage money. It is evident that this is the most important provision in the bill in its operation upon shipowners and masters; and, at the first blush it certainly appears unreasonable that, if a Captain have fulfilled all the stringent requirements of the Bill, he and his owners should be made to suffer for an event which would then happen only in the ordinary course of nature, and which no care on their parts could have prevented. On the other hand it is urged by the Committee that a provision of this kind has been the most effective protection to the emigrants under sentence of transportation to Botany Bay. The British Government, after determining that the passage money of only such convicts as were safely landed, should be paid, found the mortality on convict ships, reduced from *ten per cent, to one and a half per cent.* This certainly is a formidable fact, in support of the extraordinary provisions of this section.

The time suggested for the bill to go into operation, is in thirty days after its passage for vessels sailing from America, and sixty days for those which sail from Europe.

Should the two Governments pass Acts framed on the basis of these Reports, it will of course materially increase the expense of emigration to North America, but will at the same time give ample return for it in the increased comfort, health, and safety which will be afforded to the passengers in the stringent provisions of the Acts, and every philanthropist must rejoice to see some better arrangements made for the thousands of steerage passengers who annually leave the shores of Great Britain and Ireland and the Continent.

We have now received, in considerable detail, the emigration which has already taken place, the mode in which it has been conducted, and have given some general instructions to future emigrants. We did not purpose to extend this part of the Work to so great a length, but it was found impossible to present the subject fairly in a compass, and we were much encouraged by influential persons to give it unabridged. The subject has never before been given in its present consecutive and complete form, which will render it particularly valuable as a record and, we trust, interesting to all Latter-day Saints.

As there will, no doubt, another season of emigration transpire before this Work is complete, it is necessary to say that this review is written up to August, 1854. We shall probably issue an appendix with the last Part, bringing the history of the emigration up to that time.

CHAPTER X

[*Frederick Piercy Begins His Narrative*]

Departure from Liverpool~San Domingo~Cuba~ The Gulf of Mexico~The Mississippi River~ The Balize~Arrival at New Orleans~Attempts of "Sharpers" to Board the Ship and Pilfer from the Emigrants

On the 5th day of February, 1853, in compliance with previous arrangements, I embarked in the *Jersey* for New Orleans, on my way to Great Salt Lake Valley. My object was to make sketches of the principal and most interesting places on the Route, and Great Salt Lake City, which were afterwards to be published with suitable descriptions and statistics. On my return I was solicited to allow my narrative of the journey to be published likewise. I consented, although conscious of its want of completeness; indeed the particular object of my journey, and my limited time, entirely prevented me from gathering that variety and store of information, which might very properly be looked for in the narrative of a traveller. The original plan of the work, however, renders it a matter of secondary importance, for the editor will give historical, geographical, biographical, and statistical information as the narrative proceeds, and will write it up to the date of publication, an arrangement which cannot fail to make the work more acceptable, since it will enable him to embrace facts ulterior to the narrative.

After looking round the good ship, and taking a peep at the passengers who were to be my companions during the voyage to New Orleans, I selected a berth quite to my taste in the second cabin, a small house on deck fitted up with single berths for eight persons. I found, much to my satisfaction, that there were five or six pleasant fellows, of whom I already knew something. I was introduced to the Captain, a short, fat, fussy old fellow in spectacles, and, like most fat people with abundant corporations, he seemed to be tolerably good tempered. The first mate did not present so pleasant an appearance. His was a more angular body, all sharp points and corners. It was evident it would not do to run against him. His teeth that remained were long and pointed, his complexion, hair and eyebrows were dark, and he had the largest and lightest grey eyes I ever saw—they were absolutely luminous. He was an uncomfortable fellow to look at. All I can say of the crew is that they were a picturesque looking set of fellows, and I thought that if they were only as courageous and daring in a storm as they were in taking God's name in vain, the ship would not be lost for want of energy. The steerage passengers, of whom there were three hundred, were composed one half of English and the other half of Welsh, causing a confusion of tongues quite amusing until you were personally interested in what was said. They, however, managed very well, and most heartily and lustily helped each other in all kinds of work where more than one pair of hands were necessary for its accomplishment.

Just as I had completed my survey, there was a general muster for examination by the Government Medical Inspector, the strong and healthy strode up with confidence, answered questions promptly, and in a tone of independence, while the few who had been recently indisposed, nervously advanced, answered warily, and having passed examination, seemed to congratulate themselves, as if they had escaped from some great danger. One very old woman supported by two men was delayed a short time, but as she was only weak from the effects of old age, she was permitted to proceed on her journey of *obedience*. All were healthy, or sufficiently so to warrant them in staying on board. So we were hauled out of dock, and soon after, a pedlar and an old woman with a basket of trinkets were found "stowed away" on board. The little fat Captain, who turned out to be a choleric old fellow, flew at the man "like a Turk," punched his head, and blacked his eye, and sent both man and woman back by steam tug which took us out.

We were quickly towed down the Mersey, past the Rock Lighthouse and the Fort at the mouth, and the wind being fair, the sails were soon unfurled and filled, and we stood out to sea. Thoughts crowded my brain; of course I thought of old England. It is impossible to leave the land of one's birth without regret, or to leave one's kindred and friends, even for a few months, without a sigh. I wondered whether I should ever see them again, or if my ears would ever again be greeted with gentle words of affection in fond tones from their loving lips! I thought of perils on sea—tempest, fire, and disease; the dangers in strange cities, and risks among treacherous Indians; but again reflected and comforted myself with the assurance that it was childish and useless to fear, and that men died not by accident, that none fell without God's notice! I felt it was a worthy enterprise, and that the greater the difficulties the greater would be the honour if they were surmounted. Others had safely travelled over the same road, then why should not I? I knew that if I was wise I should look on the bright side of things, and like the artist with his pictures, should even make the shadow and gloom instrumental in adding interest and instruction to my trip. How tame and insipid would be his pictures if they were without shadow! Even so would be our lives if they were without their occasional trying circum-stances. With what intense pleasure does the safely arrived traveller look back upon his journey and call to mind the time when, after a day's travel over a sandy desert, he arrived, weary and thirsty, at a green and shady place, watered by pure bubbling springs. He thought at the time that that was the most lovely place on earth, and the water from the spring the purest and most delicious he had ever drunk. Things are good by contrast. How pleasant the green and shady place, how delicious the water, how refreshing the rest, to the jaded traveller after his day of toil! I had a chance of enduring simi-lar temporary hardships and of experiencing moments of happiness, such as those described.

Soon the land grew less distinct, and as it became more and more grey, there rose above all other sounds the voices of men and women sweetly mingling, in tones of heart-felt feeling, in the song of—

Yes, my native land, I love thee.

Then the deck became deserted, as the motion of the ship began to affect the heads and stomachs of men and women, hitherto used only to steady Terra Firma. I confess I was affected very soon. The contents of my stomach began to rebel, and at last after much threat-ening, and, as I thought, much unnecessary noise, jumped overboard. They seemed to say, "You may leave old England, but we wont." But whether they ever reached the land, I cannot say. I have a gloomy suspicion that they met with a watery grave. I went to the cabin where I found my fellow passengers already assembled, sitting on their boxes with all the gravity of men momentarily expecting the visitation of a grievous calamity. Young Joe H. was already in his berth, hugging a tin basin, and I thought, from the noise he was making, that he would soon be relieved. His brother John was sitting on his box, with his large eyes wide open, looking at Leary and seeming to say, "Am I! am I going to be sick?" While Leary with his shaven head (he had had a fever), his hands on his knees, without a vestige of colour in his cheeks, did not answer audibly, but in the same language seemed to say, *"Ditto! ditto!"* I turned into my berth and presently saw Leary start from his seat and rush out of the cabin; very soon John followed his example. I concluded that there would be no necessity for either of them to repeat the question, audibly or otherwise, and by this time, as the breeze freshened, and I became more giddy, I ceased to watch any one and of necessity minded my own business. I could not help noticing, however, as the vessel began to pitch and roll, that the tin cans and provision boxes began to travel and dance about the cabin. I thought the music they danced to was very disagreeable and earnestly entreated a man still capable of locomotion to put a stop to it. Music may have charms, but it must be of a superior description, and better timed than that was, to be appreciated, and admired.

The next day the necessary instructions were given to the emigrants, relative to the regulations deemed necessary for their comfort, health, and safety. The married men and women had already been placed in the centre of the ship, and the unmarried portion of the two extremities—the males at the bow and the females at the stern. The whole of the passengers were divided into districts of equal numbers, with a President and two Counsellors to each district. These had to see that the ship was cleaned out every morning, that all *lights* except *ship lights* were put out at eight o'clock at night, and never on any account to permit a naked or uncovered light to be in the ship. These and other precautions to prevent fire were conceived to be most essential, for in truth, no calamity that can occur is so dreadful as a fire at sea. This was forcibly impressed upon my mind by an accident that occurred during my voyage home. I give an extract from my Journal—

"December 27th, 1853.—To-day, as I was sitting down in the cabin enjoying a quiet game at chess, surrounded by several passengers who were watching the game, a cry of 'Fire' made all start; a pallor overspread their countenances, and again they were shocked, and they rushed tumultuously to the hatchway, at that repeated and dreadful cry. 'Where? where?' was the earnest inquiry of one, across whose mind the recollection flashed, that barrels of turpentine formed part of the cargo. None knew, none answered. They gained the deck, dense volumes of smoke witnessed to the truth of the cry, and showed to one partially relieved heart that it was from a house on deck, and not from below, where the cargo was. Had it been there, God alone could have saved the ship. But the wind was strong, and was sighing and moaning through the rigging, and threatened, by its force, to spread the flames beyond the chance of control, if they were not soon extinguished. The men assured the women that the fire might soon be put out, and, leaving them to their lamentations, hurried for water, while one of the officers of the ship attended to the hose. All were willing to help, buckets were abundant, soon the antagonistic elements met, and, thank Heaven, water was the conqueror. It saved the passengers, it might have been their grave."

It seems to be almost impossible to convince some of the risk incurred by having uncovered lights about the ship. The most rigid discipline should therefore be observed in this respect.

The Presidents of districts also had to see that no principle of morality was violated; to meet their districts at eight, p.m., to pray with them, and to give any general instructions thought necessary; and to daily meet in council, with the President over the whole company, to report the condition of their districts, and to consult with, and receive instructions from him.

The most scrupulous cleanliness was thought to be necessary; frequent fumigation and sprinkling of lime; and on warm days all sick persons, whether willing or not, were brought into the air and sunshine. The consequence was, that the general health, during the whole voyage, was most satisfactory, only one death occurring, and that of a very old woman, mentioned before, who was nearly dying when first taken on board.

The chief difficulty which was experienced was to rule the cooking galley. I do not believe that the Queen, with her Privy Council, and the Houses of Lords and Commons put together, could have legislated successfully for it. Two or three revolutions occurred in it. Once the cooks were forcibly expelled. The insurgents took the poker and shovel into their own hands, and as a matter of course they burned their fingers, as all meddlers in government affairs do. Too many cooks spoiled the broth; they quarrelled among themselves, and the result was that the chuckling cooks re-took their honours, and were as impartial and as unpopular as ever.

Upon one occasion while the council was sitting, an old man rushed in with a saucepan of rice, and demanded justice. "Here," said he, poking the saucepan first under one man's nose, and then under another's, "here's my rice burned again; I can't, and I won't eat it; what am I to do? I haven't had anything to eat to-day"; and seeing one man about to speak, as he supposed not in his favour, he thrust his unanswerable argument, the burnt rice, under the man's nasal organ, and, more excited than ever, shouted, "Could you eat it?" The cook was summoned, was questioned, and said that the old man was quarrelsome, *"he even quarrelled with the* WOMEN," and refused to put his rice into a cloth, so it was burned. Of course he hadn't time to keep stirring everybody's rice. The case was dismissed without damages being awarded; but as the old man had nothing cooked to eat I gave him some of my rice, with advice to obey counsel, and if he was determined to quarrel with the women, at any rate to be friendly with the cook, for to quarrel with so important a personage was absolute madness.

Considering all things, however, the little world behaved itself remarkably well. After a few days all became used to the motion of the ship. Sickness disappeared, and was only remembered to be laughed at. Merry groups assembled on the deck, and, sitting in the sunshine, told stories, sang songs, and cracked jokes by the hour together, and generally with a propriety most unexceptionable.[1]

During the whole of the voyage the weather was charming. We left winter behind us, but as we went south we were greeted by the most delicious warmth and sunshine.

[1] William Chandless, a friendly Britisher who made a voyage similar to Piercy's in 1855, wrote of the Mormons on his ship: "As a whole, they were a good, plain, honest sort of people, simple-minded but not fools, nor yet altogether uneducated; an omnium gatherum from half-a-dozen nations, containing many excellent artizans and some tradespeople, along with a number of mere labourers and some few men of talent and cultivation. . . . The better class pay their own expenses mainly; and though they join at Liverpool, do not travel in large bodies, or attract the attention with those emigrating by help of the 'Perpetual Emigration Fund' (and therefore necessarily collected in the charges of some 'elder') do; these are the poor and ignorant; and more shame for us there are so many such that poverty and ignorance are cause and effect. In the United States these people would have had a decent education, and in Utah their children will have, no matter how poor they are." *A Visit to Salt Lake; being a journey across the plains and a residence in the Mormon settlements at Utah* (London, 1857), pp. 35–36.

The most unimpressible must have been affected by the glorious rising and setting of the sun, by the beauty and vastness of the ocean, and by the power of the winds. I was much amused by an observation made to me by a lad who stammered very badly. He was standing by me one day, looking at the water, which was rather rough, when turning suddenly round to me, and rather excited, he said, "I t-t-tell y-y-you w-w-hat, it seems t-t-to me, that the s-s-sea is n-n-next to God Almighty!" Taken by surprise and rather startled, I asked him why? "Why," said he, "why it s-s-seems t-t-to me th-that it c-c-could move almost anything." I rather damped his enthusiasm at his supposed discovery by asking him, if because the sea could move almost anything, it was next to God Almighty; what was the relative position of the wind which moved the sea!

The day before we saw the first land was an exciting time for us. We had been out of sight of land so long, that some made up their minds that they would sit up all night that they might see *Cape Cabron,* on the north of San Domingo, (1)[2] the first thing in the morning. None however carried out the determination, they crept to bed one after the other, and had to be called up to see *Cape Cabron* in the morning. Soon after we came in sight of the main land of the island and old Cape Français. The green colour of the island of Tortuga was quite refreshing. We had been so long away from vegetation that even a distant glimpse of it afforded pleasure. None but those who have been absent at sea for so long a period can fully appreciate the feelings inspired by such a sight. Then we passed the island of Cuba (2) the largest of all the West Indian islands, and the principal colony of Spain. We soon left that island far behind us, and as we onward sped, buoyant with hope and anticipation of soon reaching New Orleans, the wind still continued in our favour, and we very pleasantly and swiftly stretched away across the Gulf of Mexico (3), and next began to look out for the pilot. When we got up the last morning, before arriving at the anchorage at the mouth of the Mississippi River, we found that the water had changed from its deep ocean blue, and was already contaminated by the light muddy water of the Mississippi, and then when the pilot-boat came alongside, and the pilot got on board, there came in with him a feeling of security and satisfaction. He was an assurance of safety and

---

[2] All numbered references in parentheses are to Linforth's notes to Piercy's narrative, which will be found in APPENDIX II.

seemed a sort of amphibious animal to convey us from the dangers of the deep to the security of Terra Firma.

At the bar we found a ship which had started from England two weeks before us, detained at the mouth of the river on account of the shallowness of the water. We should have remained there, too, had not our crafty old Captain represented his ship as drawing less water than she really did. The consequence was that in two or three hours a huge Mississippi steam-boat came alongside, and having bound herself to us, very soon carried us safely inside the bar. Then another boat of similar appearance took hold of us, and we began to ascend the far-famed and mighty Mississippi. (4)

We entered the river by the south-west channel, and passed the Balize or Pilot Station on the east, about three miles from the bar and the Light-house, of which the accompanying wood cut [fig. 2] is a representation, on the west, about four miles inland. Then we passed Forts Jackson, St. Philip, and St. Leon at the English turn, then the Battle-ground, where the English under command of Sir Edward Packenham were in 1814–15, so signally defeated in attempting an invasion of New Orleans.

The distance from the bar to New Orleans is from 90 to 100 miles, and the *Jersey* was four days in being towed up. For thirty miles from the entrance to the channel nothing is seen but muddy swamps and rushes, but above Fort Jackson the plantations commence, which are rather small at first, but as you approach New Orleans, they become finer and larger. The banks on the side of the river are very low, and as far up as New Orleans they present the same general appearance. I should judge, however, from the planters' large houses with their broad verandahs, that the cultivation of the sugar cane was not there an unprofitable business.

We arrived at New Orleans on the 21st of March, having had quite a pleasure trip of a little over six weeks' duration. The number of miles travelled is seldom less than 5000, although the geographical distance, from Liverpool to this port, is only about 4400 miles.

Just before we got to New Orleans, we were told to look out for thieves in the shape of boarding-house runners, and although we could not keep them off the ship, we made up our minds they should not go below. We therefore stationed four men at each hatchway, with instructions to allow none but passengers to go down. We soon found the benefit of this arrangement, as it was as much as the guards could do to keep the blackguards on deck. They swore that they had friends below, and when asked for their names, they generally gave some of the commonest Irish ones. This, however, was quite a failure, as there was not an Irishman amongst the passengers. One fellow when told that there was no Pat Murphy on board, said it was a lie, as he never knew a ship without one. But finding our guards steady and not to be intimidated, they gave it up as a bad job, and departed, vowing vengeance to the "Mormons."

CHAPTER XI

Louisiana~the City of New Orleans~Disembarkation

WE had now entered the Great Republic of the United States of North America, and had ascended from ninety to one hundred miles into the interior of the State of Louisiana (5), part of the once magnificent French "Province of Louisiana," which occupied all the valley of the Mississippi east and west, from its source to the Gulf of Mexico, and our ship was moored alongside the levée of the thriving port of the city of New Orleans. (6)

Here the emigrants were met by Elder James Brown, the agent appointed by the Church authorities to receive and forward them up to St. Louis. This gentleman rendered every assistance to the passengers in disembarking, &c., and acted in concert with the President of the company over the sea, Elder George Halliday, in giving advice to the emigrants, and protecting them from depredation. Elated with the successful termination of the voyage to this place, they soon crowded on to the levée and made their way into the city, in the hope of finding something more tempting to the palate than the ship fare. They were however especially cautioned, before leaving the ship, to be very careful and abstemious in the use of fresh meat and vegetables, a very necessary piece of advice to persons who had been living some weeks upon biscuit, salt pork, &c. They were also told to beware of swindlers and their grand instrument of attack, *ardent spirits.* As I wandered through the quaint, old-fashioned city I saw many a familiar face that I had seen on board the *Jersey,* at a street restaurant, enjoying a moderate meal obtained for five cents. Most of these places are kept by Frenchmen, and French is so commonly spoken that one may visit several cafés or restaurants without being able to converse in English. The advice given to the emigrants was so well observed that as a general thing they escaped the numerous evils with which all foreigners arriving in this place are beset. Owing to the promptness of Elder Brown, the *John Simonds* steamboat was soon engaged for the passengers. The passage for adults was two and a quarter dollars. Children between fourteen and three years old were half-price, and those under free.

Here I parted from the emigrants, for the purpose of taking sketches between this place and the camping ground.

CHAPTER XII

Departure from New Orleans~Steam-Boats~Negro-
Slavery~Carrollton~the Face of the Country~Baton
Rouge~Red River~Mississippi~Unwholesomeness
of the Waters of the Mississippi~Danger in Procuring
Water from the Stream~Washing Away of the Banks
of the River~Snags~Landing at Natchez at Night~
Beautiful Effect Caused by Reflection on the Water
of the Light from the Steam-Boat Windows~
American Taverns and Hospitality~Rapidity at Meals
~American Cooking-Stoves and Washing-Boards~
Old Fort Rosalie~An Amateur Artist

AFTER seeing as much of the sunny city of New Orleans and its
heterogeneous inhabitants as my limited time would allow, I went
on board the panting, steaming leviathan *St. Louis,* and as the sun
was going down, the boat left the levée, and I was again stemming
the stream of the father of waters, the mighty Mississippi.

The Mississippi steam-boats are eminently national, and do full
justice to the practical go-a-head people by whom they were designed
and are used. They are floating palaces, open to, and for the use of,
all who can pay, negroes excepted. A coloured man, however well
educated or wealthy, dare not show his nose in the saloon, he must
confine himself to the deck, with the deck hands and deck passengers.
The boats are propelled by two engines, one on each side, under the
superintendence of two engineers. The small house on the top of the
boat is the pilot house. Here a wheel is fitted up, connected with the
rudder by means of ropes, so that, although very much elevated, the
pilot has perfect command of the vessel. Speaking tubes and signal
bells pass from the pilot house to the engineers' department, so that
the engines can be stopped or reversed at a moment's notice. The
house just described is placed on the hurricane deck, accessible from
the cabin, or saloon, by means of staircases. In fine weather it forms

an agreeable promenade and affords a most commanding view of the river and generally of the country on each side. The deck below this is occupied by the first cabins and the ladies' saloon, which, in boats of the first class, are most luxuriously fitted up. The food supplied is of the best description and in great abundance, leaving nothing to be desired in this respect. The second cabins are of course of an inferior description, and the deck is as bad and poor an accommodation as the saloon is excellent. All that is paid for and guaranteed is a passage. Ordinary passengers are obliged to be content with lying on the boards; sometimes a berth may be obtained, but not often. Special arrangements are, however, made for L. D. S. emigrants, who are (as I myself saw in two or three instances) better provided for.

I did not see much of the Captain, as the actual business of the boat was transacted by clerks and mates. The latter curse and swear, apparently with the idea that nothing can be done without it, and certainly the materials they have to work with almost warrant the assumption. The men under them are called "Deck hands," and are, with few exceptions, composed of the most degraded class in the States, being chiefly negroes who are so stupid that they cannot be used for anything else, and Irishmen without trades. There are few Americans among them. They are divided into "watches," but when wood has to be taken in all hands turn out to the cry of "Wood pile, wood pile," which they seem to detest most heartily. Dressed in Guernsey shirts, and with knives stuck in their belts, they look grim enough for any station. Their work is most laborious and of the most harassing description, in consequence of which they get good wages, ranging from 25 to 60 dollars per month, in addition to their food. Among all the men of this description whom I saw and conversed with on the Mississippi, Missouri and Ohio rivers, I found only one at all distinguished above his class. He was evidently a thinker, and one who had read extensively, and, as might be expected, entertained the most infidel and radical notions. No veneration for existing institutions shackled his ideas, and consequently nothing could be more genuine and independent than his mode of thinking. He said that when on board a steamer he was a deck hand, but when on shore, with 300 or 400 dollars in his pocket, he begged leave to play the gentleman and enjoy life. His arguments in favour of negro-slavery were certainly of a candid description. He said that it was natural throughout creation for the strong and powerful in mind and

body to enslave those inferior to them; that it was upon this principle that animals were subdued by men, removed from their natural
sphere, made to plough, and were afterwards consigned to the
slaughter-house; and that if the principle held good with respect to
horses, oxen, &c., it was equally so with reference to negroes, who
were truly inferior animals to white men. I questioned his assertion
as to their inferiority, which he met by saying that it was only because
I had not lived among them as he had, that I differed from him. I
certainly saw no evidence of constitutional inferiority in them, either
mentally or physically. Indeed, the wonder is, considering their degraded state, that they are found so intelligent. We must take leave,
however, of this vexed question with but one remark, which is, that
considering the system was introduced into America, and firmly established by the English, French and Spanish, they should regard
American citizens with something like charity, and make themselves
acquainted with the difficulties attendant upon immediate and universal emancipation before violently insisting upon it.

I cannot refrain, here, from paying a tribute to the mirthfulness
of negroes. Their hearty laughter makes the old Mississippi ring
again. Laughing is no slight matter with a real negro, and considering the exertion attendant upon one of their performances, it is a
wonder that, having escaped shaking themselves to pieces, they ever
venture upon another. Where there is a negro there is sure to be fun,
joking and jollity. They have almost invariably a keen sense of the
ridiculous, and an enjoyment of it not to be eradicated by slavery.
They are generally very ready-witted, and full of words. Like their
betters they delight in authority, and, from what I have heard, I
conclude they are the most merciless of task-masters.

Seven miles above New Orleans, on the east bank of the river, is
situated the thriving post village of Carrollton, connected with New
Orleans by a railroad, on which trains run every few minutes during
the day and evening. It is a delightful place, and many of the business
men of New Orleans reside there. It contains a most beautiful public
garden, and hundreds from the city resort there daily. The luxuriant
foliage of the place, filled with the bright-plumaged and melodious
singing birds of the South, afford a most enchanting retreat from the
noise and bustle of the city.

Both sides of the river above this present a plain occupied by
immense sugar plantations and splendid villas with gardens and

groves of tropical fruit trees. This continues as far as Baton Rouge, the capital of Louisiana. I made a sketch of this place, which the accompanying engraving represents [pl. 11]. The large building in the centre is the State House and is certainly the finest building I saw on the banks of the Mississippi. The city stands on the east side of the river, on the first bluff seen in ascending it. It is 140 miles, by water, above New Orleans, most beautifully situated, and is said to be one of the healthiest places in the southern portion of the Mississippi valley. It contains a college and four churches, also an arsenal and barracks of the United States. Its population is about 4500, and two newspapers are supported.

In the centre of the stream, in my sketch, is seen a raft. The timber from the upper regions of this river and its tributaries is brought down in this manner by "raftsmen," and sold at New Orleans.

I left Baton Rouge in the *Princess,* and about 79 miles further on passed the mouth of Red River, (7) near the 31st parallel of N. lat., the northern boundary of Louisiana on the east of the Mississippi. From this point the traveller has Louisiana on the left-hand, and Mississippi (8) on the right.

Emigrants, crowded into steam-boats, find the difficulties of cooking anything but slight. Those will come the best off who, instead of tea and coffee, are content with cold water. Some people say that the waters of the Mississippi and Missouri rivers are unwholesome, but I invariably drank the Mississippi water fresh from the stream, and never experienced any inconvenience from it. It is certainly muddy, and any one can obtain a pretty good notion of its appearance by mixing an ounce of mud with a quart of water. However disagreeable this water may be to any palate, I would always recommend it in preference to whisky, which is abominable stuff, and far more likely to injure than to benefit. Women should be careful not to attempt to draw water from the river in buckets. The current is so rapid, that when added to the speed of the steamer through it, it requires the strength of a man to procure the water with safety. Many lives have been lost in this way, which should be a sufficient warning to those who still purpose to ascend these rivers. In most of the boats there are pumps fixed, so that there is seldom any real necessity for drawing water by hand.

Proceeding onwards, bluffs of considerable height overhang the river, a few hills are seen, and the country on both sides of the river assumes a more interesting appearance, still it is mainly monotonous, and it oppressed me very much. Day and night succeeded each other, and still the same wide, eddying, gigantic river, undiminished, and seemingly without end! I observed that it made tremendous inroads into the banks, causing vast masses of earth to fall into the stream. Of course trees fall with the soil, and either settle down as snags, or are picked up by men generally on the look-out, and, if good enough, taken to the saw-mill. A negro informed me that he was a slave, but by paying his master a fixed sum per week, he was allowed to work as he pleased, and succeeded in making a very good living by securing the drift-wood, and either taking it to the mill or chopping it up for fire-wood. As the trees are generally cotton-wood they are fit for little else than burning. The falling of the earth encroaches upon the land of the settlers and sometimes compels them to move their dwellings from the merciless destroyer. I see the time coming, however, when these banks will be jealously guarded by men who will as soon think of throwing their wealth into the river as to allow the land, which must ever be the richest possession, to be thus washed away. Added to the force of the current, there are the waves caused by the enormous paddle-wheels of the steamers, which roll up and dash against the banks, throwing the spray upon the green foliage like glittering diamonds.

I landed at Natchez (9) in the night and stood on the bank and listened to the retreating noise of the engines which had propelled in safety, thus far up the stream, the floating palace I had just left. As it moved from the shore amid the darkness, I could not help admiring its force and majesty; and as its broadside swung round to view, revealing every window brilliantly lighted, and every light reflected in the gliding stream, the effect was magical and equal in beauty to anything I ever saw.

The tavern at which I staid was kept by an Irishman apparently well to do. I found he had common sense in abundance, which is said to be uncommon with Irishmen. I was pleased to see with what apparent good feeling he welcomed a poor youngster, fresh from the Emerald Isle, in search of his fortune, and who had landed from the boat with me. He very soon told him where he could get work, but the boy said he thought of going further as he had been "ricomminded." Here I had an opportunity of becoming acquainted with the peculiar class of persons one meets with in the third-rate taverns of the States. Ten-pins, cards, drink and tobacco are the spice of life with them. One great characteristic is almost universal among "men of spirit," and that is, the practice, when means will allow, of insisting upon all persons in the room taking a drink. I was seldom in a tavern five minutes without some one saying to me, "Take a drink, stranger." To have declined these hospitable invitations would have been considered very unsociable and would most likely have given offence. I frequently saw a room full of persons thus summoned, and seldom saw any hesitation in complying with the request, the landlord, or "storekeeper," taking care to be one of the number, and charging for his own drink. The terms for food and lodging never exceed a dollar per day at this kind of house, which is very little when the varied and abundant supply of provisions is considered. The sleeping accommodation is not so good; the beds are hard, and generally as many bedsteads are put into a room as it will hold. The "boarders" are always called together by the ringing of a large bell, fixed at the top of the house, so that not only "boarders" in the house, but those who may happen to be outside and in the neighbourhood, know that "feeding time" has come. It is well known that Americans are as quick at eating as they are at most other things. However, in this case, quickness is certainly a disadvantage. It is, doubtless one cause of the universal complaint of indigestion, to which the general habit of eating bread *hot from the oven* contributes not a little. In my earliest essays at table I found myself the last to quit, and it was only by being weak enough to eat more rapidly that I could keep time with my fellow masticatory labourers. In America a man soon learns to "go-a-head," indeed he must do it in self-defence. The women also soon get into the same habit; and in household matters I think they succeed. The stoves with which they cook are a credit to the ingenious and economising spirit of America. Many English women told me that they really would not be able to manage with English stoves again, as with an ordinary American stove they could cook three times as much with a great deal less trouble. They also praised the American washing-boards which have lately been improved upon by the substitution of zinc. Wood, by repeated friction in water, becomes rough, whereas zinc is polished by the process. These washing machines certainly save labour, but I should judge that clothes are rather more injured by the use of them than by the ordinary method of washing.

While I was engaged in sketching Old Fort Rosalie, represented by the accompanying woodcut [fig. 3], an Englishwoman came from a house within sight to see what I was doing. She soon discovered that I was from England and was quite pleased to see some one who could give her news of the "Old Country." She informed me that her husband, who was at that time from home, was very fond of painting, and that he was engaged during his leisure time in painting a landscape, into which he intended to introduce every American animal and bird he could find. I thought it was rather a novel idea, and that when the painting was completed it ought to be called the happy family.

CHAPTER XIII

Perpetual Motion~Flat-Boats~Vicksburgh~
"Lynching" of Gamblers~An Hibernian's Defence of
Printing~Walnut Hills~Yazoo River~Arkansas
~Arkansas River~Tennessee~Memphis~German
Reverence for Art~Negroes; Quarrel Between Two
Rival Teamsters; Love of Finery; Piquing a White
Dandy; Negro Blood in European Veins

I took my departure from Natchez in the *Hindoo,* and on my way
to Vicksburgh I made the acquaintance of an intelligent, interesting
young man, who was returning from New Orleans, whither he had
been with a flatboat. He was the second person whom I had met
with in my life who professed to have discovered perpetual motion.
The first was in England—I saw his model, but not the sense of it.
The man strongly asserted the possibility of achieving the discovery,
but unfortunately his practical illustration, in the shape of the
model, seemed determined not to budge. It ended, as far as I was
concerned, by his very sagely informing me that if it would move
but once, *only once,* he verily believed that it would keep on. That
I did not doubt. The American, however, said that his machine was
a complete success, that although made of wood it kept in motion till
it got out of order. In reply to my question as to whether he could
make another, he said "Yes," and that an uncle of his, who had seen
the wooden one act, intended to have one made in metal. Of course
his story was difficult to believe; but of one thing he did convince
me, which was his ability to make a machine out of wood. With a
pen-knife only he cut out of a piece of wood, a chain of five or six
links, a swivel and a shackel. It was very quickly and neatly done,
and he kindly presented it to me. He was evidently a roving genius;
he had ranged from engineering to photography, and from a flat-
boat on the Mississippi he talked of going to California. Several flat-
boats may be seen in the views of Vicksburgh and Memphis [pls. v, vi].

I found the generality of flat-boat men, like their music and
dancing, wild and uncouth in the extreme. I noticed that it was

quite a common thing when a steam-boat approached a flat-boat, for the men to get up a dance or a song, the chorus of the latter being, in most cases, a wild whoop or yell, peculiar to flat-boat men and Negroes on the Ohio and Mississippi rivers.

There were some gentlemen on board who had a most disgusting and brutal method of amusing themselves. Armed with rifles, they stationed themselves upon the hurricane deck, and shot ducks and birds, when there was not the slightest possibility of obtaining them. How mean, blood-thirsty, and unworthy of men are such acts!

Arrived at Vicksburgh (10), an old man related to me several interesting circumstances concerning the "Lynching" of the gamblers who formerly infested the place.

One incident full of pathos I will mention. Just before the indignation of the citizens was excited to the utmost extent, the son of a widow visited Vicksburgh on business for his mother, with a considerable sum of money in his possession. The gamblers, with a keen scent for gold, found him out and succeeded in depriving him not only of his own, but that of his mother also. Without means, and covered with shame, he gambled to live, and was known as one of the gang. The letters of his mother entreating him to return to her were disregarded, of course with the hope that he would yet be able to regain that which he had lost. The poor mother, becoming still more concerned, sent a younger son to entreat him to return, with means sufficient to convey both of them back. The boy arrived just before the capture of the gamblers, and, having found his brother, was in the act of imploring him to leave the place with him when the mob broke into the house and took all prisoners. The eldest brother was by this time a known gambler, and being assured that he would suffer with the rest pleaded only for his youthful brother's life. Each pleaded for the other but both were disregarded and both were hung.

At Vicksburgh I met with a mongrel kind of being, half Irish and half American. Born in Ireland he had been taken over to America while very young. Finding out that I was a stranger, he soon began to question me. In reply to his inquiry I answered that I was an artist, which evidently put him on a hobby of his, for he replied immediately, "A artist! and sure what do you mean by a artist, isn't a printer a artist? In fact isn't a printer's the first trade as ever was, the baker's the second, the shoemaker's the third, and the builder's the fourth? By George, stranger," said he "I don't want to prove that you don't know nothing exactly, but perhaps you'll say I'm right, or else circumbent what I say." I was rather amused at this attack as were also the men who were standing round, for they laughingly encouraged Mike to proceed. Being in the humour to enjoy a little bantering, I answered that in my case I thought myself entitled to be called an artist, because I had attempted to produce works of art for a number of years and had lived by my profession. As to the printer's being the first trade or profession ever practised, I said as he seemed to be in possession of information which disproved assertions I had met with in some histories I possessed, I was happy that I had met with him. I told him that one ignorant author had attributed the discovery and improvement of printing to Guttenberg, Faust, Schæffer and Coster, between 1422 and 1456, and that if he would go to the library, he would there be able to read for himself. This accidental remark seemed to touch him upon a sore point, for he was out of temper immediately, and asked me if I meant to insinuate that he could not read. He told me that he had learnt *once,* some time ago, and although he never read now he talked with men who did, and that was much the easiest way of picking up information; but "he did not care what the histories said, he knew that the printer's was the first trade as ever was, and he hoped he hadn't hurt my feelings, but I had no business to put myself above a printer." I replied that I would not further dispute an assertion so ably defended, and sincerely hoped that as he thought so highly of printers, he would encourage and patronize them by purchasing and perusing their works himself, instead of being satisfied with the verbal reports of treacherous memories. Yet after all, this poor man was but a vulgar illustration of the shallow-pated hobby class who, at any and every season, lug in their poor maltreated hobbies by the head and shoulders. Then again, with what Hibernian honesty he declares his contempt for history and adheres to his opinion in spite of history and proof. He was also a genuine representative of the world-wide class who learn by hearsay and are content to believe without examining, for, as he said, it is such an easy thing!

My sketch of the city of Vicksburg being completed, I started from that place, and after a ride of two and a half miles came to Walnut Hills, which extend two miles on the river. These beautiful hills rise boldly, though gradually, with alternate swells and gullies, nearly 500 feet high. They are well cultivated, and present one of the most pleasing prospects on the lower Mississippi. I made the accompanying sketch of this scenery [fig. 4].

Ten miles further on is the mouth of the Yazoo river, which takes its rise in the north-eastern part of Mississippi. Navigation on this river is said to be safer than on any other in the south or west. The country adjacent to the Yazoo is an alluvial plain and is chiefly occupied by cotton plantations, which produce about 150,000 bales annually. Seventy-eight miles north of this, on the west of the Mississippi, is the southern boundary of the State of Arkansas (11), and at Columbia, a further distance of 42 miles, the great cotton-growing region, which occupies so large a district on both sides of the river, terminates. At 66 miles above Columbia is passed the mouth of the Arkansas river, next to the Missouri the largest affluent of the Mississippi. The Arkansas rises in the Rocky Mountains and traverses a distance of upwards of 2000 miles. It is navigable by steam-boats during nine months of the year, for a distance of 750 miles above its mouth.

Passing a number of small towns and villages, which at intervals dot the banks of the Mississippi, another 151 miles brought me to the State of Tennessee (12) on the east, and another two to Memphis (13), where I again landed. I had now travelled 750 miles up the Mississippi, and although I had heard much about the recklessness of American captains on the western rivers I was not so unfortunate as to travel in any steam-boat commanded by a man of this description, and concluded that the fatal effects which had resulted from recklessness had had the salutary effect of reforming these men as a class.

I was much pleased at Memphis with an incident which occurred from an old German's reverence for art. He was the proprietor of the ferry-boat at Memphis which conveyed me to the opposite shore. After my sketching all day within sight of the old man of course he knew that I was an artist, and when I got into the boat to return he asked me to show him my sketch, which I did with the greatest readiness. When I offered him the fare for taking me over, he drew himself up with an air of dignity, and said "No," he could not think of taking money from one who practised so noble an art. I thought how very convenient it would be for poor students if all grim, hard-hearted tradesmen entertained the same view.

While in this city I was quite amused in listening to two rival negro-teamsters quarreling. It ended in the smartest of them gaining the victory by saying to the other, "Ugh! ugh! you poor skunk, you'll be for sale soon, and then I'll buy you." Doubtless a very harmless, but evidently a most irritating threat. I remained at Memphis over the Sunday and had an opportunity of witnessing the intense love the negroes have for finery and gay colours. Ebony Apollos and sable Venuses promenaded the streets, draped in colours which reminded me of exotic flowers. One very young couple particularly attracted my attention. The husband was carrying a young infant darkie and seemed brimful of joy at possessing the treasure. He caused a great deal of merriment by going up to a white dandy at the door of a "store" and very comically requesting him to kiss the monkey-like youngster. The man's evident disgust at the proposal tickled the happy father's risibility mightily, and as the white man refused to kiss, he treated the child to a double allowance from himself. I could not help noticing that a slight existence of African blood in European veins was, in the case of females, the cause of a most attractive and charming kind of loveliness.

CHAPTER XIV

Plumb Point Bars~Missouri~Little Prairie~Kentucky ~The Ohio River~Cairo City and Ohio City~ Illinois~Cornice Rocks~Devil's Bake Ovens~ Kaskaskia River, and the Great American Bottom~ Fort Chartres~St. Louis

AFTER leaving Memphis, the first place of any particular importance is Osceola, the head of Plumb Point Bars, a distance of 87 miles. These bars are the most difficult and dangerous part of the Mississippi river. Many steam-boats have been sunk at this place, and scarcely a season passes without accidents.

Little Prairie, in Missouri (14), 44 miles further on is thought to have been the centre of the vibrations of the great earthquake of 1811–12, which were felt all over the valley of the Ohio, as high up as Pittsburgh, but especially in New Madrid county, in which Little Prairie is situated. The first shock was felt in the night of the 16th of December, 1811. The shocks were repeated at intervals with decreasing violence, until the February following. They were attended with a roaring and hissing noise. Chasms were opened in the earth, and volumes of water and steam were ejected. The waters of the Mississippi were violently driven back upon the descending current, and the sulphurated gases which were discharged during the shocks impregnated the water to the distance of 150 miles below, rendering it unfit for use, for any purpose, for several days. A number of boats on the river were sunk, and a lake, 60 miles long and several wide, is said to have been formed. On the night of the first shock, the crews of several boats which had kept in company for mutual defence against the Indians, with whom the battle of Tippecanoe had just been fought, hurried on deck, weapons in hand, thinking the Indians were rushing on board. Many boats were overwhelmed by the falling masses of earth from the banks, the crews of which perished. Great numbers were wrecked on the snags, and old trees thrown up from the bottom of the river, where they had rested for ages, and others were sunk or stranded on the sand-bars and islands. It is esti-mated that about one-half of the entire county sank several feet, which was submerged by the overflowing of the Mississippi. The capital of the county, New Madrid, 35 miles from Little Prairie, although it stood on a bluff bank, at an elevation of 15 or 20 feet above the summer floods, sank so low that the next rise of the water covered it to the depth of 5 feet. This town having suffered more than any other on the Mississippi is supposed to have been near the focus from whence the undulations proceeded. Slight shocks have been felt at intervals up to the present time.

Forty-four miles distant from New Madrid is the State of Kentucky (15), which the traveller, in ascending the river, has upon the east for about 38 miles. I observed nothing on the banks of the river in this State worthy of notice, and did not land until I came to Cairo city, situated on a point of land formed by the confluence of the Ohio (16) and Mississippi rivers, and just opposite Ohio city, in Missouri.

On leaving Memphis I determined to stay a short time at these places, thinking from their grand names that they must be places of importance. I was, however, quite disappointed in my expecta-tions, for instead of finding such cities as I anticipated, Ohio city was composed of but 6 or 7 insignificant houses, and Cairo city of not a great number more. I found that the weakness of Cairo city was the result of a habit which it had of taking too much water. It lies so low that when the river rises very high it is sure to be inundated. A levée had been raised, which is said to have cost a million of dollars. Owing to the state of the place, I thought it was wise of the man at whose tavern I put up, to take to the water altogether. He had bought a flat-boat and had fitted it up as a boarding-house, so that being always afloat it did not matter to him whether the water was high or low. His table was pretty well furnished at dinner-time, but there was one dish on it which was new to me. I was enjoying my dinner with a true traveller's appetite, and as I wanted some gravy I took some from a dish before me which sent forth a most savoury smell, when the host, looking towards me, said, "Take some squirrel, stranger." Thinking I had misunderstood him, I inquired what he had said. He informed me that he had merely asked me to take some squirrel which was on the dish before me. Horrified at having even taken the gravy, and put off my guard, I exclaimed, "Eat a squirrel!

Why I would as soon think of eating a rat." Fortunately for me it was considered a capital joke, and I afterwards learned that it was quite common to eat squirrels in America.

North of the Ohio river, the State of Illinois (17) occupies the eastern side of the Mississippi. The Cornice rocks are great curiosities. The water has worn into irregular shapes the perpendicular sides of the limestone precipices, imparting in some places a continuous formation, which has the appearance of handsome cornice work, and overhangs the cliffs, whose sides very much resemble columns and various architectural designs. Devil's Bake Oven, 67½ miles distant from Cairo city, is a large rounded mass of rocks on the Illinois shore, 50 or 60 feet in height, shaped like an oven, and thence its name.

At a further distance of 30 miles is the mouth of the Kaskaskia river, and the southern termination of the Great American Bottom, which extends northwardly on the river, for about 80 miles. The first French settlements were made in this bottom, and the town of Kaskaskia, 7 miles from the mouth of the Kaskaskia river, was founded shortly after La Salle visited the Mississippi, by Father Gravier, a Catholic missionary among the Illinois Indians, and was the capital of the Illinois country until it passed from France to Great Britain. It is now the capital of Randolph county, Illinois. Passing St. Genevieve, the oldest town in Missouri, the next point of interest is Fort Chartres, 25 miles from the Kaskaskia, and 51½ below St. Louis. This fort was originally built by the French, in 1720, to defend themselves from the Spaniards, and was rebuilt in 1756. It is now a heap of ruins, covered with a growth of trees. Originally it is said to have been a place of great strength and to have formed an irregular quadrangle, the exterior sides of which measured 490 feet in circumference.

I was anxious to make some sketches between Cairo and St. Louis, but my limited time would not permit, and I had to pass various places of interest without being able to land. I reached St. Louis (18) in safety, and as I was going ashore a man fell into the water and narrowly escaped being drowned. Being frightened, he seemed to forget that he could swim, which was the case, as the result proved. At first he raised his arms out of the water and shouted lustily, and it was only when he found that he could obtain no assistance and was being swept away by the stream that his presence of mind returned and he attempted to swim. He gained a steam-boat which was lower down, and, just as he was being carried by the stream underneath a paddle-wheel in motion, some friendly hands were outstretched, and, much to my relief, I saw him lifted to the deck. The lower decks of these river steamers are very dangerous; the sides are seldom raised more than a few inches, so that many fall into the water.

I ascended the levée and once more beheld and heard the bustle and noise of business. St. Louis, of which about one-half is shown in the view [pl. VII], has become a mighty city. I met with a number of English mechanics here, none of whom, that I remember, complained of being ill treated, but generally spoke most favourably of their American employers. Provisions being tolerably cheap, and employment abundant and usually well paid for, they did not seem to regret their separation from England. Indeed, the mere labouring man, when once comfortably settled and acclimated, has not much reason to regret the exchange.

CHAPTER XV

Departure from St. Louis~Sketching Apparatus and
Seat~American Inquisitiveness~Alton~Quincy
~Arrival at Keokuk~The Camp, its Situation and
Arrangement~"Spiritualism and Spirit Rapping"

AT St. Louis I learned that the Emigrants to G. S. L. Valley, instead
of going up the dangerous Missouri River in steam-boats would this
year (1853) start from Keokuk and cross the State of Iowa to Kanesville, and although circumstances prevented my crossing the country
with them I determined to visit the Camp, and then Nauvoo and
Carthage, places of undying interest. With these intentions I left St.
Louis in the *Jenny Deans,* and was once more afloat on the majestic
Mississippi. A ride of 17 miles brought me to its confluence with the
Missouri (19). I found that the banks of the Mississippi river, above
the mouth of the Missouri, were much more picturesque than those
below it, although the season was not far enough advanced to exhibit
nature in all her beauty.

My sketching apparatus constantly excited curiosity on board the
steam-boats. My seat, which, when closed, formed a walking stick,
was always regarded with the greatest interest, and I was constantly
requested to explain the principle of its construction. The usual
idea, previously to its being opened, was that it was a new fire arm
of unlimited shooting capabilities. Some man of exceeding sharp
practice stole it from me while I was asleep. This kind of seat, when
made of beech-wood, is sufficiently strong and is certainly the most
portable seat an emigrant can have. It is useful in every situation,
and I wonder that it is not in more general use among travellers.
Utility and portability are the qualities most essential and valuable
to an emigrant and should be kept in view in all arrangements.

I cannot leave the Mississippi and the characters I met with upon
its waters without referring to that numerous class of persons, who,
eager for the acquisition of information, are never content until they
have forced one to tell all that one knows of one's self. One, I re-

member, I was weak enough to be annoyed by, and I certainly did take pleasure in giving him equivocal answers. "Far from home, stranger?" said he. "Only about 5000 miles," I replied. "North or South?" he inquired. "Neither," said I. After a pause, and determincd to know all about me, he asked what I was doing so far from home. "Oh," I replied, "only a little business; the fact is I have a contract to make some cities and a number of steam-boats." At this, he opened his eyes, and finding that I was not to be pumped easily, he thought no doubt to shut me up in a corner by saying, "Anyhow, stranger, what State do you live in when you are at home?" "The state of matrimony," I replied, when he turned away in disgust, and I was content.

The principal places on the banks of the river, between St. Louis and Keokuk, are Alton, 5 miles, and Quincy, 139 miles, above the confluence of the Missouri with the Mississippi, both in Illinois. Alton is favourably situated for trade and is in a flourishing condition. It contains about 6 churches, a lyceum, a theological seminary, and a newspaper office. Quincy is a handsome town, and stands on a limestone bluff, 125 feet above the river, of which it commands an extensive view. It contained in 1853 a population of 11,000 and carried on various branches of business with much success. It had in the same year 18 churches, a U. S. land office, and 3 banks. Seven newspapers and periodicals were published, two of which were dailies.

I landed at Keokuk (20), about 200 miles above St. Louis, early in the morning, and although I could discover that the city was on an elevated site, it was still too grey to see any thing at a distance. I went into a small tavern, and, after inquiring as to the breakfast hour, I requested the privilege of washing myself, which was granted. I was ushered into a room already occupied by a dog and its kennel and a number of imitation dogs in plaister, with heads hung on wire, which, upon the admission of a current of air through the open door, commenced nodding their heads with the greatest solemnity and continued their salutations all the time I was occupied with my ablutions. They were the property of an Italian. These Italians make their way all through the States with plaister casts and barrel-organs, and, as they manage to live, of course it is reasonable to conclude that their efforts in sculpture and music meet with patronage.

While breakfast was preparing I sallied out in search of the Camp, which, after climbing a steep bluff on the edge of the river, I found most picturesquely situated on the top of a hill, surrounded by wood, and commanding a view of the country for miles around. The situation was admirably chosen, as there were good drainage and an abundance of wood and water combined. It was just daylight, and the guards had retired to their tents. Upon my entrance all was still in the Camp, no person was to be seen, and I had to trust to chance in finding my friend J. H.——. I therefore went to a tent at a venture, lifted a curtain hung before the entrance, and found that chance had be-friended me, for there lay sleeping just before me the man I sought. "Hallo, Jack!" shouted I, "awake thou that sleepest." He obeyed with a jump, and, staring with astonishment, grasped my hand, and in terms like my own, and almost as loud, he cried "Hallo, Fred!" He quickly dressed in the midst of a running fire of questions and answers, and as it was rather cold we had a run through the Camp, apparently to the surprise of the English, Scotch, Welsh, French and Dutch, who by this time were out of their tents and employed in making bellows of their lungs and cheeks, in the almost vain attempt to light the wood not yet freed by the sun from the dew of the previous night.

The emigrants from each nation had wisely been placed together, and those who had crossed the sea together were still associated as neighbours in Camp. I heard no complaints of sickness, and I was told that the general health was good. The Elders in charge seemed thoroughly competent, and Elders Haight and Eldredge were incessant in their labours. I particularly noticed the generosity with which Elder C. H. Wheelock volunteered the use of his teams for the public good. They were constantly engaged in transporting the luggage of the emigrants from the river to the Camp, which saved many a poor person's scanty means and rescued many a poor family from a dilemma, for as yet, there were very few oxen in the Camp, and most persons were unwilling to run the risk of their animals being worn out before the commencement of the journey.

The Camp was in excellent order, and the emigrants informed me that when the ground was not muddy they would as soon live in a tent as in a house. I saw few idlers—indeed, rather than remain unemployed until the trains moved off, those who could not get work in the town of Keokuk at their trades took advantage of the opportunity which offered of working on the roads. By this means they saved what little money they possessed, and in many instances added to their stock, and were thus enabled to obtain many little comforts which they must otherwise have gone without.

During my visit at Keokuk, I was introduced to Doctor —— and his lady, both believers in "spiritualism, and spirit rapping." They related to me many wonderful cases of such manifestations, and invited me to witness some, but for the interest of my narrative I am sorry to say that, although I attended three sittings, the spirits were most obdurate and did not bestow a single rap. One story which a gentleman present told me was so rich that it must be repeated. The doctor answered for the gentleman's veracity, and I will not exaggerate. He said that he called upon an unbelieving friend, when very soon the conversation turned upon spiritual manifestations. His friend most strenuously denied the possibility of any such thing taking place and demanded unanswerable proof on the spot—something undeniable, and which no man could fail to believe if he saw it. The narrator consented, and having requested the attendance of the spirits, and being assured that they were there, he asked what proof would be sufficient. The unbeliever requested that without any bodily connection with his visitor the table might be moved. No sooner said than done, the table, which was a heavy one, was whisked about the room with the greatest rapidity. Finding that his spiritual visitors were in the humour to make decidedly material demonstrations, he requested that one of the leaves of the table might be taken off. Obedient to his wish, one of the flaps was immediately wrenched off, and very soon, by request, the other underwent a similar fate. The man, unbeliever no longer, begged his friend to descend to the kitchen, where there was another table which he was willing to sacrifice in the same way, but at this stage of affairs the man's wife interfered and suggested the propriety of experimenting upon some more useless articles than household furniture. I considered the silence of the spirits during the three evenings I waited upon them as no sign of friendliness and therefore say nothing in their favour.

Before leaving Keokuk I made the accompanying sketch of the Camp, showing the arrangement of the wagons and tents, which, with their white covers, looked extremely picturesque amidst the spring foliage of the country [pl. VIII]. I did not purpose to cross the State of Iowa with the emigrants, but, after visiting Nauvoo and Carthage, to go up the Missouri river to Kanesville, and intercept some of the companies at the starting point on that river.

CHAPTER XVI

Visit to Nauvoo~The Temple~The Icarians~
Interview with Lucy Smith~Sketch of Her Life~
Joseph and David Smith, Sons of the Prophet~Visit to
Carthage Jail~Sketches of the Lives of Joseph and
Hyrum Smith, Willard Richards, and John Taylor

I TOOK leave of the Camp at Keokuk, and in company with 8 or 10 persons, set out to see Nauvoo (21). On the journey, I first saw what is called in America a "Plank road." It was composed of planks of equal thickness, laid close to each other. They were not nailed nor fastened in any way, and, although generally forming a very good road, it is not very uncommon for them to get out of their places and in very wet weather to float, so as to make the road thus planked almost impassable—that is, for men who have any care for their necks or their horses' legs, which, indeed, the Americans in the western States seem to have little of. This of course is the result of necessity and training, for the roads in the western States are the same as in all new countries with loamy soils, so that without a double team one is almost certain to be stalled, as I was frequently. The distance from Keokuk to Nauvoo is 12 miles. The city is first seen from the top of a hill about 2 miles from Montrose. From this point the beauty of its situation is fully realized, and one cannot wonder that Joseph Smith, as John Taylor says in his admirable song of the "Seer," "loved Nauvoo." It is the finest possible site for a city, and its present neglected state shows how little a really good thing is sometimes appreciated. The first objects I saw in approaching the city were the remains of what was once the Temple,[1] situated on the

1 The most remarkable remaining relic of the Nauvoo Temple is one of the capstones, which may be seen at the Quincy Historical Society, Quincy Illinois. A story about the faces on the capstones comes from Josiah Quincy's *Figures of the Past, from the Leaves of Old Journals* (Boston, 1883), pp. 377–400. Quincy was visiting Nauvoo with Charles Francis Adams and was honored by a tour personally conducted by Joseph Smith. As they passed the entrance to the temple they stopped before a workman who was chiseling an immense face into the capstone. "General Smith," asked the man, looking up from his task, "is this like the face you saw in the vision?"

highest eminence of the city, and which, in the days of its prosperity, must have been to it what the cap or top stone is to a building. On the banks of the river lie broken blocks of stone and shattered bricks, and the visitor's first steps are over evidences of ruin and desolation. Foundations of what must once have been substantial buildings are broken up and exposed to the light, and houses, once noted for neatness, cleanliness and order, and surrounded by flower gardens, evincing taste, care, and a love of the beautiful, after being pillaged of all that was valuable and portable, have been abandoned by their ruthless destroyers, and are now monuments of their selfish, jealous and contemptible hate.

At present the Icarians form the most important part of the population of Nauvoo. I was told while there that they were by no means in a prosperous condition, and that M. Cabet[2] had publicly said that unless they received assistance from France it would be impossible for the organization to continue. They have used the stones of the Temple to build workshops and a school-house. They live in a long ugly row of buildings, the architect of which, and of the school-house, was a cobbler. This bit of information I obtained from a dissatisfied Icarian, who seemed to think that he ought to have had the management of the affair as, when in France, he was an architect by profession. I very much question whether the Icarians will ever accomplish much. If, however, they are pleased with themselves, I am sure I will not find fault with them.

While in Nauvoo I lodged at the Nauvoo Mansion, formerly the residence of Joseph Smith, and now occupied by his mother, his widow and her family. I could not fail to regard the old lady (22) with great interest. Considering her age and afflictions, she, at that time, retained her faculties to a remarkable degree. She spoke very freely of her sons, and, with tears in her eyes, and every other symptom of earnestness, vindicated their reputations for virtue and truth. During my two visits I was able to take her portrait and the portraits of two of her grandsons also.[3] That of Joseph, the

---

"Very near it," answered the prophet, "except—[and this, Quincy said, was added with an air of careful connoisseurship that was quite overpowering] except that the nose is just a thought too broad."

[2] The Icarians were a small French communistic sect led by Etienne Cabet.

[3] Lucy Mack Smith died in Nauvoo May 8, 1855. The eldest grandson, Joseph Smith III (1832–1914) became president of the Reorganized Church of Jesus Christ of Latter-day Saints in Lamoni, Iowa, in 1860. He had three wives, who bore him seventeen children, but he was never a polygamist and stoutly opposed the institution throughout his life.

eldest son, was done on his 21st birth-day. He was born about 2 o'clock in the morning of the 6th of November, 1832, at Kirtland, Ohio. He is a young man of a most excellent disposition and considerable intelligence. One prominent trait in his character is his affection for his mother. I particularly noticed that his conduct towards her was always most respectful and attentive. The other portrait is of David, the youngest son, who was born 5 months after the assassination of his father. He was born about 9 o'clock in the morning of the 17th of November, 1844 (23). He is of a mild, studious disposition, and is passionately fond of drawing, seeming to be never so happy as when he has a pencil and paper in his hand. The other two boys whom I saw were very fine, strong, healthy fellows, and as it may be interesting to many, I will say, that during some conversations which I had with persons in the neighbourhood, I found that the whole family had obtained a most excellent reputation for integrity and industry.

From Nauvoo I went back to Keokuk and then to Carthage. The buggy I went in was not of the best description, and the harness was the rustiest and most doubtful looking which any livery-stable keeper, however obtuse and seared his conscience, could have the face to send out. The consequence was that at the first effort of the horse to pull the vehicle out of a "mud-hole," the harness snapped, the horse started, and I was left in a very decent sized pond, into which, after a little hesitation, I was obliged to jump. Having secured the horse and left it in charge of J. H——, who was with me, I went back about a mile to a black-smith's shop to get assistance, which I obtained in the shape of a young man and a piece of broken rope for which the old rascal of whom I bought it charged me 25 cents. After mending the harness with the rope, we re-attached the horse, and then our perplexity was greater than before, for the horse, finding that something was the matter, refused to pull at all. Perhaps he had lost faith in the harness. He evidently had not learned the old admonition—"If at first you don't succeed, try, try again." At last the buggy was drawn out of the hole by a four-horse team which fortunately came along. My friend, J. H——, took charge of the buggy, which the horse most obligingly consented to drag back to Keokuk, and I proceeded to Carthage with another horse. It is a post-village, and the capital of Hancock County, Illinois. It is situated about 18 miles from Nauvoo and 110 W. N. W. from Springfield, the capital of the State. The place is small and contains only about 400 inhabitants. The district of country immediately surrounding it is very fertile, and contains much stone coal. Carthage has become noted in the annals of the world, as the place at which Joseph and Hyrum Smith (24) closed their earthly career by assassination, and where the honour of a Sovereign State of the great American Union was forfeited. Not only were the lives of these two great men here sacrificed, but at the same time, and by the same fiendish multitude, two of the Twelve—Willard Richards and John Taylor (25), who refused to leave them in the hour of danger, came near losing their lives, both were wounded, but they recovered. I felt very anxious to visit Carthage, and though, like Nauvoo, somewhat aside from the route, I considered that sketches of its jail would possess undying interest for tens of thousands, and concluded not to return without obtaining them.

By accident I put up at the tavern to which the mutilated bodies of Joseph and Hyrum were taken from the jail. The landlord showed me the room where they were laid out. In life ever united, sharing reverses and prosperity, rejoicing together, and mourning in company, fate dared not separate them. They died the same death and at the same time; and while their spirits, in loving fraternity, winged their course to God who sent them down, their poor, bleeding, inanimate bodies kept mournful company, until weeping friends interred them both.

The landlord of the tavern took me to the jail and obtained admittance for me. The keeper was away, and I was shown over it by a young girl. The holes made in the wall by the bullets still remain unstopped. The bullet hole in the door is that made by the ball which caused the death of Hyrum. I was told that the stains of blood were still in the floor, but I could not see them, as the room was covered by a carpet. In this chamber the martyrs were sitting conversing with their friends when the assassins rushed into the jail. After his brother Hyrum had been shot dead at his feet, and John Taylor had been wounded, Joseph attempted to leap from the window. He was shot in doing so and fell through it, which drew the murderers from the interior, and gave Dr. Richards an opportunity to carry Elder Taylor into the inner prison and secrete him.

Having seen the place and made my sketches, I was glad to leave. Two lives unatoned for, and "blood crying from the ground," made the spot hateful.

CHAPTER XVII

Return to St. Louis—Iowa—Kanesville—The Necessity of Great Care in Procuring an Outfit—Shoeing Oxen— Costume for the Plains—Council Bluffs Ferry and Group of Cottonwood Trees—Crossing the Missouri into Indian Territory; Nebraska and Kansas—Winter Quarters— Council Bluffs and the Missouri River from an Elevation —Organizing for the Plains—Importance of Herding and Guarding the Cattle

I DID not cross the State of Iowa from Keokuk with the emigrants, but returned to St. Louis, from whence I went up the Missouri river by steamboat to St. Joseph, Mo., a distance of about 470 miles, and from thence by land to Kanesville, a further distance of about 150 miles. In travelling by land from St. Joseph I necessarily had to cross a portion of Iowa (26), and entered Kanesville, now called Council Bluffs City, by the Bluff road, and a very bad road it was. It is difficult to climb clayey hills in wet weather, so that my friends and I scrambled up and slid down alternately.

The city is situated at the mouth of a small valley, beside a stream called Indian Creek. The town was commenced by the Saints at their exodus from Nauvoo to the West in 1846, and a number of large holes, which were dug by the pilgrims in the sides of the hills as temporary dwelling places, are still to be seen. The place soon rose into some importance and continued to be occupied by the Saints until 1852, when mostly all left for Utah. A newspaper, the *Frontier Guardian*, was edited and published there by Elder O. Hyde until his departure for G. S. L. Valley.

I found Kanesville to be a very dirty, unhealthy place, and withal a very dear place to make an outfit for the Plains, notwithstanding the assertions of holders of property and merchants settled there to the contrary. They assure emigrants that their wisest plan is to take their money there to purchase their outfit, but I hope few will believe them, for as there is not much competition they get prices the very reverse of their consciences. It is nevertheless a great place for bargains. Sometimes emigrants to California get sick of the journey by the time they have arrived at Kanesville and sell out by auction in the street. The ringing of a large bell announces the sale, and it seldom fails to collect a crowd. As I said, sometimes "real bargains" may be obtained, but generally articles of the most worthless description to emigrants are offered. I saw there one infatuated lover of bargains who, although he had but one wagon and a sick wife who would be certain to occupy it always, was silly enough to attend these auctions and buy up "bargains" enough to stock a London "Bottle-wop shop." Gambling houses and lawyers abound also. Where there are so many wolves there must consequently be a number of victims. Of mechanics there are wheelwrights, blacksmiths, and others quite able to supply or repair anything necessary for the Plains. Emigrants should be very cautious and particularly with every thing they purchase, keeping in view that mistakes cannot be remedied on the journey. When a storekeeper assures you that bacon, or a ham is sweet and good, don't be content with his word, but cut into it and see for yourself. When crackers, biscuit or flour are wanted, eat some of the crackers, and smell and taste the flour. Remember that you are to be 3 months on the Plains, and that to eat bad bacon, or to live on sour bread, will be anything but healthy and pleasant. The same caution may be useful in all things, and in nothing perhaps more than in the purchase of a wagon. If you have to make the purchase yourself, you should, after deciding what weight you intend to carry, be careful to get one of proportionate strength. Rather than risk the probability of a "break down" by the way, I would prefer to have the axles stouter than would perhaps look symmetrical. If you discover a flaw or shake in the wood just say at once to the maker—"That won't do for me." Don't allow yourself to be persuaded that it will be strong enough. If you do, be assured that long before you get to the Rocky Mountains your wondering eyes will behold an awful crash. Your wagon will be tried as well as yourself, and none but good ones will get through without a great deal of patchwork. In the purchase of cows and oxen the same matter of fact principle ought to be practised. If you want a milch cow see her milked before you buy her, and be sure you taste the milk. The milk from some cows is utterly worthless and undrinkable. Some may imagine such caution as this unnecessary. To them it may be, but to a London tailor, whose knowledge of animals does not extend beyond his own goose, a hint may be useful. In purchasing, it may not always be possible to obtain those that are thoroughly trained and broken in. Indeed, except with the leading steers, it is not very essential. My opinion, however, is that well broken steers should be had to lead the team and should therefore be tried at the time of purchase. Assure yourself that they have a due respect for the authority of the whip, and that they really have been initiated into the mysteries of "geeing" and "hawing." If a good pair of leading steers are obtained, the chief difficulty with respect to the team is surmounted. All that is required then is to see that the yokes and bows fit the animals' necks. Be merciful to the poor animals, and if you can make them work easy by any contrivance, do so by all means. Well smooth the yoke where it fits on to the neck, and see that the bows are wide enough and fit well to the shoulders. Some persons, to prevent the galling of the neck, line the yoke with sheet lead, and this I should judge is likely to be effectual, as the lead admits of polish and generally retains a greasy, slippery quality. Another important matter in connection with the oxen is the shoeing of them. There are various opinions about it. Some say that all ought to be shod before starting, and others say it is best to shoe them as they begin to get sore footed and lame, as it is possible that some may not require it at all. Some say that leather shoes are best, and others that iron shoes are indispensable. It is beyond question a most troublesome matter to shoe oxen. In this respect it is far more difficult to manage them than either horses or mules. My opinion is that gutta percha would be preferable to any other material, and I think, in going over the Plains again, I should start with all the animals unshod, and immediately there was the slightest symptom of lameness, I should soften a sufficient quantity of the material and mould it around the animal's foot. This might be done at a few minutes' notice, and when you judged that the hoof had grown and recovered its hardness, the gutta percha might be easily removed. The great advantage would be that any one might do it, that it could be done without throwing the animals down or lifting them off their legs (which is the usual method), and that there would be no danger of laming them. Having obtained wagon and team, it will not be amiss to cover the wagon, so as to effectually keep out the wind and rain. A stout closely woven cloth should be used, such as is now supplied through the Presidency in England to the emigrants before leaving Liverpool. It is, however, almost impossible to get it of the same make and quality in the U. States. In addition to the outside cover, an inside lining of slighter material would prove useful in a storm. Some persons use oil cloth, but I think it hardly repays the trouble and expense.

With reference to clothing, I would say use any old clothes you may happen to have by you. But if you want to purchase, procure those that are most suitable, for instance, fustian trowsers, made so as to remain on without braces, and instead of a coat and waistcoat, made London or Paris fashion, a red Guernsey shirt, similar to those commonly worn by sailors. For a covering to the head a felt hat will be the best, and for the feet top boots will be found almost indispensable. During the first half of the journey the soles and heels of boots do not suffer much, but the toes are very soon cut out by the strong sharp grass. For this reason it would not be amiss to have a second covering put over the toes before starting. "Goggles," which are coverings for the eyes, will be found very useful as protectors from dust and sand, and also from excessive sunlight. While writing about clothing for men, it may not be amiss to mention that if they will suffer her, nature will provide them with clothing for the face and throat that will prove most useful during the journey across the Plains. I think the beard eminently useful and to most persons ornamental also. Lock up your razors and try to believe that you cannot improve God's greatest work. It is not true that the beard makes a man look like a bear or a monkey. On the contrary, the fact is, that there is not an animal in existence that is provided by nature with the moustache and beard like man. Then, while on the Plains, at least, allow your great characteristic to remain, and at the end of the journey you will thank me for my advice and be very much tempted to advocate the total abolition of razors. All that I have to recommend to the ladies is that they do not wear their dresses quite so long, and that if possible they provide themselves with India rubber goloshes and very large sun-bonnets [fig. 5].

At Kanesville I was kindly permitted to join the emigrating company, under the presidency of Elders Miller and Cooley. To Elder Miller I am indebted for numerous acts of kindness, for which I yet hope to repay him. The company being ready we drove down to Ferryville, or Council Bluffs Ferry, 12 miles distant, and just opposite Winter Quarters, at which point we crossed the Missouri into

Indian Territory, now Nebraska and Kansas (27). Short as this journey was, it was sufficient to convince some of the company that they had loaded their teams too heavily. In the view of Council Bluffs Ferry, &c., they are seen transferring the contents of their boxes to bags to lighten their load, which they ought to have done before. Their experience ought to teach those who follow after to nip in the bud their affection for strong heavy boxes. For my own use I should very much prefer strong wicker baskets of a square form, lined with zinc. They are both lighter and stronger than wood and keep out damp most effectually. Another advantage worthy of consideration is that the zinc would be useful and valuable at the end of the journey. My advice to all is to take those things which will be most serviceable on the road and valuable in the Valley. Let the beginning and end of all your thoughts be utility!

The ferry-boats are flat-bottomed and large enough to carry 2 wagons of the ordinary size. The starting point is usually chosen a considerable distance up the stream, so that the current may assist in conveying the boats to the landing place on the opposite side of the river. Ferrying is hard work. When the boat is pushed from the bank the rowers are obliged to ply their oars most vigorously, as it is no slight matter to row across a river a quarter or half a mile wide, with a current running at the rate of 4 or 5 miles an hour. Six or 8 stout fellows are required to do the work. I went 3 or 4 trips myself and found out what it was to work hard. The whole of our company crossed the river without an accident. Cattle are ferried across this river, but are compelled to swim or ford the minor streams. A few days after we crossed, the river rose several feet and overflowed the banks, which increased the difficulty of crossing ten-fold. The camping place on the west side of the Missouri was about a mile from the landing in the vicinity of 2 springs, near the site of Winter Quarters (28). I paid a visit to the old place, and found that some person had set fire to the last house that remained of the once flourishing settlement. From an elevation close by I made a sketch of Council Bluffs and the Missouri river [pl. xxi].

Before any general movement of the company can be made it is absolutely necessary that an organization should take place, that officers be appointed, and laws be made relative to travelling, camping, guarding, herding, &c. If possible, a man should be chosen as captain, possessing energy of character and intelligence. It will also prove of great advantage if he had been over the road before. He ought to have a horse constantly at his command, that he may be able to ride forward, and select the best road, and the most convenient and desirable camping places. This arrangement will prevent a great deal of confusion and unpleasantness and will save the teams much injurious delay and labour. If the company is large, it is well to organize it into divisions of 10 wagons each and to appoint not only a captain over the whole, but over each ten. This course is adopted in the emigrating companies of Saints and proves highly beneficial. In all cases it proves useful in a variety of ways. For instance, if an accident happen to a wagon, the company to which it belongs will remain behind until it is remedied and allow the main body to move on to the next camping ground. Thus, a few only will be inconvenienced, instead of the whole company. Still, if it is not possible for the 10 so left behind to join the camp the same day or night, it would be well for the main body to remain in "corral" until those left behind arrive, and if assistance is thought necessary, promptly to render it. In fact, hardly any circumstance will justify the strong part of a company in leaving the weaker portion behind for more than a day's travel. The most disastrous consequences have resulted from this injurious course being adopted. As no man would like to be left by himself, helpless and defenceless on the prairies or mountains, so no company ought to leave any individual who is willing to proceed. The company I joined was formed on the principle of mutual assistance, and, having once started, it was agreed that none should be left behind. From the fact that accidents are of frequent occurrence, it is of course wise to divide the mechanics as equally as possible among the companies, that repairs may be promptly executed.

In addition to the officers already mentioned, a sergeant of the guard should be appointed to superintend the herding and guarding of the cattle. It is his duty to see that the guard is appointed and relieved. From the time of unyoking until sunset, the cattle should be herded, that is, they should be driven a short distance from the camp to the best feeding ground, and from sunset until sunrise they should be kept in the immediate vicinity of the camp and strictly guarded. This may appear to be an immense amount of trouble, but when properly and systematically attended to, the labour being equally divided, it is not so great as it may at first sight appear to be. Still the labour, much or little, is nothing when compared with the trouble and exertion necessary to hunt up cattle in the morning if not thus attended to. If they are not carefully herded and guarded, the best part of the day will be inevitably lost, and perhaps the best part of the stock too. There is not only danger of the cattle straying away, but the probability of their being driven off by Indians also. To a very great extent the Indians live by plunder, and when once they have decided upon robbing a company they will follow up for days, lurking behind trees and hills. A remarkable instance of crafty robbery came under my notice during my return. About 50 miles from Chimney Rock, we saw 6 or 7 wagons a short distance from the road, and soon after some men came from them and inquired whether we had seen any stray cattle. Upon our replying in the negative, they informed us that a few evenings before, the herdsmen were called from the cattle to take supper, and after remaining in the tents about 10 or 15 minutes they went out, but could see nothing of any of the oxen, except those that were yoked together, all the rest to the number of 40 were gone, and that they had now given up all hope of ever recovering them. The Indians had doubtless watched for such an opportunity, and the result proved that they knew how to take advantage of it. If there are boys in the company, they, with one or two men as overseers or directors, may be used to herd the cattle. It will not, however, do to trust the more important duty of guarding at night to them. Men often go to sleep and neglect their duty, it is therefore reasonable to suppose that if men cannot or will not understand the importance of this matter, boys will be still worse. It is impossible to take too much care of the cattle; in fact it is more essential that the emigrants' animals should be healthy and strong than the emigrants themselves. In making laws for the government of the camp, it will therefore be wise to leave the number of miles to be travelled per day entirely to circumstances. Some men before starting make up their minds to travel 20 or 25 miles every day. Now this is very great folly, as every thinking man who has travelled the road must acknowledge. For the first half of the distance the feed is good, and there is a favourable opportunity, by careful and moderate driving during this part of the journey, to preserve the strength and muscle of the teams until it is really necessary from scarcity of food, water, or bad roads, to try their strength and test their powers to the utmost. In such a case forced travelling may be justifiable, but not otherwise.

To complete the organization of the company I travelled in, a chaplain was appointed, whose duty it was to call the camp together, morning and evening, for singing and prayer. The voice of prayer was heard every day, and the song of praise at the rising and setting of the sun. Many a hard feeling was then destroyed by the melting influences of spiritual instruction, and resolves to amend were made, which doubtless resulted in a better life.

CHAPTER XVIII

Departure from Council Bluffs~Six Mile Grove~
"Geeing" and "Hawing" ~Ludicrous Efforts of the
Teamsters~Pappea Creek~A Night on Guard~
Fright Among the Oxen~Elk Horn Ferry~Prairie
Dogs~Shell Creek~Accident to Henry Randell;
Surgery on the Plains~Pawnee Indians; Theft~Indian
Marksmanship~Double Team to Get Through a
Slough~Loup Fork Ferry~Elder Miller's Mules Stray;
Unsuccessful Search for Them; The Mules Found~
Prairie Creek; Dangerous Descent to the Bridge; A
Wagon Upset into the Creek~Wood River~Elm Creek
~Buffalo Hunt~Mosquitoes Impede the Progress of
the Train~Indian Subtlety~Skunk Creek~A Drink
at a Stream, and a Snake~Wide Creek~Halt for
General Repairs

IT was decided by Elders Miller and Cooley that we should start on
Thursday, the 9th of June. Operations were commenced early in the
morning, and then began the yoking of refractory cattle, and the
initiation of "greenhorns" into the art and mystery of teaming. The
whole of the cattle were driven into the "corral," and then, with
yokes and bows in hand, it was the business of the teamsters to catch
and yoke their teams, but, unfortunately, they did not know their
business. Many of them had never touched an ox before, so that the
wide-spreading horns of the untrained steers seemed to produce a
most uncomfortable nervousness. The consequence was that Elders
Miller and Cooley had to do nearly all the work, which nearly
brought noon before we could start. At length we started upon the
Plains and travelled to Six Mile Grove, where we camped. The road
was rather rough, and so were the cattle, and, in the hands of raw
teamsters, nearly unmanageable. Elder Miller was here and there
and every where, giving untrained teams and teamsters in training

many practical illustrations of the art. "Geeing" and "hawing" were most forcibly taught and of course learned in proportion to the ability of the pupil. The teamster should drive with the team to the right. When he cries "Gee," the team should go from him, and when "Haw," come towards him. When the teamster cries "Haw," it is usual with a lazy team to let them feel the whip over their necks, and when "Gee," over their backs. The consequence is that whenever a piece of rough or difficult road is encountered, the shouts and cries of "geeing" and "hawing" and the cracking of the whips are most terrific. In a large company voices of all kinds and modulations mix up in the most curious manner. When a slight movement to the right or left is required, the command to "gee" and "haw" is given in a very mild tone, but when there is danger of running against a rock, or getting a wheel locked in a tree, the command is sure to be given with the full volume of the teamster's voice. During the first few days the teams and teamsters were constantly at variance. Nearly every man had the worst team in the company! Some steers would not "gee," others would do nothing else, and then would come an appeal to Elder Miller—"O, brother Miller, do come here and try to make my lead steer 'haw,' for the stupid brute does nothing but run away from me." "Very well," brother Miller would say, "but let me see you drive a little first." Directly this request was made the raw teamster knew he was going to make an exhibition of his ignorance, and sure enough he did so, for instead of keeping behind his leading oxen he went rather before them, which was sure to frighten them and cause them to scamper to the right again. Elder Miller would bring the oxen back, and with his good-humoured smile say—"Now you are a pretty teamster, aint you, to go and place your ugly body and long dangling whip right before their eyes, instead of keeping back as you ought." Then away he would go, shouting and hallooing to a man, who, in defiance of the sacred laws of teaming, would be driving on the right hand side of his team instead of the left. Before Elder Miller could get to him, or make him comprehend his blunder, the oxen would get frightened at the strange sight of a man on the "off" side, and consequently violently swerve to the right, and cramp the wagon, and perhaps narrowly escape turning it over. Thus wisdom was gained by experience, and, however singular it may appear, a blowing up from Elder Miller only proved the kindness of his heart.

Friday, the 10th.—We left Six Mile Grove about 8 o'clock in the morning, and drove to Pappea Creek, 12 miles, without halting. After hearing so much about the Plains, of course everything was expected to look new and strange, but as yet there was nothing new or strange except the mosquitoes. Their stings are most painful and irritating. Nothing but buckskin is proof against their long probing stings. Cloth is no protection, they penetrate it easily. When I was called to take my turn at guarding, I found the mosquitoes up and rather more ravenous than was agreeable. The cattle were guarded close to the creek. While pacing round them with a rifle on my shoulder, and keeping them within bounds, the sensation of loneliness was most singular. The night was very dark and the stillness quite unbroken, except by the rustling sound of my walking in the grass. As I thought of the caution I had received about Indians, I grasped my rifle with greater energy and looked about with increased vigilance. But the night passed without any chance of testing my valour, yet I have confidence in it still.[1]

Early in the morning some one's sharp eyes discovered a good feeding ground to the left of the creek, to which the cattle were driven, and there herded.

Saturday, the 11th.—Crossed the very primitive and unsafe bridge at Pappea Creek and travelled 9 miles over a road equally primitive to Elk Horn River. The first occurrence that day was the breaking of a wagon-wheel. It was caused by the tire coming off, which, singularly enough, was not noticed by the man who was driving. He drove for a considerable distance with the wheel in that condition before he was overtaken by Elder Miller, who started off in pursuit, rolling the tire as a boy would a hoop. It was, however, too late to wedge it on as everything was strained, and one or two of the fellies were broken. The wheel was therefore taken off, and a stout piece of timber being obtained, it was securely lashed over one axle-tree and under the other, so as to allow one end to touch the ground. This answered instead of the broken wheel and supported the wagon until the evening tolerably well. About the middle of the day I saw

[1] The night watch roused special anxieties in all travellers and was frequently described in overland journals. William Chandless spoke with affection of "the whole sense of stillness and repose as one walked backwards and forwards 'through the long and pleasant grass,' now and then stopping to listen to the wolves howling, or to the monotonous munching of an ox here and there," adding with relief, ". . . the glad words flew around that it was daylight." *A Visit to Salt Lake*, pp. 83–84.

two or three wagons turn off the road and stay behind, and in the evening I heard that a fine boy had been added to our number.

The approach to Elk Horn is over a sideling road, and the descent into the lowland which borders the river is rather difficult. Another wagon was broken, and as I passed with Elder Miller's wagon and mules, which I had undertaken to drive, I saw the owner looking disconsolate and some of the "boys" rigging up the same kind of support as before mentioned.

During the process of unyoking the cattle, a slight mistake committed by one of the teamsters was the cause of a curious exhibition of fright and rage by an unbroken ox. Before taking the yoke off, the man unhooked the chain which connected the yoke with the wagon-pole, and then, having taken the yoke from the "near" ox, he was proceeding to do the same with the "off" ox, but the wild brute, feeling an unusual weight on his neck, broke away and rushed madly about with the yoke still fastened to his neck. He bellowed, and capered, and danced about in a most singular manner, and then dashed away at a headlong gallop, followed at the same pace by all the unyoked oxen in the camp. It very much astonished me, and I did not at all envy Elder Cooley, when I saw him mounted on a horse, hastening away to catch and unyoke the mad animal and bring the whole herd back. In about an hour he returned triumphant.

Arrived at Elk Horn, we camped on the east side of it until Monday about noon, resting, and repairing wagons. As there were 2 or 3 wheelwrights in the camp this was done most readily. A fine fat buck was shot by one of the "boys" and brought into camp and eaten of course. While halting at this place I made the accompanying sketch.

Monday, the 13th.—Having repaired damages we crossed the Elk Horn, which is about 9 rods wide, and 3 feet deep. The labour to the ferrymen is not so great here as at the Missouri river. On account of the narrowness of the stream they are able to stretch a rope across the river, which, being held by one or two of the ferrymen in the boat, by means of a smaller rope with a noose attached, enables them to guide the boat which is partly carried by the current, and partly dragged by them to the desired point on the opposite bank. The cattle were compelled to swim across. They were collected together on the bank and surrounded by men and boys who, with shouting and blows, tried to force them in, but they were most unwilling to commence the trip. Those in front being pressed by those behind backed and retreated from the brink until the pressure becoming overpowering there would be a flounce and a splash, an ineffectual struggle to return, and then the commencement of the voyage in earnest. Travelled 4 miles and camped on the west side of Elk Horn.

Tuesday, the 14th.—It was determined at a meeting of the camp to separate into 2 companies. Elder Jacob Bigler was chosen captain of the company appointed to go in advance. We travelled 7 miles up the Elk Horn and camped on the bank. Here I saw that curious little animal called the prairie dog. It is almost as much like a squirrel as a dog. It very much resembles a fat puppy of a light fawn colour. It burrows in the earth like a rabbit, and, it is said, usually shares his habitation with a rattlesnake and an owl: I have seen owls pop out of sight into the dog holes, but I never saw them together.

Wednesday, the 15th.—Travelled 12 miles. Detained 3 hours mending a broken wagon.

Thursday, the 16th.—Travelled 15 miles and camped on Shell Creek, which is 12 feet wide, and bridged. During the day we crossed a half dried-up creek, having mud in it of a very great depth, consequently the difficulty of crossing was great in proportion. Two or three teams were required to haul each wagon through. Considerable damage was done to chains and several wagons. A serious accident occurred to Henry Randell.

He got under his wagon to secure the tar bucket, and very carelessly left his right leg projecting outside the wheel. The team, left to itself, started on, and the wheel passed over his leg and broke it. Learning that something was the matter, I hastened to the spot, and soon saw that if I did not do something for him his chance of getting his leg set was a very poor one. I therefore took the case into my own hands and turned surgeon, although I had never before seen a broken limb. In the first place I screwed up my courage to the sticking place and bared both his legs. I then took particular notice of the exact position of the bones in the unbroken leg and the position of the foot, and placed the right leg and foot in exactly the same position, and kept them so by means of 2 boards which I nailed together. These, with the aid of thin sticks or splinters bound round the leg, with abundance of rag, seemed to answer the purpose. The continual jolting of the wagon rather retarded his recovery, but I am happy to say he got on very well.

Friday, the 17th.—Several Pawnee Indians came into camp this morning and begged all the time they remained. I asked one of the young men to give me a specimen of his skill in shooting with the bow. He fixed a small cracker on a stick which he stuck in the ground, and standing about 12 yards from it, aimed 2 or 3 times but did not hit it. A still younger one, seeing his want of skill, impatiently took his place, and split the cracker with the first arrow. Their clothing consisted of a cloth round the waist and a blanket over the shoulders. Altogether they were most villainous looking. One of them stole a gaily coloured piece of webbing belonging to me from the back of the wagon and tied it round his waist. I took it from him, but after trying to make him understand that I disapproved of his thieving, I gave it back to him, with, however, very little hope that my lesson on morals had done him any good. The whole of the forenoon was spent in repairing broken wagons. Travelled 13 miles and camped near a pond. Firewood very scarce.

Saturday, the 18th.—Commenced our day's travel with the disagreeable knowledge that we should have to double team through a deep slough. It proved much worse than our fears, for with many of the wagons a triple team was necessary. The men were over their knees in mud, and how the ladies got through I don't know and hardly dare conjecture. Elder Miller recommended me to keep in the wagon as he thought the mules could pull me through, but when in the mud-hole it was evident to me that if I remained in the wagon there we should stick, so into the mud and slush I jumped, and by plying the whip vigorously I got the team through. Once in the mud and thoroughly bedaubed I thought, I had better make the best of it, so I borrowed an ox whip, which, with putting my shoulder to the wheel, gave me healthful and useful employment until all the wagons were through. Travelled 11 miles to the Loup Fork, a tributary of the Platte, and camped on the east side, near the ferry.

Sunday, the 19th.—We remained in camp. Elder Miller's mules, always perverse and obstinate, strayed away. I made diligent search for them but could not find them. After the preaching meeting, Elder Miller started in search of them but returned without them. He had, however, discovered tracks of them, and, with his usual courage and inflexibility of purpose, supplied himself with provisions for 2 or 3 days, and, accompanied by a volunteer, set out with a determination to find them if possible. As we were to cross over to the west side of Loup Fork at this point he promised to meet us on the road, when he had either found the mules or lost all traces of them. He bade us good bye, and a few hours before sun-down started in search of his animals up the east side of the stream.

Monday, the 20th.—Elder Miller did not return, so Elder Cooley yoked up a couple of oxen to draw his wagon, and I commenced to struggle with the difficulties attendant upon the management of horned cattle. My friends must not accuse me of vanity when I assure them that the abstruse mysteries of "geeing" and "hawing" were at last comprehended and successfully performed by me. Neither should they accuse me of over cautiousness when I inform them that, finding one of the oxen afflicted with the not over amiable desire to give me a "dig in the ribs," I very prudently managed to prevent the accomplishment of his wish. We ferried both wagons and cattle over the Fork, which is a much more easy method than fording. It is a broad and comparatively shallow stream with quicksand in many places. I made a sketch of Loup Fork Ferry, which is herewith presented [pl. xxiii]. Elder Cooley lost an ox in the evening through its straying into a mud hole and getting "mired."

Tuesday, the 21st.—Looked in vain for the return of Elder Miller. The yoke of cattle under my care improved upon acquaintance, although I must confess our 15 miles' drive this day gave me enough of "geeing" and "hawing." We camped on the bank of Loup Fork.

Wednesday, the 22nd.—We travelled 17 miles this day, and camped near a slough, about a mile from Loup Fork. No timber, and water bad.

Thursday, the 23rd.—Travelled 18 miles. Camped on a small creek. Good water, but no wood. Elder Miller returned without his mules, downhearted, tired, and sorefooted. He had followed their tracks 70 miles up the east side of the Loup Fork, traced them to several islands which they passed over in crossing the river, saw the spot where they had landed on the bank, was able to detect the prints of their hoofs for some distance further, where they turned off again on the grass and all trace of them was lost. He, however, bore all the trouble and vexation like a philosopher. Late in the evening some of the "boys" discovered tracks of mules not far from the camp, which Elder Miller thought sufficient reason why he should continue the hunt.

Friday, the 24th.—Early in the morning Elder Miller started off in search of his mules. Our road was for 6 miles over sand hills, and the teams had to work exceedingly hard to get through at all. Veils and goggles were in great demand, for the wind brought the sand into our faces with blinding and choking effect. The mules were found in the course of the day, right in the road. As if tired of a wandering life, they had decided once more to submit to servitude. When I arrived at the spot, I found them in the hands of the two young Wilsons, evidently unmanageable, but when they found me at the end of the lariat they submitted quietly enough. Elder Miller early taught me that the only way to manage a mule was to administer a dose of strangulation, the consequence was they acknowledged my authority, and I harnessed them immediately. I found Elder Miller sitting on an old Indian grave, despairing of ever seeing his mules again. Travelled 15 miles and camped on a small creek.

Saturday, the 25th.—Travelled 4 miles to Prairie Creek. As the descent to the narrow bridge was very steep, all teamsters were instructed to allow no persons to remain in the wagons. I suppose these instructions were attended to in every case except one of a woman who happened to be asleep unknown to the teamster, and, as misfortune would have it, the wagon fell clean over the bridge into the creek. Of course the effect of the fall and the plunge into the cold water was a loud scream from the woman, which all thought proceeded from some person underneath the wagon. The men at once jumped into the creek, with the intention of raising the wagon, but as the woman came to her senses, she very wisely caused a commotion inside the wagon, which speedily resulted in Elder Miller's ripping up the wagon-cover with his knife and pulling her out. I urged the mules down the bank with many misgivings, for a swerve to the right or left of a few inches would have made the woman's fate mine also. We travelled 4 miles further, and with much difficulty crossed a small but very muddy creek. The "boys" close to the camp this evening shot a very fine antelope.

Sunday, the 26th.—Travelled 7 miles to Wood River and crossed over an emigrants' very bad apology for a bridge, composed of branches of trees, and foliage thrown into the river, which is about 2 feet deep and 3 or 4 yards wide. Camped close to the river. Water good and an abundance of wood. I was told that during the night an Indian was seen lurking close to the camp, and that one of the guards fired at him. I made the accompanying sketch [pl. XXIV] of our camp at Wood River (29).

[1.] New Orleans

[II.] Baton Rouge

[III.] Natchez under the hill

[IV.]   Natchez

[V.]   Vicksburgh

[VI.] Memphis

[VII.] St. Louis

[VIII.] Camp at Keokuk

[ix.] Nauvoo

[x.] Ruins of the Temple at Nauvoo

[xII.] David Smith

[xI.] Joseph Smith, Jun.

[**XIII.**] Lucy Smith

[xiv.] Joseph and Hyrum Smith

[xv.] Carthage Jail

[XVI.] Room in which Joseph and Hyrum Smith were imprisoned

[XVII.] Well against which Joseph Smith was placed and shot at after his Assassination

[XVIII.] Willard Richards and John Taylor

[XIX.] Entrance to Kanesville

[xx.]　Council Bluffs Ferry and Group of Cottonwood Trees

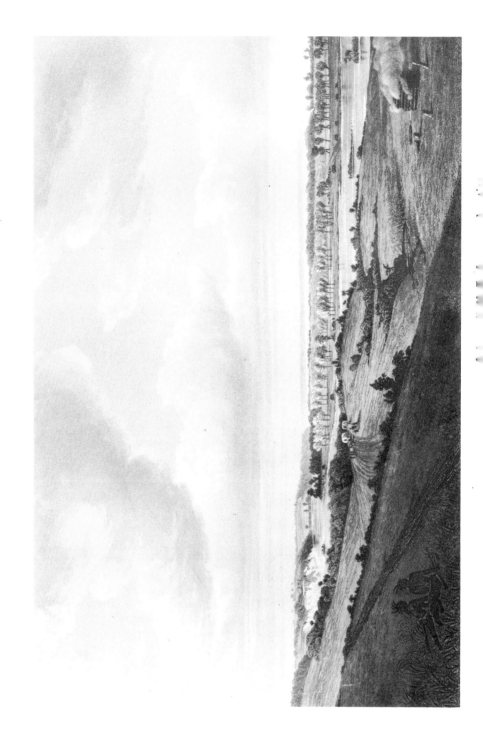

[XXII.] Elk Horn River Ferry

[XXIII.] Loup Fork Ferry

[XXIV.] Camp at Wood River

[xxv.] Chimney Rock

[XXVI.] Scott's Bluffs

[XXVII.] Fort Laramie

[XXVIII.] Laramie's Peak

[xxix.] Independence Rock

[xxx.] Devil's Gate

[xxxi.] Witches Rocks

[xxxii.] Great Salt Lake

[XXXIII.]   Great Salt Lake City in 1853, looking south

[xxxiv.] Brigham Young

[xxxv.] Heber C. Kimball and Jedediah M. Grant

[xxxvi.] Father John Smith, and John Smith, son of Hyrum

[2. Light House at the Mouth of the Mississippi]

[1. Emigrant Ship leaving Liverpool]

[3. Old Fort Rosalie]

[4. Walnut Hills]

[5. Costume for the Plains]

[6. Chimney Rock from the West]

[7. Fort Bridger]

[8. A Kanyon in the Rocky Mountains]

[9. Joseph Walker and Arapeen]

Monday, the 27th.—Travelled 20 miles over a road generally very good. A good day's travelling like this repays one for many a hardship, and when again in the noise and smoke of cities will surely be remembered with longing regret.

Tuesday, the 28th.—Remained in camp repairing wagons until 2 p.m., after which we travelled till dark, about 16 miles, over an excellent road, and camped about half a mile from the Platte river.

Wednesday, the 29th.—Travelled about 16 miles to Elm Creek, over a rough road. Came to wood and water about 6 miles from last night's camping place, and crossed 2 deep ravines.

Thursday, the 30th.—Travelled about 15 miles today, which, considering that the road was very rough and difficult, was very good work. I saw buffalo this day for the first time in my life. They are very singular in shape and run in a most grotesque manner, and apparently very rapidly. I had no chance of getting near them, but the enthusiasm of some of the hunters in the camp drew them out in chase. I wished them success, for I was tired of bacon. There was good camping at this place.

Friday, July 1st.—Travelled 8 miles to a slough, watered, and continued our journey for about 7 miles, when the train was detained a short time by our coming within convenient shooting distance of a few buffalo. The "boys" raised a cry of "Buffalo, buffalo a-head!" and away scampered men and dogs in pursuit. "Ah!" said Elder Miller, "let them go, they'll get tired without killing one I'll be bound." The buffalo, of which there were about 6 or 8, did not seem inclined to retreat until they got scent of the men, and the dogs were close at their heels. They then started off at a pace which surprised me, and in a manner closely resembling the gallop of a hog. The chase did not continue very long before the "boys" found that for speed and wind they were no match for buffalo, although so clumsy looking. They therefore separated themselves, and, urging on the dogs, succeeded at last in scattering the game. But they were green hunters, unacquainted with their rifles, and bad judges of distance. A very red-headed Welshman was the first to fire, but instead of bringing down the brute, he only made him roll away the faster. The report of the gun excited Wilson's lame bull-dog so much that he limped from under the wagon, and, warming with the exertion, increased his speed so as to catch up to the nearest animal. I saw that, unlike the other dogs, he, without the slightest hesitation, dashed at the buffalo's nose, but failing to catch firm hold was, of course, violently thrown over, and then limped back to the wagon. As yet not a horse was out. Elder Miller said it was of no use going after buffalo without one, so he remained at the camp and laughed at the "greenhorns." At last Elder Cooley got his ambition up, and taking his horse from the sheep driver, and borrowing Elder Miller's large flint-lock pistols, he joined the hunt. Although the buffalo had been chased some time, they had not succeeded in getting much further off than at first, as the river was on one side, the camp on the other, and the hunters at all points. Elder Cooley's horse carried him well, and I saw him overtake one animal, ride round him once or twice, and then extend his arm with the evident intention of firing, but there was no smoke, and no report, consequently death did not result. He stopped his horse, examined his pistols and slowly turned towards the camp; Miller gave the word to move on, the whips cracked, the wheels began to roll, and again we had to endure the certainty of fried bacon. Elder Cooley in his hurry had either shaken the powder out of the pan, or he had started without any, which was a pity, for he was a capital shot. In the evening one of the "boys" came in and reported that he had killed a buffalo, but so far off that it was useless to think of going to it. I would have brought its tongue as an evidence had I shot one, which, however, I had no ambition to do.

While I was at Winter Quarters a man named Furze requested me to call upon his friends in London, and inform them that he was well, and doing well, and was going to California. To-day I passed his grave, which had a board at its head stating that he had been killed by Indians while on guard.

Saturday, the 2nd.—Travelled 12 miles over a rough road, in some places very heavy from the previous night's rain. We camped early, on account of the sheep-driver, who was ahead, returning with the information that about a mile further on the mosquitoes were so numerous and had attacked him and his horse so furiously, that he was obliged to turn and gallop back as fast as possible. Our camping ground was near the Platte river, in a place admirably suited for the purpose.

Sunday, the 3rd.—Travelled 7 miles to heavy sand hills, which extended about half a mile, and then proceeded 7 miles further and camped close to the Platte river. We had a visitor from the camp ahead, who told us that one of their number, being about half a mile behind the camp, was attacked by Indians, who stripped him of his clothes and then gave him a kick and told him to "Puck-a-chee," which is the Indian word for Begone. It is evidently impossible to know when Indians are near. I have been told that they will follow up a camp for days, keeping on the opposite side of hills, being unseen, yet seeing all, until a favourable opportunity presenting itself for robbing, they pounce on their prey like the tiger from its lair.

Monday, the 4th.—Travelled about 6 miles to the crossing of Skunk Creek, which was not difficult to get over. Being very thirsty, and the creek shallow, I lay down with my mouth in the water, and was in the very act of taking a good draught, when a long brilliantly coloured snake glided past close to my nose. Had a professor of gymnastics been present, it is my opinion he would have spoken favourably of the rapidity with which I sprang to my feet. Travelled 7 miles further on and camped near the spring, at the head of the Pawnee swamps. No timber.

Tuesday, the 5th.—Found no timber at the place described in guides as "Last Timber." We travelled to Wide Creek, about 16 miles, and camped with the intention of remaining until all necessary repairs were attended to. Wood was obtained from the islands in the river for making charcoal, which was essential for blacksmithing purposes.

Wednesday, the 6th.—We made charcoal to-day by piling up wood, and covering it over with turf so as to burn it with as little air as possible.

Thursday, the 7th.—A forge was erected to-day and large bellows were set up. Ox shoes were made, wagon-tires were shortened, and shaky wheels were made tight, so that we were once more in travelling trim.

CHAPTER XIX

Departure from Wide Creek~Cooking with Buffalo Chips~Death of Elder Cooley's Child~A Delicate Morsel for a Cow~The "Lone Tree"~Ancient Bluff Ruins~Chimney Rock~Meeting of Missionaries from G. S. L. Valley~Scott's Bluff~Laramie's Peak~ Separation of the Company

FRIDAY, the 8th.—Having completed our repairs, we left Wide Creek and crossed Black Mud Creek, Grass Creek, two other creeks or sloughs not mentioned in guides, and North Bluff Creek, and camped near good grass and water. Distance from Wide Creek, about 13 miles. There were plenty of buffalo chips there. They are composed of grass, masticated and digested, and dried in the sun. It is a common joke on the Plains that a steak cooked on these chips requires no pepper. It is marvellous the wonders time and circumstances work. Young ladies who in the commencement of the journey would hardly look at a chip, were now seen coming into the camp with as many as they could carry. They burn fiercely and cook quite as well as wood.

Saturday, the 9th.—Our road lay through the heaviest sand-hills we had then passed over, and we found that it was preferable to make the cattle pass over rough places covered with grass than to keep them in the sandy road. We caught 2 or 3 lizards to-day, which were beautiful little creatures and appeared to be quite harmless. Crossed Buffalo Creek and camped at Shepherd's Creek, distance 11 miles. During the night Elder Cooley's child died. The poor mother's grief was very affecting. What can be more distressing than to see a poor infant struggling with death and to be utterly unable to render assistance.

Sunday, the 10th.—We buried the child and recommenced our journey at 12 o'clock. Travelled, according to Horn's Guide, 9 miles to Petite Creek, having crossed 3 creeks running between bluffs rather difficult of ascent and descent. We saw a great variety of brilliantly coloured grasshoppers, some being very large. They were very interesting to me and pleased me as much as they did the children, who hunted them with great glee.

Monday, the 11th.—A wet morning prevented our starting as early as usual, for nothing is worse for the necks of oxen than dampness. It softens the hair and opens the pores of the skin, so that a slight amount of friction causes soreness. Travelled 16 miles over a sandy and bad road, and through several creeks, none of which were difficult to cross. Camped on the bank of the Platte.

While in camp I laid a silk handkerchief upon the grass, after washing it, expecting that the sun would dry it in a few minutes, but fortune ordained otherwise. My attention was suddenly attracted to the spot where I had left it by hearing a girl cry out—"O look 'ee there! if there isn't a critter a eaten something"; and sure enough there was, for that moment I saw the bright red corners of my best silk handkerchief vanish into a cow's throat. I learned that it was no uncommon thing for these animals to appropriate such delicate morsels.

Tuesday, the 12th.—We passed over sandy bluffs which were decidedly the worst we had encountered and had to double team all the wagons except the mule-wagon. The mules were brave little fellows to pull. Travelled about 15 miles, crossing several creeks, and camped on Watch Creek.

Wednesday, the 13th.—In the guides there is a notice of a "Lone Tree." All through the journey the lone tree had been in my imagination until at last I had associated an interest, a sort of romantic idea, with it, which became quite exciting. I pictured to myself an old, weather-beaten, time-worn tree, standing in mournful solitude on a wide-spreading prairie, having to encounter alone the attacks of the elements, with no companion to share the storm, or help to break its fury. I could imagine it on a cold winter's night with its arms bare of foliage, tossing them in sorrow in the wind, being desolate and alone. Even sunshine and refreshing showers must be melancholy pleasures to a lone tree, for do not they prolong its dreary isolation! I started off ahead of the company with the intention of making a complimentary and therefore careful sketch of this tree, but I could not find it. Some unpoetical and ruthless hand had cut it down, so my hopes were blighted and my occupation was gone. We passed Ash Hollow, which is on the south side of the Platte, where we could see an immense herd of buffalo, which good judges said could not number less than 10,000. Travelled about 18 miles and camped near Calm Creek.

Thursday, the 14th.—Travelled along the Platte bottom, over a heavy road, then by the edge of bluffs to Crab Creek, a distance of 17 miles. Camped amongst arrow grass, bad for sheep, and very disagreeable to every body having sensation.

Friday, the 15th.—Travelled over a pretty good road to Ancient Bluff Ruins, which are curious natural formations, resembling ruins, as their name implies. They are fit abodes for Indian ghosts and goblins. Camped where the road joins the river, about 20 miles from Crab Creek.

Saturday, the 16th.—Travelled 13 miles and camped on the Platte. Chimney Rock in sight all day, and Scott's Bluffs in the evening. Chimney Rock is on the south side of the Platte, and on my journey home I made the accompanying sketch of it, engraved on steel [pl. xxv], which is a view taken nearer by three miles than could be obtained from the north side (30). During the day I made a sketch of it from the west, represented by the wood-cut below [fig. 6]. To the right of the rock the wagons are in corral, which is the order in which they are arranged while camping. When danger is suddenly apprehended from Indians, the cattle are driven inside the corral, but as the slightest noise from a dog, a wolf, and at times unaccountable circumstances, often cause a stampede, in which the cattle break down the wagons and rush madly from the camp, endangering the lives of the emigrants, and frequently running until they are lost to their owners or fall dead, it is much the best way to tie them up to the wagon outside the corral and picket them. In the latter method the cattle are safely guarded, and should Indians approach to drive them off or cause a stampede, they would be within range of a rifle shot all round.

Sunday, the 17th.—Travelled 6 miles, and camped on the bank of the Platte. Rain in the afternoon.

Monday, the 18th.—In the morning met 27 Elders from G. S. L. Valley on missions. They informed us that they had had a quick and an agreeable trip so far. We spent half an hour with them, and then separated, they to the rising and we to the setting of the sun. Scott's Bluffs were in view all day. They were certainly the most remarkable sight I had seen since I left England. Viewed from the distance at which I sketched them the shadows were of an intense blue, while the rock illuminated by the setting sun partook of its gold, making a beautiful harmony of colour. They present a very singular appearance, resembling ruined palaces, castellated towers, temples and monuments. In the foreground of the engraving are seen some emigrants hunting the buffalo [pl. xxvi].

Tuesday, the 19th.—Stopped to noon at Scott's Bluffs, and travelled about 4 miles to Spring Creek, making about 46 miles during the last 4 days.

Wednesday, the 20th.—Travelled over a pretty good road somewhat sandy in places. About 5 miles beyond is what is named Blue Rock. It is slightly grey, but by no means what may be called blue. Camped near the river.

Thursday, the 21st.—Saw Laramie's Peak this morning, which, by Elder Miller's account, was distant 75 miles to the south-west of camp ground. We travelled over a very sandy and difficult road. Visited a trading post kept by two Frenchmen, a few miles east of Raw Hide Creek. As the affair was made up of Frenchmen, Indians, squaws, horses, mules, oxen, dogs, trees, a shady bower, a sheep pen, a wagon, and a tent, it was most picturesque. Cattle in by no means good condition were from 90 to 100 dollars per yoke. I noticed that nearly all these trading posts were kept by Frenchmen, who were mostly married to Indian women. Camped on the bank of the Platte, 3 miles west of Raw Hide Creek. Travelled yesterday and to-day about 37 miles.

Friday, the 22nd.—Travelled about 9 miles over a good road to Laramie, and sketched what little I could see of it, but not having time to cross the river, I was unable to obtain a complete view of it until my return, when I made that which is used in this work (31). Travelled about 6 miles further, over a pretty good road, through rather a hilly country, quite different in character to that east of Laramie. Camped on the summit of a high bluff on the west side of a dry creek. I sketched Laramie's Peak, of which an engraving is given. Although its top was free from snow when I saw it, it is said to be generally covered with it, and that it "acts the part of a condenser upon the vapour of the atmosphere which comes within its vicinity, generating clouds, which are precipitated in showers upon the surrounding country."

Saturday, the 23rd.—The road was good for 3 or 4 miles, after which it became the roughest we had had. We broke one wheel, one axle, and one tongue, which Elder Miller fixed as usual. He is really a model of a captain and deserves great credit for the masterly manner in which he managed everything, and the good-humoured energy with which he surmounted every difficulty. We did not camp till after dark when, as there was no grass on the north side of the Platte, all the cattle were driven over to the south side. The night was very dark, and as it rained, all the men who would volunteer were sent over to guard the cattle, which are always more inclined to wander off in wet weather than in fine. The current of the river being very swift, none but strong swimmers ventured over. A large fire was maintained on the north side during the whole of the night, by keeping a fine old tree burning, which served as a beacon to the guards opposite. Travelled about 9 miles.

Sunday, the 24th.—We remained in camp all day. It had become apparent that our provisions would not hold out until our journey was completed, and to-day Elder Miller decided upon going ahead of the main company to bring out supplies of provisions from G. S. L. Valley. I was much gratified with this arrangement, as I had begun to doubt whether I should be able to accomplish the object of my journey the present year. This concluded upon, the mules were shod, and everything was got ready and put in order for separation from the company and the recommencement of the journey on Monday morning.

CHAPTER XX

Proceed in Advance of the Main Company~Plan of
Travel~Account of Mr. Furze's Death~Alkali Lakes~
Rock Independence~Devil's Gate~The "South Pass"
of the Rocky Mountains~Prairie Hens~Utah Territory
~Fort Bridger~Witches' Bluffs~Arrival at Great Salt
Lake City

MONDAY, the 25th.—This morning Elder Miller, Elder Bigler and
wife, and myself "rolled" out of camp to proceed in advance of the
company to G. S. L. Valley. In passing the various wagons a shower
of wishes for good luck and a quick and pleasant trip for the remainder of the journey greeted us. Travelled 15 miles and camped
with Elder Wilkin's company.

Tuesday, the 26th.—Road good to river about 15 miles. Travelled
about 33 miles, which the mules did bravely. Elder Miller's plan of
travel was most excellent. As soon as morning dawned we harnessed
up and travelled till about 8 o'clock, when we breakfasted, and the
horses and mules grazed for about an hour. We then travelled till
noon if there was good grass to be obtained for the animals, and they
were again allowed to graze for an hour or an hour and a half, when
the journey would be resumed and continued until about one hour
before sunset. A fire was then lighted and supper was taken, after
which we went on a little further till dark, and then camped without
lighting a fire. The last part of the journey was to out-manœuvre any
Indians who might have been watching us during the day, and who,
seeing a fire lighted, would naturally conclude that we had camped
for the night and act accordingly.

Wednesday, the 27th.—Rough day's travel over about 34 miles of
a very bad road. This morning we overtook the sheep-drove to which
the man who had been shot by an Indian was attached.

The captain informed me that Furze was on guard at night, when
suddenly the quiet of the camp was broken by his crying out—"Oh!
Oh!" and "Come here," and then the sharp crack of a rifle was heard,

which caused the men to run out. They found him on his hands and knees on the ground, shot through the lungs. He died almost directly without being able to communicate anything. But from the fact that no emigrants or traders were near, that the wadding used was made of dried grass, and that the rope by which a very fine horse had been fastened was severed, the captain concluded that an Indian must have committed the murder. Furze was much regretted, as he was a great favourite with all.

Thursday, the 28th.—Travelled about 30 miles, being 3 miles beyond the "Upper Ferry," where there is now a bridge over the Platte. Our journey up the north side of the Platte was much more difficult and unfavourable than it would have been (according to Elder Miller's account) over the Black Hills route, to have taken which we should have had to cross at Laramie. To-day we did not take the road described in Clayton's Guide, which leads by the Mineral Spring or lake, considered poisonous, but continued along the Platte. Found the road very hilly and rocky, but I suppose the good water of the river instead of the poisonous water of the springs amply compensated.

Friday, the 29th.—Travelled to Grease Wood Creek, 36 miles and camped. It was so dark when we had finished our supper, that we had great difficulty in finding the mules. Their wandering propensity kept me in a constant state of alarm, and every morning when I arose I fully expected to find that they had during the night become impatient of delay and had started for the Valley without us, as they did at the Loup Fork.

Saturday, the 30th.—Left Grease Wood Creek, and stopped about an hour at the Alkali Lakes to obtain saleratus. As we approached them they had all the appearance of ponds of water frozen over, and having a slight covering of snow over the ice. We then proceeded to the ford of Sweetwater, about a mile beyond Rock Independence. Forded, and then, while the company were taking breakfast, I hurried back to the Rock and made a sketch of it. It is a large rounded mass of granite, on which are inscribed the names of many passing emigrants.[1] At Devil's Gate, about 4 miles further, I remained be-

---

[1] Captain Howard Stansbury wrote of Independence Rock: "It was covered with names of the passing emigrants, some of whom seemed determined, judging from the size of their inscriptions, that they would go down to posterity in all their fair proportions." *Exploration and Survey of the Valley of the Great Salt Lake of Utah* (Philadelphia, 1852), p. 65.

hind to make a sketch of this great curiosity (32), after which, as my boots were without toes, and admitted the gravel, which cut one's feet dreadfully, I had some difficulty in catching up with the wagons. Camped on the east side of High Gravelly Bluff. Day's travel 38 miles.

Sunday, the 31st.—Breakfasted about 2 miles west of High Gravelly Bluff. Travelled till 10 p.m. and camped on east side of Ford No. 5 of Sweetwater. Wind River Mountains, which were capped with snow, in sight to-day. Day's travel 34 miles.

Monday, August 1st.—Travelled to last ford of Sweetwater, and crossed rocky ridges very rough and tedious to get over. Day's travel about 30 miles.

Tuesday, the 2nd.—Breakfasted on Pacific Creek, after crossing the South Pass of the Rocky Mountains, or summit of dividing ridge, the principal evidence of which was that, whereas all the streams we had crossed or passed until that time ran east, the Pacific Creek, which is just over the Pass, runs west. The same is the case with all the streams on the west side of the pass. The altitude of the pass is 7085 feet. We killed five prairie hens to-day, which, after being admirably cooked, made our salt bacon seem wretched indeed. Road excellent to Little Sandy, where we camped, and found good feed. Distance about 37 miles.

Wednesday, the 3rd.—Travelled about 8 miles to Big Sandy and breakfasted. While camping, a large troop of horses crossed, being driven by 2 Indian women, who were dressed in the most gaudy manner, followed a short time after by a Frenchman, whom I supposed to be the owner of both squaws and horses. Travelled about 9 miles further to Big Sandy again, dined, and then left for Green river, expecting to reach it about 6 or 7 o'clock, but much to my disappointment 6, 7, 8 and 9 o'clock came, but no river, and it was not till 11 o'clock, tired and worn out, that we came to the water. Distance 35 miles.

We had now left Nebraska, passed over the south eastern corner of Oregon, and entered the Territory of Utah (33), and although we were about 170 miles from the place of our destination, we were on our own ground, and all around assumed a closer interest as we approached Great Salt Lake City, where we were to meet anxious friends waiting to give us the hand of brotherhood and hail us welcome.

Thursday, the 4th.—Rose before the sun, and then learned from some traders that we had taken the wrong road and had come to the California Ferry. Breakfasted and turned back to the right ferry, where Elder Bigler found a relative who presented him with a very good Indian pony. There was a trading post there, and crowds of traders, gamblers and Indians, who of course all live on the emigrants.

Friday, the 5th.—Harnessed Elder Bigler's Indian pony and hitched him to our wagon. As it had never been in harness before, it was rather amusing to see it make all its movements with a jump and dart forward. By adroit management on the part of Elder Miller, it was by the evening comparatively gentle and seemed to promise to do good service. Just before arriving at Black's Fork, No. 3, where we camped, we passed a splendid range of clay bluffs which, as we passed them, seemed covered with figures in almost all attitudes—nuns confessing to priests, and warriors fighting, and transforming and varying themselves as we changed our position. Day's journey about 38 miles.

Saturday, the 6th.—Travelled about 17 miles over an excellent road to Fort Bridger, on Black's Fork, a short distance east of a bluff, very prettily dotted over with cedar. The accompanying wood-cut represents the place [fig. 7]. It is merely a trading post, then belonging to Major James Bridger, one of the oldest mountaineers in this region. The fort is built in the usual form of pickets, with lodging apartments opening into a hollow square. A high picket fence encloses a yard into which the animals of the establishment are driven for protection, both from wild beasts and Indians. The grass in the neighbourhood was abundant, but about a mile and a half from the fort Mr. Bridger had erected a board, on which was written a request for emigrants to keep a mile away from his place.

The road from Fort Bridger, described in Clayton's Guide, leads to the left of the bluff west of the fort, but the new road, the one altogether travelled now, leads to the right. East of Muddy Fork we descended the steepest and roughest hill on the road. Camped at Soda Spring, about 17 miles beyond Fort Bridger, tired enough. The wolves howled at night most dismally, causing an almost indescribable sensation. They seemed to wail and gnash their teeth for the fun of the thing. It was, however, no joke to me to be hushed to sleep with such music.

Sunday, the 7th.—Our road to-day was most tedious, with nothing but the anticipation of a quiet rest in the Valley, in 2 or 3 days, to comfort us. We passed through some droves of cattle and sheep, and fortunately got through without suffocation from the clouds of dust raised by them. I could not stop to see Cache Cave, a cave in the bluffs, which is considered a curiosity, as our teams were weary and we wanted to hurry on to Echo Kanyon, where we camped near the creek for the night. Distance about 37 miles.

Monday, the 8th.—Arose early this morning, and hastened on our journey. We crossed Echo Creek from 15 to 20 times, and most of the crossings were difficult. We passed many remarkable rocks to-day, but none I think so much so as Witches Bluffs, on the east bank of Weber river. They are more like gigantic and somewhat rude pieces of statuary in the form of women than any thing else. Out of compliment to their resemblance to the ladies I made a sketch of them. Weber River was the most important stream that we crossed after leaving the Platte. Had it been a few inches deeper our little mules must have swum for the opposite bank. Camped on Kanyon Creek. Day's journey 31 miles.

Tuesday, the 9th.—Commenced our journey this morning by getting our mules "mired" in one of the bad crossings of Kanyon Creek, and after many vain attempts to get them out, we at last succeeded by hitching Elder Bigler's horses to the wagon poles. The rest of the journey to the mouth of the Kanyon which opens into the Valley was desperate work, but we knew there were warm friends ahead, and a hearty welcome for the travelworn, so we scrambled up the mountains, and thumped and bumped over the rocks, and splashed through the streams, till we surmounted all difficulties. Signs of civilization met the eye as we proceeded along. From away up the mountain sides we could hear the sound of the axe, and in the road, chewing the cud of patience, we saw the sturdy team waiting to transfer to the busy haunts of men the foliage crowned monarchs of the solitude, perhaps then for the first time invaded. And now our journey, so full of interest and novelty to me, was nearly completed, and we were about to exchange the rude, but bracing and healthful prairie life for the comforts and refinements of the city. Just before we turned the corner into the Valley we stopped at the creek, and having bathed and changed our clothing we at last entered as the sun was setting beyond the Great Salt Lake, a steel engraving of which is herewith given [pl. xxxii], and another 5 miles brought us to the City. Day's journey about 30 miles, making a total, according to the best accounts I could keep, of 7840 from Liverpool, thus—

Liverpool to New Orleans 5000
New Orleans to St. Louis 1173
St. Louis to Kanesville 620
Kanesville to Winter Quarters 12
Winter Quarters to G. S. L. City 1035
——7840

CHAPTER XXI

Great Salt Lake City~Brigham Young~ Heber C. Kimball~Jedediah M. Grant~ Father John Smith

BY THE time we entered Great Salt Lake City (34) darkness had enveloped it, shutting out from my straining and inquiring eyes all details. I could see that the streets were broad, and hear the refreshing sound of water rippling and gushing by the road side. Occasionally a tall house would loom up through the gloom, and every now and then the cheerful lights came twinkling through the cottage windows —slight things to write about, but yet noticed with pleasure by one fresh from the Plains. A happy meeting with relatives and a few moments of wakefulness ended the 9th of August, and also ends my hastily sketched and simple narrative.

P.S.　While in the city, President Brigham Young, among other things, favoured me with the opportunity of taking for publication the portrait of himself presented in this work (35). The portrait of President Heber C. Kimball (36), and that of the late President Willard Richards are from daguerreotypes by Mr. Cannon, which were kindly furnished by Elder S. W. Richards.

After the appointment of Jedediah M. Grant (37) as successor to Willard Richards; and John Smith (38) the son of the martyr Hyrum Smith, to succeed Father John Smith as Chief Patriarch, it was considered that to give their portraits would much enhance the value of the Work. They were consequently solicited, and daguerreotypes were forwarded from G. S. L. City in time to publish with an extra Part.

The Portrait of the late Patriarch, Father John Smith, (39) is likewise from a daguerreotype in the possession of Elder S. W. Richards, which has been pronounced true to life, and which he politely permitted to be copied for the purpose of being published in this Work. The view of the City was taken with a camera lucida, from the "Bench," north of it, and just above President H. C. Kimball's house, which is seen in the foreground, a little to the left of East Temple St. The site of the city is large, and at that early period the buildings were very much scattered, rendering it almost impossible to convey any idea of the place unless a large area was embraced in the view. Consequently a favourable point was chosen, commanding the principal buildings, and the chief portion of the city which was then built upon. This, on the other hand very much reduced the size of the objects, but not to indistinctness. On the whole I think it may be presented as a faithful portrait of Great Salt Lake City in 1853.

Emigration Appendix

At the close of our review of the L. D. Saints' Emigration, which opens this Work, we intimated that we might resume the subject in the last Part, and bring the history of the same up to that time. We now proceed to do so, and take up the subject where we then left off.

With the departure of the *Clara Wheeler* in April, 1854, shipment ceased for the season, and on the 1st of July, Elder S. W. Richards was succeeded in the Presidency of the British Mission, and, consequently, the Emigration Agency, by his brother F. D. Richards, of the Quorum of the Twelve. Prior to the next season several very material changes occurred. The Eleventh General Epistle of the First Presidency, issued from G. S. L. City, April 10, 1854, recommended the Saints in Europe to emigrate at once to the United States under the instruction and direction of the Presidency of the British Isles, where they might tarry until they could go to Utah, i.e., those who could not complete the journey without detention. In addition to this, President Young, on the 2nd of August, wrote to Elder F. D. Richards with regard to a change in the ports of debarkation in the United States, as follows—

You are aware of the sickness liable to assail our unacclimated brethren on the Mississippi river, hence I wish you to ship no more to New Orleans, but ship to Philadelphia, Boston, and New York, giving preference in the order named. Whenever you ship a company, whether it be small or large, be careful to forward to Elder John Taylor, at New York City, a correct list of the names of the persons in each company, with their occupation, and approximate amount of property or means, and forward it in season for Elder John Taylor to receive it before the company arrive in port, that he may be so advised as to be able to meet them, or appoint some proper person to do so, and counsel them immediately on landing as to the best course for each and all in every company to pursue— viz., whether to tarry for a season to work in the place or immediate neighbourhood of their landing, or proceed to Cincinnati and its region, &c.

In case any should still choose to ship by New Orleans, ship them from England no later than about the 1st of December, that they may be able to get off the rivers before the sickly season sets in, for many have died off with the cholera and other diseases incident to the sickly season on the rivers, and I do not wish the brethren to be so exposed as they have been. And counsel them to hurry up the rivers, and get off from them into Missouri and Iowa to work, or on to the Plains, as the case may be, before the warm weather sets in.

The First Presidency having counselled the Saints who were unable to go direct to Utah, to gather in the meantime to various parts of the United States, and having also instructed that the emigrants be landed at Northern ports instead of New Orleans, the number of passengers was largely increased, and embarkation continued at intervals throughout the year. It was somewhat difficult, however, in the early part of it to obtain suitable ships, owing to the general derangement which then existed in the mercantile marine, incident upon the war with Russia, but the last company of through emigrants for the season was got off without any serious delay.

Elder F. D. Richards re-opened his agency by despatching the *Clara Wheeler,* on the 27th of Nov., for New Orleans with a company of emigrants for the United States. In the subjoined table we give the particulars of this ship's company, and also of each shipment made up to the close of 1855. The foreign emigration passing through Liverpool since the termination of Elder S. W. Richards's agency has altogether been shipped from Liverpool under the British agency, and is therefore included in the same table and particularized underneath it.

Referring to the Through Emigration for 1855, it will be seen that 1161 persons went out under the arrangements of the P. E. Fund Company. Of these, there are 34 who went out in the *J. J. Boyd,* who will not cross the Plains until the Summer of 1856. The sum taken from the P. E. F. Passengers, who crossed the Plains last Summer, and prepaid their passage, was £15 for all over 1 year old, and £9 for all under, which has no doubt been found on winding up the cost of the expedition quite sufficient. The number of emigrants providing their own teams, &c., who went through the same season, was about 373. The cost of 1 waggon, 4 oxen, and 1 cow was £55; and the amount of money sent forward by those persons, providing their own teams, &c., was £3853. The fitting out point for the season was Atchison, Kansas Territory; and the camping ground, Mormon Grove, about 5 miles west of it; both of which places, and the route taken to the Platte, and from thence up the south side of that river to Fort Laramie, are shown upon the map which accompanies this Work.

The American part of the journey to Utah and the purchase of teams and outfit were this year superintended by Erastus Snow, of the Quorum of the Twelve, who acted in concert with Elder Richards in the season's operations. As an intermediate assistant, Elder Richards appointed Elder John S. Fullmer, then on a mission to England, Managing Conductor, making it his duty to receive the emigrants in the United States and to forward them across the country to St. Louis, subject to Elder Snow's direction.

The total number of persons who set out from Liverpool intending to go direct through to Utah last Summer was about 1500, and the total sum of their expenditure cannot be set down at less than £30,000.

In addition to the important changes in the L. D. Saints' emigration, which have occurred since the former part of our review was published, the passage of the two new Passenger Acts—one American and the other British, has introduced other changes of almost equal importance not only to the L. D. Saints, but to emigrants to the United States generally.

The American Act came into effect in British Ports, on the 1st of May, 1855, and the British Act on the 1st of October, following. Many of the suggestions made by the respective Committees, whose reports we adverted to on pages 58 and 59, have been acted upon. In nearly all its main features, however, so far as relates to the carriage of passengers between the United Kingdom and the United States, the American Act is more than covered by the British. Some of the exceptions wherein it is not covered are that the former makes two persons between 1 and 8 years of age equal to a statute adult, while the latter makes 2 between 1 and 12 years a statute adult; that the former requires the berths to be parallel with the sides of the ship, to be 6 ft. long 2 ft. wide, and 9 in. above the deck or platform immediately beneath them, while the latter requires them to be 6 ft. long 18 in. wide, 6 in. above the deck immediately beneath, and the interval between each tier of berths, and between the uppermost tier, and the deck above it to be $2\frac{1}{2}$ ft. Both Acts prohibit the carriage of passengers on more than two decks (except the poop and deck houses, if any). The American Act requires that 16 clear superficial feet, on the upper Passenger Deck, and 18 ft. on the lower (not being an an orlop deck) if any—provided in both cases, the height between decks shall not be less than 6 ft.—shall be allowed to each statute adult. The British Act requires that 15 feet on the upper Passenger Deck, and 18 ft. on the lower, between which and the upper deck must not be less than 7 ft. in height, shall be allowed to each statute adult, and provides that no ship, whatever be her Tonnage or superficial space of Passenger Decks, shall carry more than 1 statute adult to every 5 superficial feet, clear for exercise, on the upper Deck or Poop, or (if secured and fitted on the top with a railing or guard to the satisfaction of the Emigration Officer at the Port of Clearance) on any Round House or Deck House. The 7th sec. of the American Act authorises the Captain of any Passenger Ship bringing passengers to the United States to maintain good discipline and such habits of cleanliness among them as will tend to the preservation and promotion of their health, and makes it his duty to cause the apartments occupied by them to be kept at all times in a clean and healthy state. The 14th sec. compels him, the owner, or the consignee to pay to the Government of the United States 10 dollars for each person over 8 years of age who may have died on the voyage by natural disease. This appears at first sight a singular and hard exaction, but the reader will find the arguments pro. and con. on page sixty.

The British Act has fixed the Scale of Provisions as follows, for voyages between this country and North America (except the West Coast thereof), and requires ships clearing out between the 16th of January and the 14th of October, both days inclusive, to be provisioned for 70 days, and those clearing out between the 15th of October and the 17th of January, both days inclusive, for 80 days—

DIETARY SCALE

3½ lbs. Bread	
1 lb. Flour	
1½ lb. Oatmeal	
1½ lb. Rice	
1½ lb. Peas	
2 lbs. Potatoes	Weekly to each statute
1¼ lb. Beef	adult, or every 2 chil-
1 lb. Pork	dren between 1 and
1 lb. Sugar	12 years old
2 oz. Tea	
2 oz. Salt	
½ oz. Mustard	
¼ oz. Pepper	
1 gill Vinegar	

3 quarts water daily, and 10 gallons to every 100 for cooking

The Act authorises substitution as follows—

1 lb. of Preserved Meat for 1 lb. of Salt Pork or Beef; 1 lb. of Flour or of Bread or Biscuit, or ½ lb. of Beef or of Pork for 1¼ lb. of Oatmeal, or 1 lb. of Rice or 1 lb. of Peas; 1 lb. of Rice for 1¼ lb. of Oatmeal, or vice versa; ¼ lb. of Preserved Potatoes for 1 lb. of Potatoes; 10 oz. of Currants for 8 oz. of Raisins; 3½ oz. Cocoa or of Coffee roasted and ground for 2 oz. of Tea; ¾ lb. of Treacle for ½ lb. of Sugar; 1 gill of mixed Pickles for 1 gill of Vinegar; but the substituted articles must be set forth in the Contract Tickets of the passengers.

The Act also requires each ship to be provided with *Medical Comforts,* and the following scale has been fixed upon by the Emigration Commissioners for vessels sailing from Liverpool to North America—

For Two Hundred Adults and under

14 lbs. Arrowroot	2 gallons Lime Juice
25 lbs. Sago	½ gallon Brandy
20 lbs. Pearl Barley	2 doz. Milk, in pints
30 lbs. Sugar	1 doz. Beef Soup, in lbs.
12 lbs. Marine Soap	3 doz. Pre'd Mutton, in ½ lbs.

One half the above to be added for every additional hundred

Notwithstanding it would be perfectly legal here to ticket passengers and provision them entirely after the requirements of the British Act, the agent acting for the L. D. Saints complies with the American Act, in regarding all persons of 8 years of age and upwards statute adults, and tickets and provisions them accordingly.

It is provided in secs. xxiii. and lvii. of the British Act that "no berths in a Passenger Ship occupied by passengers during the voyage shall be taken down until forty-eight hours after the arrival of such ship at the port of final discharge, unless all the passengers shall have voluntarily quitted the ship before the expiration of that time," and "that every passenger in a passenger ship shall be entitled for at least forty-eight hours next after his arrival at the end of his voyage, to sleep in the ship, and to be provided for and maintained on board thereof, in the same manner as during the voyage, unless within that period the ship shall quit such port or place in the further prosecution of her voyage."

The new Act also differs from that of 1852, in requiring 2 Cooks, when the number of statute adults exceeds 300 instead of 400, and a Medical Practitioner when the number of persons on board exceeds 300, including cabin passengers, officers, and crew, instead of 500. The subsistence money, in case of detention, has also been raised from 1s. to 1s. 6d. a day for each statute adult, in respect of each day of delay for the first 10 days, and afterwards 3s. a day, until the final departure of such ship—provided that if the passengers be maintained on board in the same manner as if the voyage had commenced, no such subsistence money shall be payable for the first two days next after the said day of embarkation, nor if they shall be maintained shall such subsistence money be payable if the ship be unavoidably detained by wind or weather, or by any cause not attributable, in the opinion of the Emigration Officer, to the act or default of the owner, charterer, or master (sec. xlix).

The framers of the present Act have no doubt produced the most perfect one that has yet appeared, regulating the carriage of passengers at sea and prescribing the mode in which the embarkation shall be effected. In order no doubt to ensure respectability among Passage Brokers, and to increase their liabilities in case of fraudulent practices, the Bond to be given to the Crown before a Licence can be obtained has been increased from £500 to £1000; and no broker can employ, as an agent in his business any person not holding from him an appointment in the form prescribed by the Act and countersigned by the Emigration Officer of the port in which the broker has his business. To protect emigrants on their arrival in port and in getting on ship-board from the numerous "sharpers" with which sea ports abound, and who are always on the alert to entrap the unwary, the Act prohibits under a penalty of £5, nor less than £1, from acting as an "Emigrant Runner," any person not duly licensed and registered for that purpose under the provisions of the Act, and defines the term "Emigrant Runner" thus— "the Expression Emigrant Runner shall signify every Person other than a licensed Passage Broker or his *bona fide* salaried Clerk, who within any Port or Place of Shipping, or within Five Miles of the outer Boundaries thereof, *for Hire or Reward or the Expectation thereof,* shall directly or indirectly conduct, solicit, influence or recommend any intending Emigrant to or on behalf of any Passage Broker, Owner, Charterer, or Master of a Ship, Lodging House, or Tavern or Shop Keeper, Money Changer, or other Dealer or Chapman, for any Purpose connected with the Preparations or Arrangements for a Passage, or shall give or pretend to give to such intending Emigrant any Information or Assistance in any way relating to Emigration." Licensed "Runners" are known by a badge worn on the breast and are prohibited from taking any fee or reward from any person for the procuring of his passage, or in any way relating thereto; if they obtain any remuneration it must be from the broker or other person for whom they "run."

The first ship sailing with a company of L. D. Saints after the American Act took effect was the *Clara Wheeler,* and after the British Act, the Emerald Isle. We now introduce a table giving a continuation of statistics up to the close of 1855 [p. 135], and a summary of the Emigration from Europe up to that period.[1]

Summary of The Latter-day Saints' Emigration from Europe,
from the Commencement in 1840, up to the Close of 1855

From 1840 to 1854 (see p. 45.)		17,195
" 1854 to 1855 (see p. 135.)	4647	
Add for persons who have emigrated between 1854 and 1855, but have not embarked under the appointed Agency.	69	
		4716
Grand Total,		21,911

The "History of Joseph Smith," or the History of the Church, a portion of which is published weekly in the *Deseret News,* having during the progress of this Work, passed the period embraced in the Table of Emigration for 1840–1, which appears on page 14, we are enabled to supply some of the particulars of which we were then deficient. We therefore give below [p. 137] a new Table for that portion of the statistics.

[1] Emigration from England continued at the same accelerated pace. The poverty of the lower classes was an important factor. One has only to thumb through the pages of the *London Times* during the year of publication of Piercy's book to see frequent reports of bread riots. See particularly February 20 and April 5, 1855. By 1860 the total number of emigrants from Great Britain and Scandinavia reached 30,000. Between 1860 and 1870 10,000 more converts left Britain for Salt Lake City. See William Mulder and A. Russell Mortensen: *Among the Mormons,* (New York, 1958), p. 334.

Franklin D. Richards, Agent. 1854—5

Date of Sailing	Vessel	Tons	Captain	Destination	President	P. E. Fund			Ordinary	Total
						Ordered	Otherwise	Total		
1854										
Nov. 27	Clara Wheeler	995	Nelson	New Orleans	Henry E. Phelps				422	422
1855										
Jan. 6	Rockaway	1162	Mills	do.	Peter O. Hanson		13	13	427	440
,, 7	James Nesmith	815	Goodwin	do.	Samuel Glasgow				24	24
,, 9	Neva	849	Brown	do.	Thomas Jackson				13	13
,, 17	Charles Buck	1424	Smalley	do.	Richd. Ballantyne	194	11	205	198	403
Feb. 3	Isaac Jeans	843	Chipman	Philadelphia	Geo. C. Riser				16	16
,, 27	Siddons	970	Taylor	do.	John S. Fullmer	15	82	97	333	430
Mar. 31	Juventa	1186	Watts	do.	William Glover	115	117	232	341	573
April 17	Chimborazo	1071	Vesper	New York	Edward Stevenson	41	154	195	236	431
,, 22	Samuel Curling	1476	Curling	do.	Israel Barlow	235	150	385	196	581
,, 26	Wm. Stetson	1146	Jordan	do.	Aaron Smethurst				293	293
June 29	Cynosure	1403	Pray	do.	George Seager				159	159
Nov. 30	Emerald Isle	1823	Cornish	do.	P. C. Merrill				350	350
Dec. 12	John J. Boyd	1311	Austin	do.	C. Peterson		34	34	478	512
						600	561	1161	3,486	4,647

The *James Nesmith, Charles Buck, Isaac Jeans, Juventa, Chimborazo, S. Curling,* and *John J. Boyd,* include in their total numbers 972 from the Scandivanian Missions, 45 from the Swiss and Italian, 75 from the French, including the Channel Islands. There are also 13 Germans and 1 Prussian. The balance are from the United Kingdom of Great Britain and Ireland.

From the same source we are also enabled to make the following extract, which gives the date of the first company's departure from England, their names, and the name of the ship —

Saturday, 6th June, 1840, a company of 40 Saints, to wit, Elder John Moon, and Hugh Moon, their Mother and 7 others of her family; Henry Moon, (uncle of John Moon), Henry Moon, Francis Moon, William Sutton, William Sitgreaves, Richard Eaves, Thomas Moss, Henry Moore, Nancy Ashworth, Richard Ainscough, and families, sailed in the Ship *Britannia* from Liverpool, for New York, being the first Saints that have sailed from England for Zion.

Brigham Young, Agent. 1840—1

Date of Sailing	Vessel	Tons	Captain	President	No. of Souls
1840					
June 6	Britannia			John Moon	41
Sep. 7 or 8	North America			Theodore Turley	200
1841					
Feb. 7	Sheffield			Hyrum Clark	235
,, 16	Echo		Wood	Daniel Browitt	109
March 17	Uleste			Thomas Smith	54
April 21	Rochester		Woodhouse	B. Young	130

It will be observed that in the previous Table and in the "Summary of the Emigration by the British Agency," on page 15, that we gave Parley P. Pratt as Agent from 1840 to 1841, which was erroneous. President Brigham Young being in England, with several others of the Quorum of the Twelve, from April, 1840, until the departure of the *Rochester*, he superintended all the interests of the Church here.

[Linforth's Notes to Piercy's Narrative]

(1) SAN DOMINGO, or, more properly speaking, Hayti, is one of the great Antilles, and, next to Cuba, the largest island of the West Indies. It lies S. E. from Cuba, and is separated from it by the windward passage, 50 m. broad. It extends from Cape Engano, lat. 18° 35′ N.; lon. 68° 20′ W. (Raper), to Cape Tiburon, lat. 18° 22′ N.; lon. 74° 28′ W.; and from Point Beata, lat. 17° 36′ 42″ N.; lon. 71° 32′ W., to Cape Isabella, lat. 19° 59′ N.; lon. 71° 1′ W.; and is about 400 m. long E. to W.; and 150 m. broad at its broadest part. Including the islands of Tortuga, Gonaive, &c., the area is about 27,690 sq. m., being nearly as large as that of Scotland.

Hayti as a whole may be said to be one of the healthiest of the West Indies islands. Its soil is rich and produces majestic pines, fine mahogany trees, fustic, satin wood, lignumvitæ, roble or oak, the wax-palm, numerous fine cabinet woods, the richest flowering plants, plantains, bananas, yams, batatas, oranges, pine apples, cherimoyas, sapodillas, melons and grapes. The scenery of the island is delightful. When Columbus and his followers came in sight of La Vega Real (Royal Valley) they supposed they had reached an earthly paradise. The native quadrupeds of Hayti are not larger than a rabbit. The animals introduced from Europe, and now in a wild state, have thriven amazingly. Cattle, pigs and dogs, in large numbers, now roam freely in the savannahs and in the mountain forests. Birds are neither numerous nor beautiful in appearance, but insects are plentiful. Numbers of caymans and alligators are found in the lakes and rivers, and whales are common in spring, in the surrounding seas. Turtles, lobsters and crabs abound on the coast. The mineral products are gold, platina, silver, quicksilver, copper, iron, magnetic iron, tin, sulphur, manganese, antimony, rock salt, bitumen, jasper, marble, lazulite, chalcedony, &c.; but all are neglected for want of capital. The geology of the island is yet but imperfectly known.

Hayti was discovered in 1492–3, by Columbus, and from an impression that it resembled his native land he named it Hispaniola, or, *Little Spain*. At Cape Isabella, on the north shore, and east of the Cape of Monte Christi, was founded the first Spanish colony in the new world. Hayti was then inhabited by a happy, docile and indigenous race of people, governed by five hereditary chiefs, named Caciques, who reigned over as many districts. The aborigines believed in a Supreme Being, but did not adore him. They paid that tribute to inferior deities called Zemes, whom they dreaded, and whom they represented by figures carved in wood or stone, or made of clay or cotton. It is said that they believed in the immortality of the soul, and expected after death, to meet their friends in an earthly paradise. Polygamy was not only practised but sanctioned. A petty king is said to have had thirty-two wives. The Spaniards by their oppression exterminated the aborigines, and introduced African slaves to cultivate the sugar cane. The pure race died out about the close of the 17th century. After the discovery of Peru, numerous colonists emigrated to South America, and the remaining inhabitants were withdrawn to the centre of the island to prevent their escape. This left the coasts free to the French, who, driven from St. Christopher, settled there in 1630. The French settlers captured the pigs and horned cattle that had become wild, sold the skins to the traders who touched on the coasts, and smoked the flesh, both for food and for sale, on a wooden grating called *boucan*, from which circumstance the settlers were called Buccaneers. They joined arms with freebooters who, in 1632, settled in Tortuga, and who were named flibustiers, from the small fast flyboats, in which their expeditions were carried on, and became marauders both by sea and land. Their successes rendered the name of Buccaneer terrible over all the West Indian seas. The island of Tortuga, and part of the mainland were claimed by the French settlers for their king, and the first governor was appointed in 1664. In 1773, by treaty with Spain, the west part of the island was guaranteed to France. The French portion prospered, but the Spanish declined. On the breaking out of the great French Revolution a contest ensued between the coloured people and the whites, the former demanding equal privileges with the latter. The slave population joined the coloured people, the whites were subdued, and the whole island ultimately fell under the power of the negro chief Toussaint L'Ouverture, first President of the Haytian Republic. He was the son of Gaou-Guino, a chief of the Arradas tribe, who had been made captive in a plundering expedition by a neighbouring tribe, and sold to the slave dealers. Gaou-Guino was brought to Hayti, and became the property of Count de Breda, owner of a sugar manufactory, two miles from Cape Français. In his state of servitude he was recognized by his fellow-slaves, from whom he received tokens of respect which they judged due to his rank. He became a member of the Catholic Church, and married a woman beautiful and virtuous. Toussaint was the eldest of five sons, and is said to have been born on the 20th of May, 1743. He had lived fifty years before he became the vindicator of his brethren's rights. He also was a Catholic, and his godfather, Pierre Baptist, communicated to him the knowledge of

French, in addition to which he acquired a smattering of Latin and geometry. He was afterwards betrayed into the hands of the French, who had sent an army to regain the position they had lost in the island, and was sent to France, and confined in the castle of Joux, where he died of starvation. The French were permanently expelled, and in 1803, the island was declared independent, and its indigenous name of Hayti was restored.

In 1821, the Spanish portion declared itself independent of the mother country, and assumed the name of Spanish Hayti, but was soon subjugated by Boyer the Haytian President. In 1842, a revolution broke out, and Boyer was compelled to flee to Jamaica; and, in 1844, the inhabitants of the Spanish portion rose, overpowered their Haytian oppressors, and formed themselves into a republic, under the name of Santo Domingo, which was proclaimed, Nov. 24, 1844. In 1848, General Soulouque, President of the Haytian republic, made an unsuccessful attempt to subdue the Dominican republic. He however in 1849 caused himself to be made Emperor of Hayti, under the title of Fanstin I. He surrounded his throne with a court and hereditary nobility, instituted orders of knighthood, &c. The independence of the Dominican republic was virtually recognized by Great Britain in the appointment of a consul to it in 1849, and it was formally recognized by a treaty of amity and commerce ratified, Sep. 10, 1850. The population of the whole island is about 940,000 of whom 490,000 are blacks, 420,000 mulattoes, or creoles, and 28,000 whites.

There are, therefore, now two distinct states in the island, the *Empire of Hayti,* and the *Republic of Santo Domingo.* The division is formed by an irregular line, drawn S. to N. from the river Anses-à-Pitre or Pedernales, on the S. coast, about lon. 71° 50′, to the mouth of the river Massacre, which flows into the bay of Mazanilla, about 10 m. S. W. of Cape Haytien, formerly Cape Français. Hayti is the portion west of this boundary, and the area is 10,081 sq. m. It is divided into six departments, subdivided into arrondissements and communes. The people are nearly all of the negro race, speak the French language, and profess the Catholic religion. Other forms of religion are tolerated. The capital is Cape Haytien, it was formerly at Port-au-Prince. The population is estimated at 740,000, females greatly predominating in numbers. The constitution of 1843 recognized the sovereign power to be in the people, but when Soulouque, in 1849 had his title changed to Emperor, the constitution was altered to suit the circumstances. The succession is hereditary, but as he has no male issue by the Empress, the amended constitution has permitted him to select his successor from among his issue.

The Republic of Santo Domingo occupies the eastern portion of the island. Its first President was General Pedro Santana, who defeated

Hérard Rivière, President of the Haytian Republic, when he attempted with 20,000 men to bring Santo Domingo again under the Haytian rule. He was succeeded in 1849, by Baez. The area of the Republic is nearly 17,000 sq. m., about the size of Switzerland. It is divided into five provinces, which are sub-divided into communes. The constitution is based upon that of Venezuela. The Congress consists of 15 Deputies, who form the Tribunado, and 5 Senators, who form the Consejo Conservador. The Executive power rests in a President, who must be a Dominican by birth, and 35 years of age. He is elected for four years. The capital is called Santo Domingo, or San Domingo, and was founded in 1496, by Bartholomew, the brother of Columbus. It was here that Bobadilla imprisoned Columbus. The principal building is the cathedral, commenced in 1514, by Don Diego, son of Columbus, and finished in 1540. The ashes of Columbus and his brother Bartholomew reposed in it for nearly two centuries and a half, but were afterwards removed to Havanna.

The history of this island is extremely interesting, and we regret that we cannot give a more extensive notice of it.

(2) CUBA is the largest of the West Indian islands and is now the most important colony of Spain. It is situated N. W. from Hayti, by the windward passage and is probably one-third larger than that island. It extends from 74° to 84° W.; and is about 750 m. in length from E. to W. Its greatest breadth is at Cape de Cruz, being 120 m., while towards its W. extremity it does not exceed 30 m. The average breadth is from 50 to 60 m. The extreme East end of the island, Pointe de Maysi, is in lat. 20° 15' N., lon. 74° 7' W. (Raper); the West, San Antonio, in lat. 21° 15' N.; long. 84° 57' 12" (Raper); and S. to N. it extends from lat. 19° 50' to 23° 10' N. Area 43,000 sq. m., of which one-seventh is said to be under cultivation and in pasture.

The population at the latest census, 1841, was 1,007,624; of whom 418,291 were whites; 88,054 free coloured persons (mixed races); 10,974 coloured slaves; 64,784 free negroes; and 425,521 negro slaves.

The coast of Cuba owing to banks, reefs, and rocks, is in general very foul, and the approach to the land is difficult and dangerous, hardly one-third of it being accessible to vessels. There are however a number of harbours including the Havanna. There are no rivers of any importance in Cuba, the largest is the Cauto rising in the Sierra del Cobre, and, after a course of only 90 miles, falling into the Bay of Buena Esperanza. None are navigable except by small boats, and then only a few miles inland.

The prevalent geological formation of the island are calcerous rocks of various kinds and qualities, but granite occurs in the south eastern part, and schistose rocks about the middle of the northern coast. Carboniferous strata are found at the west end of the island. Clays and slates are met with in some places. Copper, gold, and lead said to be rich in silver, are among its minerals. Marble of much beauty has been quarried, and crystal, flint, and a clay, serviceable in the arts, are obtained.

The soil throughout the island is mainly formed from the decomposition of calcerous rocks and is generally of great fertility. Forests of mahogany, ebony, cedars, fustic, and other useful woods abound. The principal cereal cultivated is the indigenous maize, or Indian corn. Rice is produced in considerable quantities. The articles raised for consumption and exportation are chiefly sugar, coffee, and tobacco, with some cotton, cocoa, and indigo. Oranges, lemons, shaddocks, plantains, pine apples, and other fruits are largely grown, and figs and strawberries are to be had.

The only indigenous quadruped ever known in Cuba is the huitia, which resembles a large rat, and is about 18 inches long without the tail. Oxen, pigs, sheep, goats, mules, asses, rabbits, dogs and cats have been introduced. The domestic fowls of the island comprise the cock and hen of Europe, geese, turkeys, pigeons and peacocks. The sylvan birds are numerous. Birds of prey are few, the principal is the baldheaded vulture or turkey buzzard. Sand crabs swarm in some places. Snakes and reptiles are not very numerous. Various insects abound. There are also centipedes and scorpions. The shores abound with turtles, and in the deep gulfs and bays the crocodiles and cayman are found. The manati is met with in the deep pools of fresh water, and the iguana, a sort of lizard, on the banks of streams, bays, and lagoons. Fish are said to be abundant.

The principal articles of export are sugar, coffee, molasses, tobacco, mahogany, cedar, fustic, and other valuable timber, fruits, copper, and the precious metals. The amount of sugar exported in 1847 was 575,232,000 lbs. The imports are provisions, particularly flour, rice, maize, butter, cheese, tasajo, hams, salted fish, brandies, wines, cottons, silks, woollens, hardware and machinery. The total value of exports averages about £7,000,000; that of the imports is higher. The United States holds the first place in the import trade, England the next, and then Spain.

The roads in Cuba were formerly in a most wretched condition, but have lately been improved, and internal traffic has been facilitated by the laying of railways, of which 10 have been opened in as many years. The first, from Havanna to Guines, is 46 m. long and was opened in 1837.

The revenue averages upwards of 12,000,000 dollars. The average expenditure does not exceed 8,000,000, the surplus is transmitted to Spain.

The island is divided into three intendencias—the eastern, the central, and the western. The civil and military government is intrusted to a captain-general appointed by Spain. In civil matters, however, the eastern and central intendencias are presided over by governors, who are almost independent of the captain-general, whose civil jurisdiction is mainly confined to the western intendencias. The laws are administered by a Real Audiencia (Royal Court), which has the supreme jurisdiction in all civil and criminal cases; by provincial ayuntamientos, and in the country districts by a kind of police courts. The religion is Roman Catholic. The people are devoted to cock-fighting and gambling.

HAVANNA (Spanish, *La Habana*, the haven,) is the capital. It is one of the greatest commercial ports in the Western World. It is situated on a bay on the N. W. side of the island. Its harbour is one of the best in the world. The city was founded in 1519, on a site which was then called the port of Carenas. It was surprised and burnt in 1538, by a French privateer, and was taken by the English in 1762, but was restored to Spain by the peace of 1763 and has ever since continued in her possession. It contains a cathedral, in which are deposited the ashes of Columbus which were taken thither from San Domingo in 1795, sixteen churches, and a number of other public buildings. It has numerous printing offices, and several daily papers are issued. Nearly 2000 ships are engaged in the trade of Havanna. Population (1841), 135,000.

The history of Cuba is very uninteresting. The island was first discovered by Columbus in 1492–3, who revisited it in 1494, and again in 1502. The Spaniards in 1511 formed the first settlement on the island and have retained possession of it ever since. The aborigines whom Columbus found on the island disappeared before 1560. In 1809–11 the ports were opened to the ships and trade of foreign countries. In 1850 and in 1851 a band of adventurers from the United States, under the command of a Spaniard, named Narcisso Lopez, made unsuccessful piratical attempts to seize the island. The whole 450 men who landed were either slain in fight or taken prisoners; of the latter 50 were shot, and shortly afterwards Lopez was garrotted. Owing to the position of Cuba with respect to the common routes of navigation, its possession gives an absolute control over the trade between Europe and all countries lying about the Carribean sea and the Gulf of Mexico, and consequently a great portion of the United States. The maritime powers have for many years seemed to hold a tacit agreement to leave Cuba in the possession of Spain, because, being the least powerful of them all, there could be no disposition on her part to interrupt the free navigation of these seas. An influential party in the United States has, however, declared the acquisition of Cuba to be a prominent feature of its foreign policy, and to this the President of the United States in his inaugural speech, in 1853, gave official countenance.

The Slave trade of Cuba is immense, notwithstanding the treaty with

Spain for its abolition. In 1844 not less than 10,000 slaves were introduced into the island, since then this number has been actually doubled, and there is a general impression that this iniquitous trade is not only connived at, but protected, by the Spanish Government. There are at the present time not fewer than 500,000 slaves on the island, but it is supposed that many are wrongfully held in bondage, as there is a Spanish law to the effect that every negro brought into Cuba, after a specified date, should be *ipso facto,* free. The negroes are said to be treated by their Spanish masters with great kindness, but this is denied both by Mr. Turnbull, who visited the islands in 1838, and by Mr. Madden, who visited it ten years later; they allege that the treatment is unsurpassed in rigour by any other slave-holding country. [See David Turnbull: *Travels in the West. Cuba; with notices of Porto Rico, and the slave trade* (London, 1840) also Richard Robert Madden: *The Island of Cuba: its Resources, Progress, and Prospects* (London, 1849).]

(3) The GULF OF MEXICO, is a large indentation on the east coast of North America, washing the shores of Mexico and the United States. It measures 1,000 m. from E. to W., and 500 m. from N. to S., its area is estimated at 800,000 sq. mi. The temperature is 86 deg. in summer, being 6 deg. higher than that of the ocean in the same parallel.

(4) The MISSISSIPPI, or "Great Waters," is the most important river in North America; rising in the Hauteurs de Terre, the dividing ridge of the Red River of the N., 1680 ft. above the level of the ocean, in lat. 47° N., long. 95° 54′ W., it flows through more than 18 deg. of latitude, and empties itself into the Gulf of Mexico by several mouths. Its length is 3,160 m.; but if the Missouri, above its junction with the Mississippi, be the real continuation of the latter, which is supposed by some persons to be the case, the entire length will be about 4,300 m., making the longest river in the world. Its affluents are too numerous to mention, but the Missouri is the largest and flows from the N. W. into the Mississippi, 1253 m. from the Gulf of Mexico. With its tributaries it drains an area of more than 1,200,000 sq. m. Its widest part is at the junction of the Missouri, where it is a mile and a half wide. From that point to the Ohio it is little more than half a mile wide, and from thence it varies from 600 to 1200 yards. It is stated by J. L. Riddell, in a communication to Professor Lyell to be one-third of a mile wide and 100 ft. deep opposite the Mint at New Orleans. [John Leonard Riddell (1807–1867) was an American naturalist, who in 1835 published *Synopsis of the Flora of the Western States.* Sir Charles Lyell, the distinguished British scientist, became acquainted with his observations on the Mississippi delta when he

visited New Orleans in 1848. See Lyell's *Principles of Geology,* 2 vols. (Philadelphia, 1853), p. 273. also his *Travels in North America; with geological observations on the United States, Canada, and Nova Scotia* (London, 1845).] Its source is in a small lake called Itasca, the *Lac la Biche* of the French, and its waters until it reaches the Missouri are gentle and placid; it then becomes a boiling, desolating stream and sweeps away in its progress the tender alluvial soil of the bends, with all their trees, which it deposits in other places, causing "snags and sawyers," which are dangerous to navigation. Its mean velocity between the Missouri and the Gulf is 60 or 70 m. per day, and its descent from its source to its embrouchure, averages a little more than 6 in. to the mile. The course of the river being from N. to S. it enables the traveller constantly to meet with a change of climate, while a river that flows from E. to W. has no such variety. The only falls of particular note are those of St. Anthony, 2200 m. from the Gulf, and the Rapids of Pecagama, 685 m. farther up the stream. At the former there is a perpendicular fall of 17 ft., with rapids above and below, making in all about 65 ft. descent in three quarters of a mile. The river is navigable below this with a slight obstruction above the entrance of the Des Moines. Many persons visit these falls every year to view the scenery which is said to be exceedingly grand. Although no tides enter the river, yet owing to the floods annually caused by the winter snows and spring rains in the Rocky Mountains, a great rise takes place, and sometimes the lower valley of the Mississippi is submerged, and great damage is done to property, and occasionally lives are lost. The scenery of the Mississippi is magnificent. The banks from Cairo downwards present a lovely spectacle, a rich verdure of trees runs down to the water's edge, and here and there are to be seen towns and fine plantations interspersed among them. About five hundred miles below Cairo the great cotton-growing districts commence, and below Red river, the sugar plantations. From thence to New Orleans may be seen the beautiful plantations and fine dwellings surrounded with shrubbery which attract the attention and admiration of all who journey on this noble river. A traveller, in sketches of the Mississippi, says, "The lands bordering upon it are as rich as nature can make them, being all of alluvial formation; and the soil of such a depth that there is no danger of its ever being exhausted. When we read of the myriads of people, who formerly existed in the valley of the Nile, and compare the capabilities of the Mississippi valley with it, we can comprehend the great destiny, awaiting only the development of time, in store for this already far-famed region." The Mississippi valley has obtained, from its almost unexampled fertility, the title of the "Garden of the world."

The immense fluviatile deposit at the mouth of the Mississippi, called the Delta, covers an area of not less than 14,000 sq. m., more than a quarter of the area of Great Britain. It is about 200 m. long from N. to S., and has a mean width of 75 m. from E. to W. It forms an irregular triangle, taking the line of the Atchafalaya river, from where it leaves Red river, to where it intersects the 29th deg. of N. lat., running along this parallel past all the mouths of the Mississippi, and completing the triangle by a line around Chandeleur, in St. Bernard, and N. of Lake Pontchartrain to the 31st deg. of N. lat. This vast region is composed entirely of alluvion, or sedimentary matter brought down by the floods of the river. The debris is deposited principally upon the borders of the stream, raising these portions to a much higher level than the adjoining lands. This elevation varies in width from 400 yds. to $1\frac{1}{2}$ m. This advantage has not been lost sight of, but the margin of the river has been further raised by an artificial embankment called the Levée. It commences on the right bank, at Point Coupée, 172 m., and on the left bank, 60 m. above New Orleans. The river is thus restrained within its bounds, except at the great freshets, and its current deepened. The district in Louisiana thus protected is better cultivated and more densely peopled than any other part of the State. The finer silt is carried over these heights and also down the channel to the Gulf, and it is said that it is held in its mechanical suspension long after the waters of the Mississippi have mingled with those of the ocean. This tract of land is extremely fertile, except at the tongue-like isthmus which extends into the Gulf. That is a mere sandy swamp, with a few rushes and plenty of lizards and alligators. The trees brought down the river are deposited over this lower delta. The river forces itself through the sandy swamp by four or five channels to the Gulf, but the water in them has never been equal to the requisitions of commerce, owing to the immense sandbars formed at the mouths by the sedimentary matter brought down the river, and the resistance of the Gulf waters. In consequence of these obstructions ships of the largest class are only able to get safely over the bars by the application of steam-power and literally ploughing through beds of sand.

The Mississippi and its tributaries have now upon their waters upwards of 1500 steamboats, carrying an aggregate burthen of more than twice the entire steamboat tonnage of Great Britain, and probably equal to that of all other parts of the world. The value of this enormous fleet is not less than 6,000,000 dollars.

The Mississippi river was discovered in 1541, by Ferdinand de Soto, a Spaniard. He was travelling N. W. of Pensacola with an expedition in search of gold. The first exploration of the river was made in 1673 by Marquette and Joliet, two French missionaries. It was afterwards explored to its mouth by La Salle, a native of Rouen, in Normandy. He was a gentleman of fortune, but he renounced his patrimony and joined the Jesuits, whom he left after obtaining their esteem and favour for his purity and diligence. He was a highly-gifted man, and, being exceedingly enterprising, he went to New France in quest of fame and fortune. With Marquette he entertained the idea that some of the western tributaries of the Mississippi would afford a direct route to the South Sea and thence to China. If such should be the case, the voyage around Cape Horn would be avoided. This was an object of the deepest interest to the commercial world, and all Europe was concerned in the matter. La Salle communicated his views to the Governor of New France, Count de Frontenac, who sent him to France to lay his views before Louis XIV. He obtained an audience and was well received. Letters of nobility and authority to prosecute his projected discoveries were granted. Returning to America, he made his first descent of the great river, from the mouth of the Illinois to the Gulf of Mexico, in 1682, and named the country Louisiana, in honour of his king. In 1681 he had explored the river from the Illinois to the Falls of St. Anthony. He carried the results of his discoveries to France and was then sent to colonize the country. His fleet, however, took a wrong direction, and he and his followers were carried to Texas which was thus accidentally discovered. Attempting some time afterwards to return to Louisiana on foot, he was shot by a discontented soldier. The river was first entered from its mouth by D'Iberville, in 1699.

(5) LOUISIANA is one of the southern and slave states of the United States of America, and is bounded on the N. by Arkansas and Mississippi; E. by Mississippi (from which it is partly separated by the Mississippi and Pearl rivers) and the Gulf of Mexico; S. by the Gulf of Mexico; and W. by Texas, from which it is partly separated by the Sabine river. It is situated between 29° and 33° N. lat.; and 88° 50' and 94° 20' W. lon. Its length, from E. to W., is about 292 m.; and its breadth, from N. to S., 250 m. Area, 46,431 sq. m. Scarcely one-twentieth part of the State was improved in 1850. The population in the same year was 517,763, of whom 244,809 were slaves. Nearly one-fourth part of the free population were of foreign birth, no fewer than 24,266 being from Ireland.

The State is divided into 14 parishes, and its principal cities are New Orleans, Lafayette, and Baton Rouge, the capital.

Its principal bays are Borgne, Black bay, Bastien, Barataria, Atchafalaya, Cote Blanche and Vermillion. Among its lakes are Sabine, Calcasieu and Mermentau, all which, with the above-named bays, are expansions of rivers of the same names; and lakes Pontchartrain and Maurepas, which are expansions of the Amite river. Catahoula in the centre of the State, and Bistineau and Caddo in the N. W., are the principal lakes. Small lakes, or sloughs, abound in the marshy part of the State, and along the Mississippi river. The chief rivers are the Mississippi, Red river, Washita, Sabine, Calcasieu, Mermentau, and Pearl. Numerous other rivers, branches of the larger ones, intersect the country, frequently inundating it, and causing lakes and swamps. There are very few hills, and the State nowhere attains to a greater elevation than 200 ft. above the level of the sea, and in many parts it does not average above 10 ft.

The far greater portion of the surface of Louisiana consists of an alluvial and diluvial flat. About two-fifths are occupied by the tertiary formation, and contain coal, salt, iron, ochre, gypsum and marl. Underneath the tertiary there is a saline bed. In the region around Harrisonburg have been found very large quartz crystals, many agates, abundance of jasper, sardonyx, onyx, selenite, feldspar of a splendid quality, alumine in great abundance, chalcedony, lava, meteoric stones, amorphous iron ore, and fossils of various kinds.

The soil produces the sugar cane, cotton, and rice in great quantities. The two latter flourish exuberantly in the river bottoms, which are extremely fertile, where sufficiently drained to be cultivated. The sugar cane does not flourish above 31° N. lat. In 1850 this State produced nine-tenths of the cotton and sugar raised in the whole Union.

Wherever the soil is elevated above the annual inundations, sugar can be produced, and such lands are generally devoted to this crop. The best districts for cotton are the banks of Red river, Washita, Teche, and the Mississippi. Rice is chiefly confined to the banks of the Mississippi, where irrigation is easy. The land within this State adapted to the cultivation of these three articles has been estimated as follows—sugar, 250,000 acres; rice, 250,000; and cotton, 2,400,000 acres. Some planters ordinarily realize as much as from 350 to 450 dollars annually from each of their slaves, and in some years 600 dollars have been derived. The cultivation of cotton is said to be equally profitable to the planters. The first plantations of any extent were commenced with negroes imported from Guinea, and for several years the importation of negroes was one of the most profitable monopolies of the "Western Company."

Other products are, first, indian corn, oats, peas, beans, potatoes, and butter; second, tobacco, wool, fruits, hay, bees-wax, and honey; and, third, wheat, rye, buck wheat, cheese, grass, seeds, hops, silk, and maple sugar, which however hold but a very minor place. Oranges, figs, peaches, apples, and grapes are the principal fruits, but the orange does not flourish above 30° N. lat. Other tropical fruits grow, such as lemons, limes, &c. The census of 1850 represented in the State 13,422 farms, occupying 1,590,025 acres of improved land. Two-thirds of the alluvial land is heavily timbered, and among the trees are walnut, five species of oak, sassafras, ash, mulberry, poplar, hickory, magnolia, buckeye, locust, papaw, cottonwood, willow, pine, red elm, hackberry, maple, ash, pecan, honey locust, basket elm, dogwood, tupelo, box elder, prickly ash, black locust, persimmon, and wild cane growing to the height of from 15 to 30 ft. Cyprus swamps occupy certain basins, which, having no outlet, retain the waters they receive at the floods until they either evaporate or sink into the earth.

The animals are bears, wolves, panthers, wild cats, racoons, otters, pole cats, opossums, squirrels and moles. Huge alligators and several species of turtle are among the amphibia. The principal reptiles are the rattlesnake and viper. Other snakes exist to some extent. Eagles, hawks, owls, wild turkeys, pigeons, partridges, cranes, herons, water turkeys, and wild geese are among its birds, of which there is a great variety of the smaller kinds. The fish of the lakes and rivers, and the game of the forest, are plentiful, but inferior in quality.

The manufacturers of Louisiana are very unimportant, except in the coarser sugars and molasses, which, however, are chiefly refined in the northern States.

Louisiana is said to have 2500 m. of navigable rivers within its boundaries, and consequently may not have so much need of railways as other States of the Union, but if it is to maintain its commercial position it will require them for communication with other States. There are, however, several lines of railways in operation and in progress. The natural advantages for river trade with an interior enjoyed by this State are not equalled by any other place in the world. The products of fourteen States are poured into its lap by means of the enormous river facilities it enjoys, and are transhipped at New Orleans for various parts of the Republic and foreign countries. The details of imports and exports will appear under our notice of New Orleans.

Very mild winters characterize this State, but they are more severe than are the winters in the same parallel on the Atlantic coast. The summers are long and hot, and acting on the marshes cause every autumn more or less yellow fever, highly destructive to foreigners, and, to a great extent, to the natives. The present year (1854) has been one of great mortality from this circumstance. On the whole, the seasons are very variable.

In our notice of the Mississippi river we stated that De Soto was the earliest person who visited the territory afterwards named Louisiana, by the brilliant La Salle, when he visited it in 1682. We also noticed the disastrous fate of the latter, which, with his discoveries, was not forgotten by France, though for years after his death she was too much engaged in wars and intrigues to do anything towards colonizing the country which he had visited and partially explored. At length, in 1698, an expedition for colonizing the region of the lower Mississippi was originated by the French king, and M. D'Iberville, a distinguished naval commander, was selected to head it. In the summer of the same year he entered upon the command of the enterprise, and on the 24th of September he and his colleagues sailed from Rochelle. In seventy-two days they reached Cape Français in the island of San Domingo. Here an additional ship of 50 guns was added to the little fleet of two frigates of 30 guns each, and two smaller vessels, to escort it to the shores of Louisiana. Thus strengthened, the expedition, on the 1st of January, 1699, set sail from San Domingo, and in 24 days cast anchor off the island of St. Rose. After cruising about the Bay of Pensacola, they sailed westward and anchored near the Chandeleur groups. D'Iberville and his colony landed upon Ship Island, off the mouth of Pascagoula river. He and his brother Bienville then set out to explore the mouths of the Mississippi, which had not yet been entered from the sea. On the 2nd of March they entered the river. It was then called the St. Louis. D'Iberville doubted whether they were on the mighty river of the west, but as they ascended all doubt was dispelled by finding in the hands of the Indians articles distributed among them by La Salle in 1682. After exploring the country, the party returned to Ship Island. Soon afterwards D'Iberville selected a site about 15 m. N. of this island, and 80 m. N. E. of the present city of New Orleans, and settled his colony there. He then returned to France, leaving his two brothers, Sauvolle and Bienville, the first as commander of the fort, and the other as general superintendent of the colony under him.

England was not unobservant of the attempts of France to colonize Louisiana, and an expedition and colony were despatched under Coxe, a New Jersey proprietor, to explore the mouths of the Mississippi. The expedition was escorted by a British war vessel, but being resolutely met a few miles below the present site of New Orleans by Bienville, who was exploring the channel of the river, it turned about and was seen no more by the French.

Early in the December following, D'Iberville returned from France with other settlers and troops. About the middle of February, 1700, he met with Chevalier de Tonti, who had arrived from the Illinois with a party of Canadian French. De Tonti had had some experience with the Indians and understood some of their languages. With such a companion D'Iberville determined to ascend the Mississippi river and explore its banks, and form friendly alliances with the Indians. They accordingly ascended as far as the country occupied by the Natchez tribe, where the city of Natchez now stands.

In 1702 the whole colony of Louisiana did not number above 30 families, besides soldiers. Bilious fevers had cut off many of the first emigrants, and the remainder were now threatened with Indian hostility and famine. Sauvolle fell an early victim. D'Iberville was attacked with yellow fever, and, unable to sustain the enervating influence of a tropical climate, he returned to France. More than a year afterwards he attempted to do service in the West Indies, but there he was attacked with a severe disease, and the founder of the province of Louisiana died at Havanna, on the 9th of July, 1706, a martyr to the glory of France. In his death the colony lost a friend and a hero worthy of regret.

In 1711 the government of the province was placed in the hands of a governor-general, and his head quarters were fixed at Mobile, and a new fort was erected on the site of the present city of the same name. Notwithstanding that all the extravagant expectations of the early colonists of Louisiana had met with disappointment, the Government of France still believed that it presented a rich field for enterprise and speculation and determined to place the resources of the province under the influence of individual enterprise. Accordingly, Louis XIV granted on the 14th of September, 1712, letters patent to Anthony Crozat, a great financier and merchant. The letters patent secured to him on certain conditions exclusive privileges for ten years, in all the commerce of the province. At that time the colony numbered about 400 persons. Crozat's object was to open up a trade with the Spanish ports in the Gulf of Mexico, but after much disappointment and expense, his vessels were prohibited from trading in any of the Spanish ports. Failing in all his attempts, despairing of the results of his enterprise, having accomplished nothing for the advancement of the colony, and having lost nearly 30,000 dollars, he petitioned the king to revoke his charter, or to permit him to surrender it to the crown. The latter was permitted, and in 1717 the Government of the colony reverted solely into the hands of the king's officers and Crozat retired to France.

Louisiana as claimed by the French at that period included all the regions of the United States, from the Alleghany mountains on the E. to the Rocky mountains on the W., and from the Gulf of Mexico northward to the great lakes of Canada. The population although it had nearly doubled its numbers, did not exceed 700 souls of all ages, sexes and colours.

The next scheme for colonizing Louisiana was that known by the name of the "Western Company," at the head of which was John Law, a Scotchman, and a great financier. It received a charter for 25 years. It was authorized to monopolize all the trade of that province of new France, and of all the Indian tribes within those extensive regions. Its powers were far superior to those to Crozat. Among the obligations imposed upon the Company was the stipulation to introduce into Louisiana, within the period of its chartered rights, 6000 white persons and 3000 negro slaves, and to protect the settlements against Indian hostilities. The plan of this Company was not unlike that of the East India Company, and it possessed powers and privileges nearly equal. Agriculture was now neglected, naught was dreamed of but rich mines of silver and gold, and, although the colony had been established twenty years, it was still mainly dependent upon France for supplies.

About 1719 the Spaniards and French began to disagree about their respective rights W. of the Mississippi. Each kept a jealous eye upon the other. On the E. the line between Louisiana and Florida had been agreed upon, the Perdido being the dividing stream, but on the W. the matter was still open, France claiming the territory W. as far as the bay of St. Bernard, W. of the Colorado river, and Spain, eastward from Mexico, nearly to the Mississippi itself. The French continued to claim jurisdiction of the country, westward to the Rio del Norte, up to the cession of Louisiana to Spain in 1762.

About this time also 500 African negroes were imported to cultivate the land, which Europeans, from the unhealthiness of the climate, were unable to do without suffering immensely. In 1720–22 a second cargo of negroes was introduced, and from this time the Western Company's agents continued to supply the demand for slaves. Owing now to the new interests daily awakened in France, emigration continued rapidly. Since 1719 war had raged between France and Spain, and Louisiana became involved in hostilities from which it suffered much, and the Western Company had become greatly embarrassed by the interruption of trade and the hostilities of the Indians.

In 1723 New Orleans became the provincial and commercial capital of Louisiana, and, with the consent of the "Directory," the Western Company's principal establishment was removed there. Settlements now began to concentrate around New Orleans, and houses and public buildings increased rapidly. About this time "Law's Mississippi Scheme" failed, and its disastrous effects were not only felt by the Western Company, but from the slave to the Governor himself. This Mississippi Scheme "was a system of credit, devised and proposed by John Law, for the purpose of extricating the French Government from the embarrassment under which it struggled by reason of the enormous state debt." Its failure prevented the Western Company from proceeding with the colonization and advancing the prosperity of the province.

In 1723 the province was erected into a government, independent of the jurisdiction of the governor-general of Canada.

In 1725 it had in a great measure recovered from the effects of financial embarrassments, and in 1726 agriculture began to flourish and a healthy state of trade to pervade every department. Emigrants both from Canada and France began again to arrive. In 1728 the colony was in its highest prosperity and numbered several thousand souls.

The Western Company had held the control and monopoly of the mines and commerce of the province for fifteen years, and had exercised all the rights of proprietors subject only to the approbation of the king, yet the advantage derived was not proportionate to the outlay. The last three years had been a continual source of expense and harassing vexation. The Company therefore petitioned the king to permit it to surrender its charter to the crown, which was granted, and on the 10th of April, 1732 a proclamation declared the whole province thenceforth free for settlement and trade to all the king's subjects. The settlements were now greatly extended, agriculture increased, civil government was organized, and religious instruction, which of course was of the Roman Catholic faith, was amply provided.

About 1740 cotton was introduced as an agricultural product of Louisiana, and the province continued to prosper; the Indians had become the allies of the French, and the whole Mississippi valley had yielded to their dominion. The first attempt to cultivate the sugar cane was made by the Jesuits, in 1751, who opened a small plantation for its culture just above the old city of New Orleans, and before the close of 1760 the sugar cane was one of the staple products of Louisiana. The first exportation of sugar was one ship load to France in 1765. A contest between France and England for the possession of the Mississippi valley commenced about 1754 and continued for eight years, until the eastern half of Louisiana, from the sources of the Mississippi river to the Bayou Iberville, was ceded to Great Britain. An imaginary line down the centre of the Mississippi and along said Bayou and the Amité river to Lake Maurepas, thence through Lakes Maurepas, Pontchartrain, and Borgne to the sea, was to be the irrevocable boundary between the English and French provinces. In 1762 the King of France secretly made a treaty to cede and deliver to the King of Spain the western half of the province and the Island of New Orleans on the eastern side of the Mississippi and S. of Bayou Iberville. Thus this great province passed out of the hands of the French after eighty years' dominion. From this time Louisiana, under the Spanish dominion, prospered. In 1783 Great Britain by treaty ceded to the United States, who had then gained their independence, all the territory on the E. of the Mississippi, from its sources to the 31st parallel of N. lat., which was to be the boundary of Florida on the S. All the territory E. of the river and S. of this line was now ceded to Spain. Possessed of all the territory W. of the Mississippi, and Florida on the E., and having the control of the Mississippi from the southern limits of the United States to its mouth, her policy was to obstruct its navigation by the United States as much as possible. The people of the western States needed an outlet to the sea for their rapidly increasing produce, but Spain placed such restrictions upon it and levied such imposts, that the river was almost closed against them. This led to frequent conflicts between the people of the two governments, until finally, by the treaty of Madrid, New Orleans was granted as a place of deposit for United States produce for the term of three years, which might, by subsequent negotiations, be extended. Spain, however, continued extremely jealous of the advances of the western people, and still, from time to time, imposed great restrictions upon those who wished to settle or trade within her jurisdiction. This state of things continued until at length the colossal power of France, under the great Napoleon, after having brought all southern Europe under her sway, turned her thoughts again to her former immense possessions in N. America. The people of France had never sanctioned the treaty by which, in 1762, Louisiana had been ceded to Spain. They considered it the conclusion of a dishonourable peace, and Napoleon Bonaparte determined to restore to them the vast province of Louisiana, with the same boundaries as it had when ceded to Spain. By the 3rd article of the treaty of Ildefenso, concluded on the 1st of October, 1800, between the King of Spain, and the First Consul of the French Republic, and confirmed by the treaty of Madrid, on the 21st of March, 1801, the King of Spain obligated himself to deliver the province to France. Napoleon made great preparations to formally extend over it the dominion of France, but various embarrassments delayed the departure of the fleet and troops, and fearing the powerful British Navy, which was waiting the sailing of his fleet, to destroy it, and also that as soon as Louisiana should be recognized as a province of France, the British would blockade its ports, he abandoned the project, and conceived the idea of selling the province to the United States. Accordingly, near the close of 1802 he instructed M. Talleyrand and M. Marbois to enter into negotiations with Mr. R. R. Livingston, U. S. Minister at Paris, for the sale of Louisiana to the United States. The treaty by which the sale was effected was concluded on the 30th of April, 1803, and the province was ceded to the United States for 15,000,000 dollars. On the 20th of December following the flag of the United States was hoisted in New Orleans, the Federal jurisdiction was extended over the province, and all foreign dominion ceased. The population at the time of the transfer, amounted to 49,000 souls, exclusive of Indians, New Orleans containing about 8000. William C. C. Claiborne, one of the commissioners appointed to receive the province from France, was appointed governor-general.

On the 26th of March, 1804, Congress passed an Act providing for the erection of the whole province into two territories. The section of country lying S. of the Mississippi Territory (31° N. lat.) and of an E. and W. line to commence on the Mississippi river, at the 33rd parallel of N. lat., and extending westward to the Rio del Norte, was constituted the "Territory of Orleans," and W. C. C. Claiborne was re-appointed governor. Owing to the people of the territory being mostly all of foreign origin and language, the plan of government provided for them was less democratic than it would have been had the citizens been all or mostly native Americans, which rendered it objectionable to the latter. The French population were also dissatisfied. They had expected to be speedily admitted to all the rights and privileges of an independent State; they therefore deprecated the division of the province into two territories, as that would tend to delay the period of their admission into the Union. They also deemed the extension over them of those laws of the United States which prohibited the introduction of African slaves into the territory as a blow struck at the agricultural prosperity of the province.

The Act created much opposition. Meetings were held, remonstrances made against its provisions, and a committee, consisting of three Frenchmen, was sent to Washington, to demand immediate admission into the Union as an independent State. Owing to this dissatisfaction, Gov. Claiborne met with much opposition in organizing the territorial government. The Legislature, however, met for the first time in the city of New Orleans on the 4th of December. One of its earliest creations was that of the "Bank of Louisiana," the first in the Territory of Orleans, and likewise in the whole province of Louisiana, with a capital of 600,000 dollars for 16 years.

In the meantime Congress had taken into consideration the grounds of the objections of the people to the Act organizing the territory, repealed the obnoxious law, and substituted another on the 2nd of March, 1805, by which Orleans Territory was placed on the same footing as others. The first Legislature under this act, convened for business on the 20th of June, 1805, in the city of New Orleans.

After the Territory of Orleans had been created, the remainder of the province of Louisiana was called the "District of Louisiana," and its first military commandant and civil governor was Major Amos Stoddart. His headquarters were at St. Louis, the capital of Upper Louisiana. In 1805 it was erected into the "Territory of Louisiana," and its first governor was General James Wilkinson. When the Territory of Orleans was admitted into the Union in 1812 as the "State of Louisiana," the Territory of Louisiana changed its name to "Missouri Territory," which extended from 33° to 41° N. lat., and 500 m. W. of the Mississippi. Its first governor was General William Clarke.

In the purchase of Louisiana from France its appears that the United States regarded the portion of country lying S. of the Mississippi Territory to the Bayou Iberville, and eastward from the Mississippi river to the Perdido, as a part of the ceded province, but the Spaniards retained possession of the district, which was permitted by the Federal government rather than come to hostilities with Spain. The western portion of this territory, from the Mississippi river to the Pearl, was erected into the Government of Baton Rouge, but the inhabitants, who were principally Anglo-Americans and emigrants from the Ohio region at length became tired of her despotic rule, and in 1810 threw off their allegiance. After organizing themselves into a form of State government, they applied to the Federal government for admission into the Union. Now that the people had renounced the dominion of Spain, Congress deemed it expedient to take immediate possession of the country, and the governor of the Territory of Orleans was empowered to execute their decision. The people submitted cheerfully, and the "Florida District," as it was called, was annexed to the Territory of Orleans, which increased its population to about 80,000, including slaves. In 1811 the "Planter's Bank" and the "Bank of Orleans" were chartered, the first with a capital of 600,000 dollars for a term of fifteen years, and the second with a capital of 500,000 dollars for the same term. In this year a convention authorized by Congress met to adopt a Constitution, preparatory to the admission of the territory into the Union as an independent State. They concluded their labours on the 22nd of January, 1812, and produced a Constitution differing but slightly from those of other States, except as regards slavery, which was strongly protected and sustained. The legislative powers were vested in a General Assembly, to consist of a Senate and House of Representatives. The governor was to be elected every four years by the Legislature on the second day of the session, from the two highest candidates returned by the popular vote. On the 8th of April, the Territory of Orleans, exclusive of the Florida district, was admitted into the Union under the title of the "State of Louisiana," and upon an equal footing with the original States from and after the 30th of April. By a supplemental Act, approved on the 14th of the same month, the limits of the new State were made to include the Florida district, which gave it its present boundaries. In the following June the first election was held under the new Constitution for a governor and the two Houses of the Legislature. W. C. C. Claiborne was elected first governor of the State.

Although there had been a large emigration to the new State from Kentucky and other parts of the Union, the greatest portion of the inhabitants were still Creole French and foreigners, and the whole population at the commencement of 1813 did not exceed 85,000, exclusive of

Indians. In 1812 war had been declared against Great Britain by the United States, which again retarded the growth of the population for several years. During this war Louisiana was menaced with invasion, in which the destruction of New Orleans was contemplated by the British. They were, however, repulsed with the loss of 4000 men and a vast quantity of munitions of war and naval stores. In 1815 the population numbered about 90,000, one-half of which were blacks. From this period, being freed from the danger of foreign invasion, the State began to prosper exceedingly. Its agricultural resources were developed, and the advantages of steam navigation were added to its river commerce. Enterprising emigrants and capitalists from all parts of the Union now flocked to the growing State, and its commercial importance was speedily and greatly enhanced. Anglo-Americans penetrated into every district, infusing new life and vigour into all departments, and soon the French language was superseded by the English, though many continued to use the former, and at the present time it is spoken to a great extent in New Orleans. In 1830 the population had increased to 215,740, including 126,300 blacks, and the State had advanced to quite an elevated rank in an agricultural and commercial point of view. In five years afterwards, so great had been the influx of emigrants, that the population actually numbered 400,000, inclusive of 168,452 slaves. In 1846 the Constitution of the State, formed in 1812, was considered far behind the liberal and democratic spirit which had overspread the Mississippi valley and was replaced by a new one framed upon the same basis as those of other western States, where all officers have a definite term of office and are at stated periods amenable to the people for their official conduct. Isaac Johnston was the first governor under the new Constitution. In 1850, and at the latest national census, it will be seen at the head of this article that the population of the State was no less than 517,763, inclusive of slaves. In 1852 the Constitution was again remodelled to suit the altered political views of the people. Among other things, it provides that the election of the judiciary shall be by popular vote, that the Legislature shall grant no divorce, and that there shall be a superintendent of education. Every free white male, being a citizen of the United States, 21 years of age, and a resident of the State, twelve months next preceding the election, and the last six months in the parish in which he offers to vote, has the right of suffrage in his election precinct.

The governor is elected for four years by the people and receives a salary of 6000 dollars per annum. Paul O. Herbert, of Iberville, is the present governor. The Senate consists of thirty-two members, and the House of Representatives of ninety-seven. Both are elected by the people, the former for four years, and the latter for two. The judiciary consists of a supreme court, composed of one chief and three associate judges; nine district courts with district judges, and justices of the peace. The State sends four members to the national House of Representatives and has six electoral votes for president of the United States.

The new Constitution provides that free schools be established throughout the State, and an appropriation amounting to 250,000 dollars is annually made for their support, raised by the levy of a tax of one mill on the dollar and from the imposition of a poll-tax on each white male inhabitant of the State. A fund also is established to be derived from the proceeds of public lands granted for the purpose. On the 1st of January, 1850, this fund amounted to 125,127 dollars and 47 cents. According to the census, the number of public schools in operation in 1850 was 675, teachers 845, and pupils, 25,973. There were also at the same time 142 academies, with 355 teachers, and 5379 pupils; 8 colleges, with 47 professors and tutors, and 725 students; 1 law school, with 3 professors, and 1 medical, with 7 professors and 188 students.

The most numerous religious body is that of the Roman Catholics. There are also considerable numbers of Methodists, Baptists, Presbyterians, and Episcopalians. There were in 1850, 278 churches in Louisiana, owned as follows—55 by the Roman Catholics, 12 by the Episcopalians, 106 by the Methodists, 17 by the Presbyterians, 72 by the Baptists, and the rest by a number of small denominations and Jews; giving 1 church to every 1862 persons. Value of church property, 1,782,470 dollars.

(6) NEW ORLEANS, the capital of Louisiana until 1849, is a port of entry, and the largest city of that State. It is situated on the E. bank of the Mississippi, about 100 m. above its mouth, and is built upon a bend in the river, from which circumstance it has also been called the "Crescent City." It lies 1663 m. S. W. from New York, and 1448 from Washington: 1200 m. S. of St. Louis, and 2000, S. by E. of the Falls of St. Anthony. Lat. 29° 58′ N.; lon. 90° 7′ W. According to a local census taken in 1853, the population was then 145,449, of which 29,174 were slaves and free coloured people. During the business season of the year the population is estimated at 175,000.

Our view of the city was taken at Algiers, a suburb on the opposite bank of the river, and extends the whole length of the steam-boat wharf. The site of the city is from 2 to 5 ft. below the level of the river, at the usual spring freshets. To prevent the water from overflowing, an embankment, 15 ft. wide and 6 ft. high has been made, called the levée. It extends to Baton Rouge, 123 m. above New Orleans, and to Port Plaquemine, 43 m. below it, and forms a delightful promenade. The old city was laid out by the French in 1718, and is in the form of a parallelogram, 1320 yds. long and 470 wide. The present municipal boundaries extend from 6 to 7 m. along the river, and about 5 m. back towards Lake Pontchartrain. In the old French part of the city the streets are very narrow, and the houses are built partly of wood and partly of brick, stuccoed over, and ornamented with cornices, balconies and balustrades, indicating the French and Spanish origin of the settlers who constructed them. In the more modern neighbourhoods a better style of buildings has been introduced, and the streets are mostly spacious and regular, intersecting each other at right angles. Many of the dwellings are very splendid and are surrounded with gardens of orange, lemon, magnolia, and other beautiful and luxuriant foliage of the South, which gives them an air of comfort and ease seldom enjoyed in a city. The principal squares are Jackson square, formerly Place d'Armes, Lafayette square, and Congo square, having likewise tastefully arranged gardens, grassplots, and shady walks, which constitute one of the most attractive features of the city. Many of the streets are planted with beautiful shade trees.

New Orleans has a number of costly buildings and churches. Among the former is, first, the Custom House, in course of erection, and which, when completed, will be the largest building in the United States, except the Capitol at Washington. Its four sides measure 334 ft., 252 ft., 310 ft., and 297 ft., and its height 82 ft. The business room is 116 ft. by 90, and has 50 windows. Next come the United States' Branch Mint; the Municipal Hall, built of marble, and in the Grecian style; the Odd Fellows' Hall, and the Merchants' Exchange, in which are the City Post Office, and Merchants' Reading Room. Among the latter are the Church of St. Louis, the Jewish synagogue, formerly the Canal street Episcopal church, the Presbyterian church, the new Episcopal church, and St. Patrick's church, which is a very conspicuous object in approaching the city from the river. A new Methodist church is about to be erected at a cost of 150,000 dollars. There were 38 churches in the city in 1853, of which 12 were Roman Catholic, 7 Episcopal, 6 Presbyterian, 5 Methodist, 3 Lutheran, 2 Baptist, and 3 Jewish synagogues. The chief hotels are the St. Charles, completed in 1852, at a cost of 590,000 dollars; the St. Louis and the Verandah, being also costly establishments. There are four or five theatres, the principal of which are the St. Charles, the Orleans, and the American. The principal Bank edifices are the City Bank, the Canal Bank, and the Bank of Louisiana. There are nine banks in all. There are also several fine markets; St. Mary's is 480 ft. by 42, and the Meat and Washington markets are good buildings. The cotton presses at New Orleans, for pressing that article previous to exportation, attract great attention. There are twenty of them. At the New Orleans press not less than 150,000 bales are annually pressed.

This city has many charitable and benevolent institutions, which are said to be the best conducted of any in the Union. Among them, the most worthy of notice are the Charity Hospital, the United States Naval Hospital, Stones' Hospital, and the Franklin Infirmary.

There are numerous educational establishments, which, although considered to be inferior to those of the New England States, are principally in a prosperous condition. In 1849 the University of Louisiana was established, and has connected with it a law school and a flourishing medical college. There were 40 school-houses in the city in 1853, attended by 16,885 pupils. The amount appropriated for school purposes in the same year was 188,020 dollars. About 20 newspapers, some in French, and a number of them dailies, are published in this city, and much ability is displayed in conducting them.

The cemeteries of New Orleans attract general attention from visitors. They are laid out in a handsome manner, and the most celebrated are the "French Cemetery," in the city, and the "Cypress Grove Cemetery," three miles out on the shell road, towards Lake Pontchartrain. Owing to the marshy state of the soil, graves are not dug in them; the dead are therefore deposited in tombs, built entirely above ground, to the height of about 12 ft., well cemented inside, and sometimes encased in marble, or stuccoed according to taste. There are walks between the tombs, either gravelled or covered with white shells from the sea beach, and bordered with the luxuriant shrubbery and flowers of the South, thus forming a true city of the dead. The finer feelings of nature are gratified by the respect shown in these places to the memory of the departed, by the care, taste, and elegance displayed, but "the stranger without friends, and the poor without money, find an uncertain rest, in the 'Potters' Field'; the water with which the soil is always saturated, often forcing the coffin and its contents out of its narrow and shallow cell, to rot with no other covering than the arch of heaven." The cemeteries are free to all visitors.

New Orleans is annually subject to yellow fever and other maladies, consequent upon its low situation and its climate, which greatly retard the growth and prosperity of the city. The yellow fever is particularly fatal to the unacclimated, especially those from northern latitudes. The principal business is done between the months of October and June, during which time the city is regarded as healthy for natives and foreigners, and thousands flock to it from every part of the world, for health, pleasure, or in connection with the extraordinary business of all kinds which is there transacted. In the summer all who are able leave the city, the natives going up the river and returning with the approach of the cooler season. For several weeks in 1853 the deaths from these maladies amounted to 200 daily, and during the season no fewer than 9500 persons fell victims to these terrible scourges. Their effects are said to have been still worse during the past summer (1854.)

Notwithstanding the fearful annual mortality of this city, and the difficulties of approach to it as a port, owing to the obstructions at the mouths of the Mississippi, its commerce is very great, in which it is considered to hold the third place among the ports of the United States. It stands unrivalled in its advantages for internal trade. "The Mississippi river and its tributaries afford not less than 15,000 m. of navigable waters, communicating with a vast extent of country, illimitable in its resources, exhaustless in fertility, and embracing nearly every variety of climate. Every description of craft is employed in transporting the rich products of the upper regions of the 'Father of Waters' to this great southern emporium. At one portion of its levée may be seen hundreds of flat-boats grounded on the 'batture,' and filled, some with fat cattle, horses, mules, hogs, and sheep; others with hay, corn, potatoes, butter, cheese, apples, and cider. The quay here is piled with lumber, pork, flour, and every variety of agricultural produce, as if the Great Valley had emptied its treasures at the door of New Orleans. Farther on is the steam-boat landing, a distinctive feature of this metropolis. Here all is action; the very water is covered with life. Vessels of immense size move upon its bosom, acknowledging none of the powers of air. One is rounding-to in the stream, seeking a mooring. She is covered all over, a mountain of cotton— 3000 bales, worth 180,000 dollars. Twenty more, freighted with the same national commodity, are discharging their cargoes at the wharves, while huge piles, bale upon bale, and story upon story, cover the levée. New Orleans is the greatest cotton market in the world. Immediately above and below the flat-boat and steam-boat landings is the foreign and coastwise shipping, extending two and three tier deep for nearly four miles. Here may be seen vessels from all parts of the world, each bearing at its masthead the ensign of the respective nation to which it belongs."

The foreign and coastwise arrivals at this port, for the year ending August, 1853, were, of sailing vessels and steamers, 5617, in addition to which there arrived 1044 flat-boats, laden with cattle, lumber, and various produce. The clearances for foreign ports were 1115 (tons, 544,482) of which 718 (tons, 370,741) were by American vessels. The shipping of the district—registered, enrolled, and licensed, amounted at the same date to 266,013$\frac{29}{95}$ tons.

We here give a table showing the principal articles, with their estimated total value, received at New Orleans from the interior for the year ending August 31st, 1853—

Articles	Amount	Value Dollars	Articles	Amount	Value Dollars
Apples, bbls.	48328	144984	Lead, bar, kgs. & bxs.	157	3925
Bacon, as'd. hhd. & cks.	50347	3524290	Lead, White	725	2900
Bacon, as'd. bxs.	4009	120270	Molasses, Crop, gals.	25700000	5140000
Bacon hams, hhds. & tcs.	42868	2786420	Oats, bbls. and sks.	446956	446956
Bacon in bulk, lbs.	134300	9401	Onions, bbls.	17718	35436
Bagging, pieces	64144	833872	Oil, Linseed, bbls.	508	15240
Bale Rope, coils	121553	972424	Oil, Castor, bbls.	4742	180196
Beans, bbls.	9491	66458	Oil, Lard, bbls.	14685	469920
Butter, kgs. & frkns.	44444	266664	Potatoes, bbls.	204327	408654
Butter, bbls.	2184	61152	Pork, tcs. and bbls.	316592	4432288
Beeswax, bbls.	194	9700	Pork, boxes	2074	62220
Beef, bbls.	48565	631345	Pork, hhds.	2547	178290
Beef, tcs.	30226	559181	Pork in bulk, lbs.	12985810	844077
Beef, dried, lbs.	18900	1600	Porter and Ale, bbls.	1140	11400
Buffalo Robes, pks.	17	2775	Packing Yarn, reels	2811	19677
Cotton, bales	1664864	68259424	Skins, Deer, packs	425	12750
Cornmeal, bbls.	1788	5364	Skins, Bear, packs	29	435
Corn in ear, bbls.	17620	13215	Shots, kgs.	2233	66990
Corn, shelled, sks.	1225031	1592540	Soap, bxs.	6911	20733
Cheese, bxs.	39497	157988	Staves, M.	6000	240000
Candles, bxs.	68796	447174	Sugar, est. crop hhds.	321931	15452688
Cider, bbls.	36	108	Spanish Moss, bales	3702	37020
Coal, Western, bbls.	700000	350000	Tallow, bbls.	4313	31632
Dried Apples, Peaches	2237	8948	Tobacco, leaf, hhds.	63260	6326000
Feathers, bags	2042	81680	Tobacco, strips, hhds.	10050	1306500
Flaxseed, tcs.	1279	10232	Tobacco, stems, hhds.	1700	34000
Flour, bbls.	808672	3639024	Do., chewing,kgs. & bxs.	10886	272150
Furs, hhds. bdls. & bxs.	730	300000	Twine, bdls. and bxs.	4544	36352
Hemp, bales	17648	300016	Vinegar, bbls.	142	1452
Hides	101460	202920	Whiskey	138515	1108120
Hay, bales	175000	525000	Window Glass, bxs.	13408	40224
Iron, pig, tns.	121	4840	Wheat, bbls. and sks.	47238	82766
Lard, bbls. & tcs.	118243	3074318	Other various articles		
Lard, kgs.	159672	878106	estimated at		6000000
Leather, bndls.	6309	189270			
Lime, Western, bbls.	33838	42297	Total value ...... 134,223,735 dollars.		
Lead, pigs	210287	841148			

Large quantities of coffee are imported from Rio direct and coastwise, and from Cuba direct. From July, 1852, to July, 1853, 381,513 bags were thus imported. The first brought from Rio de Janeiro was in 1835. In 1852 the United States imported for home consumption about 845,000 bags, nearly one-half being received through the New Orleans market. The aggregate sales for the year at this market amounted to upwards of 6,000,000 dollars.

The total value of American produce, exported from the district of New Orleans to foreign countries in 1853, was 67,768,626 dollars, and coastwise 30,695,466 dollars.

For several years past, although the statistics of the trade of New Orleans have shown evident signs of prosperity, the merchants and business men of the South have complained that the city was falling behind the cities of the North and West. In 1852 one of them proposed a modification of the laws bearing hardly and unequally upon capital and enterprise, the cheapening of the government, the extension of greater facilities to commerce, the establishment of manufactures, lines of steamships for Europe, munificent appropriations for railroads branching to the West, the North and the East, from a terminus at her centre, or from termini on such interior streams as are necessarily tributary to her. Much of this has been accomplished—the laws have been modified, the public debt has been decreased, and, in addition to the several railroads communicating with various points in the State, two extensive lines are now in process of construction. The first is called the "New Orleans, Opelousas and Great Western Railroad," and is to extend into central Texas; the other is called the "New Orleans, Jackson and Great Northern Railroad," and is designed to be connected with the railway system of Tennessee and of the North-western States. A charter has also been granted and a company organized for constructing a road to communicate with Mobile, through the Pontchartrain railroad.

The immense steam-boat traffic upon the Mississippi river affords every facility to emigrants to proceed to St. Louis, without detention in New Orleans more than twelve hours at the furthest, as steamers start daily for that city, and sometimes three or four times in the day. The fares are from two to three dollars on deck, and from twelve to fifteen in the cabin.

New Orleans was founded in 1718, by Bienville, Governor of Louisiana, and named after the duke of Orleans, Regent of France. It contained in 1723 about 100 cabins. In 1727 the Jesuits and Ursuline Nuns arrived. The former, on their expulsion from France, Spain and Naples were compelled to leave Louisiana, and their entire property was confiscated and sold by the court for 186,000 dollars. The same lands are now worth about 20,000,000 dollars. The city was first visited by the yellow fever in 1769, which is said to have been introduced by an English vessel with a cargo of slaves from Africa. On the 21st of March, 1778, the city was visited by a great conflagration, in which 900 houses and a vast amount of other property were destroyed. In 1794 the first newspaper, called *Le Moniteur,* was published. New Orleans is famous in history as the place intended to have been made the seat of monarchy had Aaron Burr succeeded in his treasonable attempts to cause an insurrection. In 1805 it was made a port of entry. In 1815 it was menaced with invasion by the British under Sir E. Packenham. In 1849 the seat of government was removed to Baton Rouge. From 1820 to 1853 the city more than quintupled its population and ascended by gradation to its present eminent position in wealth and commerce.

The population of New Orleans consists of Anglo-Americans; Creoles—

descendants of the French, Spanish and German settlers; Negroes; Mulattoes, and many thousands of foreigners from all parts of the world. The Creole men have less depth of character than the Anglo-Americans, but the ladies, many of them being descended from Norman ancestors, and unmixed blood, are very handsome and refined in their manners. There is another class of people called Quadroons, the offspring of Mulatto women by white men. The females are oftentimes possessed of accomplishments superior to those of the society from which they are shut out; they may be as fair as any European and have no symptoms of negro blood about them, yet the laws prohibit intermarriage with the whites. When rich, they are frequently sent to Paris in their infancy or childhood to receive their education, from whence, in numbers of cases, they return more cultivated than the white ladies from whose society they are rejected, and always too refined and over educated for the males of their own caste. They are therefore destined to be mistresses, and great pains are taken by their mothers to give them those attractions which a keeper requires. As soon as they reach womanhood, they are taken to the "Quadroon Balls," where they show their accomplishments to the white men, in dancing and conversation. Liaisons are there formed, and bargains are made with the mother, in which the man agrees to pay her a sum of money proportionate to her daughter's charms, as a fund upon which she may retire when the liaison terminates. Thus are these unfortunate females, by the tyranny of caste, committed to illicit intercourse with the whites and doomed "to bring up sons to be rejected where the father finds his equals, and daughters destined to pursue the same career which the mother has done." This must present a horrid state of society, whatever may be said of the numerous benevolent institutions and churches of the city, which are referred to with pride by its inhabitants. Indeed much has been said against the morals of New Orleans. There is no city of the Union where pleasure in so many questionable forms is pursued, and gambling indulged in to so great an extent. Bull-baiting and bear-fights are still common, and much of the Sunday is spent in these entertainments. The theatres, gambling-houses, and places of public amusement are generally open on Sunday also. It has been argued that the fact of the theatres being open on Sunday evening, is no indication whatever of a disregard of religion on the part of the Catholics, and that the latter might with equal reason reflect upon the Protestants for not keeping the doors of their churches open on week days.

(7) RED RIVER is one of the largest affluents of the Mississippi. It is formed by the Salt Fork and South Fork, which, unite near 34° N. lat., and 100° W. lon. The length of the main stream is estimated at about

1200 m. The river is navigable by large steam-packets during 8 months of the year, from its mouth to Shreveport, about 500 m., following the course of the river, from the Mississippi. The navigation is good in all stages of water to Alexandria, about 150 m. The river winds through a region of prairies with red soil covered with grass and white vines bearing delicious grapes. Much of the country is exceedingly fertile and capable of producing cotton, sugar-cane, grapes, indigo, rice, tobacco, Indian corn, &c.; but owing to the "Great Raft"—an immense swampy alluvial of the river, 70 m. long, and from 20 to 30 m. wide, commencing 30 m. above Shreveport, in which timber and fallen trees from the upper regions have for ages been brought down and embedded, the free navigation of the river is much impeded, and the prosperity of the upper valley retarded. The general government removed the obstruction in 1834–5, at a cost of 300,000 dollars, but another has since formed.

(8) MISSISSIPPI is one of the slave-holding States of the American confederacy. It originally formed part of the extensive French Province of Louisiana. It is bounded N. by Tennessee, E. by Alabama, S. by the Gulf of Mexico and Louisiana, and W. by the Pearl and Mississippi rivers, by which it is separated from Louisiana and Arkansas. It lies between 30° 20′ and 35° N. lat.; and between 88° 12′ and 91° 40′ W. lon. It is about 399 m. long from N. to S., and has an average breadth of 150 m. Area, 47,156 sq. m., of which only about 5500 are improved. The population in 1850, was 605,948, of which 309,300 were slaves. About 1⅔ per cent of the free population were of foreign birth.

The State is divided into 59 counties. It has no large towns. The principal are Natchez, Aberdeen, Vicksburg, Jackson, the capital, Columbus, Holly Springs, Port Gibson, and Shieldsborough. The Mississippi river and its tributaries drain the western part of the State, the Tombigby and Pascagoula the eastern, and the Pearl the central. The Yazoo is the largest river having its whole course within the State. The Mississippi renders the State accessible for the largest class of steam-boats for the whole extent of its western boundary. Smaller steam-boats ascend the Yazoo for 300 m., the Big Black for 50 m., the Pearl sometimes to Jackson, and the Pascagoula for a short distance. The navigation of the Pearl river is much obstructed by sandbars and shallows. Although this State has 60 or 70 m. of coast on the Gulf of Mexico it has no good harbours.

"The southern part of the State, for about 100 miles from the Gulf of Mexico, is mostly a sandy, level pine forest, interspersed with cypress swamps, open prairies, inundated marshes, and a few hills of a moderate elevation. This region is generally healthy, and by cultivation produces cotton, Indian corn, sugar, indigo, &c. As you proceed further N. the country becomes more elevated and agreeably diversified, and the soil is a deep rich mould, producing abundantly cotton, Indian corn, sweet potatoes, indigo, peaches, melons, and grapes. The natural growth of timber consists of poplar, hickory, black walnut, sugar-maple, cotton-wood, magnolia, lime and sassafras. The country in the N. part of the State is healthy and productive; and the lands watered by the Yazoo, through its whole course in the N. W., are very fertile. The Mississippi river, with its various windings, forms the entire western boundary of the State; and its margin consists of inundated swamps covered with a large growth of timber. Back of this the surface suddenly rises into what are called bluffs; and behind them the country is a moderately elevated table-land with diversified surface."

Cotton is the great staple product of the State. In 1850 there were in Mississippi 23,960 farms, containing 3,444,358 acres of cultivated land, or about 146 acres to each farm. The S. E. part of the State is famous for its cattle, being sometimes called the "Cow country."

The mineral resources of Mississippi, so far as developed, are not extensive. Gold has been obtained in Marion County, and coal and marble have been found, but only in very small quantities. In 1850, 100,000 dollars were invested in iron founderies, &c.

The climate of the State is very similar to that of Louisiana. Throughout, the paroquet and venomous snakes abound. The turtle-dove, mocking-bird and humming-bird are to be met with all over the State.

Very little internal improvement has been made. In January, 1853, there were 100 m. of railway completed, and 491 in course of construction. Brandon, Jackson and Raymond are connected with Vicksburg, and Citronelle with Mobile, by 33 m. of the finished portion of the Ohio and Mobile railroad. Some attention is being paid to plank roads.

There are very few manufactures carried on in Mississippi. In 1850, there were 866 establishments, each producing about 500 dollars annually. Among them there were 2 cotton establishments, 8 iron founderies, and 92 tanneries. The commerce of the State is chiefly carried on through New Orleans, and no table of its exports or imports can be obtained. The products of the N. W. of the State find their outlet principally at Memphis, in Tennessee, and those of the N. E. through the Tombigby river, at Mobile. A large portion of the E. and S. E. also has the same market.

De Soto was the first European that visited Mississippi, as noticed in our history of Louisiana, but no settlement was made until 1716, when some Frenchmen under Bienville formed the first permanent colony.

A general massacre of the whites by the Indians took place in 1728, which will be hereafter referred to in our notice of Natchez. Many other conflicts occurred with varying success, but eventually terminating in victory to the white inhabitants. By the treaty of Paris, in 1763, Mississippi became a part of the English territory. About the same period a number of French, from Canada, settled in the country, and in 1768 emigrants from the eastern colonies, by way of the Ohio and Mississippi rivers, began to arrive.

In 1798 that portion of the territory ceded to the United States by Great Britain, lying between the Spanish line of demarcation and a line drawn due E. from the mouth of the Yazoo river to the Chattahoochy, and having the Mississippi river for its western boundary and the Chattahoochy for its eastern, was erected into the "Mississippi Territory" and placed under the first grade of territorial government. The first governor was Winthrop Sargent. The principal white population at this early period was that of "Natchez District" and numbered about 6000 souls.

Owing to Governor Sargent's arbitrary measures, dissatisfaction was created among the people, and Congress, by special favour, passed an Act authorizing the establishment of the second grade of territorial government. A House of Representatives was now duly elected, and members of the Council having been appointed, the General Assembly was organized and convened for business in the city of Natchez, on the first Monday in December, 1800. The first regular code of jurisprudence and judicial proceedings for the use of the territory was adopted during the session of 1801–2. The first weekly newspaper was published in the Spring of 1802 and entitled the *Natchez Gazette*. It continued under different names and forms for nearly 40 years. The second was the *Mississippi Messenger*, which existed until 1810.

Education early engaged the attention of the Territorial Legislature, and a literary society was incorporated on the 8th of November, 1803, under the name of the "Mississippi Society for the Acquirement and Dissemination of Useful Knowledge." About the same time Jefferson College, the first in the territory, was organized.

Among the incidents in the early history of the Mississippi Territory was the violent death of Mason, the notorious robber. He had become the terror of the routes from New Orleans and Natchez through the Indian nations, and traders and travellers were robbed and murdered by his fearless band. His atrocities reached to such a pitch, that the governor of the territory offered a reward for him either dead or alive. Two of his band, tempted by the large reward, concerted a plan by which they might obtain it. Soon after, while Mason was counting out some of his ill-gotten plunder, one of the conspirators buried a tomahawk in his brain. His head was carried to Washington, then the capital of the territory, and recognized by many. The treacherous robbers, however, did not receive their reward, but owing to their being recognized by two young men, whose father they had plundered, they were imprisoned and finally executed. The whole band, thus deprived of their leader, dispersed.

The Protestant religion was introduced about 1798. In 1799 the first Methodist Missionary, Tobias Green, arrived from the S. Carolina Conference. In 1803 the Rev. Mr. Bowman, of the Methodist Episcopal Church, arrived from Tennessee and was most zealously devoted to the intellectual culture as well as religious instruction of the people.

In 1802 the first Presbyterian missionaries arrived, the Rev. Messrs. Hall and Montgomery, and about the same time arrived David Cooper, the first Baptist missionary, an excellent and pious man, and the Rev. Dr. Cloud, of the Episcopal Church.

Agriculture, which existed in a state of great depression when the American jurisdiction was established, had in 1807 become much improved, and cotton was introduced as a product and became the engrossing staple of the territory, which it has remained ever since.

The first joint-stock bank in the territory was chartered on the 23rd of December, 1809, with a capital of 500,000. Its title was the "Bank of Mississippi." In 1813 the Mobile District, dependent upon Fort Charlotte, was annexed to the Mississippi Territory. In 1817 on the 1st of March an Act was passed by Congress authorizing the people of the western portion of the Mississippi Territory to form a State government, preparatory to its admission into the Union as an independent State. On the 12th of December following, the constitution formed by the Convention was approved by Congress, and the "State of Mississippi" was admitted into the Federal Union. The first session of the State Legislature convened in the town of Washington, on the first Monday in October, 1817. The remainder of the territory was erected into a separate territorial government, and named "Alabama Territory." In 1820 the population of the new State, exclusive of Indians, was 75,400, of whom 33,000 were slaves. In November of the same year the capital was removed to a place near the Pearl river and was called Jackson after Major-General Andrew Jackson. In 1845 the population had increased to more than 375,000 souls, exclusive of Indians. Of this number 195,000 were slaves, chiefly engaged in agriculture, rendering Mississippi one of the largest cotton-growing States in the Union. At the close of the year the last remnant of the Indians were removed to their new lands, assigned to them in Indian Territory, W. of the Mississippi.

(9) NATCHEZ, on the E. bank of the Mississippi river, is 284 m. from New Orleans, and 1110 m. from Washington. Lat. 31° 34′ N.; lon. 91° 25′ W. Pop. 6000. The city stands on a bluff between 200 and 300 ft. above the level of the river, and is the most populous and commercial city of

Mississippi. The surface of the ground, both in the city and the surrounding country, is undulatory, which presents a striking contrast with the flat surface of Louisiana on the opposite side of the river. The streets are wide and intersect each other at right angles. The city contains a court house, 5 or 6 churches, a hospital, an orphan asylum, and a Masonic hall. The hospital was founded in 1805 and was the first charitable institution in the city. It owes its origin to the humane efforts of a few members of the medical profession, to provide relief for the increasing number of sick and indigent boatmen who were annually thrown helpless upon the city. Some of the public buildings are handsome, and the private dwellings, which are mostly built of wood, are ornamented with flower gardens and orange groves. There are 4 newspapers published, and the city boasts of a public school with about 500 pupils, and numerous flourishing seminaries, which are said to have much accelerated its growth within the past few years. As early as 1803 Natchez had become an important point for the western people, and in that year the Legislature incorporated the city. The city authorities consisted of a mayor, a recorder, three aldermen, six assistants, a clerk and a marshal, all excepting the clerk and marshal exercising the authority of Justices of the Peace.

It is now the centre of an extensive trade, of which cotton is the principal article, and steam-boats are constantly arriving at and departing from its wharves. The shipping business is carried on in the lower part of the town called "Natchez under the Hill." There are several extensive founderies in operation, and much attention has been given within the past few years to the manufacture of steam engines, cotton presses, sugar mills, &c. There is a railroad from Natchez to Malcolm, 30 m. distant.

Natchez was founded in 1700 by D'Iberville, who considered it the most suitable place for the principal French colony and the head-quarters of the provincial government. He selected the site on which the city now stands and named it "Rosalie," in honour of the Countess of Pontchartrain, who had received that name at the baptismal font. He designed to build a fort as a token of the French jurisdiction, but it was not erected until sixteen years afterwards. The ruins of this fort were visible in 1823.

The sketch of "Old Fort Rosalie" in the artist's narrative represents the remains of a terraced fort, built on the brink of the bluff just below the City of Natchez, by M. Lubois in 1730.

When D'Iberville first visited Natchez it was the residence of the "Grand Sun" or principal chief of the Natchez Indians, a powerful and intelligent tribe. Judge Peck, in his sketches of the Mississippi Valley, gives the following very interesting account of them, and of their final destruction by the French.

"They were idolaters, worshippers of the sun, and had a temple, and an altar dedicated to that luminary, on which a perpetual fire burned.

At first, they treated the French colonists with great kindness. In 1722, the Chickasaws gave them trouble, and attacked and destroyed a fort on the Yazoo. The friendly exertions of the Natchez saved the settlers. The next year, the commandant at Fort Rosalie treated them with indignity and injustice. The quarrel began between an old Natchez warrior and a soldier, about some corn. The Natchez challenged the Frenchman to single combat, who, in alarm, cried murder. The Natchez turned to depart from the camp, was fired on by the guard, and mortally wounded. No punishment was inflicted on the perpetrators, while, in other respects, the commandant rendered himself odious to the Natchez. The murder of the warrior aroused the whole tribe to seek revenge, and they attacked the French in all quarters, and killed many of them. At last the Stung Serpent, an influential chief, interposed his authority, a treaty of peace was made, and former confidence restored. The peace served to lull the Natchez into security, and gave the French opportunity to meditate and execute one of the blackest acts of treachery. The Governor of Louisiana, Bienville, ratified the treaty, and, soon after, in a most cautious and dastardly manner, arrived at Fort Rosalie, with seven hundred men, and attacked and slaughtered the defenceless natives for four days. From this time, the Natchez despaired of living in peace with the French, and secretly and silently plotted their destruction. In 1729, M. de Chopart, the commander of the fort, stung them to madness, by attempting to build a town, on the site of the village of White Apple, a large Indian town, situated about twelve miles below the city of Natchez, and three miles from the Mississippi, and which they regarded as a sacred place. He ordered their huts to be removed, and the Indians to leave the village. Among the fruitful expedients to gain time, till they could unite the warriors of the nations, and devise means to take vengeance on their enemies, they proposed to give the French commandant, each, one fowl and one basket of corn, for permission to remain till harvest. They held frequent and secret councils among themselves, and invited the Chickasaws to join them. Notwithstanding their secrecy, one of their chief women suspected the plot, and revealed it to a soldier. Still, M. Chopart disregarded the warning. The plot being matured, on the 3rd of November, 1729, the Grand Sun, with his warriors, repaired to the Fort, with the tribute of corn and fowls. They rushed into the gate, disarmed the soldiers, and commenced an indiscriminate massacre. The slaves and a few of the women and children were saved. All the men were murdered. Not a chief or warrior would stain his hands with the blood of M. Chopart, and one of the meanest of the Indians was ordered to kill him with a wooden tomahawk. The settlement contained about seven hundred French, of whom, only a very few escaped. The forts and settlements on the Yazoo and Washita shared the same fate. The news of this massacre filled New Orleans with alarm and dismay; but M. Perier, the commandant, was very active in devising the means of redress. The French gained the Chickasaws to their side, who furnished fifteen hundred warriors, which were met in the neighbourhood of Natchez, with a detachment of troops from New Orleans, under command of M. Loubois. The Natchez expected to be attacked, and had strongly fortified themselves in the fort. They professed to be desirous of peace, and much finesse was employed on both sides. At last the Natchez contrived to desert the fort at night, and, loaded with plunder, they crossed the Mississippi, and returned to a position on Red River, a few miles below Nachitoches. Here they erected a fort. M. Perier having received a reinforcement from France, marched a strong force with artillery against them. They defended themselves bravely, made several desperate sallies, but were repulsed with great slaughter. Their defence and attempts to negotiate a peace were all in vain, and they finally surrendered at discretion. The women and children were reduced to slavery and dispersed among the plantations. The remnants of this once powerful nation were finally sent to St. Domingo. Thus perished the most enlightened, civilized, and noble tribe of this continent. A few fugitives, who escaped the massacre, fled to the Chickasaws and Creeks, and became amalgamated with those tribes.

"We have already stated that the religion of the Natchez was idolatrous. One of their customs was barbarous. On the death of a Chief, or Sun, as he was called, and on some other occasions, human sacrifices were offered. Their chief suns were invested with absolute power, and there were inferior suns, that constituted a kind of subordinate nobility. The Natchez are represented by different authors as just, humane, and ready to extend relief to objects of distress. Charlevoix, who spent some days with them, in 1721, gives various details of their manners, customs, and religion. He states that on the death of a chief, or sun, his nurse, and, frequently, his body-guards, to the number of one hundred, or more, were put to death, that he might be followed to the 'spirit land' with a retinue equal to his rank on earth. Besides the sun and fire, they worshipped little wooden gods in the shape of monkies and rattlesnakes, placed on the altars." [John Mason Peck (1789–1858) was the author of the popular *A New Guide to the West, containing sketches of Ohio, Michigan, Indiana, Illinois, and Iowa*. Published in Cincinnati, it saw many editions between 1831 and 1848. See also his *Annals of the West*, published in St. Louis in 1850.]

(10) VICKSBURGH, on the E. bank of the Mississippi river, is 400 m. from New Orleans, and 50 m. W. from Jackson, with which it is connected by

the Vicksburgh and Brandon railroad. Pop. in 1850, 3,678. It is a city and a port of entry, and is situated on a hill, the highest part of which is about 200 ft. above high water mark. The ground is uneven and the city is not compactly built. It has, besides the county buildings, 4 or 5 churches and several academies for both sexes. Three newspapers are published in the city. Vicksburgh was incorporated as a town in 1825, and as a city in 1836, and within the last few years has much improved. It is now the most commercial place on the river between Natchez and Memphis and is an important mart for cotton, the recipients of which for 3 years were as follows—in 1850, 49,722 bales; in 1851, 62,134; and in 1852, 88,732. About 100,000 bales of this article are annually exported, the greater portion of which is received by railroad. The tonnage of this port, June 1852, was $213^{83}\!/_{95}$ tons enrolled and licensed and employed in steam navigation.

Steam-boats ply regularly between this place and New Orleans. The harbour is very fine, and the principal part of the business is transacted on the bottom, along the river. The Vicksburgh and Brandon railroad is to be extended eastward to Selma in Alabama. Another railroad has been surveyed from Vicksburgh to Marshall in Texas, *via* Shreveport.

(11) ARKANSAS, one of the slave-holding States, and formerly part of Louisiana, is bounded on the N. by Missouri, E. by Missouri and the Mississippi river; S. by Louisiana, and Texas; and W. by Texas and the Indian territory. It lies between 33° and 36° 30′ N. lat.; and between 39° 45′ and 94° 40′ W. long., being 240 m. in length from N. to S., and 224 m. in breadth from E. to W. Area, 52,198 sq. m., of which little better than one-fourth is improved. Pop. in 1850, 209,639, of which 46,982 were slaves.

The State is divided into 54 counties. Little Rock, the capital of the State, is the largest town, and has 3000 inhabitants. Van Buren is the most commercial town, and has 1500 inhabitants. The other towns of any importance are Fort Smith, Batesville and Camden.

Arkansas has no sea-board, but the Mississippi river coasts almost its entire eastern boundary, rendering it accessible to the sea from many points. Probably no other State in the Union is penetrated by so many navigable rivers, but, owing to the long continued droughts of the hot season, none of them can be ascended by vessels of any size more than 9 months in the year. The Arkansas is the principal river that passes wholly through the State. White River and the St. Francis with their affluents drain the N. E. part of the State. White River is navigable for steam-boats 50 m., the Big Black for 60, and the St. Francis for 300. Red

River runs through the S. W. angle of the State, receiving some small tributaries within its limits, and is navigable for steam-boats beyond Arkansas. The Washita and its affluents drain the southern portion of the State. The main stream is navigable for 375 m., and its tributary, the Saline, for 100 m. Bayous Bartholomew, Bœuf, Macon, and Tensas are all tributaries of the Washita, and have an aggregate of 635 m. of navigable water. They all rise in the S. part of Arkansas, and flow into Louisiana, where they join Red River. The Little Missouri, and Bayou D'Arbonne, are western branches of the Arkansas, the former navigable 60 m., and the latter 50 for light steam-boats.

"In the eastern part of the State, bordering on the Mississippi, and the large rivers which empty into it; the country is low and swampy, with a heavy growth of timber, and is frequently overflowed. In the central part it is undulating and broken, and in the north-western parts, the Ozark mountains, rising sometimes to the height of 1500 ft., extend across the State. The Washita Hills, N. of the Washita river have considerable elevation. The soil is of every variety from the most productive to the most sterile. On the margins of the river it is exceedingly fertile; but back of this the land is generally sterile. Prairies are abundant and of immense extent. In many parts there is a scarcity of water. Cotton and Indian corn are the staple productions; but the country is well calculated for raising cattle, wild animals, and fowls, as the buffalo, deer, elk, otter, beaver, rabbit, racoon, &c.; wild geese, turkeys, and quails are abundant. Near the centre of the State are numerous hot-springs, the temperature of which sometimes rises nearly to the boiling point." The forest trees of Arkansas are cotton-wood, ash, cypress and gum in the bottom lands; and hickory and oak on the hilly portions. Pine is found in considerable abundance on the Arkansas river, and beech on the St. Francis. Immense quantities of these woods are sent down to New Orleans. Black walnut, cherry, red cedar, dogwood, maple, poplar and sugar-maple in the north parts, which, with bois d'arc, sassafras and black locust in other parts, are found in great abundance and are very valuable.

In 1850 there were 17,758 farms in Arkansas, occupying 781,531 acres of improved land. The climate of this State in the N. and W. parts is allied to the N. W. States, while in the S. and E. it partakes of that of Louisiana. The low lands are unhealthy, but the uplands compare favourably with the most healthful regions of the western States.

The minerals of the State are principally coal, iron, lead, zinc, manganese, gypsum and salt. Near the Hot Springs is a quarry of oil-stone. The quantity is said to be inexhaustible, and the quality superior to anything of the kind in the known world. A writer in De Bow's Resources of the S. and W. states that there is manganese enough in Arkansas to supply the world. [James D. B. DeBow: *The Industrial Resources of the Southern and Western States* (New Orleans, 1852–1853).]

This young State has made very little internal improvement, and she is not extensively engaged in manufactures. In 1850, there were only 271 manufactories, of these three were engaged in the manufacture of cotton, consuming raw material to the amount of 8975 dollars, and producing 81,250 lbs. of yarn, valued at 16,637 dollars. There were no manufactures of wood or iron reported. Home-made manufactures to the value of 646,938 dollars were produced, and 51 tanneries, employing 42,000 dollars capital, and consuming raw material worth 35,230 dollars, produced leather to the value of 78,734 dollars. The State has no foreign commerce, although it has considerable boating trade with New Orleans, engaged in the export of her productions.

There are no colleges in the State, nor has she yet organised a system of public schools. In 1850 there were 187 churches, owned as follows— 73 by the Baptists; 73 by the Methodists; 25 by the Presbyterians; 7 by the Union Church; 6 by the Roman Catholics; 2 by the Episcopalians; 1 by the Free Church. At Little Rock there is a State penitentiary, which has been once or twice burned down by the convicts. There were no banks in Arkansas in January, 1852.

Arkansas was originally settled by the French, at Arkansas Post, as early as 1685, and formed part of the great French province of Louisiana, and afterwards of Missouri Territory, from which it was laid off in 1819, and subsequently organized into the second grade of territorial government. Colonel James Miller was appointed first governor. This territory was known as "Arkansas Territory." For many years Arkansas was considered to be the extreme confines of civilization in the S. W., and population advanced slowly. Ten years after its organization the population only numbered 30,388 souls, including 4576 slaves. From this period, circum-stances for its colonization were more favourable, and in 1836, the population having reached about 60,000, a Constitution was formed, and the "State of Arkansas" was admitted into the Federal Union as an inde-pendent State, and was in point of time and order the 25th in the Con-federacy.

The first governor of the State was James S. Conway, with Robert A. Watkins, Secretary of State. "Like the Missouri Territory, Arkansas had been a slave-holding country from the earliest French settlement, and the institution was sustained by the new Constitution. After the admission of the State into the Federal Union, her population and wealth continued to increase, and settlements gradually extended over the unoccupied districts, and rapidly occupied the fertile regions upon all the tributaries of the White river, and the St. Francis, N. of the Arkansas river, as well as upon the tributaries of the Washita and Red River, S. of that river."

The governor is elected by the people for 4 years, and receives a salary of 1800 dollars per annum. The present (1854) incumbent is Elias N. Conway. The Senate consists of 25 members, elected for 5 years, and a House of Representatives of 75 members, elected for 2 years, both by the people. The judiciary consists of a supreme court, composed of a chief justice, and 2 associates, elected by the legislature for 8 years; and second, of 6 circuit courts. The circuit judges are elected by the people for 4 years, and the prosecuting attorney for 2 years. The State sends 2 members to the national House of Representatives and is entitled to 4 electoral votes for President of the United States.

(12) TENNESSEE, one of the western States of the American Confederacy, is bounded on the N. by Kentucky and Virginia; E. by North Carolina, from which it separated by the Alleghany mountains; S. by Georgia, Alabama, and Mississippi, and W. by the Mississippi river. It lies between 35° and 36° 30' N. lat.; and between 81° 40' and 90° 15' W. lon.; being about 430 m. long from E. to W., and 110 broad. Area, 45,600 sq. m., of which only about one-fifth were improved in 1850. Pop. in 1850, 1,002,625, of which 239,460 were slaves. About 1 per cent. of the free population were of foreign birth. Tennessee is the second State in point of population in the Mississippi valley and is divided into 79 counties. Nashville is the capital and its largest town—pop. in 1850, 10,478. The other principal towns are Memphis, Knoxville, Chattanooga, Columbia, Murfreesboro, Jackson, Clarksville, Bolivar, Charleston and Carthage.

The principal rivers are the Tennessee, which twice crosses the State and has a course of nearly 900 m., about 400 of which are within the State, and 700 navigable for steam-boats (with the exception of that portion in Alabama, called the Muscle Shoals) to its junction with the Holston in E. Tennessee; the Cumberland, rising in Kentucky, navigable for 400 m. for steam-boats, to Carthage, about 50 m. above Nashville in a direct line; the Forked Deer navigable 150 m.; the Big Hatchie, above 100, and the Obion 60. The Holston, Clinch, French Broad and Hiawasse are branches of the Tennessee. The tributary streams are all more or less navigable, and all the waters of this State ultimately reach the Mississippi, though generally by a circuitous route.

"Tennessee is very agreeably diversified with mountain, hill and plain, containing within its limits fertility of soil, beauty of scenery, and a delightfully temperate climate. In the E. it is separated from North Carolina by different ridges of the Appalachian chain, passing under the various local names of Stone, Iron, Bald and Unaka mountains. Then follow the valleys of the Holston and other rivers, forming the head waters of the Tennessee. Next succeed the Cumberland mountains, an outlying ridge of the Alleghenies, which enter the State from Kentucky, and cross it in a S. W. direction into Alabama. The height of these mountains, which spread over about 50 miles, is variously estimated at from 1000 to 2000 feet. They are wooded to the tops, and embosom delightful and fertile valleys. Their summits are often rounded and cultivated, while others are too rugged for tillage. Middle Tennessee, lying between these mountains and the Tennessee river, is moderately hilly, while the section between the river last named and the Mississippi, called West Tennessee is either level or gently undulating."

"The soil of Tennessee is generally arable, and of a good quality. In E. Tennessee much of the land among the mountains is poor and ill adapted to cultivation, but even here the valleys are very fertile. This section is favourable to grazing, and great numbers of live stock are exported from thence to the Atlantic States. A greater number of mules are raised in Tennessee than in any other State in the Union. Middle Tennessee has much good land. Western Tennessee has a rich black mould, and on the shores of the Mississippi and Tennessee are extensive brakes of gigantic cane. Indian corn, tobacco, and cotton are the great staples. In 1850 Tennessee produced more hogs than any State in the Union, was fifth in the amount of Indian corn produced, fourth in that of tobacco, and fifth in cotton. The other articles cultivated are wheat, rye, oats, buckwheat, barley, potatoes, sweet and Irish, wool, maple sugar, flax, hemp, hay, cheese, butter, wine, whisky and fruits. Of the latter, apples, pears, and plumbs." The forest-trees are pine, sugar maple, juniper, red cedar, savine, poplar, hickory, walnut, oak, beech, sycamore, locust, cherry, &c.

The animals are deer, racoons, foxes, squirrels, and sometimes, although rarely, bears in the wilder sections of the State.

The minerals are iron and coal in abundance, lead, silver, zinc, manganese and magnetic iron ore. There is also gypsum of a fine quality; beautiful varieties of marble, nitre, slate, alum, burrstones, and limestone, which forms the bed of a large portion of the State. Salt springs exist, though not of a very rich quality. There are some valuable mineral springs. The iron business is coming into note. There were on the Cumberland river, in the early part of 1853, 21 furnaces, 9 forges, and 2 rolling mills; manufacturing 44,500 tons of metal, and 1400 kettles, valued together at 1,678,000 dollars. Rich deposits of copper are found in the S. E. part of the State, which are now being extensively worked.

Tennessee has numerous caves, several of which are at least 100 ft.

below the surface, and 1 m. in extent; some are several miles in length, and one has been descended for about 400 ft., where was found a stream of sufficient force to turn a mill. Another on the top of Cumberland mountain has never been sounded. In one, called Big Bone Cave, the bones of the Mastodon have been found.

The internal improvement of this State has been favourably progressing for years. In January, 1853, it had 185 m. of completed railway, and 509 in course of construction. When the several lines which are now in progress are completed, uninterrupted communication will be opened between the Atlantic Ocean, and the great Mississippi and Ohio valleys. The natural water-power of this State and its abundance of coal and other fuel, will, no doubt, as soon as the railway connections with the Atlantic States are completed, make it a great manufacturing section. In 1850 it had 2789 manufacturing establishments, each producing 500 dollars and upwards annually. Of these, 33 were cotton factories, 81 furnaces and forges and 364 tanneries. Home-made manufactures were produced of the value of 3,137,810 dollars—the highest in the Union.

Tennessee has very little foreign commerce; its few exports are chiefly live stock, pork, bacon, lard, butter, ginseng, cotton-bagging, flour, Indian corn, fruits, tobacco, cotton, hemp, feathers, and saltpetre. Five steamers were built in the fiscal year ending June 1852, the total tonnage of which was only $479^{61}/_{95}$. The tonnage of the state at that time was $40829^{2}/_{95}$. Her foreign imports were 256,054 dollars.

There were in this State in 1850, 9 colleges, with an aggregate of 551 students, and 27,056 volumes in their libraries; 1 theological, with 24 students, 1 law, with 56, and 2 medical schools, with 590. The number of children in the state was 288,454, of public schools 2,713 and of academies 278. The school-fund amounts to about 1,321,655 dollars, and the annual expenditure to 114,718. There were 5100 vols. [in the] school libraries. In the same year there were 1939 churches in the State, owned as follows—831 by the Methodists, 611 by the Baptists, 357 by the Presbyterians, 57 by the Christians, 28 by the Free Church, 17 by the Episcopalians, 15 by the Union Church, 12 by the Lutherans, 3 by the Roman Catholics, and the balance by the Africans, Friends, Protestant Evangelicals, and Dunkers, making one church to every 517 inhabitants. Value of Church property, 1,208,876 dollars. There are not many public institutions. The principal are a penitentiary at Nashville on the silent system, and a deaf and dumb asylum at Knoxville. Twenty-one public libraries with 47,376 volumes existed in 1850.

This state was the first settled by Anglo-Americans, W. of the Alleghanies, emigrants having built Fort Loudon as early as 1757. Formerly it formed part of the possessions of N. Carolina, which State ceded it to the General Government in 1783, but afterwards revoked the grant. The inhabitants then attempted to form an independent State under the name of Franklinia. It was finally ceded to the U. S. Government and formed part of the S. W. Territory, till its admission as a sovereign State in 1796, forming the 16th of the Confederacy. Its first governor was John Sevier. From the adoption of the State government until the present time, Tennessee is said to be surpassed by no State in the rapid development of its natural resources and in the patriotic chivalry of its citizens. It took an active part in the war of 1812. General Andrew Jackson, one of the heroes of that time, and since so celebrated as President of the United States, and James K. Polk, the 11th President, were both natives of Tennessee. This State is sometimes called the mother of States, from having contributed more largely to the colonization of the valley of the Mississippi than any other State of the Union.

In January, 1852, there were 23 banks in the State, with an aggregate capital of 8,405,197 dollars.

The governor of Tennessee is elected by the people for 2 years, and receives a salary of 2,000 dollars per annum. The present (1854) governor is Andrew Johnson. The Senate consists of 25 members, and the House of Representatives of 75, both elected by the people for 2 years. The judiciary consists of a supreme court, presided over by 3 judges, elected by a joint vote of the two houses of the legislature for 12 years; a court of chancery, presided over by 4 chancellors, and of 14 circuit courts, presided over by as many judges. The judges of the inferior courts are elected by the legislature for 8 years. Davidson county, in which is the city of Nashville, has a special criminal court, and the city of Memphis has a common law and chancery court.

(13) MEMPHIS, 751½ m. from New Orleans, and 422 below St. Louis, on the E. bank of the Mississippi, in the state of Tennessee, is a port of entry, and the most populous and important city on the river, between St. Louis and New Orleans. Pop. in 1853, 12,000. The city is situated on the 4th Chickasaw bluff, which is elevated about 30 ft. above the highest floods. The base of the bluff is washed by the river for a distance of 3 m., and a bed of sandstone projects into the stream, forming a convenient landing. Memphis, as will be seen from our engraving, taken on the opposite side of the river, has a remarkably fine appearance. Many signs of activity and commercial improvement are here exhibited, and the population has doubled itself since 1845. Large quantities of cotton are grown in the surrounding country, for which Memphis is the principal mart and port of shipment. About 120,000 bales are annually shipped. From this point to its mouth the river is deep enough to float the largest

ships of war, and the United States have recently established a naval depôt at this place. Steam-boat building has been commenced and there are cotton, iron, and rope manufactories in operation. The western terminus of the Memphis and Charleston railroad is at this city. A railroad to Nashville is in course of construction, and another to Little Rock, Arkansas, has been projected. Steam-boats make frequent passages between this and other ports on the river.

The city contains 6 or 7 churches, an academy, a medical college, 2 banks and a telegraph-office. Six weekly, and several daily newspapers are published. The site of Memphis was formerly Fort Assumption, used for protecting the country against the Chickasaws. A French army consisting of nearly 4000 white, red, and black were gathered here to chastise these Indians. They remained inactive from the summer of 1739, to the spring of 1740, during which time hundreds sickened and died, when in March of the last named year peace was concluded.

(14) MISSOURI is one of the largest of the United States, and the first formed wholly W. of the Mississippi river. It is bounded on the N. by Iowa, from which it is separated for about 130 m. E. N. E., by the Des Moines river; on the E. by the Mississippi river; on the S. by Arkansas; and on the W. by Kansas and Nebraska territories. It lies (with the exception of a small projection between the St. Francis river and the Mississippi, which extends to 36°,) between 36° 30' and 40° 36' N. lat.; and 89° 10' and 96° W. lon.; being about 285 m. in its greatest length from E. to W., and 280 in width, from N. to S. Area, 67,380 sq. m., of which only about one-eighteenth part was improved in 1850. Pop. in 1850, 682,244, of which 87,422 were slaves. More than one-eighth of the population at that time were of foreign birth.

There are 101 counties in Missouri. Jefferson city is the capital. St. Louis, with a pop., in 1853, of 88,000, is the largest city of the State. The other principal towns are Hannibal, Lexington, Castor, Weston, Palmyra and St. Genevieve.

By means of the Mississippi river, Missouri can hold commercial intercourse with the most northern territory of the Union, the Ohio valley, some of the Atlantic States, and the Gulf of Mexico. By means of the Missouri, which divides the State into two portions, its internal commerce may be extended to the Rocky Mountains. Both the Mississippi and Missouri rivers are navigable for large steamers far beyond the limits of the State, though the navigation of the latter is impeded by the swiftness of its current. The Missouri receives a number of tributaries within the State, the principal being Chariton and Grand rivers, from the N., and the Osage and Gasconade from the S. The Osage is navigable for boats of light draught, 200 m. The principal tributaries of the Mississippi within the State are the Salt river N., and the Maramec, S. of the Missouri. The St. Francis and White rivers drain the S. E. part of the State and pass into Arkansas.

Missouri "presents a great variety of surface and soil. Alluvial or bottom land is found on the margin of the rivers; receding from them the land rises, in some places gently, and in others very abruptly, into elevated barrens or rocky ridges. In the interior, bottoms and barrens, naked hills and prairies, heavy forests and streams of water, may often be seen at one view, presenting a diversified and beautiful landscape. The southeast part of the State has a very extensive tract of low marshy country, abounding in lakes, and liable to inundation. Back of this a hilly country extends as far as the Osage river. This section is rich in minerals. The lead region covers an area of more than 3000 sq. m. In St. Francis county is the celebrated Iron Mountain, elevated 300 ft. above the surrounding plain; it is a mile and a half across its summit, and has 80 per cent of its mass pure iron. Five m. distant is the Pilot Knob, 300 ft. high, and with a base a mile and a half in circumference, of the same species of rich ore. Between the Osage and Missouri rivers, is a tract of country very fertile and agreeably diversified with woodland and prairie, and abounding with coal, salt, &c. The country N. of the Missouri is emphatically 'the garden of the West.' There is no part of the world where a greater extent of country can be traversed more easily, when in its natural state. The surface is for the most part delightfully undulating, and variegated, sometimes rising into picturesque hills, then stretching away into a sea of prairie, occasionally interspersed with shady groves and shining streams."

The non-metallic minerals of the State are limestone in great abundance, beautifully veined and crystalline marbles, gypsum, red and white sandstone, sienite, saltpetre, sulphate of baryta, kaolin, and inferior clays. There are vast veins of cannel coal, one of which consists in one place of a solid stratum 24 ft., and in another 75 ft., in thickness, and is supposed to be the largest body of cannel coal discovered. The interior of the State is not very well known, but there is much to interest the tourist, in the wild bluffs, both of the Missouri and Mississippi rivers, which vary in height from 50 to 300 ft. There are also many inducements to geologists for a visit. Near the head waters of White River there is a cave, which Schoolcraft thus describes—"The opening appeared to be 85 or 90 ft. wide, and 30 ft. high. A vast gloomy rotunda opened before us, which very soon after entry increased to a height of 60 or 70 ft., and in width to 150 or 200 ft. This hall extended into the rock southerly, branching off into lateral avenues. We explored the main gallery for 500 or 600 yds., when we met with obstructions." [Henry Rowe Schoolcraft. See his *Journal of a tour into the interior of Missouri and Arkansas . . .*1818 and 1819 (London, 1821).]

The climate of Missouri is very variable; in winter the thermometer sinks below zero, while the summer is excessively hot, but the air pure and dry. During the autumn, bilious and remittent fevers are common on the river bottoms.

In 1850 there were in the State 54,458 farms, occupying 2,924,991 acres of improved land, being less than 60 acres to each farm. The soil is, generally speaking, good and of great agricultural capabilities. The great staple is Indian corn. More hemp is produced than in any state except Kentucky. The principal products are wheat, oats, tobacco, wool, peas, beans, Irish and sweet potatoes, fruits, butter, cheese, pork, hay, flax, honey and beeswax; considerable quantities of rye, buckwheat, market products, grass seeds, maple sugar; with some rice, barley, wine, hops, silk and molasses. The oak, elm, ash, hickory, cotton-wood, linn, and white and black walnut grow luxuriantly on the river bottoms. The white and pin oak, and sometimes forests of yellow pine, grow in more barren parts. The crab-tree, papaw, persimmon, hazel and pecan are abundant. Among the fruits are three species of wild grapes, apples, pears, peaches, apricots and nectarines.

The manufactures of Missouri are unimportant. In 1850 it had 3030 establishments, each producing 500 dollars and upwards annually. In this number there were 2 cotton factories, and 1 woollen, 13 iron forges and founderies, and 148 tanneries. Home-made manufactures in the same year amounted to the value of 1,674,705 dollars.

On the 1st of January, 1853, this State had not a mile of completed railroad. In 1854 there were three railroads in course of construction. First, "the St. Louis and Pacific," of which about 38 m. are completed westwardly from St. Louis; second, the "Iron Mountain," from St. Louis to Missouri, length about 75 m.; third, the "Hannibal and St. Joseph," connecting the Missouri and Mississippi at the points named in the title of the road, length 280 or 300 m. The State has lent its credit to the first road to the amount of 3,000,000 dollars; to the second, 750,000, and to the third, 1,000,000. The following railroads are undergoing survey—the "North Missouri", from St. Louis to the northern boundary line of the State, 250 m.; and the "South-Western," from St. Louis to Springfield, about 300 m. Plank roads are coming much into vogue.

The commerce of Missouri is rapidly advancing with the increasing settlements on its two great rivers, and chiefly concentrates at St. Louis. The foreign imports (a very small part of its trade) amounted in 1851–2 to 914,826 dollars. Its exports consist for the most part, of lead, pork, flour, wheat, tobacco, and live stock. An active caravan trade has long been carried on between this State and Santa Fé.

There were in this State in 1853, 6 colleges, with about 378 students, and 18,400 volumes in their libraries, and 2 medical schools, with 164 students. The State University is at Columbia. Howard High School is a flourishing and successful establishment. The school-fund amounts to upwards of 500,000 dollars, yet the common school system is very defective. There is also a seminary-fund of 100,000 dollars. In 1850 there were 59,927 children in the State, 39,983 of whom were in the schools. The annual expenditure for school purposes amounts only to 88,124 dollars, and there are only about 6000 volumes in school libraries. There were 773 churches in the State in 1850, owned as follows—283 by the Baptists, 200 by the Methodists, 108 by the Presbyterians, 64 by the Roman Catholics, 51 by the Christian Church, 21 by the Lutherans, 13 by the Free Church, 11 by the Union Church, 10 by the Episcopalians, and the balance by the German Protestants, the German Evangelical Church, the Independents, the Jews, the Latter-day Saints, and a number of minor bodies, giving 1 church to every 882 inhabitants. Value of Church property 1,558,590 dollars. The public institutions are the State Penitentiary at Jefferson city, 19 public libraries, with 37,506 volumes, a lunatic asylum, and a deaf and dumb asylum at Fulton.

Missouri was originally a part of the great province of Louisiana, whose history and vicissitudes we have previously noticed at some length. The first settlers were French, and as early as 1719 a fort was built by order of the commandant-general of Louisiana, to protect the settlements against invasion from the Spaniards, who then occupied Texas. Fort Orleans, as it was called, stood on an island in the Missouri river, above the mouth of the Osage, and near the site of the present Jefferson city. The lead mines of this region were commenced to be worked in 1720. St. Genevieve, the oldest town in the State, was settled in 1755. In the following year St. Louis was settled, and in 1780 was exposed to an invasion from the British. After the territory of Orleans had been detached from Louisiana, the remainder of the province was designated as the "District of Louisiana," and Major Amos Stoddart was appointed military commandant and civil governor. His head-quarters were at St. Louis. Up to this period nearly the whole of this immense district of country was an unknown wilderness of forests and prairies, traversed only by a few roving bands of savages, and a few French traders. The first American exploration was that of Lewis and Clark, in 1804–5, who penetrated the sources of the Missouri, and thence to the Pacific Ocean through the Columbia river. In the meantime the District of Louisiana had been erected into the "Territory of Louisiana," with the first grade of territorial government. The first governor was General James Wilkinson, and the head-quarters were at St. Louis. In 1812 Congress passed an act providing for the organization of a representative grade of territorial government upon the W. side of the Mississippi. This territory extended from 33° to 41° N., and was named "Missouri Territory." Its western limit was the Indian and Mexican territories, in the remote West, 500 m. beyond the Mississippi. St. Louis was made the seat of government, and the head-quarters of the "Governor, and Superintendent of Indian affairs." The first governor was General William Clark. The first delegate to Congress was Edward Hempstead. Under this new state of things many Anglo-American people emigrated from the western States and territories, augmented the population, and introduced American manners, customs, laws and usages, which soon changed the aspect of the country, yet St. Louis, as late as 1814, had not lost its French population, aspect, nor usage.

The application of the Missouri Territory for authority to assume a regular State government raised one of the most alarming political storms ever witnessed in the United States, between the friends and enemies of the institution of Negro slavery. "Experienced statesmen were apprehensive that even a dissolution of the Union might result from the untempered zeal of the enemies of slavery." The non-slave-holding States required the people of Missouri to renounce the institution or forfeit their right to be admitted into the Union as an independent State. They likewise called upon the government to restrict the extension of servitude W. of the Mississippi. After the question had agitated the Halls of Congress for 2 years and induced much angry debate, it was agreed that the institution of slavery should be recognised in the present State of Missouri, and no further N. or W., but only S. of lat. 36° 30'. On the 6th of March, 1820, the people of the territory were authorized by Act of Congress to form a State Constitution preparatory to their admission into the Union as an independent State, with its present boundaries. The Convention met at St. Louis on the 12th of June, 1820, and organized with David Barton as president, and W. G. Pettus as secretary. In five weeks the Constitution of the State of Missouri was adopted, and under its provisions Alexander McNair was elected first governor. The population at that time was 66,586, including 10,222 slaves. In framing the Constitution a provision had been introduced requiring the legislature to pass a law "to prevent free negroes and mulattoes from coming to and settling in the State." When the Constitution was presented to Congress this provision was strenuously opposed, but after much debate Missouri was admitted on condition that it should pass no laws to prevent any free citizen of the U. States from enjoying those rights within that State to which they were entitled by the Constitution of the U. States. After its admission into the Union, Missouri rapidly increased by emigration from Kentucky, Tennessee, Virginia, North Carolina, &c., and after the lapse of 10 years it had increased its population to 140,455 souls, including nearly 26,000 slaves and persons of colour. Trade and commerce had sprung up in all the river towns, and agriculture, manufactures and arts had extended to the extreme frontier settlements. Before the close of 1833, nearly 30,000 Germans had settled within the State. From that period up to the present it has been increasing in agricultural and commercial importance.

It appears from the Revelations of the Lord, given to Joseph Smith, the Prophet, that Missouri is the land which has been consecrated for the gathering of the Saints in the last days, and where the city of Zion, with its Temple, will ultimately stand; all other gathering places of the Latter-day Saints being merely Stakes of Zion. In compliance with a commandment of the Lord, given in 1831, between 20 and 30 Elders of the Church commenced their journey by different routes, westward from Ohio, with a view to meeting in the western part of Missouri. About the middle of July, Joseph Smith and several of the Elders arrived at Independence, Jackson County, which was pointed out as the place for the city. The spot for the Temple was a short distance from the Court House and was dedicated on the 3rd of August. The settlement in Jackson county continued to receive immigrants, who flocked in from Ohio and other parts. Lands were purchased, several hundred houses were built, and extensive improvements made; but 2 years had not elapsed before an organized mob, consisting of the highest officers in the county, civil and military, undertook to drive them from it. After plundering the Saints of their property, laying their cultivated fields waste, and burning their houses, they accomplished their object. No other reason was assigned for this relentless persecution than the objection entertained to the religious belief of the Saints; and so well satisfied were the mobbers of the illegality of their proceedings, that they declared that the arm of the civil law did not afford them a sufficient guarantee in the undertaking. They therefore pledged themselves to each other to rid their society of the Saints, "peaceably if they could—forcibly if they must." The number thus banished was about 1200. Settlements were then made on the other side of the Missouri river, in Clay, Caldwell, Carroll, and other counties. These lawless proceedings met with no check from the constituted authorities of the State; but Lilburn W. Boggs, who had acted a prominent part in the expulsion from Jackson County, was elected governor. The people were now encouraged to renew their murderous attacks, and men and women were driven from place to place, robbed of their all, and left houseless and unprotected, until many expired under their sufferings. Governor Boggs was again and again applied to for protection, but instead of bringing the perpetrators of these crimes to justice, and protecting the Saints in their constitutional rights, he issued an order for their *extermination* and *banishment*. The militia were called out and placed under General Clarke, and under shadow of authority, laid fields of corn waste, burnt houses, shot the cattle, butchered many of the Saints, and ravished the women. About 100 leading members of the Church were thrown into dungeons, and were, in some instances, fed on human flesh. The property of the Saints was confiscated; and they, numbering about 15,000, were, in the winter of 1838–9, expelled from the State at the point of the bayonet. Before their final expulsion, the Saints, unwilling to believe that American citizens could appeal in vain for a restitution of liberty cruelly wrested from them by tyrants, petitioned the State legislature, then in session, but instead of its hearing the cries of these 15,000 suffering and wronged people, it actually sanctioned the unconstitutional acts of the governor, and appropriated 200,000 dollars to defray the expense of extermination. The subject was afterwards laid before the President and Congress of the U. States, but without redress; the President, Martin Van Buren, replying to the delegation, "Gentlemen, your cause is just, but I can do nothing for you."

The governor and lieutenant-governor of Missouri are elected by popular vote for 4 years. The former receives 2000 dollars per annum and the use of a furnished house. The present governor (1855) is Sterling Price. The lieutenant-governor receives 4½ dollars per day, during the session of the Senate, of which he is ex-officio president. The Senate consists of 18 members, and the House of Representatives of 49; the former elected for 4 years, and the latter for 2, by the people. The sessions of the legislature are biennial. One year's residence in the State is necessary to qualify for the suffrage. Missouri sends 7 members to the National House of Representatives, and has 9 electoral votes for President. The Judiciary consists first, of a supreme court, composed of 3 judges; second, of 14 circuit courts, the courts of St. Louis, and the common pleas court of Hannibal city; and third, of county courts. In 1853, this State had 1 bank with 5 branches—capital 1,210,622 dollars, 69 cents.

(15) KENTUCKY is one of the western States of the U. S., and the second admitted into the Union after the revolution. It is bounded on the N. W. and N. by Illinois, Indiana, and Ohio, from which it is separated by the Ohio river; E. by the Big Sandy river and Cumberland mountains, which divide it from Virginia; S. by Tennessee, and W. by the Mississippi river. It lies between 36° 30′ and 39° 10′ N. lat.; and between 81° 50′ and 89°

26′ W. lon., being about 300 m. in length, from E. to W.; about 180 in
its greatest breadth and 150 in its average. Area nearly 37,600 sq. m., of
which not quite one-half were improved in 1850. Population in 1850,
982,405, of which, 210,981 were slaves. About 4 per cent. of the free
population were of foreign birth.

Kentucky is divided into 100 counties. The capital is Frankfort. The
largest and most commercial town is Louisville, with a population, in
1853, of 51,726. The other populous towns are Lexington, pop. about
12,000, Covington, pop. 9408, Newport, Maysville and Paducah.

This State is washed along its entire northern boundary by the Ohio
river, which gives it a steam-boat navigation of 600 m., and opens to it the
inland commerce of the Ohio valley. By means of the Mississippi river,
which coasts its western boundary, it has access to the trade of the immense valley bearing the name of that river. The Cumberland river rises
in the S.E. part of the State, is about 600 m. long, and is navigable for
steam-boats to Nashville, and sometimes to Carthage. Keel-boats ascend
still higher. The Tennessee rises in Kentucky and flows about 70 m.
within it. It is navigable for steam-boats far beyond the limits of this
State. The other rivers are the Licking, Kentucky, Salt and Green; commencing at the E. and having N. W. courses, varying from 100 to 350 m.,
of which, except the Licking, there are severally navigable for steam-
boats, 62, 35, and 150 m. The Big Sandy, a tributary of the Ohio, forms
the eastern boundary for about 100 m., of which 50 are navigable. All the
important streams of Kentucky are tributaries of the Ohio.

The central and northern counties of Kentucky are hilly or undulating,
while those W. of the Cumberland river are mostly level. A range of hills
runs almost parallel with the Ohio river, with intervals of bottom land
between it and the river, varying from 10 to 20 m. wide. The Cumberland mountains form the S. E. boundary of the State, and several outlying
ridges traverse the S. E. counties, but none of them are more than 2000 ft.
high. Kentucky enjoys a medium climate, having neither the severity of
northern States nor the enervating heats of the southern. It has but 3
months' winter, and spring and autumn are mild.

The soil of Kentucky is mostly a black mould, without sand, and often
2 or 3 ft. deep; and is said to rival in fertility the most favoured parts of
the Mississippi valley. An injudicious system of culture has prevented
this State from becoming one of the leading agricultural States of the
Union. The staple products are Indian corn, tobacco, flax and hemp;
besides which, great quantities of wheat, rye, oats, wool, peas, beans, Irish
and sweet potatoes, barley, fruits, market products, butter, cheese, hay,
grass seeds, maple sugar, beeswax, and honey; and some buckwheat, rice,
wine, hops, cotton, silk and sugar-cane are produced. The quantity of flax

and hemp raised is larger than that of any other State. The quantity of tobacco is second only to that of Virginia; but if population and area are relatively considered, it is greater than that of Virginia. In the growth of Indian corn, Kentucky ranks next to Ohio, which is the first in the Union. In 1850 there were in the State 74,777 farms, occupying 11,368,270 acres of improved land.

Kentucky is generally well timbered, and in parts the cane grows to a height of 12 ft., forming extensive cane brakes, so dense that it is often difficult to pass through them. At its first settlement it was one of the best wooded of the western States. Its forest trees are the black walnut, oak, chestnut, buckeye, sugar-tree, elm, papaw, honey-locust, mulberry, ash, yellow poplar, coffee-tree, cottonwood and white-thorn. The fruit trees are the apple, pear, plum and peach. White grapes are abundant.

The geological formation of the State partakes of the carboniferous rocks, characteristic of the Mississippi valley. Below the mountains "it has at the usual depth of 8 ft., a bed of limestone, which has frequent apertures, through which the waters of the rivers sink into the earth, causing some of them to disappear for a time, and others to be greatly diminished in the summer season. The rivers have generally worn deep channels in the calcareous rocks over which they flow. The precipices formed by the Kentucky are in many places stupendous, presenting per-pendicular banks of solid limestone, 300 ft. high, above which is a steep and difficult ascent several times as high. In the S. W. part of the State, between Green and Cumberland rivers, are several remarkable caves. One called the Mammoth Cave, 130 m. from Lexington, on the road to Nash-ville, has been explored for a distance of 8 or 10 miles."

The minerals of the State are an abundance of coal, and iron, some lead, iron, pyrites, marble, freestone, gypsum, conglomerate, and cliff limestones. Salt and medicinal springs are particularly numerous in this State. Salt is extensively manufactured from these springs, and large quantities of saltpetre were procured from the Mammoth Cave during the war of 1812. It is said that probably no western State presents so great a variety of interesting objects to tourists, whether its mere pic-turesqueness, or the wild and more striking deviations from the ordinary course of nature, are regarded.

Kentucky has but few manufactures, although the amount of capital invested is considerable. In 1850 it had only 3471 establishments, each producing 500 dollars and upwards annually. Home-made manufactures amounted to 2,487,493 dollars. Of the above establishments, there were 8 cotton factories, and 25 woollen, 45 forges and furnaces and 275 tanneries.

This State has not kept pace with others, N. of the Ohio, in constructing works of intercommunication; it has, however, been fully alive to the importance of providing a cheap and expeditious means of transport for its products. In January, 1853, it had 94 m. of railroad in operation, and 661 in course of construction. The railways completed connect Frankfort with the commercial capital Louisville and Frankfort. Those projected are to connect Louisville with Chattanooga, Danville and Jeffersonville; Covington with Lexington; and Maysville with Big Sandy River and Danville.

Kentucky carries on an active trade with New Orleans and other towns on the Mississippi and Ohio rivers. The exports are hemp, salt beef, pork, bacon, butter, cheese, hogs, horses and mules. Large numbers of the two latter animals are annually driven to the Atlantic States for sale. Cotton bagging and hemp cordage are also extensively exported. In 1852 there were built in Kentucky 27 steam-boats, with an aggregate tonnage of $73127\frac{7}{95}$. The tonnage owned in the State in the same year was $11,818\frac{80}{95}$, and the foreign exports amounted to 185,559 dollars. In 1853 Louisville owned a steam marine of 26 vessels and a tonnage of 14,529, all high pressure.

In 1852 the common school fund of Kentucky amounted to 1,400,270 dollars. The number of children in the State between 5 and 16 yrs. old was 215,195, of whom 194,963 had attended the schools, but the average attendance was only 69,825. It had in this year 8 colleges, with an aggregate of 656 students, and 37,000 volumes in their libraries; likewise 1 theological school, with 18 students; 2 law schools, with 125; and 2 medical schools, with 590, showing a larger number of law and medical students in colleges than in any other State S. or W. There were, in the same year, 1818 churches owned as follows—789 by the Baptists, 522 by the Methodists, 222 by the Presbyterians, 117 by the Episcopalians, 112 by the Christians, 48 by the Roman Catholics, 32 by the Free Church, 31 by the Union Church, 15 by the Methodist Episcopal, and the balance by the African Church, German Protestants, Jews, Lutherans, Republicans, Shakers, Dunkers, Unitarians and Universalists, giving one church to every 540 persons. The public institutions are the State Lunatic Asylum at Lexington; a Deaf and Dumb Asylum at Danville; and a Blind School at Louisville. A second Lunatic Asylum has been erected at Hopkinsville, at a cost of 180,000 dollars. The State Penitentiary is at Frankfort.

Kentucky was originally included in the territory of Virginia, from which it was separated in 1790. The first English settlement was made by Col. Daniel Boone, in 1775, on the banks of the Kentucky. It was originally the battleground of the Northern and Southern Indians, and from this circumstance, together with their numerous forays upon the Whites, it was called the "Dark and bloody ground," or Kentucky. In 1792, it was admitted into the Union, as an independent State. The first governor was Isaac Shelby. The population, which at that time was about 90,000 persons, has continued rapidly to increase, until it now numbers nearly 1,000,000, and is highly prosperous and wealthy. The State now has hundreds of towns and villages.

Kentucky was the central scene of the imputed intrigues of Aaron Burr and his coadjutors to form a Western Republic. The Kentuckians, however, frank and brave in character, were not the material from which to manufacture rebels, nor was the State that gave Henry Clay to the national councils one to foster disunionists. In 1799 the present Constitution was formed. The governor is elected by the people for 4 yrs., and receives a salary of 2500 dollars per annum. The present (1855) is Lazarus W. Powell. The Senate consists of 38 members, elected for 4 yrs., and the House of Representatives of 100 members, elected for 2 yrs. The judiciary consists first, of a court of appeals, composed of 1 chief and 4 associate judges; second, of a court of chancery, presided over by a single chancellor; and third, of 12 circuit courts. All these officers are elective. The State is entitled to 10 members in the national House of Representatives, and to 12 electoral votes for President of the U. States. Its banking capital, in 1853, was 7,656,700 dollars.

(16) The Ohio river is formed by the junction of the Alleghany and Monongahela rivers at Pittsburgh. Its entire length following its windings is 950 m. Tributary rivers and creeks, to the number of 75, empty into this river, and between Pittsburgh and its mouth there are an hundred islands, besides a number of tow-heads and sand-bars. It is one of the most important rivers in the United States, having, with its tributaries, not less than 5000 m. of navigable waters, and draining an area of 200,000 sq. m. Its confluence with the Mississippi is at lat. 37° N., and lon. 89° 10′ W.

The French called this river *La Belle Rivière*, "the beautiful river," which it is said corresponds to that of the Indian appellation "Ohio." "No river in the world rolls for the same distance such a uniform smooth and placid current. Its banks are generally high and precipitous, rising into bluffs and cliffs, sometimes to the height of 300 ft. Between these bluffs and the river there is generally a strip of land, of equal width, called *bottom*. These bluffs exhibit a wild, a picturesque grandeur, which those who have never viewed nature in her primitive and unspoiled state can hardly imagine. Dense and interminable forests—trees of the most gigantic size, casting their broad shadows into the placid stream; the luxuriant and mammoth growth of the timber in the bottoms; the meanderings and frequent bends of the river, and the numberless beautiful wooded islands, all of which, in rapid succession, shift and vary the scene to the eye as you float down the endless maze before you; are calculated to fix upon the mind an indelible impression."

(17) ILLINOIS is one of the western U. States. It is bounded on the N. by Wisconsin; E. by Lake Michigan and Indiana, from the last of which it is partly separated by the Wabash river; S, by the Ohio river; and S. W. and W. by the Mississippi river. It lies between 37° and 42° 30′ N. lat., and between 87° 30′ and 91° 40′. W. lon., being about 380 m. in extreme length, from N. to S., about 200 in its greatest breadth, and 140 in its average. Area 55,405 sq. m., of which little more than one-sixth were improved in 1850. Population in 1850, 851,470, of which about one-eighth were of foreign birth. The State is divided into 100 counties, and has a number of thriving towns, rapidly increasing in population. Chicago is the largest city, and had a population in 1853 of 50,000. Other large towns are Quincy, Galena, Peoria, Springfield, the capital, and Alton.

The Illinois river, formed by the junction of the Fox and Des Plaines rivers from the N., and the Kankakee from Indiana, is the largest in the State. It has a course of 400 m., and is navigable a distance of about 250. The other rivers are Rock River, rising in Wisconsin, and flowing 300 m., mostly in Illinois; and the Kaskaskia, rising in the middle of the State, and having a course of 250 m., of which 150 are navigable for boats. Both of these, with the Illinois, empty into the Mississippi, which coasts the entire western boundary. The Ohio forms the entire southern boundary, and the Wabash part of the eastern. Little Wabash has a course of 130 m. and empties itself into the Wabash. Peoria Lake, through which the Illinois flows about 150 m. from its mouth, is a beautiful sheet of water 20 m. long and 2 broad.

"The surface of the State is generally level. It has no mountains, though the northern and southern parts are hilly and broken. The portion of the State south of a line from the mouth of the Wabash to the mouth of the Kaskaskia, is generally covered with timber, but north of this the prairie country predominates. The eye sometimes wanders over immense plains covered with grass, with no other boundary of its vision but the distant horizon, though the view is often broken by occasional woodlands. The dry prairies are generally from 30 to 100 ft. higher than the bottom lands on the rivers, and very fertile. A range of bluffs commences on the margin of the Mississippi, a short distance above the mouth of the Ohio, and extends N. beyond the Des Moines rapids, sometimes rising abruptly from the water's edge, but generally a few miles distant from it, leaving between the bluffs and the river a strip of alluvial formation of inexhaustible fertility. The banks of the Illinois and Kaskaskia, in some places, present sublime and picturesque scenery."

Illinois has a great variety of climate, extending as it does through more than 4° of lon. The seasons, though milder than those of the Atlantic States in the same lat., are very irregular. The southern part is much warmer than the northern, and cattle are frequently unhoused during the whole winter. Illinois is said to be surpassed in agricultural capabilities by no State of the Union. The great American Bottom, lying S. of the Kaskaskia, is of exceeding fertility, and has been cultivated for 100 yrs. without apparent deterioration. The number of farms in the State in 1850 was 76,208. The great staple product is Indian corn, in which Illinois stands third in the Union in the absolute amount raised, and first if the population and number of acres under cultivation are regarded. The other products are wheat, oats, Irish potatoes, hay, butter, and cheese in great quantities; rye, wool, beans, peas, barley, buckwheat, fruits, garden vegetables and some tobacco; sweet potatoes, wine, grass seeds, hops, hemp, flax, silk, maple sugar, and molasses, beeswax and honey, and the castor bean. The indigenous fruits are a variety of berries, plums, grapes, crab apples, wild cherries, persimmons and the papaw. Of orchard fruits, the apple and peach flourish the best, but pears and quinces are cultivated with facility. The shellbark, hickory, walnut and other nuts abound. The forest trees are black and white walnut, ash, hackberry, elm, sugar maple, honey locust, buckeye, catalpa, sycamore, cottonwood, pecan, hickory and oak in the bottomlands; post-oak, blackjack, hickory, black and white walnut, linn or basswood, cherry, &c., in the uplands; white and yellow poplar in the southern part of the State; and cypress on the Ohio bottoms.

The minerals of Illinois are lead, which abounds in the vicinity of Galena, bituminous coal, in almost every county, copper in abundance, and iron. The other minerals are lime, zinc, some silver, marble, freestone, gypsum and quartz crystal. There are several salt and medicinal springs.

Illinois presents few objects of interest to tourists except its wide spread prairies, decked with flowers of every hue that can please the eye; and the river bluffs, which inspire a sense of rugged grandeur. There is a cave in Hardin county, on the banks of the Ohio, called "Cave-in-Rock," which, in 1797, was the abode of a band of robbers who sallied out to rob the unfortunate boatmen and emigrants. It has since been used for the same purposes by other bands of robbers.

This State is not largely engaged in manufactures, though there are many facilities for carrying on this branch of industry. According to the census of 1850, it had 3099 manufacturing establishments, each producing

500 dollars and upwards annually. Of these establishments 16 were woollen factories, 31 were furnaces and forges, and 96 were tanneries. Homemade manufactures in the same year amounted to 1,115,902 dollars.

In 1853 Illinois had 269 m. of railroad in operation and 1772 in course of construction. Chicago, its largest city, is already connected either directly or indirectly with Detroit, Cincinnati, New York, Philadelphia and Boston, beyond the limits of the State; and with Rockford, St. Charles, Aurora and Peru, within it. There are also railroads uniting Springfield with Jackson, Naples and Alton, and Quincy with Columbus. Lines of railroad will soon exist from Chicago to almost every point in the State, and that city will have, through connection with other railroads, communication with St. Louis, Terre Haute, Louisville, Nashville, New Orleans, Mobile, Savannah and Charleston.

This State is most favourably situated for commerce, being able to communicate with the western, southern and central parts of the Mississippi Valley by means of the Mississippi, Missouri and Ohio rivers; and with the northern and eastern States, by way of the great lakes. The total tonnage of the State, in 1851, was 25,209$\frac{3}{9}$⁄$_{95}$. The imports from the lakes, in 1851, amounted to 7,820,953 dollars, and the exports to 4,435,012. The foreign exports in the same yr. amounted to 51,325 dollars, and the imports to 4832, both very inconsiderable items. Chicago does an immense business in lumber and general trade, and the tonnage of the district amounts to about 16,000. The domestic exports from Galena in 1851 amounted to 1,800,358 dollars, of which seven-ninths were lead.

In 1852 there were 3076 common schools reported in the State, and 78 district libraries. The number of children taught in these schools was 139,255, and the amount paid to teachers 310,806 dollars, of which 113,500 dollars was public money. The school fund amounted in 1852 to 951,504 dollars and 7 cents, derived from the public lands and the surplus revenue of the U. States. In the same year there were 4 colleges in the State, with an aggregate of 198 students, and 14,800 volumes in their libraries; 1 theological school (Baptist), and 1 medical. The number of churches in Illinois in 1850 was 1167, owned as follows—389 by the Methodists, 265 by the Baptists, 198 by the Presbyterians, 67 by the Christians, 58 by the Roman Catholics, 46 by the Congregationalists, 40 by the Lutherans, 31 by the Unionists, and the rest by the Africans, Concordists, German Reformed, Independents, Latter-day Saints, &c. The public institutions are the State penitentiary at Alton, and 27 libraries, with an aggregate of 19,916 volumes.

Illinois was colonized by the French, about the same time as Philadelphia. Father Marquette, a Catholic Missionary among the Indians, visited the country as early as 1673, and settlements were made at Cahokia and

Kaskaskia at the close of the 17th century. The Illinois country, as it was called, passed with the other portion of eastern Louisiana, into the hands of the English at the treaty of Paris in 1763, and into the possession of the U. States at the revolution in 1775. Settlers from Virginia located themselves in the territory, and in 1787 it became a part of the North-West Territory then created, and which embraced all the country N. of the Ohio river.

In 1800 it formed part of Indiana Territory, from which it was detached in 1809, and erected into a separate territorial government, under the title of "Illinois Territory." Ninian Edwards was the first governor under this organization and held office for 3 terms. The population at this time was about 5000. In 1818 the present State was organized and admitted into the Confederacy. The first governor of the State was Shadrach Bond. The executive power is vested in a governor and lieutenant-governor, elected by the people for 4 yrs. Joel A. Matteson is the present (1855) incumbent of the former office, and receives a salary of 1500 dollars per annum. He is also *ex-officio* fund commissioner. The legislature consists of a Senate of 25 members, and a House of Representatives with 75, both elected by the people, the former for 4 yrs. and the latter for 2. The Judiciary consists of a supreme court of 3 divisions, presided over by as many judges, and 15 circuit courts, with as many judges. All white male citizens 21 years of age and having resided in the State 6 months next preceding an election are qualified voters. Illinois sends 9 members to the national House of Representatives and has 11 electoral votes for President of the U. States. At the close of 1852 there were 17 banks in the State.

After the expatriation of the Latter-day Saints from Missouri, they found in this State a shelter and protection from their merciless and unrelenting foes. The city of Quincy and other neighbourhoods acted in a benevolent manner towards the refugees as they crossed the Mississippi, and prosperity again smiled upon them. At length Nauvoo was built and incorporated, and many other thriving settlements made; but few years had elapsed before the Saints were again subjected to annoyances and persecution in this State. In 1844 Joseph and Hyrum Smith were assassinated at Carthage while under the protection and pledge of safety of the governor of the State, Thomas Ford; and in 1846 the Saints were as ruthlessly expelled from Illinois as they had been from Missouri. These transactions, however, will be further noticed under Nauvoo and Carthage.

(18) St. Louis is the largest city of Missouri, a port of entry, and the seat of justice of St. Louis county. It is situated in lat. 38° 37′ 28″ N., and lon. 90° 15′ 16″ W., and is, by Conclin's River Guide, 1173½ m. from

New Orleans, although it is usually called 1200. [George Conclin's *New River Guide, or a gazetteer of all the towns on the western waters: containing sketches of the cities, towns, and countries bordering on the Ohio and Mississippi rivers . . . with forty-four maps* was published in Cincinnati. It saw four editions between 1849 and 1855.] It is 17 m. below the Missouri river, and 128 E. from Jefferson City. Pop. in 1850, 77,850, of which 2650 were slaves, and 40,414 were born in foreign countries. According to a writer in the *St. Louis Republican* of July 14, 1854, the population was then estimated at 120,000. The situation of St. Louis is very beautiful; it rises from the river by two plateaux of limestone formation, the first 20 ft., and the other 60, above the floods of the Mississippi. The first rises rather abruptly, but the second more gradually, spreading out into a large plain affording fine views of the city and river. The city and suburbs extend nearly 7 m. by the curve of the river, and about 3 back, but the thickly settled portion is only about 2½ m. in length and 1¼ in breadth. The streets, which are well laid out, are 60 ft. wide, and Front Street, running along the levée, is 100. They chiefly intersect each other at right angles. Front, Main and Second Streets, parallel to each other and the river, are occupied with the principal wholesale establishments. Fourth Street is the fashionable promenade and contains the finest retail stores. The streets parallel with the river and Front Street are named Second Street, Third Street, &c., and those to the right and left of Market Street, and at right angles with the river, generally bear the name of some forest trees. The only square is Lafayette, in the southern section of the city. St. Louis is handsomely built, and the principal material used is brick, although limestone is used to some extent. It is said to have improved more rapidly in the style of its public buildings than any city of the Union. A writer before referred to says—"In beauty, strength and durability, in adaptation to the various purposes for which it is designed, few cities even now excel St. Louis, and we are every year advancing." A new court-house has lately been built at a cost of nearly 500,000 dollars. It is built of Genevieve limestone and occupies an entire square. The "Centre Market Buildings," a handsome structure, has lately been erected to supply the place of the former "Market and Town-house." In 1829, there were 4 churches in the city, the Catholic, the Presbyterian, the Episcopal, and the Baptist; they are all now pulled down, and in 1854 about 65 existed, several of which cost above 100,000 dollars. They are distributed among the Catholics, Methodists, Presbyterians, Episcopalians, Unitarians, Jews, Evangelicals, L.D. Saints, and others. The finest of these are St. George's (Episcopal); the Catholic Cathedral; the Church of the Messiah, a Gothic edifice, belonging to the Unitarians. The Cathedral is 136 ft. long, and

84 wide, with a front of polished freestone, 58 ft. high, adorned with a Doric portico. It has a chime of bells, weighing 2600 lbs. The U. S. Arsenal is a large and imposing building inclosed by handsomely ornamented grounds. Jefferson barracks are about 13 m. below on the bank of the river. The chief hotels are the Planter's House, the U. States hotel, the Virginia hotel, the Missouri hotel, and the Munroe House.

Improvements have gone on so rapidly in this prosperous city, that the value of real estate has advanced at an amazing ratio. For instance, in 1833 a block situated between Fourth and Fifth Streets and Locust and St. Charles Streets was sold for 6000 dollars, and is now worth 182,000. Land in many situations which 15 or 20 yrs. ago sold for 33 or 34 dollars per front foot now realizes 600 dollars. Real estate investments on Front and Main Streets vary from 700 to 800 dollars per front foot. The revenue of the city 20 yrs. ago was 4765 dollars and 98 cents, now the assessed valuation is 39,397,186 dollars, upon which a tax of 413,670 dollars is collected. From the sales of licenses 46,000 dollars more is raised. In 1853, the assessed value of merchandise amounted to 8,744,786 dollars and 64 cents. In 1829 the highest tax paid by any individual was 532 dollars, now one gentleman, J. H. Lucas, pays in his own name a city tax of 14,000 dollars, and conjointly with others a still further sum. The Water-works are of considerable importance and embrace 35¼ m. of pipe. The main reservoir is capable of containing 5,000,000 gallons of water. In addition to this, arrangements are being made to construct a new reservoir with a capacity of 52,000,000 gallons, the cost of which it is estimated will be about 100,000 dollars. Gas-works of great magnitude have also been put in operation within the past 6 yrs. Already 33 m. of street pipe are laid in the city. The levée 20 yrs. ago was a mere mud bank. Great expenditures have been made upon it, bringing about very important changes. Last spring the governmental authorities made an appropriation of 200,000 dollars for its improvement. The harbour also is undergoing considerable improvement. A roadway from the Illinois shore to and across Blood Island is approaching completion and will be 3 ft. above high-water mark.

Although manufactures are in an infantile state in St. Louis, they are scarcely less important than its commerce. In 1850 there were 1300 establishments in operation, comprising about 100 different manufactures, which amounted in value to 15,000,000 dollars, and it is supposed that at the present time the business of 1852 has been doubled in amount. The manufactures of iron exceed those of any other city on the Mississippi, if not in the West. During the last year as much as 100 tons of that metal were daily melted in the various founderies of the city, and lead pipe was manufactured to the amount of over 2,000,000 lbs., and sheet lead 1,250,000 lbs. St. Louis supplies the whole valley of the Mississippi with the latter article. There is one shot tower in the city, which made in 5 months 2,422,835 lbs. of shot of all sizes. Belcher's sugar refinery is one of the largest in the Union, and in 1852 produced 6563 bxs., 7658 hhds., 12,457 bls., and 29,848 bags of refined sugar, besides 103,550 pkgs., and 10,567 bls. refined from molasses and cane syrup. Other manufactures are the flouring business, of which more is done than in any city of the Union; chemicals and oils; tobacco; hemp and ball rope. Coopering and meat packing are also important businesses in the city.

St. Louis enjoys great natural advantages for a commercial emporium, being situated almost at the focus, at which converge the Mississippi, Missouri, Ohio, and the Illinois rivers, and nearly in the centre of the fine agricultural region drained by those streams. With such facilities and the completion of the vast system of railroads now contemplated, together with those already in operation, it cannot but increase in wealth and prosperity, at a much greater ratio than it has hitherto done. Each stream which contributes to the commerce of this port has its regular packets, and for the most part, a separate place of landing. The aggregate arrivals of steamboats at St. Louis during 1852 was 3184. The shipping owned in this district in the same year amounted to 37,861$\frac{51}{95}$ tons, enrolled and licensed, of which 32,646$\frac{18}{95}$ were employed in steam navigation. The following table will show the leading imports for the yr. ending December, 1852—

Articles	1852	Articles	1852
Pork, bbls. and tierces	69,010	Lead, pigs	409,314
Beef " "	17,709	Sugar, hhds.	35,283
Lard " "	42,515	Sugar, bbls. and bxs.	27,672
Lard, kegs	11,815	Coffee, bags	96,240
Bacon, casks and hhds.	11,215	Molasses, bbls.	54,935
Bacon, pieces	18,809	Salt, sacks	266,616
Flour, bbls.	135,333	Salt, bbls.	42,281
Wheat, bushels	1,591,886	Hides	97,148
Corn, "	689,440	Whisky, brls.	46,446
Oats, "	646,162	Barley and Malt, sacks	47,264
Hemp, tons	8,187	Bagging, pieces	3,650
Rope, coils	42,121	Nails, kegs	42,201
Tobacco, hhds.	14,053	Lumber, feet	16,810,575

Other principal domestic imports are butter, cheese, tallow, hay, furs, fruits, beans, seeds, potatoes, onions, feathers and beeswax. This port is also one of the most important in the West for the shipment of cattle; over 300 head a week were sent in 1853 to southern markets. The following table represents the foreign merchandise entered at the Custom House for the year ending December, 1852—

Articles	1852	Articles	1852
	Dols.		Dols.
Sugar and Molasses	413,172	Burr stones	420
Hardware, cutlery, &c.	118,276	Drugs and Medicines	756
Railroad iron	132,894	Cigars	5,773
Earthern and glass ware	80,729		
Tin-plate, tin, iron, copper, &c.	59,826	Total	954,946
Dry and fancy goods	110,814	Duties collected	290,168
Brandy, wine, gin, cordials, &c.	32,985		

The bank of the State of Missouri (whose charter expires in 1856) is the only chartered Banking institution in St. Louis or Missouri.

The benevolent institutions of St. Louis are scarcely commensurate with the demands made upon public charity. Among the principal may be mentioned the City Hospital, the Marine Hospital, the Sisters Hospital, the House for the Friendless, the House of Refuge, and about 9 Orphan Asylums.

The literary and educational institutions of St. Louis are said to be, considering their recent origin, excellent in a high degree. St. Xavier's college, now known as the St. Louis University, under the direction of the R. Catholics, is "a well ordered, well sustained, and efficient institution." The medical department of the Missouri University is located in this city. It was founded in 1840, and had, in the winter of 1852–3, 92 students attending its lectures. The Mercantile Library Association of St. Louis, organized in 1846 and incorporated in 1851, occupies a fine building in the Italian style and has upwards of 7000 volumes in its library, besides serials and newspapers. The number of members is about 800. The common schools are the pride and glory of St. Louis and are attended by upwards of 5000 pupils. The property belonging to them amounts to about 500,000 dollars, and the income in 1853 amounted to 43,000 dollars. There are about 25 publishing officers in the city. Seven or eight newspapers are published daily. The *Times* and *Republican* have tri-weekly and weekly editions, and several have weekly editions. Four or five are printed in the German language.

The site on which St. Louis stands was selected on the 15th of Feb., 1764, as one possessing peculiar advantages for the fur trade and for defence against the Indians. The confluence of the great rivers in the immediate neighbourhood, which was a desideratum in the estimation of the trappers, has contributed much to render it a place of great importance as a centre for agricultural and manufacturing enterprise. On the 11th of August, 1768, Rious, a Spanish officer, and a company of Spanish troops, took possession of St. Louis and Upper Louisiana, in the name of his Catholic Majesty, and on the 26th of March, 1804, it was transferred to the U. States. At this time its population was about 1000 souls. In 1813 the first brick house was built, but as late as 1815 "St. Louis was a French town extending along the river, in long narrow, and sometimes filthy streets, lined with frail wooden tenements, contrasting strongly with the few large stone houses, plaistered and whitewashed, near the river, and the romantic circular stone forts in the rear, also whitewashed with lime." In 1817, the first steam-boat arrived. In 1822 St. Louis was chartered as a city, under the title given to it by Laclede in honour of Louis XV of France. During the 5 years between 1825 and 1830 emigration from Illinois began to be of importance, and from this State St. Louis received its first great commercial impulse and still derives much of its support. With 1829 the keel-boat disappeared. The steamer *Yellow Stone* about this time ascended to the Great Falls, and was succeeded by the *Assinaboine* and others. It was between these two periods that St. Louis laid the foundation for the fast increase in wealth and population which has so distinguished it. The town had already become the great emporium of the upper Mississippi in trade, arts and manufactures, and, in point of commercial importance, as well as population, stood second only to New Orleans. In addition to its advantages as a commercial port and the depôt of the American Fur Company, it carried on a great trade with Santa Fé and the Mexican States, by means of caravans, across the great American desert, via Independence, Mo. But the introduction of steam power in the navigation of the Mississippi and its tributaries gave a new and powerful impulse to St. Louis, increased its importance, and caused it to advance in a direct ratio to the successful extension of steam navigation on the western waters.

About 1840 the manufactories for the supply of materials used in the construction of steam-boats began to rival those of Pittsburgh, Cincinnati and Louisville, and before the year 1844 the most splendid specimen of western steam-engines and boat-building issued from this port. The population and prosperity of the city have continued from that time to increase in a regularly progressive manner, until it has reached its present wealthy and populous position, and it is becoming a general opinion that St. Louis will ere long take its place as the western metropolis of the U. States. Since the great emigration to California, Oregon, and Utah commenced, it has been the mart at which the emigrants have chiefly made their purchases for their outfit.

St. Louis has been for years the residence of numbers of L. D. Saints, some of them emigrants from different parts of the world on their way to Nauvoo, Council Bluffs, or Utah, and many of them American converts. Owing to the rapid advancement of the city, the unemployed have found labour, and many have thus completed their outfit for the remainder of their journey. At the present time there are between 1300 and 1400 in the city and vicinity, presided over by Elder Milo Andrus, from G. S. L. City, and formerly a missionary to England.

At a General Conference of the Church, at G. S. L. City, commencing April 6, 1854, St. Louis was named as a place to which the L. D. Saints might gather with approbation who were unable to go directly through to Utah, and Elder Erastus Snow, one of the Twelve Apostles, was appointed to superintend all the interests of the Church in that part of the U. States. In pursuance of these instructions, President Snow held a Conference in Fourth Street Chapel, commencing on the 4th of Nov., 1854, at which St. Louis was organized as a Stake of Zion. Elder Milo Andrus was appointed President, and Elders Charles Edwards and George Gardner Counsellors. The following Elders were appointed for the standing High Council—James H. Hart, Andrew Sprowle, John Evans, William Morrison, James Sherlock Cantwell, William Lowe, Samuel James Lees, Edward Cook, James Brooks, William Grove, John Clegg, and Charles Chard. Elder Kleber Worley was ordained to the office of Bishop, and Thomas Harris and Edmund Holdsworth were appointed to be his Counsellors. Elder Robert Windley was set apart as President of the Elders' quorum; Priest William Becker, as President of the Priests' quorum; and Teacher Seal, as President of the Teachers' quorum. While in session, the Conference voted to adopt the law of Tithing throughout the Stake. President Snow edits and publishes a weekly paper in St. Louis, entitled the *St. Louis Luminary*, devoted to science, religion, general intelligence and news of the day.

(19) The MISSOURI RIVER ("Mud River") is the largest tributary stream in the world and has its source in the Rocky Mountains, nearly in the same latitude as that of the Mississippi. (47° N.) The bed of the river commences at the confluence of three small streams—Jefferson, Madison and Gallatin, running nearly parallel to each other, and not far from the head-waters of the Columbia, which flows W. to the Pacific Ocean. Its entire length from its source until it reaches the Mississippi, is computed to be about 3785 m., and steam-boats have navigated it for a distance of 2200 m. Its course is first circuitously along the base of the Rocky Mountains, then E. till it reaches the N. W. extremity of Minnesota; thence it flows S. S. E. and separates that territory, the State of Iowa, and a part of that of Missouri, from Nebraska and Kansas territories on the W., traverses the State of Missouri, and joins the Mississippi 17 m. above St. Louis. Its affluents are very numerous, but the most important are the Yellow Stone, the Nebraska or Platte, and the Kansas. At a distance of about 400 m. from the source of the Missouri are what are termed the Gates of the Rocky Mountains. For a distance of about 6 m. the rocks

rise perpendicularly from the water's edge, to a height of 1200 ft., the river is compressed to a width of 150 yds., and for the first 3 m. there is but one spot, and that only a few yds. in extent, on which a man could stand between the water and these perpendicular walls. The scenery at this place has an aspect of extreme loneliness and grandeur. About 110 m. below are the Great Falls, next to those of Niagara, the grandest in N. America. Throughout the greater part of its course the Missouri is a turbid stream, but there is no serious obstacle to navigation from its mouth to the Great Falls, except, perhaps, its shallowness in times of drought. There is a succession of minor falls and rapids below the Great Falls, causing a descent of 357 ft. in 16½ m. The flood from the Missouri does not reach the Mississippi, until the rise in the Red, Arkansas and Ohio rivers has nearly subsided. Its stream is so rapid and sweeping in its course, and its bed is composed of such masses of sand, that it is continually shifting its bars, and a chart of it one year is a poor guide for navigating it the next.

The bottoms of the river are higher, more sandy, and not so wet as those of the upper Mississippi, while its alluvions are somewhat narrower, their medial width being for the first 500 m. about 4 m. It seldom overflows its banks in this distance and is little inclined to be swampy. There are fewer lakes, bayous and small ponds than along the Mississippi, and there are no prairies to be seen on its banks for the first 400 m. of its course. Within the State of Missouri the banks of the river are heavily timbered, but beyond that distance they are very destitute of wood. The river sometimes washes the bases of the Dark Hills of a friable and crumbling soil. Its first explorers, Lewis and Clark, found here many singular petrifactions, both animal and vegetable, and on the top of one of the hills the petrified skeleton of a fish 45 ft. long. The entire extent of area drained by this river is estimated about 500,000 sq. m.

(20) KEOKUK is situated at the S. E. corner of the State of Iowa, at the foot of the "Lower Rapids" of the Mississippi river, which are 11 m. in extent, in the course of which the river has a fall of 24 ft. It is a very flourishing town, and at the head of navigation for the larger class of steamers, and the natural outlet of the fertile valley of the Des Moines, the most populous part of the State. Magnificent steam-packets ply between St. Louis and this place, and the number of arrivals at Keokuk in 1852 was stated to be 795. The town contains the medical department of the State University, 6 or 7 churches, 3 academies, several public schools, and a hospital. There are about 90 stores in the town, 2 flouring mills, and 2 iron founderies. The reported sales of merchandise at this place in 1852 amounted to 1,345,000 dollars. A railroad to Dubuque,

180 m. in length, is in course of construction. There are two weekly papers, and one medical, published in this town. Opposite Keokuk the Mississippi is about 1 m. wide. The river flows on a bed of limestone and is bordered by bluffs, which rise abruptly nearly 100 ft. high. Between these bluffs there is an island 1700 ft. wide.

Up to 1853, the point of outfit for the plains for the L. D. Saints had been at Kanesville, Council Bluffs, on the Missouri river, at the western boundary of Iowa. The merchants and traders of this place had commenced a system of inordinate speculation upon emigrants, which, in connection with the somewhat dangerous ascent of the Missouri and the sickliness of its bottoms, caused the point of outfit to be changed to the Mississippi river. Elder Isaac C. Haight, who had charge of the emigration over the Plains in 1853, selected Keokuk for that purpose, being a healthy locality, and otherwise suitable. This change, however, increased the land travel the whole breadth of Iowa which lies between Keokuk and Council Bluffs. Arrangements were made by Elder Haight with the St. Louis packet line to take the Saints with their luggage, on their arrival at St. Louis, from one boat to another, so that they might not be detained there more than 24 hours. The company which left England in the *Jersey* was not detained there over one night. Excellent arrangements were also made at Keokuk and Sugar Creek for camping and organizing the emigrants, previously to departure for G. S. L. Valley, and owing to the liberality of the inhabitants of those places no expense was incurred. The Mayor of Keokuk and other influential men rendered every assistance and seemed highly gratified and pleased with the temporary residence of the Saints among them. At Sugar Creek a field of 2000 acres was placed at the service of the emigrants by one gentleman.

Before setting out from Keokuk, it was necessary that an organization should be made of the Camp, and consequently Elder Haight appointed captains of hundreds, of fifties, and of tens. Each had a certain number of teams to preside over and likewise had a general superintendence of all things pertaining to the journey. Pioneers were selected to go in advance to search out suitable camping grounds. Chaplains were appointed to accompany the Camp, to see that the regular Church services, especially that of the Lord's Supper, were attended to on the Sabbath day, that all persons attended meetings, and to visit the sick, &c. Guards were selected to stand watch at night when the Camp came to a halt, and to announce the hours. A council of the whole Camp, presided over by the President of the entire company, had jurisdiction in all cases of dispute or of conduct unbecoming Saints.

The healthfulness of Keokuk was such that few deaths occurred while the emigrants were encamped there. The last company of teams started on the Plains about the 20th of June, and reached the Missouri river about the 20th of July, at which time the water was high, the spring freshets having been higher in the previous spring than was ever known since white men had set foot upon its banks. The emigrants were remarkably healthy on arriving at this point, and only about 100 chose to remain behind, "some to apostatize and others to go on the next season." The road between Keokuk and Council Bluffs lies to the N. W., and passes through beautiful woodland scenery and prairies with grass varying from 1 to 7 ft. in height, affording good feed for cattle.

In 1854 Elder Wm. Empey, who conducted the European emigration over the Plains selected as the point of outfit, Kansas on the Missouri river, on the western frontiers of the State of Missouri, and 14 m. N. W. of Independence, which again introduced some portion of the route avoided in the previous year, and much sickness and death resulted, chiefly, however, from cholera. The inhabitants of Kansas were hospitable to the emigrants, and rendered them some assistance. The route taken from this point was to the Big Blue river, and thence to the Nebraska or Platte river—through the present newly organized territories of Kansas and Nebraska. A few American companies of Saints started from Fort Leavenworth and pursued a road which intersects that above named, beyond the Big Blue. These routes from the Mississippi and Missouri rivers will be found marked on the map which will be issued before the completion of this Work.

(21) NAUVOO, or the *Beautiful,* is situated on the E. bank of the Mississippi, in Hancock county, Illinois, near the head of the Lower Rapids. By Conclin's guide, it is 192 m. above St. Louis. The site of Nauvoo is one of the most beautiful on the river. The ground rises gradually from the river and presents a smooth and regular surface with a plain at the summit. [Nauvoo is a Hebrew verb form with the root meaning "comely" or "beautiful." Joseph Smith, who had studied Hebrew with Joshua Seixas in Kirtland, Ohio, in 1836, disliked the name Commerce, and changed it to Nauvoo in 1839.]

Nauvoo was first settled by the L. D. Saints, in 1839, at their expulsion from Missouri. At this time that district of Illinois was very thinly populated, and a little settlement called Commerce, the spot first settled by the Saints, was the name given to the whole neighbourhood. There extensive purchases of land were made of Dr. Isaac Galland, Mr. White, D. H. Wells, and others, on which the Saints located. Joseph and Hyrum Smith removed there directly after their escape from jail in Missouri. At first the situation was extremely unhealthy, and the Saints, having suffered much from persecution and otherwise, were easy victims to sickness; but the place afterwards became more congenial to health. On the 5th of October, at a General Conference of the Church, Joseph Smith presiding, Commerce was appointed a stake of Zion and place of gathering for the Saints. William Marks was appointed president of the Stake, and George W. Harris, Samuel Bent, Henry G. Sherwood, David Fullmer, Alpheus Cutler, William Huntington, Thomas Grover, Newel Knight, Charles C. Rich, David Dort, Seymour Brunson and Lewis D. Wilson, members of the High Council. Newel K. Whitney was appointed Bishop of the middle ward, Edward Partridge of the upper, and Vinson Knight of the lower. On the 21st of October James Mulholland was appointed Clerk of the Land Contracts, and Henry G. Sherwood, to sell town lots, of which 500 dollars was to be the standard value—none were to be sold for less than 200, nor more than 800. In November the first number of the "Times and Seasons," the first paper published in Commerce, was issued by Ebenezer Robinson and Don Carlos Smith. On the 21st of April, 1840, the Postmaster-General of the U. S. changed the name of Commerce to that of Nauvoo, and George W. Robinson was appointed postmaster. The whole settlement then contained 250 houses and was rapidly increasing in population.

On the 3rd of October following, it was resolved at a General Conference to petition the State Legislature to incorporate the town of Nauvoo, and Joseph Smith, John C. Bennett and Robert B. Thompson were appointed to draft a petition and a bill. At the same Conference it was resolved to build a "House of the Lord," and Reynolds Cahoon, Elias Higbee and Alpheus Cutler were set apart for the building committee. A resolution was passed to commence it within 10 days from that date, and to appropriate every 10th day to the building of the edifice. On the 14th of September, Nauvoo and the L. D. Saints throughout the world were called to mourn the death of the first Patriarch of the whole Church —Joseph Smith, Senr., who died in that town, after sharing in all the troubles and persecutions of the L. D. Saints from their first existence. The bill for the incorporation of the town was presented to the Legislature and passed the House of Representatives with only one or two dissenting voices, and the Senate with no opposition whatever. The Charter for the "City of Nauvoo," including charters for the "Nauvoo Legion," and the "University of the City of Nauvoo," was signed by Governor Thomas Carlin on the 16th of December, 1840, and took effect from the 1st of February following. The 4th Sec. of the Act provided for a city council, which consisted of a mayor, 4 aldermen, and 9 councillors, who held office for 2 yrs., or until their successors were appointed. By the 7th Sec. all free, white, male inhabitants, who were of the age of 21 yrs., who were entitled to vote for state officers, and had been residents of the city

60 days next preceding an election, were entitled to vote for city officers. The 24th Sec. empowered the City Council to establish within the limits of the city, an institution for the teaching of the arts, sciences and learned professions, to be called the "University of the City of Nauvoo." The 25th invested it with power to organize the inhabitants of the city, subject to military duty, into a body of independent military men, to be called the "Nauvoo Legion." The Legion was to perform the same amount of military duty, as was then, or thereafter might be, required of the regular militia of the State, and was at the disposal of the Mayor, in executing the laws and ordinances of the City Corporation and the laws of the State; and at the disposal of the Governor for the public defence, and the execution of the laws of the State and of the U. States, and was entitled to its proportion of the public arms. The Legion was exempt from all other military duty. On the whole, the Act was said to be very broad and liberal, and to confer most plenary powers on the corporators. Joseph Smith, in speaking of it himself, says—"I concocted it for the salvation of the Church, and on principles so broad that every honest man might dwell secure under its protective influence, without distinction of sect or party."

Having laid this foundation for the gathering of the Saints, a proclamation was issued on the 15th of January, 1841, by the First Presidency of the Church—Joseph Smith, Sidney Ridgon and Hyrum Smith, inviting the wealthy to remove to Nauvoo and neighbourhood, and establish and build up manufactories in the city, and purchase and cultivate farms in the country, that a permanent inheritance might be secured, and the way prepared for the gathering of the poor. At this time the population of the city was upwards of 3000. John C. Bennett, M.D., was elected first mayor. An early ordinance, passed by the Corporation, was one in relation to religious liberty. It provided that all religious sects and denominations should have free toleration and equal privileges within the city, and that any person ridiculing or abusing another on account of his religious belief, should, on conviction thereof before the Mayor or Municipal Court, be fined in any sum not exceeding 500 dollars, or imprisoned not exceeding 6 months. On the 3rd of February ordinances were passed organizing the Nauvoo Legion and the University, and on the 15th, one was passed regulating the sale of intoxicating liquors, with a view to prevent the introduction of drunkenness into the city. On the 10th of March the State Legislature passed "An Act to incorporate the Nauvoo Agricultural and Manufacturing Association, in the county of Hancock." The object of this association was the promotion of agriculture and husbandry in all their branches, and for the manufacture of flour, timber and such other articles as were necessary for the ordinary purposes of life. Capital 100,000 dollars, with power to increase it to 300,000. On the same date the "Nauvoo House Association" was chartered, capital 150,000 dollars.

At a General Conference in Nauvoo, on the 6th of April, the foundation of a temple, the ruins of which are shown by our engraving, was laid, according to the resolution taken at the previous October Conference, and in the meantime, on the 19th of January, a revelation from the Lord on the subject had been given. The day was most anxiously looked for, and many strangers assembled to witness the ceremony. At length the day arrived, and was ushered in by loud peals of artillery calling to the field the Legion, consisting of 14 companies and 2 volunteer companies of militia from Iowa. About half-past 9 o'clock the military were reviewed by Joseph Smith, Lieut-General of the Legion; after which the procession was formed, and marched to the Temple ground as follows—Lieut-General Smith, Brig-Generals Law and Smith, aides-de-camp and conspicuous strangers, general staff, 2nd Cohort (infantry), ladies eight abreast, gentlemen eight abreast, 1st Cohort (cavalry). The oration was delivered by President Rigdon. The S. E. corner stone was laid by the First Presidency; the S. W. by Pres. Don C. Smith and his counsellors of the High Priests' quorum; the N. W. by the High Council, representing the Twelve Apostles who were then in Gt. Britain; and the N. E. corner by the Bishops. The vast assembly then separated, the whole having passed off in harmony, and no contention or discord having appeared. Persons unconnected with the Church for once forgot their prejudices and took pleasure on the occasion.

President Heber C. Kimball, writing from Nauvoo in July, 1841, described the appearance of the city at that time in the following language—"You know there were not more than thirty buildings in the city when we left about two years ago; but at this time there are 1200, and hundreds of others in progress, which will be finished soon. On Friday last 70 Saints came to Nauvoo, led by Lorenzo Barnes, from Chester county, Pennsylvania, in wagons, living in tents by the way. On the next day, a company came in wagons from Canada, all in good spirits, and in two or three days after, they all obtained places to live in. They are coming in from all parts of this vast continent daily and hourly, and the work is spreading in all of this land and calls for preaching in all parts. You will recollect when we built our houses in the woods there was not a house within half a mile of us. Now the place, wild as it was at that time, is converted into a thickly populated village." Another account of the rapid progress which Nauvoo had then made, and of its thriving condition, we quote from the *St. Louis Atlas*—"The population of Nauvoo is between 8000 and 9000, and of course the largest town in the State of Illinois. How long the Latter-day Saints will hold together and exhibit their present aspect, it is not for us to say. At this moment, they present the appearance of an enterprising, industrious, sober and thrifty population, such a population, indeed, as in the respects just mentioned, having no rivals east, and we rather guess, not even west of the Mississippi." In July, 1842, Dr. J. C. Bennett was expelled from the Church, in Nauvoo, for disgraceful conduct. [Dr. John C. Bennett later wrote an extremely damaging book, *The History of the Saints; or an Exposé of Joe Smith and Mormonism* (Boston, 1842). It was first printed as a series of letters to the *Sangamo Journal*. Much of what he said about polygamy was later inadvertently verified by Mormon historians themselves, but the book remains difficult to judge because Bennett was such a scoundrel.] He had previously resigned the office of mayor; and was succeeded by Joseph Smith. Before the close of 1842 a vast improvement had taken place. The city, which then extended 3 or 4 m. on the river, and about the same distance back, had been regularly laid off into blocks, containing 4 lots of 11 by 12 rods each, between 700 and 800 houses had been erected, and the population numbered about 15,000. Two steam mills and 2 printing presses existed, and buildings for various manufactures were rapidly going up. In the meantime, the Temple and Nauvoo House were progressing. The city had been settled scarcely 3 yrs., and by a people who came to it nearly destitute of every worldly thing, but it is impossible that any city could present a greater claim for improvement effected in the same amount of time by the industry of its own inhabitants than did Nauvoo. It is true, there were then no expensive mansions nor finished public buildings, but the city presented, in its numerous well-built houses and well cultivated farms and gardens, "a pattern of mechanical skill, domestic economy, practical temperance, common intelligence, and every day virtue." Nor was the mercantile business great, but that circumstance only promoted the increase of home manufactures and self-reliance.

Notwithstanding all these signs of industry and of consequent prosperity, the people of Illinois imbibed the same persecuting spirit which had followed the L. D. Saints in all their wanderings. On the election of Thomas Ford to the office of Governor of Illinois, he expressed himself dissatisfied with the privileges granted to Nauvoo in the Charter of incorporation, under which the citizens had prospered and brought Nauvoo to an eminence above that of all other cities of the State. Some members of the Legislature talked of modification, and others, more rabid, of annulling all the charters granted to the city. The bias of the public mind in Illinois was not, however, fully against the people at that time, and consequently the charters were not interfered with, and the citizens, anxious to believe that the unfounded prejudice against them would ultimately wear itself out, continued in their usual avocations, all tending to increase the importance of Nauvoo. Occasionally, honourable individuals, who had visited the city, would publish accounts which contradicted many of the false reports in circulation against the people, which in many cases enlisted the sympathies and respect of persons far and near, and, in some measure, postponed the day of calamity which awaited it and its citizens. A Mr. Prior, a Methodist minister, who visited the place in the spring of 1843, wrote of it and the people as follows— "At length the city burst upon my sight, and how sadly was I disappointed. Instead of seeing a few miserable log cabins and mud hovels, which I expected to find, I was surprised to see one of the most romantic places that I had visited in the west. The buildings, though many of them were small and of wood, yet bore the marks of neatness which I have not seen equalled in this country. The far-spread plain at the bottom of the hill was dotted over with the habitations of men with such majestic profusion, that I was almost willing to believe myself mistaken; and instead of being in Nauvoo, of Illinois, among Mormons, that I was in Italy at the city of Leghorn (which the location of Nauvoo resembles very much), and among the eccentric Italians. I gazed for some time with fond admiration upon the plain below. Here and there arose a tall, majestic brick house, speaking loudly of the genius and untiring labour of the inhabitants, who have snatched the place from the clutches of obscurity, and wrested it from the bonds of disease; and in two or three short years, rescued it from a dreary waste to transform it into one of the first cities in the west. The hill upon which I stood was covered over with the dwellings of men, and amid them was seen to rise the hewn stone and already accomplished work of the temple, which is now raised 15 or 20 ft. above the level of the ground. The few trees that were permitted to stand were now in full foliage, and were scattered with a sort of fantastic irregularity over the slope of the hill. I passed on into the more active parts of the city, looking into every street and lane to observe all that was passing. I found all the people engaged in some useful and healthy employment. The place was alive with business—much more so than any place I have visited since the hard times commenced. I sought in vain for any thing that bore the marks of immorality; but was both astonished and highly pleased at my ill success. I could see no loungers about the streets, nor any drunkards about the taverns. I did not meet with those distorted features of ruffians, or with the ill-bred or impudent. I heard not an oath in the place. I saw not a gloomy countenance; all were cheerful, polite, and industrious. I conversed with many leading men, and found them social and well-informed, hospitable and generous. I saw nothing but order and regulation in the society. Where then, I exclaimed, is all this startling proof of the utter profligacy of Nauvoo? Where, in the name of God, is the immorality charged upon the citizens of it; and what dreadful out-breaking crimes have given men the license to deprecate this place as much as they do? Where is the gang of marauders, horse thieves and ruffians, the drunkards and vicious men of Nauvoo? Where are the horrid forms of human beings distorted with hellish rage and maddened ire? Where are the dark and diabolical superstitions? Where are those specimens of credulity and ignorance? Where are those damning doctrines of demons? Where, in fine, is this slough, this sink of iniquity of which I have heard so much? Surely not in Nauvoo. They must have got the wrong place, or wilfully lied about it. I could but blush with disappointed shame for my friends who had so misinformed me, and very soon made up my mind, like the Queen of Sheba, not to believe any reports of enemies but to always, like her, go and see for myself."

Indeed, Nauvoo was now rapidly advancing in population, wealth and every other characteristic of a great city. An Englishman, who saw it at that time, and wrote a letter to the *Times and Seasons,* said—"Look and see what they have done at Nauvoo during the comparatively short time they have been there. If they are enabled to proceed as they have commenced, their town ere long will become a mighty city. I do not believe that there is another people in existence who could have made such improvement in the same length of time under the same circumstances."

The happiness and prosperity of the people of Nauvoo, however, were frequently interrupted by the unrelenting persecution of Joseph Smith and the Saints by their old enemies, the Missourians. Various demands for Joseph were made upon the Governor of Illinois, by the Governor of Missouri, and, although he was not given up, it subjected him to numerous law-suits, entailing fearful expense, which impoverished the Saints. There were also troubles arising out of the conduct of various individuals—W. Law, F. M. Higbee, Dr. Robert D. Foster and others, in Nauvoo, professedly members of the Church. At length matters reached the culminating point, in the assassination of Joseph and Hyrum Smith at Carthage, on the 27th of June, 1844, by which Nauvoo was deprived of two of its great master spirits, under whose wise policy and judicious watch-care it had risen from the wilderness to a city of 15,000 or 20,000 inhabitants. The immediate circumstances which produced this event are too lengthy for us to detail here, but we may remark that the individuals above named after having failed in their attempts, before the Municipal Court of Nauvoo, to fasten charges of immorality upon Joseph Smith, united in the establishment within the city of a newspaper, called the *Nauvoo Expositor,* having for its object the defamation of the citizens who were not of their party. [Only one issue of the *Nauvoo Expositor* appeared. It was devoted in large part to a description of the polygamous activities of Joseph Smith, much of which seems to have been accurate.] The foulest libels upon Joseph Smith's private character, and that of other persons, appeared in its columns, and its prospectus actually proposed the repeal of the City Charter; with a view, no doubt, to the destruction of the place. The City Council falling back upon their prerogatives, contained in the Charter (Sec. 13) and in the Legislative Powers of the City Council (Sec. 7), declared the *Expositor,* on account of its filthy contents, a nuisance, and ordered its abatement, which was carried out by the City Marshall and the police. Its proprietors then went to Carthage, the county seat, and sued out a writ against the Mayor, Marshall, and police for a riot! The constable from Carthage executing the writ was requested by Joseph and his companions to return them anywhere else but Carthage, as that place had become the rendezvous of the most hostile opponents of the Saints, and fatal consequences were apprehended if he and the other defendants were taken thither. The constable, however, refused, upon which the Municipal Court sued out a writ of *Habeas Corpus,* which the Charter (Sec. 17) empowered them to do, "in all cases arising under the ordinances of the City Council," and an investigation was had before that court. It resulted in the dismissal of the prisoners, as no riot had been committed, they having only acted in the discharge of a duty imposed upon them by the City Council. The mobbers refused to recognize the writ of *Habeas Corpus* and the decision of the Municipal Court, and sent runners through Hancock and the surrounding counties to ignite the already inflammable materials which everywhere abounded in the shape of virulent opposers of the truth and haters of Joseph Smith and Nauvoo. By this means a mob was rasied to again arrest Joseph, or lay the city in ashes and literally exterminate its inhabitants. Volunteers were actually invited from Missouri to join in the unlawful proceeding. This was a critical moment for Nauvoo, and Governor Ford, who was applied to for advice in the matter, was absent from home. In this emergency the Legion, amounting to between 3000 and 4000 men, was placed under arms to defend the city against the mob, until the Governor should do something in his official capacity. These prompt measures induced the mob to remain in Carthage and Warsaw. This was the position of the parties when the Governor appeared in Carthage. Instead of the mob being dispersed and the ringleaders arrested, it was actually mustered into regular service, the Governor placing himself at its head. His first act was to disband the Legion, whose men were standing in defence of their own lives, those of their wives, children, and of the citizens generally. He then requested the Mayor, Marshall and policemen who had been before arrested and discharged, as related, to repair to Carthage and appear before a magistrate to answer the charges preferred against them in the writ; thus, in his capacity of governor and the representative of justice trampling upon the rights of a chartered city, *Habeas Corpus* and all. Was there ever a greater instance of barefaced despotism in the aristocratic nations of the old world? The prisoners were taken to Carthage on the 24th of June, 1844, the public arms were demanded from the Legion, and the city was left defenceless within half a day's journey of an infuriated mob. The prisoners arrived at Carthage late at night, and on the morning of the 25th were apprehended on a charge of treason, founded on the affidavits of Henry O. Norton and Augustine Spencer. In the afternoon the prisoners appeared before R. F. Smith, J.P., to answer to the charge of riot, but by the advice of counsel and to prevent further excitement, they voluntarily entered into recognizances in the sum of 500 dollars each for their appearance at the next term of the Circuit Court for the county. Joseph and Hyrum had not been at liberty above half an hour before they were waited upon by constable Bettersworth who had arrested them in the morning upon the charge of treason. He insisted upon their going to jail with him, but their counsel, Messrs. Woods and Reid, objected to it, as they were entitled to an examination before they could be sent to jail. The constable holding a mittimus from justice Smith, they were conveyed to jail, "there to remain until discharged in due course of law." The next day the said justice commanded the constable to bring them before him for examination. The jailor could find no law authorising him to deliver up to a justice of the peace persons committed to his keeping "until discharged by due course of law," and refused to give them up. The justice then sent a body of "Carthage Greys," of which he was captain, and they by intimidation and threats, procured Joseph and Hyrum, and brought them before him. The counsel for the prisoners expressed a wish that the examination should be gone into and asked for subpoenas for witnesses from Nauvoo, which were granted, and the examination was postponed until 12 o'clock on the 27th. In the course of the day the return of the subpoenas was altered to the 29th, but on the following day, between 5 and 6 o'clock, the mob rushed upon the jail, overpowered the guard, and shot Joseph and Hyrum dead. Elder John Taylor was wounded with 4 bullets, and a fifth struck his watch, which saved his life. The fingers pointed to 5 h., 16 m., 26 sec., leaving on record the exact time when the tragedy occurred. On the first day of their imprisonment Joseph and Hyrum were visited by Governor Ford, who, after a lengthy conversation upon the leading causes which had given rise to the difficulties, promised them protection, *and pledged his word, and the faith and honour of the*

State that they should be protected. He had made this pledge on a previous occasion. The Governor also stated that he intended to march into Nauvoo at the head of the force which had assembled, to gratify them, and that the prisoners should accompany him, and afterwards return to attend the trial before the magistrate, which he said had been postponed until the 29th to allow time for that visit. This intention was not, however, fully carried into effect. The troops were disbanded except two companies—one from McDonough county, the other the Carthage Greys. At the head of the first the Governor marched to Nauvoo, but without the prisoners; they were left in prison with the Carthage Greys to *protect them*—the same men who had just previously mutinied and come near shedding their blood in the Governor's presence. In a statement to the people of Illinois after the tragedy had occurred, Governor Ford gave as a reason for not marching the troops into Nauvoo, as he originally intended to do, that he was satisfied that nothing but the entire destruction of the city would satisfy a portion of them, and pretexts for commencing hostilities would not be wanting. After his arrival in Nauvoo, he called the citizens together, and addressed them for about 20 minutes in a most insulting manner, and, as he says himself, *"told them what they might expect if they designedly or imprudently provoked a war!"* While the outraged citizens of Nauvoo were listening to this harangue the Prophet and his brother were being murdered in jail, notwithstanding *the word of the Governor, and the honour of the State* were pledged for their protection! [For Governor Thomas Ford's own account see his *History of Illinois* (Chicago, 1854).]

The news of the assassination met the Governor on his return from Nauvoo to Carthage, and on his arrival he found that many of the inhabitants had fled, and that others were preparing to do so, justly fearing an attack from Nauvoo. It was not until the following morning that the people of Nauvoo were made acquainted with the melancholy occurrence. A letter was addressed at 12 p.m. to Mrs. Emma Smith, by Willard Richards, John Taylor and Samuel H. Smith, informing her and the Saints of the event and earnestly entreating them to be peaceable and stay at home. To this letter Governor Ford appended the following— "Defend yourselves until protection can be furnished necessary, June 27th, 1844." M. R. Deming, Brig.-General of the militia of Illinois, appended another postscript, addressed to Mr. Orson Spencer, requesting the citizens to be prudent and quiet, lest they should be attacked from Missouri, and assured them that the horrible crime just committed would "be condemned by three-fourths of the citizens of the county."

On receipt of the news the Legion was immediately called out and was addressed at 10 a.m. by Judge Phelps, Col. Backenstos of Alton, the

Governor's aide-de-camp, and others, which allayed all excitement. Preparations were then made to receive from Carthage the bodies of the martyrs, which arrived in the city about 3 o'clock. They were met by a great assemblage of people E. of the Temple, on Mulholland Street, under the direction of the City Marshal, followed by their brother Samuel H. Smith, Willard Richards, and Mr. Hamilton of Carthage. The wagons were guarded by 8 men. A procession was then formed which followed the bodies to the Mansion House in the following order— The City Council, the Lieut.-General's Staff, the Major-General and Staff, the Brig.-General and Staff, the Commanders and Officers of the Legion, and several thousand citizens. Wailing and lamentation ascended from all, and on arrival at the Mansion the scene was indescribable. Between 8000 and 10,000 people were assembled, and were addressed by Willard Richards, Judge Phelps, Messrs. Woods and Reid of Iowa, and Col. Markham. The vast assembly then separated, "resolved to trust to the law for justice, for such a high handed assassination, and if that failed to call upon God to avenge them of their wrongs." It was generally believed that the citizens would avenge themselves of the death of their leaders, but they had no such intentions. On the 1st of July a meeting was held by the City Council, to act upon instructions received from Governor Ford through Col. Fellows and Capt. A. Jonas. At this meeting it was resolved to rigidly sustain the laws and the Governor, so long as he sustained the citizens in their constitutional rights; to request the Governor as he had taken from the inhabitants of Nauvoo the public arms, to do the same with the rest of the militia of Illinois; to reprobate private revenge on the assassinators of Joseph and Hyrum Smith, and not to appeal to arms but the majesty of the law, &c. The resolutions of this meeting were submitted to Messrs. Fellows and Jonas, who publicly addressed the citizens, in a conciliatory spirit, in the afternoon of the same day. Elder Daniel Spencer succeeded Joseph Smith in the mayoralty of Nauvoo.

At this momentous period of the history of Nauvoo, only two of the Twelve Apostles were present. The other ten were absent on missions, but soon returned, and on the 15th of August an Epistle was issued in which it was distinctly stated that Nauvoo and the Temple were to continue to be built up according to the pattern on which they had been commenced. The hostile spirit of the mob relaxed a little, and the citizens were permitted for some months to pursue their usual avocations with but slight interruption. Besides the Temple, the other public buildings in the city at that time were the Seventies Hall, the Masonic Hall and Concert Hall. The population numbered about 14,000 souls, of whom probably nine-tenths were L. D. Saints.

At the county court of Hancock, Levi Williams, Thomas C. Shary, Mark Aldrich, Jacob C. Davis, William N. Grover, John Allyer, William Davis, John Wills, and William Galliher were indicted for the murder of Joseph and Hyrum. *The Illinois State Register,* in adverting to the charge against them said—"We understand, upon good authority, that it will be proved on their trials, that a part of their plan in killing the Smiths was to have the Governor murdered in Nauvoo by the Mormons, they supposing that the Governor had some hand in the business. This expected murder of the Governor the assassins anticipated would raise a great multitude against the Mormons, and would lead to their expulsion. A plan more devilish, treacherous, cowardly and malignant, could not have been conceived. Notwithstanding this plan to have the Governor murdered, these same treacherous scoundrels, about the middle of August last, procured George T. M. Davis, Mayor of Alton, to write the Governor a letter, informing him distinctly, that, if he encouraged prosecutions against the assassins, they intended to implicate him as a *particeps criminis.* This information we got from the Governor himself. We further learn from him that he offered himself to submit to the law, if any person had any assertion to make. He told the people of Hancock that he would take no advantage of the force he had with him, nor would he run away to Missouri to avoid inquiry." Under such circumstances as these, the result of the trial might readily be anticipated—that no convictions would be made. Such was the case, the trial terminated on Friday, May 30th, 1845, and the guilty wretches, whoever they were, escaped for the present the penalty commensurate with their crimes, if indeed any penalty they might undergo could be considered equal to them.

The reduction of Nauvoo and the expulsion of the Saints therefrom was the one great aim of the mobocrats, and their next plan to bring about these events was to charge upon Nauvoo all the real and supposed crimes of the whole community, and so raise a tide of influence against it that should bring about its ruin. The City Council, therefore, met on the 13th of Jan., 1845, and passed a number of resolutions to the effect that they believed that the greater part of the thefts complained of were not true in fact, but trumped up by inimical persons to cover their aggressive doings, and defined the world to substantiate a single instance, where they had concealed criminals or screened them from justice. Persons who had lost property and had good reason to suppose that it was secreted at Nauvoo were invited to make diligent search within the city, to trace out the guilty parties, and the Council pledged itself to legally assist in so laudable a work. It was the opinion of the Council that many disreputable persons had been induced, from reports published in the *Warsaw Signal,* to flock into Hancock county to carry on their vile practices, knowing that it would be charged upon the Saints, and the Mayor of Nauvoo was instructed to increase the police to any number not exceeding 500, and the citizens were called upon to use renewed diligence, that if any such persons were found within the city they might be brought to justice. On the following day the citizens held a meeting, expressed their approval of the doings of the City Council, and pledged themselves to assist the public in bringing offenders to justice. Fifty delegates were selected and sent to the surrounding country to assure the people of the falsity of the accusations made against the Saints, and to request their aid in ridding the country of the thieves and counterfeiters that infested it. On this subject we quote the opinion of Governor Ford, given in his message to the legislature of Illinois, after he had made two visits to Nauvoo for the purpose of investigating the charges of promiscuous stealing—"Justice, however, requires me here to say, that I have investigated the charge of promiscuous stealing, and find it to be greatly exaggerated. I could not ascertain that there were a greater proportion of thieves in that community, than in any other of the same number of inhabitants, and perhaps if the city of Nauvoo were compared with St. Louis, or any other western city, the proportion would not be so great." The deputy sheriff of Hancock, J. A. Kelting, also exonerated the Saints from the same charges, and distinctly stated that stolen property was brought by way of Nauvoo from the country, crossed over the Mississippi, and carried 10 or 12 m. into the interior of Iowa Territory, where the thieves had friends to conceal the property, and that there seemed to be a connection of these friends on the Illinois side of the river, who, with 5 or 6 in the city, had a line for running stolen property through Nauvoo, but that they were not L. D. Saints, nor fellowshipped by them. Notwithstanding these proceedings of the citizens of Nauvoo, and the unqualified and unquestionable statements of Governor Ford and the deputy sheriff that the Saints were not guilty of the charges of theft preferred against them, but were equally as good as their neighbours, evil still lurked in the hearts of the people against Nauvoo, and, before January had elapsed, the Illinois legislature repealed the charter and left the city completely exposed to mobocratic fury and violence. It was fully expected that Nauvoo could not live without a charter, but business proceeded as briskly as ever, union and perseverance characterized the population generally, and the prosperity of the city was never more apparent than during the summer of 1845. On the 24th of May, at 6, a.m., the cap-stone of the Temple was laid amidst great rejoicings. In the month of September hostilities again commenced in earnest by the burning of the houses and property of the Saints residing in Morley settlement. On the 11th about 29 houses were burned down, and the families compelled to lie out all the night, which was a rainy one. Sheriff Backenstos stated on the 16th that "the Mormon community had acted with more than ordinary forbearance, remaining perfectly quiet, and offering no resistance when their dwellings, their buildings, stacks of grain, &c., were set on fire in their presence, and that they had forborne until forbearance was no longer a virtue." The *Quincy Whig* said—"These outrages should be put a stop to at once; if the Mormons have been guilty of crime, why punish them, but don't visit their sins upon defenceless women and children. This is as bad as savages." The mobbers, however, among whom were senators, military and civil officers, and ministers of the Gospel (?), continued their depredations. Sheriff Backenstos, who, with a small posse, was vigilant in arresting the course of those desperadoes, was frequently attempted to be murdered, but by his spirited and determined resistance of the course of the lawless incendiaries was making headway against them. He was interrupted, however, in this duty by Gen. J. J. Harden, a governmental officer, commissioned by the Executive of the State, and apprehended and tried for murder several of the mobbers and incendiaries having fallen during his attempts, in his official capacity, to restore order. The mob now rapidly increased by reinforcements from the surrounding counties, all was commotion, and naught but extermination or death was predicted for the citizens of Nauvoo. A meeting was held at Quincy on the 22nd of September, which deputed Messrs. H. Asbury, J. P. Robins, A. J. Pearson, P. A. Goodwin, J. N. Ralsten, M. Rogers, and E. Conyers, to communicate with the presiding authorities of the Church and request them to state their disposition and intention with regard to the removal of the citizens to a place where the peculiar organization of the Church would not be likely to engender so much strife and contention, as unhappily existed at that time in Hancock and some adjoining counties. A council of the authorities of the Church was convened on the 24th to consider the communication. In this council the troubles the Saints had waded through and the apparent impossibility of again living in peace in Illinois were taken into consideration, and it was resolved to leave the State, under certain conditions as to the sale of property, &c., early in the following spring. This was announced to the Quincy committee, and the Governor and people of Illinois generally, and caused a partial cessation of hostilities. In the meantime the Temple was so far finished as to allow a General Conference of the Church to be held in it on the 6th of October. At this Conference the subject of the evacuation of Nauvoo was canvassed before the Saints, and committees for the sale of houses, farms, lots, &c., were appointed. On the 1st of November a statement appeared in the *Times and Seasons,* detailing the persecutions of the previous part of the year, naming the propositions made to the

Quincy committee for the abandonment of Nauvoo, and stating that, notwithstanding the conditions on which those propositions were made had been violated by the mobbers, in their continued depredations upon the citizens and their property, every exertion would be made by the Saints to preserve the law and their engagements sacred, the event being left with God; also that the continued abuses, persecutions, murders and robberies practised upon them by a horde of land pirates with impunity in a Christian republic and land of liberty had brought them to the solemn conclusion that their exit from the U. States was the only alternative by which they could enjoy their share of the elements which God had created for all.

Notwithstanding all these concessions to gratify the wishes of an unprincipled populace, embracing rulers as well as ruled, the Saints were perpetually embarrassed by their persecutors, who had not patience to wait for spring to arrive, to wrest their possessions from them. On the 20th of Jan., 1846, the High Council issued a Circular, stating that early in March a company of pioneers would be sent out to the western country, to put in a spring crop, build houses, and prepare for the reception of those families who would start as soon as grass should be sufficiently grown to sustain the teams. It however became necessary, to assuage the wrath of the mobbers, to commence the evacuation earlier, although they had accepted the proposition for the removal to take place in the spring. Consequently, early in Feb., the Twelve Apostles, the High Council, and about 400 families, led the way to the far distant West, many crossing the Mississippi on the ice. The Twelve and High Council crossed on the 11th. As soon as spring opened, a general departure took place, but as summer approached, purchasers for the property of the exiles became scarcer, and of course many were unable to go from want of the means. There was also the committee remaining which had been appointed to superintend the sales and exchange of property. This excited the mob still further, and many depredations and acts of barbarity were committed. Major Warren, who had been stationed at Hancock county, with about 20 men by Governor Ford, to prevent depredations and keep the peace, during the evacuation reported in the *Quincy Whig,* of May 30th, as follows—"The Mormons are leaving the city with all possible dispatch. During the week four hundred teams have crossed at three points, or about 1350 souls. . . . The demonstrations made by the Mormon population are *unequivocal.* They are leaving the State, and preparing to leave, with every means God and nature have placed in their hands. . . . This ought to be satisfactory. . . . A man of near 60 years of age, living about 7 miles from this place, was taken from his house a few nights since, stripped of his clothing, and his back cut to pieces with a whip, for no other reason than because he was a Mormon, and too old to make a successful resistance. Conduct of this kind would disgrace a horde of savages."

In the meantime, the Temple, having been completed externally, even to the gilding of the angel and trumpet at the summit of the spire, and the main court of worship having been quite prepared, was dedicated according to the Holy Order of Priesthood, revealed through the Prophet Joseph Smith, and public services were held in it on the 1st and 2nd of May. Elder Orson Hyde, of the quorum of the Twelve, who had been deputed to remain and superintend in Nauvoo after their departure, presided at the ceremony of dedication. [In addition to the public ceremony of dedication, there were elaborate secret rituals, including many polygamous marriage ceremonies. These were recorded in one of the most remarkable of all Mormon manuscripts, "The Nauvoo Temple Record, 1846," which is now in the Church library in Salt Lake City.] The building was erected of light grey limestone, about as hard as marble. It was 128 ft. long, 88 ft. broad, nearly 60 ft. high, and to the top of the tower about 200 ft. It had 30 hewn pilasters, which cost about 3000 dollars each. The bases of the pilasters were crescent new moons, and the capitols, near 50 ft. high, were suns with human faces in bold relief, $2\frac{1}{2}$ ft. broad, and ornamented with rays of light and waves, the whole surmounted by 2 hands holding 2 trumpets. There were 2 stories in the clear, and $2\frac{1}{2}$ stories in the recesses over the arches, 4 tiers of windows, 2 Gothic and 2 round. The baptismal font, supported on 12 carved oxen, was in the basement story, and, with the oxen, was intended to be gilded with gold. On the west front of the building was inscribed in golden letters—

"THE HOUSE OF THE LORD:
BUILT BY THE CHURCH OF JESUS CHRIST OF LATTER-DAY SAINTS.
HOLINESS TO THE LORD."

The amount said to have been expended on this building by the Saints, exceeds 1,000,000 dollars.

This much accomplished, the Saints were contented, having fulfilled the commandment to build the holy edifice, and immediately after, all who were able to do so crossed the Mississippi and followed their predecessors in the exodus. Col. Kane thus describes the day on which the largest band left the city—"From morning to night they passed west-ward like an endless procession. They did not seem greatly out of heart . . . ; but, at the top of every hill before they disappeared, were to be seen looking back, like banished Moors, on their abandoned homes, and the far-seen Temple and its glittering spire." [Colonel Thomas L. Kane was a consistent friend of the Mormons, who often interceded on their behalf in Washington, D.C.]

The glorious 4th of July was now approaching, and the citizens of Hancock county, while plundering and banishing many thousands, and murdering others of their fellow citizens, were preparing to celebrate the birth-day of their boasted Republic and national independence. On the 6th of June a preparatory meeting was held at Carthage, at which a resolution was passed to the effect that "as the Mormons were not yet all removed from the county, its citizens were not free; and therefore, *public rejoicings for the blessings of freedom would be out of place.*" The meeting adjourned to meet on the 12th, "to inquire why the Mormon population had not all left the country by the 1st of May," and to adopt some method to facilitate their departure. The day on which the adjourned meeting was held had been appointed by the Governor, to assemble the militia of the county to raise volunteers for the Mexican War, and this circumstance suggested the idea to some persons that it might be converted into a demonstration against the Saints. The suggestion was taken up by the military officers present, and by the 19th about 500 men were assembled and marched to Golden's Point, within 5 or 6 m. of Nauvoo, but owing to a report that Col. Stephen Markham and many others from the camp of the Twelve had crossed the river from Iowa, the expedition became terrified and retreated to Carthage. The truth was Col. Markham and several men had merely returned from Council Bluffs with a team for some Church property, but Markham's name was a terror to these banditti, and they fled when there was really no pursuit.

After the failure of the "Golden's Point expedition," as it was called, the mob camp disbanded, pledging themselves to return promptly at the call of their officers. This was followed by the resignation of the military committee, appointed at a Convention of delegates from 9 surrounding counties, held at Carthage on the 2nd of Oct., 1845, to facilitate the extermination. The resignation stated that the period for which the committee had been appointed had expired and that the members thereof regarded their functions at an end. It is thought, however, that the real cause of their resignation was that the people had acted in the Golden's Point affair without consulting them or that they were chagrined at the cowardly retreat. The mob were now again without an organization, but possessing the same violent feelings towards the Saints, they soon found an occasion to renew the excitement. They had laid an injunction upon the Saints not to leave the bounds of the city except on their removal westward, but a few of the citizens, some of them not Saints, but new residents, disregarded it and went armed into the country 6 or 8 m. to harvest a field of wheat, and while doing so were attacked by a party of the mob, over-powered, severely beaten with hickory gads, and robbed of their arms. This circumstance created a great stir in Nauvoo, and the new citizens made common cause with the Saints in bringing the offenders to justice. Warrants were issued, and several were apprehended, but were removed by writ of *Habeas Corpus* to Quincy for trial. While the prisoners were remaining in Nauvoo in charge of the officers, the mob kidnapped Phineas H. Young, his son Brigham Young, Richard Ballantyne, James Standing and Mr. Herring, ran them into the woods, and detained them 14 days almost without rest, sleep, or food. They were handed from one band to another, and frequently threatened with instant death if they opened their mouths, but finally, falling into the hands of less vigilant keepers, they made their escape. Among the men apprehended for the outrage at the harvest field was Major McCalla, and in his possession was found a singularly stocked rifle, which was at once recognized by Wm. Pickett and others to have been stolen from the harvest men, and it was taken from him. The mobbers then charged them with theft, obtained a warrant for the apprehension of Clifford, Furness and Pickett, and a man named John Carlin was made a special constable to arrest them. The mob had a great aversion to Pickett, and he was marked by them. Information was given to him that the warrant was merely a trick to get him into their hands, and that they intended to waylay him and kill him. The officer was asked by Pickett whether he was willing to guarantee his safety, which he replied to in the negative; consequently, Pickett resisted the officer, but went afterwards in company with several of the citizens to the magistrate at Green Plains, by whom the warrant purported to have been issued, but he had no record of it and refused to take him into custody. The other two persons accompanied the officer and on the way to the magistrate were met by a large body of armed men, who called out for Pickett, but finding themselves disappointed in their prey, turned upon Clifford and Furness, and it was with great difficulty their lives were preserved. The charge against them was not sustained, and they returned to Nauvoo. It being now fully evident to the citizens of Nauvoo, new and old, that these arrests were merely pretexts to get up an excitement, the demands of Carlin were denounced and disregarded. He then proceeded to call out the *posse comitatus* and on the 17th of Aug. issued a proclamation for the people of the county to meet him in Carthage on the 24th, armed and equipped, and provided with necessary provisions. The *posse* commenced to assemble agreeable to the proclamation, and on the same day the Governor, who had been applied to for protection by the citizens of Nauvoo, sent Major Parker to the city, with a small company of men to guard it against attack. The Major therefore issued a proclamation on the 25th, calling upon all good citizens to return to their homes and keep the peace of the county. Carlin replied to the proclamation by letter, stating that he was a legal officer, acting in obedience to the requirements of the law, and did not acknowledge the authority of any one to interfere with him in the discharge of his duty. Major Parker replied that unless the *posse* dispersed he should regard them as a mob and treat them as such. He also stated that he was prepared to assist in the execution of any writ that might be required in Nauvoo and that it could be effected by 4 men. On the 29th a proclamation to the public was issued by 9 leaders of the mob from 4 counties, justifying and upholding Carlin, and denouncing and defying the authority of Parker. The arrest of Pickett was not the chief aim of the mob, but the final extermination of the Saints, as the following from the *Quincy Whig* fully indicates—"Carthage, Illinois, Aug. 27th, 1846. Mr. Bartlet. Dear Sir—I arrived in this place at eleven o'clock this forenoon, and found about 550 men under arms, and reinforcements arriving every hour. They all express a determination to stick together until they accomplish the object for which they assembled, 'if it takes until next spring.' There is a feeling of determination among them that never existed before. It is a general saying, 'that if the resolution of the Carthage Convention cannot now be carried out, they will leave the country, or turn Jack-Mormons.' Notwithstanding all the Anti-Mormons have suffered, they still dislike to shed blood if it can possibly be avoided; that is, if the Mormons will give up Pickett and others to be dealt with according to law, *and remove themselves peaceably from the State.* Every assurance of protection will be given them if they agree to do this."

The force collected by Carlin was placed under the command of Cols. Singleton and Chittenden. A treaty of peace was next arranged between the people of Nauvoo and the leaders of the mob, some of the terms of which were, that the Saints should leave within 60 days, that all hostilities should cease, and that all bodies of armed men should be dispensed with. The mob, however, would not stand by the treaty, but rebelled against their leaders, in consequence of which Cols. Singleton and Chittenden withdrew, declaring that the "Mormons" had done all that could in justice be required of them. The multitude were again in the hands of Carlin, who gave the command to the *Rev.* S. Brockman, who was elevated to the dignity of a general. A proposition was now made by Carlin and Brockman that the Saints should leave in 30 days. From the rank of special constable we have seen this Carlin rise within a few days to an eminence from which he defied the Executive of the State, disregarded all the rights of his fellow citizens, and ordered the expulsion within 30 days of hundreds of them equally as free as himself. The particular duty which he was charged to perform—the arrest of Pickett, was no longer the motive which directed his course, but, making common cause with the mob, he became their leader, for which he ought to have been arrested and tried for treason against the State. The crisis had now come. The force under Carlin and Brockman had increased to about 1000 men, with 6 pieces of cannon, and was drawn up within a mile of Nauvoo. The force in the city did not number over 300, with 5 pieces of cannon, made out of some old steam-boat shafts. On the afternoon of the 10th a few shots were exchanged, and on the 11th, 12th and 13th, a regular siege ensued, in which William Anderson, his son about 15 years old, and one named Norris fell on the part of Nauvoo. There were a few wounded, but none mortally. The loss on the side of the mob is said to have been heavy, as the citizens of Nauvoo fought valiantly and repulsed them at every point. On the 14th a committee arrived from Quincy to settle the matter if possible without any more bloodshed, and a treaty was finally concluded, by which it was agreed that the Saints and the new citizens who had taken part in the defence of Nauvoo, should lay down their arms and leave the State in 5 days, their arms to be restored to them as soon as they should cross the river. A committee of 5, with clerks, were to be allowed to stay in Nauvoo to settle the business of the expelled, and the mob were to be allowed to enter the city on the 17th, which they did, numbering 1625, and most of the Saints departed the same day, leaving many of their things behind them.

Thus was this unconstitutional and unhallowed purpose of the mob accomplished, and the miserable remnant of the Saints in Nauvoo—the sick, the widow, the orphan, and such as were merely tarrying to sell what little property they possessed, to enable them to follow the main body of the exiles, forced to yield, at the point of the bayonet, to the terms of their persecutors, who seemed to have lost every sense of humanity and all regard for the laws and institutions of their country. The Governor of Illinois was laughed to scorn, and the entire State seemed to be, in respect to the Saints, ruled by the mob, so that there was no help in this the last hour of their affliction previously to quitting its confines. Soon after the expulsion, the following comment upon the matter appeared in the *New York Sun*—"Some excuse can be found for the religious and personal outrages of the Goths and Vandals, or for the cruelties and persecutions of the darker ages; but in these enlightened times, in a country of laws and free institutions, where the largest liberty is secured to every citizen—that a community of 12,000 or 15,000 people, without having been charged with any legal delinquency, should be driven by force of arms from their houses and property as outcasts, and that the strong arm of the State should not be held forth for their protection, is a stain on our annals, and on our country at large, which we apprehend will take years to wash out. We have no parallel to it in the history of our country.

But the tale does not end here. Riot, drunkenness and crime signalized the victory of the Anti-Mormons! A reckless body of men seized upon the Mormon property, took possession of their farms, desecrated their Temple, and the poor, the sick, the aged, and the infant, were driven half famished into the woods, and the safeguards of domestic and social life were thus outraged and broken down. If recent statements respecting their condition and character be true, the State of Illinois is bound in honour and in law to restore them to their homes and property, and the Legislature, for the sake of justice and humanity—for the character of the State, and the institutions of the country, should direct the Governor to issue a proclamation inviting the Mormons to return to their homes, and offering to guarantee their safety against every attempt to injure or molest them. They are now, by the injustice of the State, dying in the wilderness of sickness and starvation—a prey to savage Indians and beasts of prey. Many are lying on the bare earth opposite Nauvoo, while brigands have possession of their property. Let Illinois move in the good work, before public opinion everywhere unite in demanding for the Mormons indemnity for the past, and security for the future."

Illinois regarded not this public censure and admonition, but the Saints were permitted to wend their way across the desert, as best they might, to a new and distant home, where, after much privation, prosperity and peace have abounded unto them. A stain is nevertheless imprinted upon Illinois, which it will be difficult to remove, and henceforth it will be classed with Missouri for the barbarity of its people and the imbecility or unwillingness of its rulers to protect the oppressed.

After the surrender of Nauvoo by the Saints, it gradually dwindled away in importance, until it became what our Artist found it. On the 10th of Nov., 1848, the Temple was fired by an incendiary, and on the 27th of May, 1850, a tornado blew down the N. wall, and so shook the building that the Icarians, who had been engaged in rebuilding the edifice for their use, deemed it advisable to pull down the E. and S. walls, leaving only the W. wall which our engraving represents. This beautiful ruin is all that is left of what was once a work "the most elegant in its construction, and the most renowned in its celebrity, of any in the whole West," and which had been built by the L. D. Saints in the midst of poverty and persecution.

(22) LUCY SMITH, mother of the Prophet Joseph, was the daughter of Solomon and Lydia Mack. She was born at Gilsum, Cheshire, New Hampshire, on the 8th of July, 1776, and was the youngest of 8 children —4 of whom were girls. Solomon Mack had just attained his majority when the war between France and England, which grew out of disputed

N. American territory, was proclaimed. He entered the British army and had 2 teams in the service of King George II., employed in carrying Gen. Abercrombie's baggage, and was present in 1758, at the engagement on the west side of Lake George. He was engaged more or less in military pursuits until 1759, when he was discharged, and married an accomplished school teacher, Lydia Gates, the mother of the subject of this memoir. She was the daughter of Nathan Gates, a wealthy man, living in East Haddam, Conn. She was of a truly pious disposition and had an excellent education, which peculiarly fitted her for the duties of a preceptress to her children, especially at a period when schools were rarities in the half cleared and thinly settled districts. Lucy profited by the talents and virtues of her mother. On the 24th of Jan., she was married to Joseph Smith and received from her brother, Stephen Mack, and John Mudget, his partner in business, a marriage present of 1000 dollars. Her husband owned a good farm at Tunbridge, on which they settled. The fruits of this marriage were 7 sons—Alvin, Hyrum, Joseph, Samuel H., Ephraim, William and Don Carlos; and 3 daughters—Sophronia, Catherine and Lucy. All the sons except William are now dead.

In 1802 Lucy Smith, with her husband, moved to Randolph, Vermont, where they opened a mercantile establishment. Mr. Smith here embarked in an adventure of ginseng to China, but was robbed of the proceeds and was much involved thereby. To liquidate his debts, he had to sell his farm at Tunbridge, to which he had then returned, and to use his wife's marriage present, which till then had remained untouched. From Tunbridge they removed to Royalton. They remained there a few months and then went to reside at Sharon, Windsor County, where Joseph the Prophet was born. They again returned to Tunbridge and Royalton successively, but in 1811 their circumstances having much improved they quitted Vermont for Lebanon, in New Hampshire. Here their children were all seized with the typhus fever, though none fatally, and Joseph was afflicted with a fever sore. When health was restored to the family their circumstances were very low, and they returned to Vermont and began to farm in Norwich. The first two years the crops failed and the third the frost destroyed them, which determined Mr. Smith to remove to the State of New York. His wife and family did not remove until he had made preparations for them in Palmyra. Here the whole family set themselves industriously to repair their losses—Mr. Smith and his sons to farming, and Mrs. Smith to painting oil cloth coverings for tables, and were so prospered that in 2 years they were again comfortably situated. After 4 years had elapsed, they removed to Manchester. In these alternate scenes of adversity and prosperity, the subject of religion was a constant theme with both Mr. and Mrs. Smith, though the former never subscribed to any particular sect. Both were occasionally favoured of the Lord with dreams or visions of the approaching work which He was about to commence on the earth, which prepared them for the mission of their son Joseph and the important part they were destined to take in it. Lucy Smith and several of her children joined the Presbyterian body in the year 1819, but after Joseph had received the first visitation of the angel and communicated the matter to his parents, she manifested intense interest in it, and from that time her history became identified with the mission of her son. She and her husband were baptized in April, 1830, and she removed to Kirtland, Ohio in 1831 with the first company of Saints, where she rejoined her husband, who had previously gone there in company with his son Joseph. Mr. Smith was several times torn from his wife by the enemies of the Saints, and unjustly imprisoned, but she manifested on all such occasions a calm assurance that all would end well. In 1838 all the family set out for Far West, a tedious and unpleasant journey, mostly through an unsettled country. They remained in Missouri until the extermination of the Saints from the State, participating in their numerous trials. On the occasion of the last arrest of her sons Joseph and Hyrum in that State by the mob in Oct., 1838, and when a court martial had decided to shoot them and others, she and her husband could distinctly hear the horrid yellings of the mob, which was encamped at a short distance from their house. Several guns were fired, and the heart-broken parents supposed the bloody work was accomplished. Mother Smith thus describes these moments—"Mr. Smith, folding his arms tight across his heart, cried out, 'Oh, my God! my God! they have killed my son! they have murdered him! and I must die, for I cannot live without him!' I had no word of consolation to give him, for my my heart was broken within me—my agony was unutterable. I assisted him to the bed, and he fell back upon it helpless as a child, for he had not strength to stand upon his feet. The shrieking continued; no tongue can describe the sound which was conveyed to our ears; no heart can imagine the sensations of our breasts, as we listened to those awful screams. Had the army been composed of so many blood-hounds, wolves and panthers, they could not have made a sound more terrible." As the reader is aware, Joseph and Hyrum were not shot at that time, but were carried to Richmond, and thence to Liberty. At their departure from Far West, the heart-stricken mother pressed through the crowd to the wagon containing her sons, exclaiming—"I am the mother of the Prophet —is there not a gentleman here, who will assist me to that wagon, that I may take a last look at my children, and speak to them once more before I die?" With her daugher Lucy she gained the wagon and grasped Joseph's hand, which was thrust between the cover and the wagon-bed, but he spoke not to her until she said—"Joseph, do speak to your poor mother once more, I cannot bear to go till I hear your voice." At this he sobbed out—"God bless you, mother"; and while his sister Lucy was pressing a kiss on his hand, the wagon dashed off. Mourning and lamentation now filled the old lady's breast, "but," says she, "in the midst of it I found consolation that surpassed all earthly comfort. I was filled with the Spirit of God." Shortly after this, Mr. Smith removed his family to Quincy, Illinois, to which place most of the Saints had previously fled, and in common with them suffered the hardships and privations which characterised the extermination from Missouri. From Quincy the family removed to Commerce (Nauvoo), and on the 14th of Sept., 1840, Mr. Smith, after blessing his children individually, closed his earthly career. Mother Smith felt this bereavement keenly. In 1843 she took up her residence with her son Joseph and was shortly afterwards taken very sick and brought nigh to death. She had scarcely recovered when she was called to suffer almost overwhelming grief for the assassination of her sons Joseph and Hyrum. When she was permitted to see the corpses of her murdered sons, her sorrow was great indeed. "I was," she says, "swallowed up in the depths of my afflictions; and though my soul was filled with horror past imagination, yet I was dumb, until I arose again to contemplate the spectacle before me. Oh! at that moment how my mind flew through every scene of sorrow and distress which we had passed together, in which they had shown the innocence and sympathy which filled their guileless hearts. As I looked upon their peaceful, smiling countenances, I seemed almost to hear them say—'Mother, weep not for us, we have overcome the world by love; we carried to them the Gospel, that their souls might be saved; they slew us for our testimony, and thus placed us beyond their power; their ascendancy is for a moment, ours is an eternal triumph.' " She had reared 6 sons to manhood, and only one remained, and he was at a distance from Nauvoo. Not one was near to console her in this trying hour. Some time after, she completed a very interesting little work, which she had for some time been preparing, entitled *"Biographical Sketches of Joseph Smith the Prophet, and his Progenitors for many Generations,"* which has since been published. [Lucy Smith's *Biographical Sketches of Joseph Smith the Prophet and His Progenitors for Many Generations* (Liverpool, 1853), is one of the most valuable source books for a study of Joseph Smith. Brigham Young, realizing perhaps that it contained items which could be damaging to the reliability of Joseph Smith's own story, had it suppressed. There have been several reprints.]

At the last General Conference in Nauvoo, Mother Smith was permitted to address the Saints. She reviewed the scenes through which her sons and the Church had passed, exhorted parents to exercise a proper care over the welfare of their children, and she expressed her intention to accompany the Saints into the wilderness, and requested that her bones after her death should be brought back and be deposited in Nauvoo with her husband's, which President Young, and the whole Conference by vote promised should be done. She had not, however, gone to Utah in 1853, but was living at the Nauvoo Mansion with Emma Smith, where our Artist found her, and made the sketch for the portrait which we give of this venerable and extraordinary woman.

(23) It is stated in *Biographical Sketches of Joseph Smith*, &c., that David was born on the 18th of Nov., but as the Artist was personally informed by Mrs. Emma Smith that it was on the 17th, we have given that date.

(24) JOSEPH SMITH was the fourth child of Joseph and Lucy Smith, and was born at Sharon, Windsor County, Vermont, on the 23rd of Dec., 1805. When about 7 years old he came near losing his leg through a fever sore, but by opening the leg, and extracting several pieces of affected bone, amputation was avoided. In this excruciating operation he exhibited that courage which, united with tender feeling, always marks the character of the great and good. Previously to commencing the operation, the surgeons requested to be supplied with cords to bind Joseph to the bed, but to this and to their request that he should drink some brandy or wine, he entirely objected, remarking—"I will not touch one particle of liquor, neither will I be tied down; but I will tell you what I will do; I will have my father sit on the bed and hold me in his arms, and then I will do whatever is necessary in order to have the bone taken out"; and looking at his mother, his eyes swimming with tears, he continued— "Mother, I want you to leave the room, for I know you cannot bear to see me suffer so, father can stand it, but you have carried me so much, and watched over me so long, you are almost worn out. Now, mother, promise me you will not stay, will you? The Lord will help me, and I shall get through with it." He soon commenced getting better after the extraction of the pieces of bone, and, when able to travel, he was sent to live with his uncle Jesse Smith at Salem, for the benefit of the sea air. Only one more circumstance of interest marked his boyhood. At the age of 14, when passing one evening through the door yard of his father's dwelling, he was shot at, but the balls missed him and lodged in the head and neck of a cow. No trace of the person who attempted the murder was ever found, and no reason could be assigned for the attempt. Owing to the adversities of his parents and the difficulty in giving chil-

dren an education in newly-settled districts, Joseph's advantages for
learning were few indeed, but his mind was active in observing and re-
flecting. On the subject of religion his ideas began to develop themselves.
The aspect of the religious societies around him, however, did not com-
mend either of them to his judgment sufficiently to induce him to become
a member. He had the greatest partiality for the Methodists and sometimes attended their meetings. In the midst of this indecision, he had recourse to his Bible, and there read in St. James—"If any of you lack wisdom let him ask of God, that giveth to all men liberally, and upbraideth
not, and it shall be given him." He felt the force of the passage, it gave
heavenly confidence, and he resolved to test the promise. Accordingly, on
the morning of a beautiful clear day in the spring of 1820 he retired to
the shade of a wood near by, and after kneeling began to offer up the
desires of his heart to God. While thus engaged two personages stood
before him, clothed with ineffable brightness, and one pointed to the
other, saying—"This is my beloved Son, hear him." Joseph then made
known the object of his prayer, and he was informed that he must join
neither of the sects, for they were all wrong, and their creeds an abomina-
tion in the sight of God. Many other things were communicated by the
heavenly personages, and on leaving Joseph they again forbade him to
join any of the sects. We have said that he was more partial to the
Methodists than any other religious body, and after receiving this vision
he informed one of their preachers of it, but met only with ridicule and
opposition. He experienced the same in all quarters, and he was led to
ask—"Why persecute for telling the truth?" Again—"I had actually seen
a vision, and who was I that I could withstand God?" Thus things went
on until the evening of the 21st of Dec., 1823, when he received a visitation from the angel Moroni, who informed him that God had a work
for him to do, that his name should be had for good and evil among
all nations, and revealed to him who were the aborigines of America, and
where was deposited their sacred Record—the Book of Mormon. The
angel informed him that this Record contained the fulness of the Everlasting Gospel, and that he should be the instrument in bringing it
forth, and have power given him to translate it. The vision was twice
repeated during the same night. He was commanded to tell his father
all he had seen and heard, but fearing his father would not give credit
to it, he did not do so, and before the next day had transpired the
angel stood by his side and admonished him of this neglected duty.
After he had communicated to his father what he had been commanded, he repaired to the place where the plates which contained the
Record were deposited and was permitted to view them, but it was not
till the 22nd of Sept., 1827, that the angel delivered them into his hands.

In the meantime, in 1825, Joseph had engaged himself with a Mr. Stoal, who set him to work digging for a silver mine, which it was reported the Spaniards had opened in Harmony, Susquehannah county, Pennsylvania, and from this circumstance arose the opprobrious epithet of a "Money Digger." While thus engaged, Joseph boarded with a Mr. Isaac Hale, whose daughter Emma he married on the 18th of Jan., 1827. After the plates were entrusted to Joseph, he met with the utmost difficulty in preserving them from his excited persecutors, and was finally under the necessity of leaving Manchester, and going with his wife to Susquehanna County, Pa., which place he reached in December, and immediately commenced copying some of the characters from the plates. In April, 1828, he commenced to translate, and Mr. Martin Harris to write for him. Subsequently and chiefly, Oliver Cowdery was his scribe. In May, 1829, Joseph Smith and Oliver Cowdery were baptized, and, by John the Baptist, ordained to the Aaronic Priesthood. His words in ordaining them were— "Upon you my fellow servants, in the name of Messiah, I confer the Priesthood of Aaron, which holds the keys of the ministering of angels, and of the Gospel of repentance, and of baptism by immersion for the remission of sins; and this shall never be taken again from the earth, until the sons of Levi do offer again an offering unto the Lord in righteousness." They were shortly afterward ordained to the Melchisedec Priesthood by Peter, James and John. At length, after having passed through many vicissitudes, the translation of the Record was completed, and, in 1830 an edition under the title of the BOOK OF MORMON was published.

The next great event in Joseph Smith's life was the organization of the Church of Jesus Christ of Latter-day Saints, on the 6th of April, 1830, in the house of Mr. Peter Whitmer, Fayette, Seneca County, New York. The Mission which he had been called to perform soon began to make great progress and excite corresponding hatred in the hearts of its opposers. In Jan., 1831, he removed to Kirtland, Ohio, where he found a branch of the Church, numbering about 100 members. There, among other things, he was engaged in translating the Holy Scriptures. On the 19th of June, in company with his wife and Sidney Rigdon, Martin Harris, Edward Partridge, W. W. Phelps, Joseph Coe, and A. S. Gilbert and wife, he set out, in compliance with a commandment of the Lord, for Missouri, where it was promised that the place for the City of the New Jerusalem should be revealed. It was revealed in July, that Independence, Jackson County, was the place, and that the spot for the Temple to be built upon was a lot lying a little W. of the Court House, and on the 3rd of August it was dedicated. After spending until the 9th of that month in receiving revelations for the Church and giving instruction for its guidance, he returned to Kirtland, where he arrived on the 27th. His time was now much occupied in travelling and preaching in various places by which numbers of converts were made. He also continued the translation of the Scriptures. In March, 1832, while living in Hiram, a mob gathered about his house, and, having dragged him from it in the dead hour of the night, tarred and feathered him and left him on the bare ground. The next day being Sabbath, Joseph preached as usual, his flesh all scarified and defaced. Many of those concerned in the affray of the previous night were present, and 3 persons were baptized during the day. He then left again for Missouri, on the 2nd of April, and arrived on the 24th, where he met with a welcome "only known to brethren and sisters united as one in the same faith, and by the same baptism, and supported by the same Lord." On the 6th of May, he set out to return to Kirtland, and on the way the horses of the stage in which he and the other brethren were travelling took fright. Bishop Whitney jumped out, and in doing so caught his foot in the wheel, by which his foot and leg were broken in several places. Joseph jumped out, but cleared himself. This accident detained Joseph with Bishop Whitney at Mr. Porter's tavern at Greenville 4 weeks, and while there Joseph nearly lost his life by poison mixed with his dinner, either intentionally or otherwise, but it is supposed intentionally. They recommenced their journey the following morning and arrived some time in June. On the 23rd of July of the following year the corner stones of the Kirtland temple were laid. On the 24th of Feb., 1834, Joseph received a revelation from the Lord concerning the troubles that the Saints in Missouri were experiencing, by which he was commanded to select not less than 100 men to go up to their relief. Accordingly, on the 26th he started from home to obtain volunteers for this purpose, and on the 5th of May he set out with about 100 men, with clothing and other necessaries for the Saints, who were suffering in Missouri. After a long and difficult journey, he again set foot in Jackson County, on the 1st of July, and proceeded to organize a High Council for the City of Zion and otherwise arrange the affairs of the Church in that place. While he was there, the High Council by his direction addressed an appeal on behalf of the Church to the authorities of the State and of the nation and to all people, for peace, and praying for protection while they sought to obtain without force their rights, privileges and immunities. On the 9th, Joseph set out again for Kirtland, having held a meeting in the E. of Clay County on the 8th.

On the 27th of March, 1836, Joseph dedicated the Lord's house in Kirtland. At this dedication he stated that he had completed the organization of the Church. With Oliver Cowdery he was favoured to behold a vision of the Lord; one of Moses, who committed unto them the keys of a dispensation for gathering Israel from all parts of the earth; one of Elias, who committed unto them the Gospel of Abraham; and another of Elijah, who committed unto them the keys of a dispensation to turn the hearts of the fathers to the children, and the children to the fathers. Many other persons saw glorious visions on the occasion. About the 1st of June, 1837, assisted by his colleagues, in the First Presidency, Joseph set apart by prayer and the laying on of hands H. C. Kimball and Orson Hyde, two of the Twelve, as a mission to England. This was the first foreign mission appointed by the Church. At the time of their departure he was seized with a severe illness, which continued for some days. In the following September he quitted Kirtland for Missouri, in company with Sidney Rigdon, to fulfil a mission appointed them by a conference of Elders on the 18th of that month. The object of the mission was to lay off new stakes of Zion for the rapidly increasing members of the Church to gather to. On his return, about the 10th of Dec., he found "apostacy, persecution and confusion" prevailing to an alarming extent. He states that the new year dawned upon the Church in Kirtland, in all the bitterness of apostate mobocracy, which continued to rage, so that it was necessary for Elder Rigdon and himself "to flee from its deadly influence, as did the Apostles and Prophets of old, as Jesus said—'When they persecute you in one city flee to another.' " They started from Kirtland about 10 o'clock in the evening of the 12th of January, 1838, on horseback, and reached Norton, Medina county, Ohio, 60 m. distant, by the next morning. Here they tarried until the arrival of their families, and on the 16th continued their journey in wagons to Far West. Joseph had only resided there about 6 months before the troubles the Saints had been wading through for several years reached their highest pitch, and he was betrayed into the hands of the mob leaders on Wednesday, the 31st of October. On the next day his brother Hyrum was arrested and brought into camp. A court martial was then held, and they were condemned to be shot on Friday morning, on the public square in Far West, as an example to the "Mormons," but, owing to the dissension of Gen. [Alexander] Doniphan, the sentence was not put into execution. They and 5 other brethren were carried off to Independence under a strong guard, from whom they suffered many indignities by the way. From thence they were taken to Richmond, where they arrived on the 9th of Nov. Gen. [John B.] Clark, the head of the mob, who had the brethren in custody, determined to shoot them three days after their arrival, but by the influence of some parties he was intimidated, and after searching through a military code of laws and finding that preachers of the Gospel who had never done military duty could not be subject to court martial, he delivered them over to the civil authorities, to be tried as persons "guilty of treason, murder, arson, larceny and theft." They underwent a mock trial and were then sent to Liberty, in Clay county, where they were put into jail and confined about 5 months. Poison was given to them many times, and even human flesh, in several instances, during this imprisonment. In the following April they were removed to Davies county, to have a trial, as it was said, but it was a mere farce—the grand jury who sat upon their case during the day acted at night as their guard and boasted over the bloody deeds they had committed at Haun's Mill and other places of sad memory. They were, however, indicted for "treason, murder, arson, larceny, theft and stealing," on which they asked for a change of venue to Marion county, but it was refused and one given for Boone, in removing to which place the sheriff who had them in charge told them that he had been requested by Judge Birch, of Davies county, never to carry them to Boone, and gave them permission to escape, which they availed themselves of, and Joseph and Hyrum arrived in Quincy, Illinois, in 9 or 10 days afterwards, and were welcomed by the embraces of their families and the congratulations of the Saints and sympathizing friends. In the short period of Joseph's residence in Missouri, upwards of 50,000 dollars were paid to lawyers to conduct or defend the cases growing out of his persecutions, and that too without any very adequate services being rendered in return, for sometimes the lawyers were intimidated by the mob and at others so intoxicated as to be utterly incapable of business. Three times during their imprisonment in this State were Joseph and Hyrum and other brethren with them sentenced to be shot; but it was overruled by the all-wise God.

On the 9th of May, Joseph and his family left Quincy for Commerce, and on the 10th took up their residence in a small log house on the bank of the river, about a mile south of the town. About this time the Saints were making out statements of their losses and sufferings in Missouri to present to the President of the U. States, with a petition to Congress for redress, and on the 29th of Oct. Joseph left Nauvoo for Washington with Sidney Rigdon and Elias Higbee, the three having been appointed a committee to present the petition. After arriving in Washington they had an interview with President Martin Van Buren, and subsequently with J. C. Calhoun. It was at this interview that Mr. Van Buren, uttered the well known words—"Gentlemen, your cause is just, but I can do nothing for you." Early in Feb. 1840, seeing all his efforts ineffectual to obtain redress for the wrongs the Saints had endured, Joseph left the Capitol for Nauvoo. The remaining 4 years of his life may be said to have been chiefly occupied in the building up of that city as a gathering place for the Saints, during which period, the Foreign Missions of the Church were only 2 in number—the British, and a special one to Jerusalem. We have noticed the chief events of his life, connected with the history of Nauvoo, in our note on that place. His chequered life, however, was characterized until his tragical death by many things not merely confined to Nauvoo, but affecting the L. D. Saints universally, and of deep interest to them. Referring to the circumstance of his escape with his brother Hyrum from Missouri, it may be mentioned that that State made no public demand for them until nearly 2 years had elapsed, when Gov. Boggs made a demand on Governor Carlin of Illinois for Joseph Smith, Sidney Rigdon and others. A writ for their apprehension was issued, but the sheriff could not find them. They were not fugitives from justice but "from the hand of a cursed, infuriated set or race of beings who were enemies to their country, to their God, to themselves, and to every principle of righteousness and humanity." The writ was returned to the Sheriff and the matter dropped at that time, probably owing to public opinion, which, out of Missouri, was then with few exceptions utterly against the Nero of the West. The press came out plainly on the subject. The *Quincy Whig* spoke thus—"Reason, justice, and humanity, cry out against the proceeding. We repeat that compliance on the part of Governor Carlin, would be to deliver them not to be tried for crime, but to be punished without crime, and that under those circumstances they had a right to claim protection, as citizens of this State."

In pursuing the most remarkable events in Joseph Smith's career, we have scarcely been able, for want of space, to refer to the numerous Revelations he received from the Lord, for the guidance of the Church at large, in which were restored the true order of Priesthood and a knowledge of the ordinances pertaining to Eternal Life. We cannot, however, pass over one received on the 19th of Jan., 1841. In that, after being acknowledged as acceptable in the sight of the Lord, he was commanded to immediately make a Proclamation of the Gospel to all the Kings of the world, to the President and Governors elect of the U. States, and to all the nations of the earth. It pointed out the duties of various prominent members of the Priesthood; required a boarding-house to be built for the accommodation of strangers who should go up to Nauvoo to contemplate the work of the Lord; called upon the Saints to come from afar with their wealth and means, to help to build a Temple to the Lord, in which, among other ordinances of salvation, might be administered Baptism for the Dead; called Hyrum Smith to take the office of Priesthood and Patriarch to which he had been previously appointed by his father, and appointed him to be a Prophet, Seer, and Revelator; appointed William Law, Second Counsellor to Joseph; and admonished Sidney Rigdon of his duty as First Counsellor.

In the following June, in returning from Quincy to Nauvoo, he was arrested on the writ before referred to, for the purpose of being delivered up to Missouri. A writ of *Habeas Corpus* was obtained, and the case was heard at Monmouth, Warren county, before Judge Douglas, of the U. States Supreme Court, which resulted in his immediate discharge, as the writ on which he had been arrested was null and void, from having been previously returned to the Executive. The Hon. O. H. Browning, in addressing the court for the defence, eloquently referred to the cruelties of Missouri. He concluded with the following language—"And shall this unfortunate man, whom their fury has seen proper to select for sacrifice, be driven into such a savage band, and none dare to enlist in the cause of justice. If there was no other voice under heaven ever to be heard in this cause, gladly would I stand alone, and proudly spend my latest breath in defence of an oppressed American citizen."

In the summer of 1842 Joseph Smith succeeded J. C. Bennett in the Mayoralty of Nauvoo, which office he retained until his death. On the 6th of May of this year, L. W. Boggs, Ex-Governor of Missouri, was shot at and wounded at his residence in Independence, Mo. Still as relentless as ever in his purpose to destroy Joseph, he charged him with being accessory before the fact, and applied to Thos. Reynolds, Governor of Missouri, to make a demand upon the Governor of Illinois for him, and a writ was served upon him on the 8th of August. An investigation into the matter was had on writ of *Habeas Corpus,* in Jan. 1843 at Springfield, before the Hon. N. Pope, judge of the Circuit Court of the U. S. for the district of Illinois, which ended in an honourable acquittal, the judge requesting, "that the decision of the court be entered upon the records in such a way, that Mr. Smith be no more troubled about the matter." Missouri, however, still true to her purpose, continued to excite the public mind against Joseph and made another demand upon Illinois to deliver him up to her for trial on a charge of treason, and in June, while he was visiting at Inlet Grove, 12 miles from Dixon, J. H. Reynolds, sheriff of Jackson county, Mo., and Harman Wilson, of Carthage, Ill., appeared with a writ from the Governor of Illinois and arrested him. They drove him to Dixon in a wagon and frequently struck him with their pistols on the way, and would have immediately carried him into Missouri to be murdered, but for the interference of the people. With much difficulty a writ of *Habeas Corpus* was procured at Dixon and made returnable before the nearest tribunal, in the 5th judicial district, authorized to hear and determine upon such writs, which was at Nauvoo. On arriving there a writ was sued out and made returnable before the Municipal Court, and upon examination Joseph was discharged from arrest upon the merits of the case and upon the further ground of substantial defects in the writ issued by the Governor of Illinois. Missouri was not yet satisfied but made a requisition upon Governor Ford of Illinois, to call out the militia to re-take Joseph. To this the Governor objected, as the laws of the State had been fully exercised in the matter, and everything had been done which the law warranted. The affair cost Joseph upwards of 3,500 dollars. At Dixon he sued out a writ against Reynolds and Wilson for false imprisonment and using unnecessary violence in arresting him. On the 9th of May, 1844, the case was called up for trial, and a verdict for the plaintiff was recorded, with 40 dollars damages and the cost of the suit.

On the 12th of July 1843 the Prophet Joseph received from the Lord the great Revelation on "Plurality of Wives," and the true order of the marriage covenant, but it was not published to the world until 1852.

The growing importance of Nauvoo, the increase of members to the Church in all parts of the Union and in this country, together with the perplexity caused by false friends and apostates in Nauvoo, made Joseph's duties truly multifarious; but in the midst of all, his love for the Saints was constant, and his regard for their interest ever wakeful. The Presidential chair of the U. States at this time was about to be vacated. Among the new candidates were J. C. Calhoun and H. Clay, and to ascertain what would be their rule of action to the Saints as a people, Joseph wrote to each, setting forth how they had been persecuted by Missouri and had failed to obtain redress, though they had petitioned from the State courts to Congress itself. Very exceptional replies were returned, and Joseph rejoined at some length, severely commenting upon them. The number of votes which the Saints could give was not unknown to the rival parties —whig and democrat, and they were courted by both; but the Saints could not feel justified in giving them to either and put Joseph Smith forward as a candidate. On the 7th of Feb., 1844, he issued an address to the American people, declaring his views on all the great leading political topics of the times. This, and the correspondence between him and Calhoun and Clay, are published in the 4th and 5th vols. of *Times and Seasons,* and are documents of much interest. Though Joseph was not elected, this course prevented political demagogues from making a target of the Saints, as had been the case at previous elections, and also enabled them to vote for one whom they considered "honourable, fearless, and energetic," and "that would administer justice with an impartial hand, and magnify and dignify the office of Chief Magistrate." We have now reached the period in the life of the Prophet, at which we strike directly the train of circumstances which led to his death at Carthage. One Francis M. Higbee, a member of the Church, had been accused by Joseph Smith, some time in 1842, of seducing several women, and of other evil conduct, and was brought before Presidents B. Young and Hyrum Smith and others, which much enraged him. Similar charges were preferred

against the notorious J. C. Bennett. They both confessed and asked for-
giveness. Their repentance was not sincere, and they secretly determined
to ruin Joseph. The thing festered in Higbee's mind until May, 1844,
when he sued out a writ, from the Circuit Court of Hancock county, for
the arrest of Joseph, on the plea of defamation of character. The damages
were laid at 5,000 dollars. Joseph was accordingly arrested, but petitioned
the Municipal Court of Nauvoo for a writ of *Habeas Corpus,* that the
whole matter might be thoroughly investigated. An examination took
place before that court and resulted in his discharge; first, from the illegality of the writ, upon which he was arrested; and secondly, from its
being fully proved that the suit was instituted through malice, private
pique, and corruption, and ought not to be countenanced. This led, in
quick succession, to the establishment of the *Nauvoo Expositor,* its
destruction, the arrest of Joseph and Hyrum, and their assassination on
the 27th of June, all which we have detailed, as far as space permits, in
the note on Nauvoo.

On leaving Nauvoo for Carthage, Joseph expressed himself thus—"I
am going like a lamb to the slaughter; but I am calm as a summer's
morning. I have a conscience void of offence towards God, and towards
all men. I shall die innocent, and it shall yet be said of me—he was murdered in cold blood." His eventful life was about closing, and it seemed
as though he had a strong premonition of it. His presence of mind never
forsook him, nor did his firm reliance upon the Lord depart from him.
His last expression was an ejaculatory prayer—"O Lord my God." His
whole life was one of extraordinary activity. In about 20 years he brought
forth and translated the BOOK OF MORMON; received numerous Revelations, from which the BOOK OF DOCTRINE AND COVENANTS was compiled;
caused his mission to be proclaimed in the 4 quarters of the globe,
and saw, according to many authorities, more than 100,000 persons receive it; founded and built up a great city, to which upwards of 20,000
people gathered; and built one temple in Kirtland and partially another
in Nauvoo. From first to last he was involved in about 50 law-suits, arising out of the persecutions of his enemies, but came out of the legal
furnace "without the smell of fire, or a thread of his garment scorched."
For a period in 1842 he edited the *Times and Seasons* and at his death
was mayor of Nauvoo; Lieut.-General of the Nauvoo legion, a portion of
the State militia; one of the regents of the Nauvoo University; and a
member of the Nauvoo Agricultural and Manufacturing Association. He
had 4 sons, Joseph, Frederick G. W., Alexander, and Don Carlos, and a
fifth, David H., was born about 5 months after his assassination. He was
tenderly attached to his family and in private life was always cheerful
and agreeable. In a public capacity he was courteous and affable and

allowed that all men were honest, which drew around him many hypocrites and designing wicked men, who caused him much sorrow and were the source of his chief persecutions. He was truly inspired of God and commensurate with his holy calling, so that "without learning, without means, and without experience, he met a learned world, a rich century, a hard hearted, wicked and adulterous generation, with truth that could not be disproved; revelations, whose spirit had so much God in them, that the servants of the Lord could not be gainsaid or resisted, but like the rays of light from the sun, have tinged every thing they have lit upon, with a lustre and livery which have animated, quickened, and adorned."

HYRUM SMITH was born in Tunbridge, Vermont, on the 9th of Feb., 1800, and married Jerusha Barden, on the 2nd of Nov. 1826, by whom he had 6 children, Lovina, Mary, John, Hyrum, Jerusha and Sarah. He became a widower on the 13th of Oct., 1837, while absent at Far West, and married Mary Fielding, the same year, by whom he had 2 children, Joseph and Martha. Like his brother Joseph's, Hyrum's early years were spent in agricultural labours, and nothing of particular note characterized that period of his life. He speedily became a believer in Joseph's mission, and by him was baptized in Seneca Lake, in June, 1829. He was one of the 8 persons permitted to view the plates from which the BOOK OF MORMON was translated, and his name is prefixed to it as a witness. On the 3rd of Sept., 1837, at a Conference assembled in committee of the whole Church, at Kirtland, he was appointed one of the Presidents of the Church. On the 19th of Jan., 1841, he was called by revelation to take the office of Patriarch over the whole Church, to which he had been appointed by his deceased father, by blessing and also by right, and was likewise appointed a Prophet, Seer and Revelator. He was personally connected with many of the principal events of the Church, up to the time of his death, and in the various offices he filled won the love and esteem of all persons. In the Revelation calling him to be the chief Patriarch, the Lord thus spoke of him—"Blessed is my servant Hyrum Smith, for I the Lord love him, because of the integrity of his heart, and because he loveth that which is right before me, saith the Lord." He was tenderly attached to his brother Joseph, whom he never left more than 6 months at one time, during their lifetime. He was arrested with him at Far West, and imprisoned with him at Liberty, and finally at Carthage spilt his blood with him. In this catastrophe he fell first, exclaiming—"I am a dead man," and Joseph responding—"Oh dear! brother Hyrum!" In the *Times and Seasons*, we find the following beautiful eulogy—"He lived so far beyond the ordinary walk of man, that even the tongue of the vilest slanderer could not touch his reputation. He lived godly, and he died godly, and his murderers will yet have to confess, that it would have been better for them to have had a mill-stone tied to them, and have been cast into the depths of the sea, and remain there while eternity goes and eternity comes, than to have robbed that noble man of heaven of *his life*." At his death he held various military and civil offices in the Nauvoo Legion and in the Municipality. In closing this brief memoir of Hyrum Smith, we may appropriately name that his son John was appointed at a Special General Conference, held in G. S. L. City, June 27th and 28th, 1854, Patriarch over the whole Church, and on the 18th of Feb., 1855, was set apart "to hold the keys of the Patriarchal Priesthood."

(25) WILLARD RICHARDS was the son of Joseph and Rhoda Richards, and was born at Hopkinton, Middlesex county, Massachusetts, on the 24th of June, 1804. Owing to the teachings of his parents he was early the subject of religious impressions, and at the age of 17 years set himself industriously to investigate the principles of religion as he saw it around him, especially in the Congregational Church, which resulted in the conviction that "none of the sects had the fulness of Truth." Under these circumstances he kept himself aloof from all religious societies, and felt assured that God would shortly have a Church upon the earth, whose creed would be the Truth, and the whole Truth. In the summer of 1835, he obtained from his cousin, Lucius Parker, of Southborough, a copy of the BOOK OF MORMON, which Brigham Young, then President of the Quorum of the Twelve, had left with him. In 10 days he had twice read the book through and was convinced of its divine authenticity. At that time he was living in Boston, in the practice of medicine, but he immediately commenced to settle up his affairs, to remove to Kirtland, a distance of 700 m., to give the doctrines of the Church a more thorough investigation. He was prevented by a stroke of the palsy from carrying out this intention for a few months, so that he did not reach Kirtland until October, 1836. The following December, on the last day of the year, he was baptized by his cousin, President Brigham Young, and on the 6th of March, 1837, was ordained to the office of an Elder. Shortly after his ordination, the mission to England, the first foreign mission of the Church, was formed, and on the 12th of June, he was set apart under the hands of the First Presidency to accompany it. He laboured in this country with much success in establishing the work, and in organizing Branches and Conferences of the Church. On the 14th of April, 1840, he was ordained at Preston one of the Twelve Apostles, having been chosen by revelation, through the prophet Joseph, some time previously. After his return to America, he was chosen Historian and General Church Recorder, for which avocations he was eminently gifted. His tenacious

memory enabled him to record events, dates, and circumstances, with re-markable accuracy, and his various attainments gave him that discrimina-tion and judgment so much required in an historian. He retained this office until his decease. In all his deportment he manifested a teachable and humble spirit. His many natural gifts and acquirements were con-secrated with a full soul to the building up of the kingdom of God. Such a man could not escape the particular notice of the Prophet Joseph, nor fail to win his esteem. He became his intimate friend and close com-panion. "He was in the same prison, side by side, with the two martyred Prophets, when they fell under a shower of bullets; and a bare drop of his own blood mingled with theirs on that memorable occasion. The blood of his brethren, that flowed copiously around him, the mangled body of his fellow survivor, Elder John Taylor, and the hideous spectacle of painted and armed murderers, found in Dr. Willard Richards, on that occasion, an embodiment of Priesthood, of presence of mind, of quick-ness of conception, and boldness of execution, that will never be forgot-ten. During that catastrophe of Joseph and Hyrum's death, and the emer-gency into which the Church was suddenly thrown, Doctor Richards felt the burden of giving direction to the affairs of the Church in Hancock county, in consequence of the absence of the Twelve Apostles. Though standing in the midst of the murderous mob at Carthage, with the mangled bodies of his martyred friends, and that of Elder Taylor, under his charge, his letters and councils at that time indicated great self-com-mand and judgment. His ability was happily commensurate with such an occasion.

"In the spring of 1847, he was enrolled in the memorable Band of Pioneers, under President Young, that first marked out a highway for the emigrating Saints to the Great Salt Lake. He submitted to the hardships and privations of that rugged enterprise, in common with his associates."

"At a Conference held in Iowa, commencing on the 24th of December, 1847, he was elected as Second Counsellor to the First President," in which position he stood until his decease, "ever shedding light and consolation in his sphere, upon the minds of thousands and tens of thousands to whom he ministered."

After the settlement of Great Salt Lake Valley by the Saints, and when the State of Deseret was organized, he was elected Secretary of State, and after its organization as the Territory of Utah, though not the nominal Secretary, the chief of the duty was performed by him. He was also a member of the Council of the Legislative Assembly, and presided over that body until his death. The last day he ever left his house was to address the Council, it being the close of its session. He remarked—"I will go and perform this last duty, if, like John Quincy Adams I die in the attempt, but no one knows the aggravated extent of my bodily malady." He took farewell of the Council and never left his house again alive. Among other offices which he filled were those of Secretary of the Perpetual Emigrating Fund Company and Postmaster for Great Salt Lake City. In the latter office his judgment touching postal arrangements throughout the Territory of Utah was much respected by the Postmaster General of the U. States. The *Deseret News,* the organ of the Church at head quarters, was edited by him, and his "might emphatically be called the pen of a ready writer." Though he lived many years a dying man, he strove hard against the ravages of his disease, that he might uphold the hands of his superiors and encourage and direct the Saints generally, by sending forth through his pen rays of light and truth to the remotest corners of the habitable earth. The labours of this distinguished man, however, were brought to a close in the prime of life. The palsy with which he had been afflicted since he first became acquainted with the BOOK OF MORMON, in conjunction with dropsy, terminated his earthly career on the 11th of March, 1854. He had frequently felt that his change was near at hand. In his farewell address to the Legislature he remarked—"Death stares me in the face waiting for his prey." He fell asleep without a pang, or discoverable sensation of pain, in the midst of a numerous and affectionate family, and circle of friends, whose grief was shared by the Church throughout the world. We are indebted to the *Deseret News,* from which we have already made several extracts, for the following beautiful panegyric on this great and good man—"That ardent love of truth, and intuitive perception of the same, which impelled him to investigate the claims of the everlasting Gospel in the beginning, grew with his passing years, and became more and more manifest, by his unwavering and unflinching adherence to it, in the most perilous and troublesome times of the Church's history in after life.

"He possessed a calm and even mind, and yet was rather reserved, and naturally diffident of his own superior ability. This diffidence may have caused the early part of his ministry to be undervalued, when the revelations of eternity lifted up, to his astonished and enraptured understanding, that vail which had long hung over the inhabitants of the earth. The reflection of such light and intelligence upon his mind unfolded, in unmistakable characters, the corruption and deep ignorance of all men without the light of immediate revelation, and so deeply did he feel the folly of his own wisdom, that he said he often conceived himself thrown back into another childhood, where he had to unlearn what he had previously subscribed to, and commence afresh and entirely anew the science of life and salvation.

"From being familiar with the minutia of the medical profession, and a careful observer of clerical deportment, and a handsome proficient in science generally, the change that swept over his past attainments and brought him down to the altar of revelation by the Holy Ghost, showed forth the reality of a new birth personified in all his subsequent life. On great and rare occasions, his masterly energies came forth like a well disciplined and invincible troop, that knew their place, and prerogative to act in defence of the truth. But he is gone. A pillar in the Church is removed from its mortal tenement, and a great man in Israel is gone! The great archer has been allowed to single out a distinguished victim! His numerous and sadly bereaved family should not miss the blessings of a grateful multitude, who appreciate the great value of the departed Willard." [For a sympathetic modern biography of Willard Richards see Claire Noall: *Intimate Disciple, Portrait of Willard Richards* (University of Utah Press, 1957).]

JOHN TAYLOR was the son of James and Agnes Taylor, and was born at Milnthorpe, County of Westmoreland, England, on the 1st of Nov., 1808. His parents owned a small estate at the village of Hale, in that county. They were members of the Church of England, and he was brought up in the doctrines of that Church until he was about 15 years old. He then joined the Methodists, and was soon after appointed a local preacher, and continued as such until he left England about the year 1828 or 1829. His father's family had left about 2 years previously and gone to the neighbourhood of the city of Toronto, Upper Canada. After a short residence in New York, Brooklyn and Albany, he visited his parents in Canada and took up his residence at Toronto. At that city he married Miss Leonora Cannon, daughter of Captain Cannon, of the Isle of Man, who was a member of the Methodist society to which Mr. Taylor had attached himself on his arrival at Toronto. Here he united with a few sincere and well educated gentlemen in the search of the Scriptures, some of whom belonged to the Methodist society. In the course of their researches they became convinced of many important truths, such as the Gathering of Israel, the Restoration of the Ten Tribes, and the Personal Reign of Jesus on the earth. They came to the conclusion that the churches of the day had departed from the order of God and were consequently corrupt and fallen, and that if the Bible were true the religion of the day was false. With these convictions they fasted and prayed much that if God had a Church on the earth He would send a messenger unto them. Mr. Taylor heard, investigated, and rejected Irvingism, and shortly after was waited upon by Elder Parley P. Pratt, with a letter of introduction from a merchant of their mutual acquaintance. Having heard of the stories current about the Book of Mormon and Joseph Smith he received Elder Pratt cautiously. After a rigid scrutiny, however, he and several of his friends believed the doctrines laid before them and were baptized. Mr. Taylor was ordained an Elder by Elder Pratt, and was shortly after ordained, by Elder Pratt and O. Hyde, presiding Elder in Upper Canada. During a visit of Joseph Smith, Sidney Rigdon, and T. B. Marsh, the latter then being President of the Quorum of the Twelve, to Toronto in 1837, Elder Taylor was ordained a High Priest under their hands. He paid several visits to the Temple at Kirtland and was Joseph Smith's guest while there. At the time of the great apostacy at Kirtland, in 1838, he was designated by revelation for the Apostleship. By request of the Prophet he removed to Kirtland, and from thence to Missouri, and on his way to the latter place preached the Gospel and organized a Branch of the Church near Indianapolis, Indiana. On arriving in Missouri, he and his party, numbering about 24, encountered a part of the mob, numbering about 150, led by Abbott Hancock, a Baptist minister, and Sashiel Woods, a Presbyterian minister. He reached Far West, and at a Quarterly Conference, held there on the 6th of Oct., 1838, it was voted that he fill the vacancy in the Quorum of the Twelve, occasioned by the apostacy of Elder John Boynton. The High Council of Zion voted the same on the 19th of Dec. following, and he was ordained to the Apostleship by Brigham Young and Heber C. Kimball.

While in Missouri Elder Taylor suffered in the persecution of the Saints and witnessed the mobbings at Caldwell and Davies counties, and at Adam-ondi-Ahman and Far West. He was one of a small company of men selected to go and protect Adam-ondi-Ahman from a portion of the mob, which numbered some thousands, and, notwithstanding their overwhelming numbers, retreated before the little army of the Saints. During the imprisonment of Joseph and Hyrum and other brethren at Liberty jail he paid them several visits. Before leaving Missouri for Illinois with the body of the Saints, he was appointed, by those of Caldwell county, one of a committee to draft and sign a memorial to the Legislature of the State, setting forth the most prominent features of the persecution and praying for redress. He was also appointed, in connection with Bishop Edward Partridge, by the High Council of Zion, to draft a petition to the General Government.

Soon after Elder Taylor's arrival in Quincy he returned to Far West, in company with 4 of the Twelve and other Elders. They went to fulfil a Revelation given on the 8th of July, 1838, requiring the Twelve to take farewell of the Saints on the 26th of April following, on the building spot of the Lord's house in Far West, and go from thence over the "Great Waters" to promulgate the Gospel. The mob loudly boasted that this

Revelation could not be fulfilled, as no "Mormon" was then permitted to be in the State. It was, however, fulfilled. The brethren arrived at the spot early in the morning of the day appointed, soon after midnight, and held a Conference, at which a number of persons were disfellowshipped from the Church; the foundation of the temple was recommended to be laid; Wilford Woodruff and Geo. A. Smith were ordained to the Apostleship, and Darwin Chase and Norman Shearer to the office of the Seventies. This done, the Twelve offered up prayer respectively, took leave of the Saints present, and departed immediately. Elder Taylor started from Illinois for England on the 8th of August, leaving his family in a soldiers' barracks at Montrose, Iowa. On his journey he was sick for 11 weeks; the rest of the Twelve were also sick, which, indeed, was the case at that time with most of the Saints who had suffered so much in Missouri.

On the 11th of January, 1840, he arrived in England and immediately began to preach and baptize in Liverpool and other places. He was the first who reared the standard of the Gospel in Ireland and the Isle of Man. His labours also extended to Scotland. While in this country he corrected the proof sheets of the Book of Mormon, and, with Presidents Young and Kimball, arranged the first edition of a Hymn Book for the Saints in the British Isles. He also wrote several tracts in reply to false charges against the Church. He returned to Nauvoo in July, 1841, and found his wife at the point of death. He called in 20 Elders, who prayed for her, and she recovered. At a conference in Nauvoo, in October, 1841, he was appointed, with Elias Higbee and Elias Smith, a committee to petition Congress for redress of wrongs and injuries received in Missouri. He was appointed also to present the petition. By appointment of Joseph Smith, he edited the last three volumes of the *Times and Seasons*. He also edited and published the *Nauvoo Neighbour*. In Nauvoo he was a member of the City Council, one of the Regents of the Nauvoo University, and Judge Advocate of the Legion. Under all circumstances he was firmly attached to the Prophet Joseph, and attended him in many scenes of persecution and trial, and finally at his place of assassination. In attempting to leap out of the window of the jail when the mob was firing into the chamber in which he had been sitting with Joseph and Hyrum, he was wounded with four bullets and would, in all probability have been killed by a fifth but for his watch in the left pocket of his waistcoat, which prevented the ball from entering his vitals. In his wounded condition he was carried by Dr. Richards into the inner prison and secreted from the mob.

At the expulsion of the Saints from Nauvoo Elder Taylor left with others of the Twelve, and proceeded to Winter Quarters. He assisted in organizing the Mormon Battalion for the Mexican war. Just about this period, at a particular juncture in the history of the Church in the

British Isles, he was deputed with Elders O. Hyde and P. P. Pratt, to come to England, where he again landed on the 3rd of Oct., 1846, having left his family in the wilderness in tents and wagons. He returned in the following spring, and went to G. S. L. Valley with Elder P. P. Pratt, in the first companies, where he remained two years. On the 12th of March, 1849, he was elected one of the Associate Judges under the Provisional State of Deseret, and in the following Oct., agreeable to appointment by a General Conference, he left G. S. L. City, with Elders C. E. Bolton and John Pack, on a mission to France, passing through England on his way. During this mission the Book of Mormon was translated under his direction into French and was published by him at Paris. He also edited and published a monthly paper called *L'Etoile du Deseret*. Several Branches of the Church were organized during his mission in France. Prior to finally quitting the Continent he went to Hamburg, and introduced the Gospel, where, by his direction, the Book of Mormon was translated into German, and published in that city. A periodical, *Zions Pionier*, was also commenced there by him to advocate the faith of the Saints.

On his first appearance at Boulogne he was challenged to discussion by several clergymen, which he accepted, and a report of the proceedings was published in pamphlet form at Liverpool. Another work, *The Government of God*, written while on this mission, was published after his return home. He arrived in G. S. L. Valley again on the 11th of August, 1852, and was elected in 1854 a member of the Council of the Legislature, which office he resigned to come to New York on a mission, without purse or scrip, to preside over the Saints in the eastern States, superintend emigration, and publish a paper, the first number of which, under the significant title of *The Mormon*, appeared on the 17th of February, 1855. We have now traversed the chief events in the career of this eminent minister of Jesus until the present time, trusting that his life, which he had never held dear for the Truth's sake, may long be spared to the people whom he has ever nobly represented in adversity and prosperity. [John Taylor (1808–1877) became president of the Church after the death of Brigham Young. He stoutly defended polygamy till his death, and the institution was not formally abandoned by the Church until 1890, during the reign of his successor Wilford Woodruff.]

(26) Iowa is bounded on the N. by Minnesota; E. by the Mississippi river; S. by Missouri; and W. by Minnesota and Nebraska Territory. It lies, with the exception of a small projection in the S. E. between the Des Moines and Mississippi rivers, between 40° 30′ and 43° 30′ N. lat., and between 90° and 97° W. lon., being about 300 m. long from E. to W., and 208 broad. Area, 50,914 sq. m., of which little better than a

fortieth part was improved in 1853. Pop. in 1852, 230,000, of which 10 per cent. were of foreign birth.

The State is divided into 100 counties, of which 70 have been regularly organized. The State Capital is at Fort Des Moines. Its largest town is Burlington, with a population of about 5000. Other towns are Dubuque, Keokuk, Muscatine, Davenport, Iowa City and Council Bluffs City.

Iowa is watered by several important rivers which cross it in a S. E. direction, and fall into the Mississippi, of which the Des Moines is the principal, and whose source is in Minnesota. The other rivers are the Skunk, Iowa, Red Cedar, a branch of the Iowa, Wapsipinicon, Makoqueta, Turkey, Upper Iowa and Little Sioux. The Iowa is navigable for steam-boats for 110 m. and the Cedar for 60. In the N. and W. of the State there are a few lakes.

"The surface of Iowa is generally composed of rolling prairies, having nothing within its limits which approaches a mountain in elevation. The highest ground in the State is a plateau in the N. W., called 'Couteau des Prairies,' which enters the State from Minnesota. A small portion in the N. E. on the Mississippi is rugged and rocky, and Table Mound, a conical elevation, with a flat summit 3 or 4 m. from Dubuque, is perhaps 500 ft. high. The State, however, may be generally described as a rolling prairie, crossed by rivers whose banks are skirted by woods. There are said to be some swamps in the N. W. portion of the State. The prairies, though sometimes 20 m. across, are rarely more than 5 or 10. The soil is generally good and easily cultivated, though in the N., near the confines of Couteau des Prairies, the highlands are covered with gravel, and support a scanty vegetation, and the low grounds are wet or marshy, and without timber."

In 1850 there were in the State 14,805 farms. The principal products are Indian corn, wheat and live stock; besides which are produced considerable quantities of rye, buckwheat, barley, butter, cheese, hay, wool, maple sugar, bees' wax and honey; and some rice, tobacco, fruits and silk. The ash, elm, and white maple grow in alluvial belts of a quarter of a mile to 1 m. in breadth on the river banks. The poplar, oak, walnut, hickory, locust, ironwood, cottonwood, lime or basswood, and a little pine grow in the northern parts of the State. The grape, gooseberry, and wild plum are indigenous. The peach grows too luxuriantly and blooms too soon to admit of culture to advantage.

Iowa is rich in minerals. Lead ore is abundant, but is deeper than in Illinois and Wisconsin. Zinc and copper are found in connection with the lead. The great coal field of Iowa and Missouri has an extent in the former State of near 200 m. from E. to W. and 140 from N. to S. Although this State has an abundance of coal and water-power, two very important elements in manufactures, they have scarcely yet been turned into any very great account. In 1850 there were 482 manufacturing establishments, producing 500 dollars or upwards annually. Of these, 3 were engaged in the manufacture of iron, and 1 in that of woollen. As regards internal improvements they have scarcely extended yet beyond opening common and laying plank roads. A railroad from Dubuque to Keokuk is projected. The State has no foreign trade, but exports grain, flour, lead and pork.

The School fund, in 1850, amounted to 250,230 dollars, and the annual expenditure to 41,963. Of the 64,336 children then in the State, only about one-third were attending school. The school libraries had 278 volumes. An appropriation has been made for Iowa University, which is to be perpetual. In the same year there were 148 churches in the State, owned as follows—50 by the Methodists, 24 by the Presbyterians, 17 by the Roman Catholics, 16 by the Baptists, 14 by the Congregationalists, 8 by the Christians, 5 by the Friends, 4 by the Episcopalians, 4 by the Lutherans, and the balance by the German reformed, Moravians, Unionists, and Universalists, giving about one church to every 1298 persons. The State has 5 public libraries, with an aggregate of 2660 volumes. In June, 1852, there was but one bank in Iowa. Its capital was 200,000 dollars.

Iowa originally formed part of the Louisiana purchase and afterwards part of Missouri, Wisconsin, and Iowa Territory successively. The first white settlement was made in 1832 at Fort Madison. The increase of population was very rapid and said to be unprecedented in the history of western colonization. In 1838 the "District of Iowa" was erected into a territorial government under the title of "Iowa Territory." The first governor was Robert Lucas, formerly Governor of Ohio, who was very favourably disposed towards the L. D. Saints, who were then just settling in Illinois, on the opposite side of the Mississippi. When they applied to the Government of the U. States in 1839 for an investigation into the Missouri wrongs, he furnished the deputation with a letter of introduction to President M. Van Buren, setting forth that while the Saints dwelt in Ohio they were always believed to be an industrious and inoffensive people, and since the settlement of a number of families in Iowa he had no recollection of any of them having been charged as violators of the law.

Although the population of Iowa Territory in 1844 warranted an application to the Federal Government for admission into the Union as an independent State, and a Constitution was formed, they were not admitted until several years afterwards, owing to a difference respecting boundaries. The people of Iowa afterwards assented to the restrictions named by Congress, and the "State of Iowa" was admitted in Aug., 1846. The first State election was by proclamation of Governor Clarke, held on the 26th of Oct. following. The governor of Iowa is elected every 4 years and receives a salary of 1000 dollars per annum. The Senate is composed of 19 members, elected every 4 years, and the House of Representatives of 39 members, for 2 years. The Sessions of the Legislature are biennial. The Judiciary is composed, first, of a Supreme Court, presided over by one chief justice, and two associate judges; and second, of District Courts, presided over by a single judge. The judges of the Supreme Court are elected for 6 years, by joint vote of the Legislature, and the district judges for 5 years, by the voters in their respective districts. Iowa sends 2 members to the national House of Representatives.

(27) INDIAN TERRITORY. This vast tract of country extending in 1853 from the confines of Iowa, Missouri, and Arkansas on the E., to Texas, New Mexico, Utah and Oregon on the W.; and northward from Texas and New Mexico, to the North West Territory and Minnesota, and having an area of 181,171 sq. m., had been set apart by the Government of the U. States as a permanent home for the Indian tribes removed from the E. of the Mississippi, as well as those indigenous to the territory. The eastern portion was chiefly occupied by the tribes removed thither, and included, among others, the Choctaws, Chickasaws, Creeks, Cherokees, Senecas, Shawnees, Seminoles, Quapaws, several Miami tribes, Potawatamies, Ottawas, Delawares, Kickapoos, Sacs and Iowas. The country directly W., with a small portion in the N.E., was occupied by the Osages, the Kansas, or Konzas, the Ottoes, Omahas or Mahas, Pawnees and the Puncahs, all indigenous tribes. The central and western portions were roamed over by the Comanches, Kioways, Pawnees, Arrapahoes, Utahs, Cheyennes, Gros Ventres, Arickarees or Rickarees, and some other nomad tribes. The number of Indians on the Plains and in the Rocky Mountains was estimated at 63,000. "Some of the removed tribes have made considerable advance in agriculture and the industrious arts, and have established schools and churches, while others are relapsing into indolence and vagrancy, and, following the common fate of the savage, when in contact with the civilized man, are fast diminishing under the influence of intemperance and vicious connection with abandoned whites."

Although this tract of country was set apart for the Indian tribes and was not free for settlement by the citizens of the U. States, still many of them crossed the boundary and "squatted" on the Indian lands. This was encouraged by various statesmen, among whom was Senator Benton. In June, 1845, and in March 1853, attempts were made in Congress to organize a territory by the name of Nebraska, but without success. On the 25th of May, 1854, an act was passed, and on the 30th of the same month was approved by the President of the U. States, organizing the greater portion of Indian Territory and all North West Territory into two territories, Nebraska and Kansas. The boundaries of Nebraska are the 40th parallel of N. lat., on the S.; Utah, Oregon and Washington Territories, on the W.; the 49th parallel of N. lat. on the N.; and the territory of Minnesota, and the States of Iowa and Missouri on the E., from each of which it is chiefly separated by the Missouri River. The boundaries of Kansas are the 37th parallel of N. lat. on the S.; the territories of Utah and New Mexico on the W.; Nebraska on the N.; and Missouri on the E., from a small portion of which it is separated by the river of the same name. The Bill provided that the rights and property of the Indians within the said territories should be respected, until their titles to the lands should, by treaty between the respective tribes and the Government of the U. States, be extinguished. Various tribes of the Nebraska Indians have transferred their lands to the U. States. In 1854 the Omahas and Ottoes ceded about 10,000,000 acres, for which they were to receive 52,000 dollars annually for thirty years. The Omaha purchase extends northwards from the Nebraska or Platte river to Iowa Creek, and westward from the Missouri river to the Loup Fork. The land reserved for the future homes of the Omahas is a tract embraced between Iowa Creek and Neobrarah River. The Ottoe purchase lies S. of the Platte. The land which this tribe reserved for its future occupancy lies due W. from Old Fort Kearney, upon the W. side of the Big Blue. It is 10 m. wide, and runs W. indefinitely. It was fully expected that the whole valley of the Platte would be opened to the settlement of white men by May, 1855.

The Executive power of these territories is vested in a governor, appointed by the President of the U. States for 4 years, with a salary of 2500 dollars annually. The first appointees were, for Nebraska, Gen. W. G. Butler of Kentucky, for Kansas A. H. Reeder, of Pennsylvania. The present Governor of Nebraska is Mark W. Izard. The Legislature consists of a Council, numbering 13 members, elected for 2 years; and a House of Representatives, numbering 26 members, elected for 1 year. The latter may be increased by the Legislature to 39 members, according to the increase of population. The Judiciary consists of a Supreme Court, District Courts, Probate Courts, and Justices of the Peace. The Supreme Court consists of a Chief Justice and 2 Associates, appointed by the President for 4 years.

In the passage of this Act the memorable "Missouri Compromise," which prohibited the institution of Negro slavery further north than 36° 30′ was repealed, and the new territories were left free to form their own domestic institutions. In its progress through Congress the Act met with violent opposition from the Anti-slavery party. The Pro-slavery party were equally zealous in getting it passed. Contention rose so high, both in Congress and out, that a dissolution of the Union was threatened and seriously talked of by both parties. The Northern States contended that the Constitution gave Congress the power to prohibit slavery in the States and Territories, while the Southern States denounced it as an unconstitutional interference, and that, therefore, the Missouri Compromise ought never to have been made. The Nebraska-Kansas Bill agitation, however, was not the first step to the abandonment of the Compromise. In 1850, when the Union was nearly rent asunder by the vexatious slavery question, Congress passed what is frequently called the "Omnibus Bill," by which California, with a Constitution excluding slavery, was admitted into the Union as an independent State; Utah and New Mexico were erected into Territories, with a provision in the organic Acts, that when they are admitted into the Union as States, it shall be with or without slavery, as the voice of the citizens may determine at the time of admission; the slave trade, but not slavery, was abolished in the district of Columbia; and the Fugitive Slave law was passed, requiring persons bound to service in one State and escaping to another to be given up. The *New York Herald*, in commenting upon the passage of the Nebraska-Kansas Act, held this language—"The passage of the Nebraska Bill is one of those great events which, in a nation's history, inaugurate a political revolution and a new cycle in political affairs. It is the triumph of a great principle over temporising expedients—of the Constitution over sectional fanaticism, and popular sovereignty over the usurpations of Congress. . . . It is a substantial declaration by Congress that they have no power over slavery, neither in the States, nor in the Territories, but that in the Territories, as in the States, it is a subject which belongs entirely to the people. This is the true constitutional doctrine, and the Constitution is a rock upon which the country, the North and the South, may securely stand." Such a clear and practical enunciation of the doctrine of Congressional non-interference with the domestic institutions of the States and Territories, forever settles the question with regard to the institution of Plurality of Wives in Utah.

Though the people of Nebraska and Kansas are left to decide whether Negro Slavery shall exist among them or not, it is not very probable that the institution will ever flourish much in Nebraska, for the climate and productions are not such as to make slave labour profitable. The case, however, is different in Kansas. The most disgraceful scenes which could be conceived of have been enacted there. Abolitionists, or free-soilers, have been intimidated at the polls by Missourians, who have crossed the

State line, and, in "Squatter Sovereignty," carried all before them. Newspaper offices have been torn down, and blood has been spilt in a number of instances. The Pro-slavery party declare that abolitionists and free-soilers shall not reside in Kansas, and that it shall be a slave State, which from present appearances is very likely to happen.

Any description of the topography, soil, and climate of these new territories must necessarily be very imperfect in their present thinly settled state. The E. of Nebraska is in many respects similar to Western Iowa, in soil, climate, fruits and productions. The interior or western part is more mountainous or barren, almost entirely destitute of timber, and really of little or no value except for grazing. The geological formation of the territory is limestone in the E., sandstone in the S. and W. of the Missouri, and rocks of the Diluvian period N. and W. of it. The Missouri river rises in Nebraska, in lat. 45° N., and flows northwards for about 500 m.; then E. N. E. to lat. 48° 20′, from which point, at its junction with White Earth River, it forms the entire eastern boundary of the territory. The principal rivers, having their whole course within the territory, are the Platte and the Yellow Stone, both having many large tributaries. The Platte is the longest affluent of the Missouri and rises in the Rocky Mountains by two branches termed the North and South Forks, which unite about 800 m. from the source of the former and principal fork. The whole length is about 1200 m. It is a very shallow stream except in floods and may be forded in almost every part. The Yellow Stone is said to have its source in Sublette's Lake in the Rocky Mountains. It is the largest affluent of the Missouri and is about 1000 m. in length, for about 800 of which it is navigable.

The principal settlements of Nebraska at present are Omaha City, the capital, opposite Council Bluffs City, in Iowa, Nebraska City, formerly Old Fort Kearney, Bellevieu, Plattsmouth, Mount Vernon, Florence, formerly Winter Quarters, Fort Calhoun, Desota, Tekama and Fontenelle.

The face of the country in Kansas is a continued succession of gently undulating ridges and valleys. In the valley of the Kansas river for about 200 m. up "the soil is very rich and productive, and the country exceedingly beautiful. Along the river, extending for a few miles on each side of it, the country is densely timbered, and so also are the small streams which empty into the river from either side. On leaving the margins of the streams, the country is high rolling prairie. The soil is good, but the want of timber and water will be found a serious drawback to the rapid settlement of that portion of the Territory." West of this for about 350 m. the country is sandy and wholly unfit for agricultural purposes. A district E. of, and skirting the base of, the Black Hills, is extremely fertile, and said to be one of the most lovely and desirable regions upon the Continent. In the tract of country between the Black Hills and the Rocky Mountains, there is every variety of aspect and soil—stupendous mountains and beautiful valleys, "fruits and flowers spangle the greensward; vines hang in festoons from tree to tree; cascades spring in rainbow hues from the cliffs; pines and cedars, the growth of ages, spread their sombre shade upon the mountain sides, and the stupendous peaks shooting up into the skies are crowned with a glittering coronet of snow." A few hours' travel from this scene of primeval beauty leads to one of intense contrast, where there is a sterile sandy expanse of many miles in extent, producing only stinted artemisia, and a few other miserable plants, where the rivulets are lost as they descend from the bare ridges around, and their hollow murmurs may be heard beneath the feet. The surrounding peaks are immense piles of bare granite, which seem to have been thrown together into inextricable confusion.

The geological formation of Kansas is but very partially known. For some distance westward it is limestone, and afterwards sandstone. The great coal fields of Missouri, S. of the Missouri River, extend 30 or 40 m. into this territory. Its chief river is the Kansas, formed by the junction of the Republican and Smoky Hill Forks near lat. 39° and lon. 96°. The entire length of the Kansas is about 1200 m., for 900 of which it is navigable. Its tributaries are not numerous, and there are few other rivers of importance in the territory.

A number of settlements have already been formed in Kansas. The capital is at Fort Leavenworth, the oldest military post on the Missouri, having been established in 1827. At Atchison, a new town in this territory, on the western bend of the Missouri, about midway between Weston and St. Joseph, and 500 m. from St. Louis, the emigrating Saints are this year (1855) fitting out for the Plains.

(28) WINTER QUARTERS. This name was given to the place by the L. D. Saints who wintered there in 1846–7, in their progress from Illinois to the West. At that time it formed part of the lands belonging to the Omaha Indians, an insignificant tribe of the Grand Prairie, who then did not number more than 300 families. Upwards of 1000 houses were soon built —700 of them in about 3 months, upon a pretty plateau overlooking the river, and neatly laid out with highways and byways, and fortified with breastwork and stockade. "It had too its place of worship, 'Tabernacle of the Congregation,' and various large workshops, and mills and factories provided with water power." At this time the powerful Sioux were at war with the Omahas, and it is said that the latter hailed with joy the temporary settlement of the journeying Saints among them. At any rate, the encampment served as a sort of breakwater between them and the

destroying rush of their powerful and devastating foes. The Saints "likewise harvested and stored away for them their crops of maize," and with all their own poverty frequently spared them food and kept them from absolutely starving. Always capricious, and in this case instigated by white men, the Indians, notwithstanding they had formally given the Saints permission to settle upon their lands, complained to the Indian Agents that they were trespassing upon them, and they were requested to remove. From this circumstance is attributable the rise and rapid growth of Kanesville, leaving Winter Quarters again entirely to its savage inhabitants, and only its ruins to point out its former prosperity, and now its situation.

In the annals of the Church of Jesus Christ of L. D. Saints, this halting place in the wilderness must always fill an important and interesting page. It was from this spot that the Pioneers took their departure on the 14th of April, 1847, in search of a location W. of the Rocky Mountains, upon which the exiled Saints might re-assemble themselves, far from the haunts of persecuting Christendom, and where the foot-prints of a white man had scarcely ever before been seen. While tarrying here, the first General Epistle of the Council of the Twelve Apostles, written after the expulsion from Nauvoo, and dated Dec. 23, 1847, was addressed to the Saints of all the world; and lastly, the re-organization of the principal authorities of the Church was effected before the end of the same month at a conference held at the Log Tabernacle, in Iowa—Brigham Young being acknowledged President of the Church, and Heber C. Kimball and Willard Richards, his counsellors. The Presidency left Winter Quarters for G. S. L. Valley in the following May, many of the Saints having previously left for that place, and others having re-crossed the river into Iowa. Since the organization of Nebraska Territory, an effort has been made, owing to the desirable situation of Winter Quarters, and its good ferriage and water facilities, to build a city by the name of Florence upon the old site.

(29) WOOD RIVER is about 150 m. a little S. W. of Council Bluffs. It is a general stopping place on the great emigrant route through the Platte valley, and in order to afford Post Office facilities to parties of emigrants, the Government of the U. States established a Mail Station there in Jan., 1854. It is called the Nebraska Centre P.O. The mail goes to and from Council Bluffs twice a week.

(30) Captain Stansbury thus describes Chimney Rock—"This singular conformation has been, undoubtedly, at one time a portion (probably a projecting shoulder) of the main chain of bluffs bounding the valley of

the Platte, and has been separated from it by the action of the water. It consists of a conical elevation of about one hundred feet high, its sides forming an angle of about 45° with the horizon; from the apex rises a nearly circular and perpendicular shaft of clay, now from thirty-five to forty feet in height. The cone has, I think, been formed by the disintegration of the softer portion of the bluffs, arranging itself at its natural angle in a conical form, while the remainder of the earth has been carried away by the floods and distributed over the plain, leaving the broad valley which is at present formed between it and the main bluff. The Chimney, being composed of more tenacious materials, has been left standing in a vertical position, and has been worn into its present circular form by the gradual action of the elements. That the shaft has been very much higher than at present, is evident from the corresponding formation of the bluff, as well as from the testimony of all our *Voyageurs*, with whom it was for years a landmark or beacon visible for forty or fifty miles, both up and down the river. It is the opinion of Mr. Bridger that it was reduced to its present height by lightning, or some other sudden catastrophe, as he found it broken on his return from one of his trips to St. Louis, though he had passed it uninjured on his way down."

(31) FORT LARAMIE, a military post and post office, is situated on Laramie River, at its confluence with the Platte, in lat. 42° 12′ 10″ N., and lon. 104° 31′ 26″ W., and is 522 m. from Winter Quarters, and 509 from G. S. L. City, being about midway between these two points. From Fort Kearney it is 335 m. and from Fort Leavenworth 647. After leaving Scotts Bluffs the country rises much more rapidly than on the east. The elevation of the fort is 4090 ft. above the level of the sea.

Fort Laramie was formerly known as Fort John, and was established and owned by the American Fur Company for the protection of their trade. Its walls are built of *adobe* or sun burnt brick, being about 15 ft. high and of a rectangular construction, inclosing a court of about 130 ft. sq. The walls form a portion of a range of houses opening on the inside. In 1849 it was sold to the U. States and was improved and extended by the erection of additional quarters for the troops, of which about 100 with officers, &c. are generally stationed there. Opposite the fort is old Laramie Ferry, considered the best crossing of the Platte river on the route to the South Pass. The proprietors of the ferry have also a blacksmith's shop and do considerable business in supplying emigrants with horses, mules, grain, outfitting goods, &c. The road on the other side of the Platte crosses the Laramie Fork 1 m. below the fort. Laramie river is a small mountain stream, of pure, clear, cold water, which makes a pleasant contrast with the yellow and muddy waters of the Platte.

Among the events connected with the history of Fort Laramie is that of a treaty made there in Sept. 1851, by D. D. Mitchell, superintendent of Indian affairs, with 8 of the mountain tribes. The number of Indians present was from 8000 to 12,000, and they were together about 8 days. A confederated treaty was concluded between themselves, as well as with the government of the United States, which has been generally kept in good faith.

The country in the vicinity of Laramie is described by Captain Stansbury as follows—"The general flora indicates a much drier atmosphere; the grasses especially are brown, and burned up wherever the earth is not directly moistened by proximity to some stream. The soil around Fort Laramie appears to be sterile, owing no doubt to the extreme dryness of the air, and the almost total absence of dews. The great quantity of coarse conglomerate, too, which, by its disintegration, leaves the surface covered with gravel, must operate as a great impediment to cultivation. The rocks however contain the elements of fertility, being composed of limestone, clay and sand; and I have no doubt that, with the aid of irrigation, the bottom lands of Laramie Creek might be made to produce most abundant crops. Hay is cut about eight miles up the stream in quantity sufficient for the wants of the garrison.

"A short excursion of some seven miles up the Laramie river showed that the sections of the bluffs presented strata of sandstone conglomerate, formed, in some cases, of the detritus of sandstone and calcareous rocks, cemented in an argillaceous matrix. The general direction of the strata was nearly horizontal, but there were evident local displacements, caused apparently by subterraneous upheavings. In some cases the strata were declined as much as 30°, and in opposite directions, within a short space. In many places large quantities occurred of the fragments of primary rocks, resulting most probably from the decomposition of conglomerate: the sandstone was often good, although generally too scaly for building purposes."

In journeying on the N. side of the main stream of the Platte, the artist considers it best to cross at Laramie to the south side, and take the old Oregon road to the upper crossing of the Platte, 124 m., by which a very bad, sandy and hilly road is avoided. This was the route taken by the first company of Saints who went to G. S. L. Valley and has generally been used. Since the change in the starting point for the overland journey, from Winter Quarters to Kansas, and more recently to Atchison, by which the S. side of the river is approached in a north-westerly direction, it is used altogether.

(32) We quote from Capt. Stansbury the following description of

Devil's Gate—"A short distance beyond [Rock Independence] was a range of granite hills, stretching entirely across the valley, and continuous with a range extending to the north. Through this range the Sweetwater passes in a narrow cleft or gorge, about 200 yards in length, called the 'Devil's Gate.' The space between the cliff, on either side, did not in some places exceed 40 ft. The height was from 300 to 400 ft., very nearly perpendicular, and, on the south side, overhanging. Through this romantic pass the river brawls and frets over broken masses of rock that obstruct its passage, affording one of the most lovely, cool, and refreshing retreats from the eternal sunshine without, that the imagination could desire. It is difficult to account for the river having forced its passage through the rocks at this point, as the hills, a very short distance to the south, are much lower, and, according to present appearance, present by no means such serious obstacles as had been here encountered. It is probable that when the canyon was formed, stratified rocks obstructed it in that direction, and that these rocks have since disappeared by slow disintegration. The granite rocks of the pass were traversed in many places, by dikes of trap, which were, in some instances 20 ft. thick, whose direction was east and west. South of the pass, at its eastern extremity, stratified rocks, consisting of conglomerate, were observed, in a nearly horizontal position, without exhibiting the least evidence of having been disturbed by the igneous rocks around which they were placed; indeed, they could be traced in close contact with the granite, without any displacement of the strata, proving that their formation must have been subsequent to that of the granite, from the disintegration of which they were composed. The conglomerate is of the same character as that which was observed before coming upon the carboniferous rocks. The rocks were not observed to have any marked dip. It is highly probable that they belong to a period subsequent to that in which the carboniferous rocks were formed, and that the eruption of granite took place after the latter formation, but that of the conglomerate. No dikes of trap were observed in the granite, except in the immediate vicinity of the "Devil's Gate."

(33) UTAH TERRITORY is bounded on the N. by Oregon; E. by the territories of Nebraska, Kansas, and New Mexico, from which it is separated by the Rocky Mountains; S. by New Mexico; and W. by California. It lies between 37° and 42° N. lat., and 105° 30', or 106° and 120° W. lon., being about 650 m. long from E. to W., and 350 broad from N. to S. Area 225,000 sq. m. There is no recent data from which to ascertain the amount of the population, in 1855, but it is variously estimated at from 40,000 to 60,000.

The Territory was originally divided into 12 counties—Weber, Davis,

Desert, Green River, Great Salt Lake, Utah, Tooele, Juab, Millard, San Pete, Iron and Washington; since when Carson and Summit have been added.

The principal cities and settlements, beginning in the N. and proceeding S. to a distance of about 360 m., are Box Elder, Ogden, Farmington, Great Salt Lake, Drapersville, David, Lehi, Lake, Pleasant Grove, Provo, Springville, Palmyra, Payson, Nephi, Manti, Fillmore (the capital), Parowan, Cedar and Harmony. Tooele City stands about 32 m. W. of G. S. L. City. Besides these there are numerous small but thriving settlements intervening and east and west.

The general face of the country in Utah is that of an elevated tableland, divided into unequal portions by the Sierra Madre mountains, the largest portion lying to the W. of them. This section is known as the Great Basin, and is hemmed in by mountains on all sides—the Blue mountains of Oregon on the N.; the Wahsatch mountains on the E.; the Sierra Nevada on the W., and nameless mountains on the S. This remarkable depression has an area of 500 m. from N. to S., and 350 m. from E. to W., and a general elevation of from 4000 to 5000 ft. above the level of the sea. It has its own system of lakes and rivers, which, contrary to others, have no communication with the ocean. Detached parallel mountain-ranges, having a N. and S. direction, again divide this section into a number of valleys, imparting an Alpine scenery to the landscape. The principal range is the Humboldt River Mountains, near the centre of the Basin, elevated from 2000 to 5000 ft. above the level of the surrounding country. The Wahsatch mountains attain to an elevation of from 4000 to 7000 ft. above the neighbouring valleys, and some reach the height of perpetual snow.

From Lieut. Gunnison's "History of the Mormons in the Valley of the Great Salt Lake" we make the following extracts for a general description of the eastern portion of the Basin—"Along the western foot of the Wahsatch range, for three hundred miles, is a strip of alluvion, from one to two miles in width,—and, in the valley of the Jordan, this is widened by what can be reclaimed by irrigating from its waters; and the spots similarly situated, in other valleys, furnish the only land suited to cultivation in the Utah Territory. This arises from the want of rain during the growing season; and water for the crops is only to be procured from the numerous streams that flow down the mountain gorges, fed during the spring and into midsummer, by the melting snows. The higher mountains retain the snow, and irrigate the bases the longest time, and where the streams cannot be taken at the kanyon mouths, and led off for the farmer's use, the ground is lost to the plough. Most of these creeks are absorbed in the porous alluvion before they have reached a mile from the base, and frequently re-appear in very diminished quantity in springs, at too low a level for use, in the arid plain that borders the salt pools or lakes. The land around Salt Lake is flat, and rises imperceptibly on the south and west for several miles, where it is not broken up by the abrupt hills, and is a soft and sandy barren, irreclaimable for agricultural purposes. On the north the tract is narrow, and the springs bursting out near the surface of the water, the grounds cannot be irrigated; but the eastern side, above the line of overflow when the lake rises with the spring freshets, is fertile and cultivated between the mountain and shore.

"On the south of the lake, and above the alkaline barrens lie the more fertile valleys of the Jordan and Tooele, separated by the Oquirrh Mountain; and these are divided from the plains which lie to the south, between the same ranges, by the Traverse Mountain, which is a cross ridge, diminishing in height to the westward. Here is fine grazing during the entire year, and the east of Jordan Valley is watered by bold streams that traverse a strip of alluvion 20 m. long, by 8 in width, to the banks of the Jordan. This great stream rushes with a foaming torrent through the kanyon cut in the cross range, and descends about 100 feet in a distance of 2 m. where the current becomes more gentle and winding to the great lake below. The banks are steep and high, immediately below the kanyon, but gradually retreat and slope away to the Oquirrh hills, and a canal can easily be carried on the level of the kanyon, winding on a curve to Spring Point, 20 miles from the city. The chalky waters of the Jordan can be used for irrigating 80 additional square miles in the valley, and furnish water-power very accessible, and to any required extent, for milling, machinery, or manufactures. Ascending the Traverse range, a beautiful panorama of lake, plain, and river, embosomed with lofty and romantic mountains, bursts upon the view. Here is the lovely Utah Lake and its winding outlet; and the Timpanogas, with four other rivers, fringed with cottonwoods, a sight so seldom seen in these regions, and by contrast, enchanting. All the valley on the east side of the lake is fertile, and the waters throughout fresh and sparkling, as they rapidly descend to the quiet reservoir.

"The valley affords perennial pasturage, but the hill-sides furnish the bunch grass only during the warm months of the year.It seeds in summer, and is germinated by the autumnal rains, and grows under the snowy covering of winter. In the spring, as the snow-line retreats up the slope, under the melting influence of the approaching sun, the cattle and wild grazing animals follow it to the mountain peaks until midsummer, to be driven down again as the accumulating snow, beginning on the summits about the equinox, descends in a few weeks to the base. When it rains on the valleys, the snow falls on the mountains and, during winter, an im-

mense quantity is drifted into the kanyons, and passes, to the depth sometimes of hundreds of feet, blocking up the roads, and making prisoners
at home, those who sojourn in those solitudes.

"This position of these two descriptions of land, the cultivated and the
waste, renders the people there residing, equally a pastoral and an agricultural community. All the cultivated lands, that is, those brought under
irrigation, can be allotted to raising cereals and vegetables. The flocks
and herds driven to the hills in summer, and fed upon the plains in
winter, will furnish one half the provisions required to sustain the population that can be accommodated on the cultivated belt between the
pastures. The soil, in its mineral composition, is of the most fertile description, having been formed out of disintegrated feldspathic rocks of
the summits, and mixed with the debris and decomposed limestones from
the lower altitudes.

"In order to estimate the probable amount of population which can
well be sustained in the territory, we may safely rely on an equivalent of
two thousand pounds of flour to the acre of the plowed lands, and, drawing the meat part of the ration, or one half, from the herds fed elsewhere,
there could be fed four thousand persons on the square mile. Such a
density of inhabitants it can hardly be supposed will ever be attained
there; but, modified by the peculiar circumstances of the case, and social
character of the people, and giving a far less amount to the mile, we may
calculate that the territory of Utah will maintain, with ease, a million
inhabitants. Stretching southward from the point we have been noticing,
and passing over the rim of the Great Basin into a cotton-growing region,
and where it is contemplated to try the sugar-cane; having abundant iron
mines every where in its whole extent, and inexhaustible beds of coal in
the Green River Basin—with hill pastures, the finest in the world for
sheep and wool raising—with water-power for manufactures on every
considerable stream—there are elements for a great and powerful mountain nation." [Lieutenant John W. Gunnison (1812–1853), who accompanied Captain Howard Stansbury on his exploring expedition to the
Great Basin in 1849, and who wrote a friendly account, *The Mormons
or Latter-day Saints, in the Valley of the Great Salt Lake* (Philadelphia,
1852), was ambushed and slain by Indians in Central Utah in 1853.]

Captain Stansbury thus describes the country stretching about 70 m.
W. of the shores of the Great Salt Lake—"the examination just completed proves that the whole western shore of the lake is bounded by an
immense level plain, consisting of soft mud, frequently traversed by small,
meandering rills of salt and sulphurous water, with occasional springs
of fresh, all of which sink before reaching the lake. These streams seem
to imbue and saturate the whole soil, so as to render it throughout miry

and treacherous. For a few months, in midsummer, the sun has sufficient influence to render some portions of the plain, for a short time dry and hard: in these intervals the travelling over it is excellent; but one heavy shower is sufficient to reconvert the hardened clay into soft, tenacious mud, rendering the passage of teams over it toilsome and frequently quite hazardous.

"These plains are but little elevated above the present level of the lake, and have, beyond question, at one time formed a part of it. It is manifest to every observer, that an elevation of but a few feet above the present level of the lake would flood this entire flat to a great distance north and south, and wash the base of the Pilot Peak range of mountains, which constitute its western boundary; thus converting what is now a comparatively small and insignificant lake into a vast inland sea. This extensive area is, for the most part, entirely denuded of vegetation, excepting occasional patches of artemisia and greasewood. The minute crystals of salt which cover the surface of the moist, oozy mud, glisten brilliantly in the sunlight, and present the appearance of a large sheet of water, so perfectly, that it is difficult, at times, for one to persuade himself that he is not standing on the shore of the lake itself. High rocky ridges protrude above the level plain, and resemble great islands rising above the bosom of this desert sea.

"The mirage, which frequently occurs, is greater here than I ever witnessed elsewhere, distorting objects in the most grotesque manner, defying all calculation as to their size, shape, or distances, and giving rise to optical illusions almost beyond belief. With the exception of the two valleys, lying at the south end of the lake, the country is, as a place of human habitation, entirely worthless. There is, however, one valuable use to which it may and perhaps will be applied: its extent, and perfectly level surface, would furnish a desirable space on which to measure a degree of the meridian."

In order to convey a more particular description of the Territory, we give a detailed account of the various districts and settlements, and of their topography, agricultural facilities and improvements. We shall also note the advances made in manufactures, the provision made for education, &c.

Great Salt Lake Valley was the first district settled by the Latter Day Saints. It lies between the Great Salt Lake and a traverse range of mountains which separate it from Utah Valley, and through which the Jordan river flows to the Great Salt Lake. The timber, which is principally pine and fir, is plentiful on the mountains and in the kanyons, but not easy of access. The land is generally rich and fertile, adapted to the cultivation of every kind of grain, especially wheat. Flax and hemp have done well.

By "using the proper exertion in taking out the streams, and economising the water during the season for irrigation, the greatest part of the valley might be made susceptible of a high cultivation and capable of sustaining a large and dense population." Much of it has already been cultivated, and it is now dotted with the thriving farms and beautiful gardens of the inhabitants.

The principal city and settlement in this valley, as also of the Territory, is Great Salt Lake City, of which we shall hereafter give a separate notice.

Leaving Great Salt Lake City and proceeding about 16 m. almost directly N., we come to the town of Farmington, the county seat of Davis Co. It is situated near the mouth of North Cottonwood Kanyon. A stream furnishes water for irrigation and mill privileges and waters a large tract of the choicest land. The Wahsatch Mountains rise on the E. to nearly a mile in height. At the close of 1854 the town contained 1 circular-saw mill, 1 water-power threshing machine, 1 shingle machine, 1 cooperage, 2 cabinet shops, and an extensive tannery. There was a grist mill in operation just above the town. Its Court House, 35 ft. by 45 ft., built at a cost of 5500 dollars, was the first erected in Utah. The town has a school house, 20 ft. by 32 ft., well finished, which was attended by 80 scholars.

At the foot of the same chain of mountains, about 22 m. further N., in Weber Valley, is Ogden City, laid out on both sides of the Ogden, and some 4 or 5 m. above the mouth of that river, where it meets the Bear and Weber rivers. The soil is rich and fertile. In 1854, 10,000 bushels of wheat were raised. The city was incorporated in February, 1851, by the General Assembly of Deseret, and it is now the county seat of Weber Co. It has 2 school houses, with about 120 scholars. Not far from Ogden are Bingham's Fort, Odgen Hole, and Willow Creek. The Fort contains about 800 inhabitants, and is surrounded by an abundance of good farming land. Ogden Hole is a sort of broken kanyon, in the mountains, N. of Weber kanyon. This settlement has about 47 families, and is, considering its population, one of the most flourishing in the Territory. In 1854 it raised 16,000 bushels of wheat. The settlement contains 1 threshing machine, and one school house, with about 50 scholars. [Ogden Hole, now known as Ogden Valley, a renowned beauty spot in Utah, is of special interest to this editor, who spent her childhood there.] At Willow Creek there are 35 families, who raised 12,000 bushels of wheat in 1854. Box Elder, about 25 m. N. of Ogden, is the last northern settlement of the territory. It contains about 60 families.

The crossing of the Bear River is about 15 or 20 m. N. of Box Elder, where the road turns N. W. across the river to ford the Malade, and then a trifle S. of W. to California. Lying between Bear river and its tributary the Malade is a valley, named after the latter river, 5 or 6 m. wide. Passing eastward through a passage made in the Wahsatch mountains by the Bear river, we enter Cache Valley, in Green River Co., which is both beautiful and picturesque, and is diversified by numerous clumps of willow. The soil is principally a rich alluvion with much vegetable mould. "Facilities for irrigation are very great, and water could be obtained to a large extent for farming purposes." To the S. of this valley, from the Wahsatch mountains on the W., to the eastern boundary of the Territory, very little exploration has been made, but it is thought to be a very sterile region.

We re-enter the great Basin, and 17 m. W. of G. S. L. City the road that crosses the Great Western Desert nears the Lake at Black Rock. Here are some springs of fresh, cold water on the shores of the Lake, oozing out of its bed, and sometimes washed by its waters. Doubling a point of low mountains at Benson's mill, about 7 m. further on, and travelling 6 m. in a S. S. W. course, we find Tooele City, in Tooele County and Valley.

Tooele Valley forms an excellent pasturage for numerous herds of cattle, which are wintered there, under charge of keepers. The grass is very abundant, and numerous springs are found on both sides of the valley. There are also many salt springs in various parts of it. Tooele City is the principal settlement, and was incorporated in Jan., 1853. Other settlements are Grantsville, 12 m. W. of Tooele, and Richville. Excellent crops of wheat and abundance of vegetables are raised there. From Tooele city the road turns N. to round a low mountain that juts towards Great Salt Lake and then crosses over a plain about 15 m. wide, called Spring Valley, by Capt. Stansbury, and Lone Rock Valley, by the inhabitants of the Territory, from a large rock, almost equal to Independence Rock, standing alone in the centre of the plain, and once, no doubt, a small island of the Lake. This valley extends northward to the southern shore of the Great Salt Lake and is shut in toward the S. by a range of comparatively low hills which connect two mountain ranges that form its eastern and western boundaries. In some places, owing to salt springs, it is marshy and wholly impassable. Capt. Stansbury, in noticing the Lone Rock, writes—"I remarked on our left, in the middle of the valley, a curious isolated mass of rocks, resembling a small fortification, or redoubt; it was surrounded by marshy meadow-land, and could, in case of need, be defended by a small force against almost any number of Indians. Numerous springs broke out from the mountain and at the edge of the prairie; but they were all saline, with a temperature of 74°, and totally unfit to drink. To this place we gave the name of 'Spring Valley.' Near the point of the mountain was a very large spring, which discharged its waters northward into the Lake. The water was very salt, nauseous and bitter, with a temperature of 70°; notwithstanding which it swarmed with innumerable small fish, and seemed to be a favourite resort for pelicans and gulls." The road then threads through the mountain range forming the western boundary of this valley and enters upon the Great Western Desert. The Desert is 70 m. long, for which distance there are no springs. Forage and water must be carried for cattle, and the journey begun in the P.M. and continued through the night. This route to California was first taken in 1845 by Capt. Frémont, who lost 10 mules and several horses in effecting the passage. It was taken a year afterward by a party of emigrants under a Mr. Hastings, from whom it is named "Hastings Cut Off." "The road to California from this point follows around the southern end of the ridge, passes to the N. of another high mountain, and thence to the head of Humboldt's or Mary's river." [For the story of Lansford W. Hastings and his "cutoff" see Dale L. Morgan: *The Great Salt Lake* (New York, 1947), pp. 154 ff.]

Commencing again in G. S. L. Valley, we find the settlements of Big Cottonwood, on the creek of that name; Union, on little Cottonwood Creek; and Drapersville, on South Willow Creek, at the respective distances of about 8, 12, and 21 m. nearly S. of G. S. L. City, and all good farming districts. Twenty-five miles south of G. S. L. City the southern State road rounds a point of the mountains that separates G. S. L. Valley from Utah Valley, and where the Jordan passes and opens into the latter.

Utah Valley is about 40 m. long from N. to S., and 12 m. broad, from E. to W., and is thus described by Capt. Stansbury:—"At the outlet of the Lake there is a reed marsh, which, by early cutting the dense growth, a pretty hay can be made. It will be difficult to obtain irrigable land until we reach the Spring creek, and we have to rely on the American fork for water to irrigate with. A beautiful and wide bottom land lies along the Lake shore, for some miles under the control of this stream, and from the crossing to the heads of Pomont-quint is a rich alluvial soil mixed with vegetable mould. A series of rolling round hills now occur between the Pomont Creek and Timpanogas well grassed for cattle ranges. On the Timpanogas bottom wheat grows most luxuriantly, and root crops are seldom excelled. A continuous field can be made thence to the Wa-ke-te-ke Creek, and the lovely Utah Valley made to sustain a population of more than a hundred thousand souls. The west of the lake is grazing land." This valley is in Utah County, and the principal settlements are David City, on Dry Creek, 28 m.; Lehi City, on Dry Creek (W. of David), 30 m.; Lake City, on American Fork, 34¾ m.; Pleasant Grove, on Battle Creek, 41 m.; Provo City, on the S. side of Provo or Timpanogas River, 46¼ m.;

Springville, on Hobble Creek, 53½ m.; Palmyra, on the N. side of Spanish Fork, 59½ m.; and Payson, on both sides of Peteet-neet Creek, 64½ m. distant from G. S. L. City. Of these, Provo, the capital of Utah County, is by far the most populous and important. Its population in 1854 was about 2500. It was incorporated on the 6th of February, 1852, by the General Assembly of Deseret, and the municipality is now divided into 4 wards. It is organized into one school district. The excellent facilities which the Provo affords for manufacturing purposes have been taken advantage of, and there are already flouring and other mills, driven by water power. A woollen factory, a machine shop, a pottery, and various other manufactures have already been established and are prospering. Education has, to some extent, been provided for, but not adequately to the number of scholars. One seminary and 5 or more common schools exist; and the attention of the citizens has lately been directed to the introduction of others. A public library has been opened, and music and the drama have found encouragement. A Music-Hall has been built, and a Dramatic Association formed. Besides the Music Hall, the principal public buildings are the Town-Hall, the Meeting Hall, Seminary, and Tithing Office. The city contains two or more hotels. Among the improvements of the locality, bridges have been erected over the Provo, which, however, have not been sufficiently strong to withstand the rapid current, and at the present time are being replaced by more suitable ones. That across the main stream is 120 ft. long, and over which the new military road through the Territory passes. The contract is 6500 dollars. There have been two companies chartered in this city by the Legislature. One is the "Provo Manufactiuring Company," shares 50 dollars each. Capital not to exceed 1,000,000 dollars. The other, the "Provo Canal and Irrigation Company," shares, 200 dollars each. Capital not to exceed 200,000 dollars. The other settlements of this valley are likewise in a prosperous state and constantly increasing in population and importance. School houses, tithing offices, meeting halls, and other public buildings are rapidly springing into existence to meet the wants of the inhabitants.

Contiguous to Utah Valley, we find Juab Valley and County, separated from Utah by a ridge of mountains, on which runs Summit Creek, where a settlement has been attempted. Juab is a long, moderately wide, and well grassed valley. "It is regular in form, has several springs in it; amongst them one named by the Indians, 'Punjun Spring,' which their traditions regard as bottomless, and in the evening they report the slight wailing of an infant is often heard to proceed from it. The west side of the valley is nearly destitute of timber, on the east old Mount Nebo raises his hoary head covered with snow, and in the ravines of the mountains large timber is seen. Salt Creek runs through pretty near the centre of the valley. Its banks are steep, the stream is rapid and muddy. On its sides are willows and many cedars interspersed to beautify the landscape." A mountain of salt exists in Salt Creek Kanyon, a trifle to the left of the road leading to Manti, and about 4 m. distant, a spring yielding pure salt. The valley also contains gypsum. Nephi City, the principal settlement of the valley and capital of the county, is situated on Salt Creek, which is 25 m. S. of the Peteet-neet. It was commenced in Sept. 1851", and incorporated Mar. 6, 1852. Its barometric attitude is 4425 ft. Here the San Pete road turns into the Kanyon, from whence issues Salt Creek. Taking a meandering course about S. E. by S., we enter San Pete Valley and County, and by travelling 5 m. reach Manti City. The valley "is generally level and filled with sage and rabbit weed, except a strip on the immediate banks of the creek, and a few marshy places. The hills are low and well studded with cedars, pine, and other timber, which can be procured with but little trouble in comparison to G. S. L. Valley." It contains plenty of limestone, and good salt is obtained from springs on the San Pete Creek, and from beds and springs about 30 m. S. of Manti." Coal has this year (1855) been discovered W. of the crossing of San Pete Creek on the road to Manti. It is clean, bituminous, and very similar to the best Alleghany coals of Maryland. There is an immense quantity of it, and one vein has been found 5 ft. in thickness. In addition to the mineral wealth of San Pete County, it is also highly productive in wheat, corn and vegetables. It is thought that the vast facilities of the San Pete and its branches must ere long render that county the granary of the Territory. Melons, squashes, pumpkins and tomatoes also grow luxuriantly. Manti City is the capital of the county and principal settlement of the valley. The city is beautifully located on the banks of the San Pete, which runs through it and waters its farms. It is, by the road, 78 m. from Fillmore City, and 130 m. from G. S. L. City. It is in Lat. 39° 16′ 32″, and has an altitude of 4848 feet. It was commenced in 1849 and incorporated Feb. 6, 1851. Having an abundance of stone admirably adapted for building, it is chiefly used for that purpose. Various branches of manufactures are already carried on in this city, and its saw and grist mills are said to be as good as any in the Territory. Another settlement of this county is Fort Ephraim, 7 m. N. of Manti, containing about 30 families. In this vicinity is a delightful country both for agricultural and grazing purposes. It is also well timbered. A coach, with the United States Mail, runs weekly between G. S. L. City and Manti, calling at the intermediate settlements.

From Nephi City, travelling S. about 25 m. brings you to the Nicollet or Sevier river, noted for the lamented massacre of Capt. Gunnison and party. An excellent bridge, 162 ft. long, having 4 abutments, well filled with stone, was erected over the river in 1852. Crossing the river, we ascend gradually and pass through a depression in the mountain range, which lies between the Sevier and Lake Valley, and the latter opens to view about 15 m. long, in a N. N. W. and S. S. E. direction, and from 1 to 4 m. wide. It is well grassed, and the mountain slopes on either side are well wooded. Leaving this valley we pass through a kanyon, about 5 m. long, on a gradual ascent, and then descend some miles to Cedar Springs, in Pauvan Valley, Millard County, one of the most delightful counties in the Territory.

Pauvan, Indian Pah-Van-te, is a fine rich valley, and is said to be the most delightful for extent and beauty of scenery of any in the Territory. It is beautifully studded with mounds of various sizes. Its forests of cedar extend into the plain, and it has all the varieties of soil and landscape, from the lofty mountain and rich valley, to the level plain and bleak desert. The Kanyon of Chalk Creek, when the valley was settled, contained an extensive supply of red and white pine timber. There are 7 or 8 fine streams of water, and the hills and plains are covered with bunch grass. An inexhaustible supply of sandstone and limestone, well adapted to building purposes, is found at the base of the mountains. At 37 m. from the Sevier we find Fillmore City, the capital of the county, and of the Territory, situated on Chalk Creek, Indian, Nu-quin, a branch of the Sevier River, which gives it its irrigation and mill water. In Fillmore, one of the greatest objects of notice to a mountaineer, is the uncommon fact in Utah that one can look in any direction without seeing mountains. Looking a little N. of W. from this city, you see an extended plain uninterrupted by a single hill. It is a common expression on arriving at Fillmore, that one is in an open sea, out of sight of land—that is, in that one direction only. This is thought to extend over the Great Western desert.

Fillmore City is in lat. 38° 58' 40", N., and is 151½ m. from G. S. L. City, about 600 m. E. by N. of San Francisco, and 1200 m. W. of St. Louis. The city site was determined upon Oct. 29, 1851, by commissioners appointed by the Legislature for that purpose. It is divided into blocks of 10 acres each, subdivided into 8 lots of 1¼ acres each, with streets 8 rods wide, crossing at right angles, N. and S. and E. and W. Saw and grist mills have been erected, also a City Hall and School House. The State House in course of erection will be equal to any and superior to many in the Union. It is being built of stone, laid in lime mortar, and one wing is nearly completed, the dimensions of which are, in the basement, 41 ft. 4 in. wide and 61 ft. 8 in. long. It has three stories, whose respective heights are first, 10 ft.; second, 12 ft.; third, 14 ft. 6 in. to the spring of the arch. The side walls are 43 ft., in height, and are, in the basement,

3 ft., and above it, 2 ft. in thickness. There are pilasters on three sides of the building which impart a grand appearance. It is estimated that the cost of this one wing will not fall short of 40,000 dollars. Ten miles south of Fillmore is Corn Creek, the head quarters of Kanoshe, the Pah-Van-te chief, but without settlements. The chief however lives in a respectable house, and, with his men, cultivates a farm.

Travelling from 30 to 40 m. S. we enter Iron County, and at about 10 m. further meet the Beaver river, which is the only stream of much importance until you come to the settlements. It is the largest county of the Territory and has an estimated area of 7000 sq. m. It extends entirely across the Territory, having California on the W. and the Rocky mountains on the E. It is watered by the Green and Grand rivers which unite near its southern borders to form the Rio Colorado, and likewise by several minor streams. The surface on the eastern and central parts is mountainous, and contains rich iron ore and stone coal. The Kanyons contain plenty of limestone, with plaster of paris and flintstone, and several kinds of clay, salt and alum have been found. Specimens of pottery, made at some anterior date, have been found, indicating that material for this kind of work exists. Timber, the finest in the Territory, is abundant, covering the mountains and filling the kanyons. While this county is so rich in minerals, its soil is equally fertile in producing wheat, corn, potatoes, squashes, pumpkins, turnips, beets, &c. Wheat averages 40 bushels to the acre, and 65 have been produced. Indian corn likewise has done well. The climate of the country is very salubrious, and during a part of the winter, which is short, resembles an Indian summer in the States. The spring is early.

Little Salt Lake Valley contains the principal settlements. It is about 60 m. E. of the meadows of Santa Clara, between 37° and 38° of N. lat., and 113° and 114° of W. long., and is about 5000 ft. above the level of the sea. It is thus eloquently described by Mr. Carruthers a resident of Cedar City—"The view from the mountains on the east of the city presents the beholder with a scene truly picturesque and imposingly grand. The prospect to the west and north exhibits, in all the pride and glory of mountain grandeur, an extensive and beautiful valley carpeted with a luxuriant herbage, stretching far and wide, flinging its ample green skirts upon the broad bases of the towering mountains, and terminating amid their curvatures and kanyons. A small portion of this wide-sweeping plain is studded with gentle undulations and a few rocky cliffs, thrown up by some great convulsion of nature, presenting on their rugged brows, and gently sloping bases, the black vertical stratum of the magnetic iron ore— the hope, and when manufactured, the staple production of our locality. To the south you again behold the valley stretching itself, like an arm of the mighty deep, amid the mountains, bearing majestically upon its proud bosom all the inviting inducements that possibly could be offered to encourage and gladden the heart of the settler—a rich soil, luxuriant pasturage, abundance of timber, short and mild winters, mountains of iron ore, extensive strata of stonecoal, a healthy and pure atmosphere, not to say anything of the gold and silver, the copper, the zinc, &c., &c., which are only some of the things of the ancient mountains and the lasting hills. The valley I have been describing is encircled with a broken chain of beautiful mountains; on the south and east they are lofty, romantic and grand, presenting on their sloping sides up to their towering summits a variety of vivid colours—the scarlet the orange and the green. They are densely covered from the base to a considerable distance up the acclivity, with trees of cedar and pine, which are beautiful evergreens. To the west they recede in the distance as they approximate to the extremity of the great California basin. To the north you again behold them as far as the eye can penetrate, towering above their fellows, shooting into the ærial regions their pyramidical forms, crowned with the eternal snows—crowns too which bid defiance to the melting influences of the effulgent beams of the regal sun. On the east, at a distance of from three to six miles, the mountains are cleft asunder into beautiful kanyons, the storehouses of immense quantities of timber, and the great reservoirs of those cooling and crystal rivulets which are poured forth in rapid torrents on the plains below."

Parowan City, handsomely laid out on a beautiful stream called Centre Creek, at the mouth of its kanyon, on the E. of the valley, about 96 m. S. of Fillmore, and 247 of G. S. L. City, was the first settlement. It was commenced Jan. 22, 1851, as a farming district to provide for the wants of the persons who might be employed in the Iron Works which were about to be formed some 20 m. distant. The colony numbered 120 men with some 30 families, under the superintendence of Elder George A. Smith, and the first year they had to endure all the rigours and hardships of a mountain winter, without houses, but succeeded well in the enterprise. Mr. Carruthers describes the vigorous operations of the first year as follows—"After looking out and selecting a location, we formed our waggons into two parallel lines, some seventy paces apart. We then took our boxes from the wheels, and planted them about a couple of paces from each other, so securing ourselves that we could not easily be taken advantage of by any unknown foe. This done, we next cut a road up the kanyon, opening it to a distance of some eight miles, bridging the creek in some five or six places, making the timber and poles (of which there is an immense quantity) of easy access. We next built a large meeting-house in the form of two rectangles, lying transversely, two stories high, of large pine trees, all well hewn and neatly jointed together. We next built a large square fort, with a commodious cattle carrel inside the inclosure. The houses built were some of hewn logs, and some of adobies, all neat, comfortable and convenient. We next inclosed a field some five by three miles square, with a good ditch and pole fence. We dug canals and water ditches to the distance of some 30 or 40 miles. One canal to turn the water of another creek upon the field, for irrigating purposes, was seven miles long. We built a saw and grist mill the same season. I have neither time nor space to tell you of one-half of the labours we performed here in one season. Suffice it to say that, when the Governor came along in the spring, he pronounced it the greatest work done in the mountains by the same amount of men." The city was incorporated Feb. 6, 1851, and is the capital of Iron County. It now possesses a thriving population, and has School Houses, a Tithing, Store, a Council House, 38 ft. by 46, in the form of a Greek cross and a Dramatic Association. It has also an Iron Foundry, a Tannery, Machine and Cut Nail Shops, and a Cabinet and Sash Manufactory. Much of the work is done by Piede Indians, who, as the Indians of several other settlements, are being gradually taught the arts of civilised life and reclaimed from their wandering propensities.

In the fall of the same year that Parowan was founded, some 35 men were detailed to go to Cedar, on Coal Creek, 20 m. S., to do the same work there, and to build iron works. Deeds worthy of everlasting remembrance were performed by these hardy pioneers of Iron County. A kanyon was opened, a fort was built, 500 acres of land were enclosed, extensive canals and water ditches were cut, crops were sown and harvested, and the foundation of the iron works was laid in an incredibly short period. In the meantime, in the Spring of 1852, Elders E. Snow and F. D. Richards, then in England, in compliance with instructions from the First Presidency of the Church, contained in the Sixth General Epistle, organized the Deseret Iron Company, with a subscription amounting to £4000, in shares of £500 each, and, on returning to Utah, obtained a liberal charter for the same from the Legislature, for 50 years, confirming the price of the shares, and leaving the extent of the capital to be regulated by the requirements of the business. The Company having previously associated with them the interests and labours of the persons who had commenced the manufacture of iron, were now prepared to proceed, and develop with vastly increased efficiency the mineral resources of Iron County, and soon established their works at Cedar City, where now they have so far succeeded as to be able to produce 1700 lbs of good iron every 24 hours. As many as 150 additional men were called for in the Spring of the present year (1855). To encourage the manufacture of this staple article, the Territorial Legislature has already made two appropriations amounting together to 6840 dollars, and both the Legislature and the Church, through its Trustee in Trust, have taken shares in the concern. The city, as already stated, is situated on Coal Creek, about two m. from the mouth of its kanyon. The iron ore, in qualities varying from 25 to 75 per cent of pure iron, is found in a chain of mountains which commence about 8 m. W. of the city, and excellent coal mines have been opened about 7 m. E. of it. A Tithing Store and School Houses have already been erected, and a Seventies Hall is about to be built by subscription, shares, 25 dollars each.

Several other beautiful valleys in this county have been partially explored, among which the principal are the Beaver Valleys, watered by the river of that name. One of these, called Beaver Valley, No. 2, situated about 200 m. S. S. W. from G. S. L. City, is about 60 m. long, and 15 m. wide, and is said to have the richest soil known in the mountains. The river is about 25 ft. wide and 5 ft. deep, with a rapid current, and it could easily be made to irrigate the whole valley, if necessary, though much of it will not require it. On the adjacent mountains are found cedar and other wood, and in the upper kanyons, timber for building.

Leaving Cedar City, and travelling about 25 m. S. by W. we come to Harmony Settlement, Washington County. It is situated on Ash Creek, 20 m. N. of the Rio Virgen. The settlers are building houses for the Indians and teaching them to cultivate the land for their subsistence, which is well received, and many of them are believing the Gospel and becoming Latter-day Saints.

The Southern route to California after leaving Cedar turns a little to the W. and then proceeds across the N. W. portion of New Mexico to the eastern boundary of California, but it is intended that it shall pass through Harmony. Small settlements exist at Carson Valley, Carson County, on the extreme W. of the Territory; at the White mountains, W. of Fillmore; at Fort Supply, on Green River, in Green River County; and quite recently one has been made at the Elk mountains, on the left or S. bank of Grand River, near where it unites with Green River to form the Rio Colorado. It is situated in a valley about 10 m. long, and 2½ m. wide, with the Elk mountains about 10 m. to the S. E. "Elk Mountain and Pack Saddle Creeks unite near the centre of the valley, and empty into Grand River where it enters a kanyon in the mountains S. of the settlement. The river runs through the N. W. end of the valley and is ruggedly kanyoned at its entrance and exit."

In addition to the settlements we have described, there are many more in different parts of the Territory, where the valleys have been explored and agricultural facilities exist.

Of the geology and mineralogy of the Territory our information is yet necessarily limited. It is stated in Cap. Stansbury's work that the specimens collected on the islands and shores of Great Salt Lake give a good idea of the general geological features—i.e., we presume, of the neighbourhood of G. S. Lake. The specimens referred to are metamorphic rock, consisting of talcose and mica slates, hornblende rocks, and a few specimens of granitic and sienitic character. In some localities the metamorphic strata appear to be overlaid by a coarse conglomerate, or coarse sandstone, partially altered, and assuming the character of a quartz rock. The more elevated portions of the shores of G. S. Lake and the mountain ranges consist of carboniferous limestone, in some places threaded by calcareous spa. Fossils, particularly corals of the cyathophyllideæ, abound in the limestone, which is said to rest on coarse sandstone. Near the Fort Hall road from the States where it intersects the road to G. S. L. City, there is said to be a mountain of marble of almost every hue and colour, and equal in quality to any procured in Italy. From an exploring tour South, made by President Young and others, in 1851, we learn that, "from the head waters of Dry Creek, in Utah Valley, to near Salt Creek Pass, the mountain ranges are composed of a very hard, compact, variegated sandstone, alternating with limestone. From the pass to the Sevier, the low mountain range on the W. side of Juab Valley, the higher range between Juab and San Pete Valleys, and the still higher one E. of San Pete, and much of that between the Sevier and Lake Valley, are of an entirely different lithological character, being composed of the softer sandstone, the more earthy limestones, the various coloured marls, and an indurated clay. It is in this formation that the coal and beds and springs of salt are found. The portion of the mountain range, lying E. of the road between Pauvan Valley and Lake Valley and the left or western branch of the Sevier has the same composition and characteristics as the range first described."

We have already stated that a rich mine of coal has been discovered in San Pete County and that excellent coal and iron abound in Iron County. Other minerals of the Territory are gypsum, or plaster of paris, alum, brimstone, and saleratus and salt in great quantities. Gold is reported to have been obtained in Carson County. There is every probability that the mineralogical resources of Utah are immense. The boiling and hot springs which will be hereafter referred to indicate the proximity of volcanic fires.

In treating of the waters of the Territory, the Great Salt Lake claims our first attention, both from its size and other peculiarities. This inland sea has not inaptly been compared to the Dead Sea of Palestine, except that it lies about 4200 ft. above the level of the sea, instead of 1000 ft.

below, as is the case with the latter. It lies in a N. E. direction from the centre of the Territory, and is about 70 m. long from N. to S., and 30 m. wide from E. to W. The water of this lake is so saline that no living thing can exist in it. Persons who are engaged in salt boiling state that they procure 2 measures of salt from 3 of brine. An analysis of the water made by Dr. L. D. Gale shows that it "contains full 20 per cent of pure chloride of sodium, and not more than 2 per cent of other salts, and is one of the purest and most concentrated brines known in the world." Its specific gravity is 1.17, but it slightly varies with the seasons, being doubtless affected by the immense floods of fresh water which, in the spring, rush from the melting snows in the mountains. "The brine is so strong that the least part of it getting into the eyes, produces the most acute pain, and if accidentally swallowed, strangulation must ensue." This large body of water has no outlet, except by evaporation, which, in hot weather, leaves a thick incrustation of salt on the shores. Some of the salt has been anlayzed by Cap. Frémont and found to contain in 100 parts, 97.80 of chloride of sodium, or common salt; 1.12 of sulphate of lime; .24 of magnesium; and .23 of sulphate of soda. The Lake has a number of bays, whose shores in summer "are lined with the skeletons and larvæ of insects, and the few fish that venture too far from the mouths of the rivers; and these form banks that fester and ferment, emitting sulphurous gases, offensive to the smell, but not supposed deleterious to health; and these, often dispersed by storms, are at last thrown far up the beach to dry into hard cakes of various dimensions, on which horses can travel without breaking them through; the underside being moist, the masses are slippery and insecure." It has also several, beautiful islands, two of which, Antelope and Stansbury's, are of considerable magnitude, "with a mountain ridge through the centre 2000 ft. high, and fresh springs of water, which have caused them to be selected by the shepherds and herdsmen for their occupation."

About 38 m. S. of G. S. Lake is Utah Lake, connected with the former by the Jordan, a beautiful body of fresh water, nearly 30 m. long, and 15 m. broad, with a smooth uniform bottom, and a depth varying from 7 to 15 ft. It abounds with suckers, salmon trout, and various other kinds of fish, which are caught in large quantities. On the slope of the Sierra Nevada mountains is Pyramid Lake, so named from a rock which rises from its midst. It is said by Frémont to be 700 ft. higher than G. S. Lake. There are several small lakes in the interior of the Basin, which receive its streams and are frequently mere sinks or sloughs. The most important yet known are Nicollet or Sevier Lake and Lake Ashley. Mud, Pyramid, Carson's and Walker's Lakes, near the E. base of the Sierra Nevada, receive the waters of the eastern slope of those mountains. Humboldt's

Lake is about 50 m. E. of Pyramid Lake, and is formed by the Humboldt river. These lakes have no visible outlet, except by evaporation.

The rivers of the Basin have no apparent communication with the ocean, but either discharge themselves into the lakes, or are absorbed by the sands of the deserts. The largest of these streams is the Humboldt or Mary's River. It has its source in the W. declivities of the Humboldt mountains, and flows S. W. about 300 m. to the lake of the same name. The Nicollet river rises in the S. part of the Territory, flows N. and then W., for nearly the same distance as the Humboldt, and empties itself into Nicollet Lake. Bear River, the principal tributary of G. S. Lake, enters the Territory from Oregon in the N. E. of the Basin. Weber River and the Timpanogas rise in the Wahsatch mountains; the former empties into G. S. Lake, and the latter into Lake Utah. The Ogden is a tributary of the Weber. [It is an error to say that the Ogden River is a tributary of the Weber. Both empty into Great Salt Lake at approximately the same point, but they are independent rivers draining separate valleys.] East of the Great Basin, we find Green River, whose source is in the S. E. of Oregon, and Grand River, whose source is in the Rocky mountains. These two unite near lat. 36° N. to form the Colorado which flows into the Gulf of California. Before the junction, Grand River has a course of about 300 m., and Green River of 400 m. These streams with their affluents drain the entire eastern division of Utah.

Objects of interest to tourists, especially to men of science, abound in the Territory of Utah. In a geographical point of view, it is one of the most interesting countries in the world. It has all the characteristics of the Holy Land of the Scriptures—its Dead Sea, its Jordan, its sea of Gallilee, &c., but on an infinitely larger scale. Its extremely mountainous character, affording scenes of the wildest and sublimest grandeur, impresses one forcibly with the beauty, sublimity, and permanence of the works of nature, when compared with the feeble imitations of man. Lieut. Gunnison has eloquently portrayed the appearance of the landscape while he was surveying G. S. L. Valley—"Every day of the year has a different landscape for the eye, in the variety of light and shade cast by the sun, as he approaches toward, and recedes from, those frowning cliffs and snow-clad peaks—and the different coloured garb of the seasons, *nature's* change of fashions, so much imitated by the lovers of dress, on whom her lessons are not bestowed in vain, comes to aid in breaking up the monotony. On the south-east rises the lofty head of the Lone Peak, with double buttressed pillars on the summit, that look like an open portal to giant chambers in the clouds; and not far off, on the north, stand the Twin Peaks, side by side, like conjugal partners hesitating awhile on earth, before they pass through this inviting door to mansions amid the stars. When these barren masses of grey rock are viewed near at hand, the mind labours under its load of sublimity, grandeur and awe—but when standing on some distant eminence, the eye seems to grasp the infinite before it, and distance softens the harsh outlines into wavy curves, with closing vistas between, lost in the horizon's edge; the senses become enraptured for awhile with vastness and beauty combined; but soon there comes welling up from the depths of the soul the feeling that something is still wanting, and coldness, sterility, and vacuity brood over the landscape. The full charm is not there—for the accessories of art spring not forth to make an agreeable variety, nor the forest-trees pointing to the skies, under whose shady retreats the weary of earth may contemplate their destiny." The improvements of the settlers have now given, in a great measure, life and animation to some of these vast solitudes, imparting an Alpine scenery to the country. As in the deserts of the Old World, so in Utah, on the barren plains and arid valleys, the mirage takes up objects and distorts them in the most fantastic manner. "A small stick close at hand, will start up an immense giant at a distance, and far off things mock you with their retreatings as you endeavour to reach them."

The fastnesses and gorges of the Rocky, Wahsatch, Humboldt, Sierra Nevada, and other mountains, reveal scenes, as they are explored equal in interest to any that have yet been discovered by civilized eyes. The gorges, or kanyons, some of which have perpendicular walls from 600 to 1500 ft. high, present scenes of the utmost wildness. They are in some instances nearly half a mile wide, and in others, only a few rods, which would, if necessary, enable a handful of resolute men to defend them against a host. Echo kanyon, which terminates on the Weber, is 25 m. long, and half a mile wide. We here introduce a sketch made in Parley's kanyon, one of the passes into the G. S. L. Valley. It is in the kanyons that the timber is usually found.

The most remarkable object of interest in the Territory will, perhaps, be considered the G. S. Lake. The salineness of its waters, the circumstance of its having no outlet, and being fed from another smaller and fresh water lake, afford to the scientific abundance of materials for reflection. Pyramid Lake, "embosomed in the Sierra Nevada mountains, with its singular pyramidical mount rising from its transparent waters to the height of about 600 ft., and walled in by almost perpendicular precipices, in some places nearly 3000 ft. high," is said to have nothing similar to it in the U. States. Cap. Frémont describes the Boiling Springs, in about 117° 30′ W. long., and 39° N. lat., as boiling up at irregular intervals with much noise. He states that the largest basin is several hundred feet in circumference and has a circular space at one end 15 ft. in diameter, entirely occupied with boiling water, whose temperature near the edge is 206°. Its depth near the centre is more than 16 ft. Lieut. Gunnison thus describes the Warm and Hot Springs of G. S. Lake Valley—"At the base of the hills, around the lake, issue numerous warm springs, that collect in pools and smaller lakes; inviting aquatic fowl, during the winter, to resort to their agreeable temperature, and where insect larva furnishes food at all times; and the soil is so heated that snow cannot lie in their vicinity. In some places springs of different temperatures are in close proximity, some so hot that the hand cannot be thrust into them without pain; and near the Bear is a depression, in which issue three fountains between the strata, within a space of thirty feet; of which one is a hot sulphur, the next tepid and salt, and the uppermost, cool, delicious drinking water—the three currents unite, and flow off through the plain, a large and bold river. There are also warm 'breathing' or gas-intermitting fountains, chalybeate and gypsum springs, of high and low temperatures." The water of the Warm Spring in the northern confines of the city has been conducted by pipes into a bath house for the use of the public. It is said by Dr. Gale, who has analyzed it, to be a Harrowgate water, abounding in sulphur. We cannot pass over one other object of interest, though not equal in importance to those named. We refer to the frequent junction of rivers in this Territory, or the "Meeting of the Waters," having beautiful vales between them. For instance, the union of Bear and Weber Rivers, Green and Grand Rivers, and many other minor streams. A similar circumstance in the county of Wicklow, Ireland —the union of the Avoca and the Avon, has made the Vale of Avoca immortal in all lands. One of the tenderest and most beautiful of Moore's Irish Melodies, "The Meeting of the Waters," has made it classic ground, and tourists would as soon think of neglecting to visit the Lakes of Killarney as the Vale of Avoca. The Territory has also, in various localities, evidences of a period, long since past, when a people more advanced in the arts of civilized life occupied its lands than the present tribes of Indians who roam over them, affording objects for antiquarian study.

As regards the climate of Utah it has been said that the great plateau between the Rocky and Sierra Nevada mountains has many of the characteristics of the Great Tartar Plains of Asia. On the mountains it is exceedingly cold; in the winter the snow falls to many feet in depth and fills up the smaller mountain passes, but seldom lies in the valleys for more than a few days. In midsummer it is dry and hot, the heat ranging at mid-day from 90° to 105°, with cool mornings and evenings, refreshed with mountain breezes. Winter commences in the first half of November and continues until March. The thermometer seldom falls below zero. Seed time is from April until the 10th of June. Harvesting commences about the 4th of July. "Spring and autumn, though mild, are subject to sudden changes and the wind is very variable. Rain seldom falls between April and October, but when heavy showers do come, they are generally accompanied by thunder and hail, and sometimes with strong winds." The lightness of the atmosphere in G. S. L. Valley renders breathing a real luxury, and the inhabitants enjoy generally as good health as those of the most salubrious countries.

The general products of Utah may be enumerated as follows—the fine bunch grass of perennial growth, affording fodder for cattle, during summer and winter, wheat, rye, barley, oats, buckwheat, Indian corn, beets, and garden vegetables, in which it surpasses most countries in abundance and quality; potatoes cannot be found generally so good in any other part of the United States. Flax and hemp do well, the former, in some parts of the Territory, may be seen growing wild, and is used by the Indians in making fishing nets. In 1853 the Legislature awarded two premiums for raising flax seed. Wm. S. Muir, who obtained one of them, had raised 27½ bushels of seed, and 500 lbs. of flax lint, from 1 acre of ground. Throughout the whole Territory, timber is scarce, except on the mountains, and is composed, as elsewhere stated, of pine and fir trees. In the bottoms of the principal streams, groves of cottonwood and box elder are found, and in some of the valleys, a scrub cedar. Indian corn and vines are liable to be caught by early and late frosts. Much laudable exertion is being made in establishing nurseries and in cultivating orchards, and peaches, plums, grapes, currants, apples, &c., have been raised. A currant found extensively in the mountains is equal to the English currant.

Animals indigenous to the Territory are the antelope, elk, deer, and mountain sheep which supply excellent meat for table use; the black and grizzly bears, panthers, foxes, wolves, and wolverines, and smaller animals of prey. Among its feathered tribes are numerous pelicans and gulls, blue herons, cranes, and the brandt. Water fowl are abundant on the lakes, some of which, with others of the feathered tribes, are used for the table. Numerous quantities of eggs are deposited in early summer among the reeds of the marshy flats by the goose, the duck, the plover and the curlew; and on the islands of Salt Lake, by the pelican, gull, &c. Fine fish abound in the fresh water lakes and rivers—salmon trout in the mountain streams, and perch, pike, bass, chub, &c., in the lakes and calmer currents of the plains.

The manufactures of so young a Territory must necessarily be limited, but the progress already made is really surprising. The distance intervening between it and the great depots of commerce has served much to encourage domestic manufactures and develop the resources of the Territory. Beside the Iron Works, Foundries, and Machine Shops of Iron

County already described, there are extensive Sugar and Woollen Manufactories in progress in Great Salt Lake County, the machinery for which
has been taken from Great Britain and the U. States, at a cost which will
probably not fall short of £40,000. The Sugar Works can grind, press,
and boil 1000 bushels of beets and make 2½ tons of sugar in 24 hours.
There are also Woollen Manufactories in various parts of the Territory.
Other manufactures are leather, cutlery, earthenware, nails, combs from
mountain mahogany horn and bone, hats and caps of the finest furs, glue,
and firearms. Excellent flouring and saw mills exist in all the settlements,
and cabinet shops, cooperages, &c., in some of them, now affording many
of the conveniences of civilized life.

Much encouragement is given to home manufactures, and thousands of
yards of stuffs are annually woven in the habitations of the citizens and
worn by them, the best families of the Territory setting the example. In
one winter alone, 700 yards were woven in Governor Young's family, and
in 1854 the family of President H. C. Kimball made about the same
quantity. At present many articles of constant use have to be supplied
from the eastern States and California, at a great advance upon their
original cost, owing to the distance they have to be carried. An idea may
be formed of the increasing prosperity of the country from the fact that in
1854 in G. S. L. City alone the 22 merchants and store keepers who were
then doing business there employed a capital of about £260,000.

As to exports, Utah can scarcely be said to have any yet, but much trade
has been carried on with the overland emigrants to California, and considerable stock is annually driven to that State and sold. Exploration of the
Colorado has shown that it is navigable for steamers of light draught above
the Rio Virgen, in New Mexico, which at some future day may open up a
trade down its waters with the west coast. The Pacific railroad, should it
pass through any part of the Territory, particularly G. S. L. Valley, may
also have a tendency to promote the same desirable object.

Internal improvements have had considerable attention wherever a
settlement has been formed. The principal streams have been bridged,
and also many of the minor ones, and public roads, of which there were
of course none in the Territory when the L. D. Saints entered it, have
been made. In 1854 Congress appropriated 25,000 dollars for the construction of a military road through the Territory, and the southern
State road passing through all the settlements on the way to California
has been adopted by Col. Steptoe, the Government Commissioner. Two
canals are in course of construction in G. S. L. Valley—one on the W.
side of the Jordan, to connect Utah and G. S. Lakes; and the other on
the E. side, to connect Big Cottonwood Creek and City Creek, and cross
the intermediate streams, all of which flow into the Jordan. Both canals

are intended to be large enough for boats to be used in the transportation of rock, lumber, &c., as well as to facilitate the irrigation of land and to afford advantages for machinery.

For the purpose of education, no Territorial tax has yet been levied, but each city or settlement has made its own regulations. A University has been chartered under the title of the University of Deseret [now the University of Utah]; and there are some few parent schools and numerous common schools. Religious, scientific, and literary institutions have been recently founded. The most prominent is the Deseret Theological Institute, Brigham Young, president, and then follow the Universal Scientific Society, Wilford Woodruff, president, and the Polysophical Society, Lorenzo Snow, president.

The public institutions are the State House, at Fillmore, already described; the Public Library, for which Congress has made two appropriations, amounting to 5500 dollars; the Penitentiary, situated on Big Kanyon Creek, for which, Congress has appropriated 20,000 dollars; and the Arsenal, to which a Military School is attached.

The Indian tribes which roam over Utah, may at present be classified under two great heads—the Utahs and the Shoshonee (or Snake) Diggers, subdivided into numerous small bands with their respective chiefs. The former range over the district S. of G. S. Lake, and from New Mexico to California; the latter have the district N. of the Lake, especially the vicinity of Humboldt or Mary's River. The two tribes are perpetual foes to each other. The Utahs are united by a common language and affinities and numerous intermarriages. They are a superstitious race and have many cruel customs. They have likewise many traditionary notions of almost all the prominent events in the history of the world, such as the Creation, the Flood, Elijah's being fed by ravens, and the death and resurrection of Christ. They are great believers in dreams, and in healing, laying on of hands, &c., &c. The Diggers have made very little depredation upon the white settlers, while the Utahs have several times attempted to destroy them and uproot the settlements, which we shall further notice in our history of the Territory. An official visit to the Humboldt River Indians by Dr. G. Hurt, the Indian Agent for the Territory, has just been satisfactorily concluded, and it is expected travellers to California, via the Humboldt river, will now meet with less molestation. Some of the bands of the Utahs are the Utahs proper, now under Arapeen and Sau-e-ette; Yampah Utes, under White Eye; Timpanogas Utes, under Peteet-neet and Washear; Pe-ar-a-wats; Pau-van-tees, under Kanoshe; Pah Utes; and Piedes. The late Joseph Walker, one of the leading chiefs of the Utahs, was generally very friendly to the L. D. Saints, and so also is Arapeen, his successor. We here introduce their portraits sketched from a painting in possession of the late Elder W. W. Major. Walker, who appears with his cap on, had made himself rich by horse-stealing, and had succeeded by his aggressions upon the minor bands in gaining great influence over them. After the L. D. Saints colonized Utah both he and Arapeen requested baptism, and became united with the Church. By the politeness of Mr. Dimick B. Huntington, Indian Interpreter, we are enabled to append a short memoir of Walker, most of the facts in which we understand came from the chief himself. [For a first-hand description of Chief Wakara, or Walker, see Solomon Nunes Carvalho: *Incidents of Travel and Adventure in the Far West* (New York, 1858), pp. 185–194. Carvalho had the good fortune to accompany Brigham Young when he negotiated a truce over trouble arising from the murder of John W. Gunnison. He sketched portraits of both Wakara and Kanosh, chief of the Pahvant Indians.]

It appears that Joseph Walker was born on Spanish Fork (Pequi-nary-no-quint is the Indian name, and signifies Stinking Creek) in Utah County, U. T., in or about the year 1808. When he was about 12 years old the deer, he used to say, were very thick, and the buffalo more numerous than the Mormons' cattle. The first horse he ever saw was brought to Utah by the Spaniards. His father, whose name is unknown, obtained the animal, and lest it should run away, kept it tied up to the corner of his hut until it starved to death, not knowing anything of the nature of the animal, or that it required anything to eat. When the first white man came among them, the Timpanogas Utes, to which he then belonged, were quite numerous. In his earlier days, as far back as he could remember, he was with his father in many battles with the Snake Indians, who then occupied the country in the vicinity of G. S. Lake Valley. When he was about 20 years old a portion of the tribe to which he belonged broke off and joined the Snakes, among whom was one of Walker's own uncles and other relatives. This small band of seceders intermarried with the Snakes, and their children are what are now called Diggers—the low race found among the settlements at the present time. They also assisted the Snakes against the Timpanogas band, who were at that time located on the Timpanogas or Provo River, and as Walker and his father's relatives had some scruples about fighting their own relatives who were in the ranks of the Snakes, about 40 in number left the Timpanogas and went on to Spanish Fork to live, that they might not have occasion to join in warfare against the Snakes. This gave offence to the remaining portion of the tribe, who commenced a war with Walker's band, and a company of them stole upon Walker's lodge and shot his father in the back while smoking. Walker carried his father and buried him in Rocky Kanyon, about a mile S. of Spanish Fork. Soon after this, he and his brother

Arapeen, whose proper name is Senior-roach, stole into the Timpanogas Utes lodge in the night, and shot 4 persons of the tribe. At his father's death Walker assumed the command of the band. About 2 years after, he went over into Uintah Valley, about 150 m. S. E. of G. S. L. City, to some white traders who were there, where, according to his account, he was taken sick and died. His spirit was absent from his body a day and a night, during which time his body remained warm. While absent from the body his spirit went to heaven where he saw God and a great multitude of angels or beings dressed in white. None of the angels spoke to him, but God talked with him and told him that he must come back to the earth again, for his work was not done, and that some white friends were coming to see him. Before he returned God gave him a new name— Pannacarra-quinker, which signifies Iron Twister. This circumstance occurred about 2 years before the L. D. Saints entered the valleys of Utah, after which time he had occasional skirmishes with the Snakes, but maintained friendly feelings generally towards the whites and boasted that he had never shed the blood of white men. He died on the 29th of January, in the present year, 1855, on Meadow Creek, about 6 m. from Fillmore, of a cold which had settled on his lungs. He died with a good spirit and spoke affectionately of President Young. The Utahs killed 2 squaws, 2 Piede children, and about 15 of his best horses on the occasion. He was buried with all his presents and trinkets, and a letter which he had received the previous day from President Young.

Arapeen was about 2 years younger than Walker at his death and had been with him nearly all his days consequently the history of one is the history of the other to a great extent. He has succeeded his brother in the chieftainship, is more daring than he was, and is very passionate when excited, becoming almost ungovernable. He is admitted to be a beautiful orator and has considerable influence.

Utah is a portion of what was formerly called Upper California, belonging to Mexico, and was acquired by the United States from that country in 1848, by the treaty of Guadaloupe Hidalgo, at the close of the war. The first white settlers were unquestionably the L. D. Saints. A band of pioneers, consisting of 143 men, embracing several of the Twelve Apostles, and with the First Presidency at their head, had preceded the main body, in search of a suitable location in the far distant West. On the 24th of July, 1847, they entered Great Salt Lake Valley. The pioneers, after dedicating the land and themselves to the Lord, commenced with the few implements of husbandry they had carried with them to cultivate the ground, and put in potatoes and other seeds. A few days afterwards, the site of G. S. L. City was laid out.

The old mountaineers and trappers said that agricultural facilities necessary to the sustenance of a civilized community did not exist, but the weary and exiled pilgrims remained and formed the nucleus of the present rising Territory of Utah. In September and October following, an addition of about 4000 souls, was made to the colony, and immediately after about 2000 bushels of wheat were sown. In 1848 another large company arrived under President B. Young, who had in the meantime returned to Winter Quarters. Agriculture and building were now vigorously prosecuted. The winter of 1847–8 was extremely mild, allowing much tilling to be done, and flocks and herds throve well upon the abundant grass; but the succeeding winter was like a New England winter for severity, and snow fell to a depth of from 1 to 3 feet. The season also commenced earlier than was anticipated and found many of the inhabitants without houses or fuel. A people so lately robbed of all their earthly possessions as they had been, and being so far distant from where supplies could be procured, would naturally be ill prepared for this vicissitude, despite their magnanimous industry and perseverance since their arrival in those primeval solitudes. The wilderness might afterwards blossom as the rose and become like the Garden of Eden, but then all was in embryo, and the immense labour done and the provisions raised were totally inadequate to the demand of the numerous recently arrived and almost destitute colonists. This circumstance was much aggravated by crickets having during the previous summer destroyed much of their grain, and which would no doubt have all been destroyed, but for a marvellous interposition of Providence in the shape of gulls "who came in flocks to feast on the banquet which was so bountifully spread for their reception." These birds would arrive in early dawn from the islands of G. S. Lake, feast upon the crickets to satiety, disgorge the meal, return with fresh appetites and renew the repast, until the setting sun would gild the mountain tops in the west, when they would retire to their insular retreats. This operation was repeated from day to day, until the little destroyers were themselves exterminated.

Fearful apprehensions being entertained as to a scarcity of food, the Bishops, early in the following February, took an inventory of the quantity of breadstuffs in G. S. L. Valley, when it was found that there was not more than ¾ lb. per day from then to the 5th of July for each individual. This was a trying time, and much suffering ensued. Many persons dug side by side with the Indians for roots, which they ate with old hides taken from the ditches and from the roofs of the houses. The harvest of 1849 proved abundant, both for consumption and sale to the crowds of emigrants passing through to California, and from that time to 1854 an abundance of all cereals was raised. The harvest of this year will be limited, owing to grasshoppers, aided by crickets, having made

great havoc with the crops as they appeared above ground; but by per-
severingly sowing over and over again, in some instances to the extent of
four times, it is expected there will with economy be sufficient for the
inhabitants.

In the beginning of 1849 the commencement of a series of Indian hostilities was made by a marauding party of Utahs. A skirmish between
them and the settlers took place in the kanyon immediately E. of Battle
Creek, which derives its name from that circumstance. The settlers were
commanded by Col. John Scott, and 5 Indian warriors were killed. One
was taken prisoner, but afterwards released.

The members of the renowned Mormon Battalion had now chiefly
returned from the Mexican campaign, and a portion of them, who discovered the gold mines of California, had brought considerable gold dust
with them, which was deposited with the authorities, and a paper cur-
rency was issued, the old notes of the "Kirtland Safety Society" being
again on a par with gold, for public convenience. Thus was fulfilled a
prophecy made by Joseph Smith at Kirtland, that although the "Kirtland
Safety Society" had become bankrupt, its notes would again be on a par
with gold.

Notwithstanding the country had now been ceded to the United States,
and the great influx of emigrants, no recognition had been made of the
colony by Congress, either by providing for it a Territorial government
or otherwise, the inhabitants, therefore, being chiefly L. D. Saints, were
left entirely to the guidance of their ecclesiastical leaders, and justice
was administered and enforced solely by the Church authorities. But the
citizens were anxious that a civil government should be formed, and a
Convention was called "of all the citizens of that part of Upper California lying E. of the Sierra Nevada mountains to take into consideration
the propriety of organizing a Territorial or State government," which
met at G. S. L. City on the 5th of March, 1849, for that purpose. This
convention adopted a Constitution which ordained and established a
Provisional Government by the name of the STATE OF DESERET, with legislative, executive, and judicial powers. Brigham Young was elected Governor, and, with all other officers elected under the Constitution, took
an oath to support the Constitution of the United States. On the 2nd of
July the Legislative Assembly met and elected A. W. Babbitt delegate to
Congress, who was forthwith despatched to Washington with the Constitution and a Memorial to that body, setting forth, among other things,
that, in view of their own security, and for the preservation of the constitutional right of the U. States to hold jurisdiction there, the people had
organized a Provisional State Government, under which the civil policy
of the nation was duly maintained; that there was then a sufficient num-

ber of individuals residing within the State of Deseret to support a State Government, thereby relieving the general Government from the expenses of a Territorial government in that section, as an evidence of which, they had already erected a legislative hall; and asking Congress to consider their interests, and, if consistent with the Constitution and usages of the Federal Government to ratify the accompanying Constitution, and admit the State of Deseret into the Union on an equal footing with other States, or provide such other forms of civil government as their wisdom and magnanimity might award. In the meantime, the Provisional State Government went immediately into action under the Constitution adopted, and its jurisdiction was extended over and submitted to by the inhabitants.

In the following August Cap. Howard Stansbury, of the Topographical Engineers of the U. States army, with Lieut. Gunnison, and other assistants, arrived by order of the U. S. Government to make a survey of G. S. L. Valley. The Captain is since deceased, but his memory is cherished by the inhabitants of Utah, for his able and disinterested defence of them from many malignant aspersions made against them.

Before the close of the year, Utah, Sanpete, and Tooele Valleys had been occupied, and flourishing farms opened, and mills erected. The settlements north had also been extended. The Indian aggressions, which commenced in the early part of the year, had now begun to assume a more serious aspect. In the southern settlements, cattle were driven off, and all attempts to recover them were resisted. Finally the settlers were fired upon, while engaged in their ordinary pursuits. Many conciliatory overtures were made to the Indians, but all in vain. The Governor and other authorities were greatly averse to harsh measures, but acts of kindness were construed by the Indians into an evidence of cowardice, which emboldened them in their depredations. In this emergency the Governor applied to the U. S. officers at Fort Hall, in Oregon Territory, and they promised to chastise the aggressors, but the snow was so deep that no troops could move down from that quarter. Cap. Stansbury was then applied to for his views of the policy of the inhabitants forming an armed expedition for that purpose, and he states in his work that he did not hesitate to recommend the contemplated expedition as a measure not only of good policy, but one of absolute necessity and self preservation. The Governor accordingly organized a force of 100 men, under Gen. D. H. Wells, of the State Militia, and Lieut. Howland, of the Mounted Rifles, U. S. army, was detailed from Cap. Stansbury's command to accompany it as adjutant. The little army then moved down to Utah Valley and found the Indians rudely fortified on the banks of the Timpanogas, to receive the attack of the troops in February, 1850, and from whence they purposed to carry on an exterminating war upon the settlers. From the great amount of underwood, as well as standing and felled timber, it was an admirable position. The Indians could see and sally out and not be seen, unless when some of the more daring would advance and raise their heads to take aim. It was here that young Higbee was killed, the first of the white settlers that fell by the hands of the Indians. General (then Major) Geo. D. Grant commanded the expedition until they were routed from the Timpanogas, and General Wells continued it into the mountains and around the Utah Lake. The lake was then frozen over, and a lively skirmish occurred upon it between a small party of cavalry and a few mounted Indians. In this war the Indians state that they had from 25 to 30 of their number killed, among them some of their leading chiefs. The leader of the band (Lake or Timpanogas Utes) Old Elk, then a celebrated war-chief, was afterwards found dead in his wick-e-up. It was supposed that he had died of measles. Some 12 or 15 horses and about 63 prisoners, women and children, were taken, and afterwards, at a treaty held by the Governor, were restored, save a few who died through change of diet. On the side of the whites there was 1 man killed, and 5 or 6 wounded, and 7 horses killed. This convinced the Indians of the superiority of the settlers over them, even in their own mode of warfare, and decided the question of the existence of settlements S. of G. S. L. Valley, and probably of any in the country. In the following March the Legislature passed an ordinance prohibiting the sale of arms, ammunition, or spirituous liquors to the Indians, and a temporary cessation of hostilities ensued.

Various mercantile concerns now began to be established, which, with the immense quantity of goods exchanged by the emigrants passing through to California for the produce of the valley, supplied the citizens with good clothing and many other articles of which they stood in great need. Indeed so eager were the emigrants to procure fresh meat, vegetables, and horses with which to complete their journey, that they parted with their goods at prices infinitely below what they could be procured for in the eastern cities, to say nothing of the cost of transit. The inhabitants had now become rich again. President B. Young had prophesied in 1846 that they should be better off in 5 years than ever they were before, and his prediction had during 1849 a most palpable fulfilment, though when it was uttered, naught but starvation and death, humanly speaking, stared them in the face.

On the 15th of June, 1850, appeared No. 1 of the *Deseret News,* the first paper published in the country. It was edited and published by Dr. Willard Richards, whose memoir appears on pp. 237–240.

The thousands of persons attracted by gold to California also formed a Constitution for a State Government, their delegates meeting for that purpose at Monterey, on the 1st of Dec., 1849, and forwarded the same to Congress, by John C. Frémont and William M. Gwinn, senators elect. This petition was not presented until some months after that forwarded by the Convention which met at G. S. L. City, but it was favourably entertained—President Z. Taylor expressing to Congress a hope that it would be granted, while the latter was entirely disregarded or rejected. It may also be observed that the relative permanent populations of Deseret and California were at that time in the ratio of 5 to 3.

Deseret, California, and New Mexico were now before Congress each applying for a government, and forthwith a question was started as to whether Negro Slavery should be recognized in the new commonwealths. The advocates and opposers of this instituion, in and out of Congress, marshalled on the arena of political warfare, which was carried to such extremes that a dismemberment of the Union was openly talked of. Senator Foote, of Mississippi, publicly declared that a Constitution had been adopted for the "United States South." However, on the 7th of Sept., 1850, after mutual concessions and compromises by the contending parties, California, with a Constitution excluding slavery, was admitted into the Union as a State; and Deseret, under the Indian appellation of Utah, and New Mexico, were erected into Territories, with a proviso in the Organic Acts, that when they applied for admission into the Union, as independent States, it should be with or without slavery as their Constitutions might prescribe at the time of admission.

On the 9th of Sept., the Act for Utah was approved by President M. Fillmore, President Taylor having died while the compromise measures were pending. Thus were her people who had been driven by unrelenting persecution, sanctioned by the whole Republic, upwards of 1000 miles beyond the borders of civilization; who, on their weary march, when every man was needed, had been deprived of 500 men to increase the armies of their persecutors in the war with Mexico; who had "toiled for rocks and snowy lands, contended with the red men, and subdued the desert for a residence"; who had enriched the land acquired by the U. States from Mexico, while California had merely worked a number of mines; and who had evinced the most unmistakable signs of loyalty to the General government, as witness the unflinching and generous statements of Stansbury and Gunnison and a host of others—thus were the people of whom so much can be said, deprived of the right of self-government. Not only was this the case, but the boundaries were altered to those given at the head of this note, depriving Utah of all seaboard and important river navigation.

The Act is similar to those granted for other Territories of the Union.

The Executive is vested in a Governor, holding office for 4 years, or until his successor is appointed. He is also Commander-in-chief of the Militia, and Superintendent of Indian Affairs. All laws passed by the Legislature must be approved by him before they can take effect, and a copy of the same must be transmitted by the Secretary of the Territory to Washington, where they are subject to veto. The Legislature is vested in a Council, consisting of 13 members, and House of Representatives, consisting of 26 members, who are elected by the white male citizens of 21 years old and upwards, not including military officers and soldiers in the United States service. The Judiciary consists of a Supreme Court, consisting of 1 Chief Justice and 2 Associate Justices; 3 District Courts, each presided over by a Justice of the Supreme Court; Probate Courts; and Justices of the Peace. The Governor, Secretary, Chief and Associate Justices, Attorney, and Marshal are appointed by the President of the U. States. The first appointee for Governor was Brigham Young, with a salary of 1500 dollars as Governor, and 1000 as Superintendent of Indian Affairs. He took the oath of office on the 3rd of February, 1851. The Act provided for the election of 1 delegate to Congress by the voters qualified to elect members of the Legislative Assembly, and lastly extended the laws of the U. States over, and declared them to be in force in the Territory, so far as the same, or any provision thereof, might be applicable. Congress appropriated 20,000 dollars for the erection of a State House.

On the 26th of March, 1851, Governor Young, in a special message to the General Assembly of the State of Deseret, notified them of the passage of the Act organizing the Territory of Utah, and held the following language—"Upon the dissolving of this Legislature, permit me to add, the industry and unanimity which have ever characterized your efforts, and contributed so much to the pre-eminent success of this government, will, in all future time, be a source of gratification to all; and whatever may be the career and destiny of this *young* but growing republic, we can ever carry with us the proud satisfaction of having erected, established, and maintained a peaceful, quiet, yet, energetic government, under the benign auspices of which unparalleled prosperity has showered her blessings upon every interest."

The Assembly was dissolved on the 5th of April, and the State of Deseret merged into the Territory of Utah. On the 19th of July Messrs. Bernhisel and Babbitt, with some government officers for the Territory, arrived from Washington, and on the 4th of Aug., Dr. Bernhisel was elected first delegate to Congress from Utah. The first session of the Legislature of the Territory convened, in pursuance of a proclamation by the Governor, on the 22nd of September. Among their earliest acts they located the seat of government at Fillmore City and legalized the laws of the Provisional State of Deseret.

No sooner had the U. States officials for the Territory arrived than mischief again began to brew for the citizens. At a General Conference of the Church of J. C. of L. D. Saints, held early in September, Perry E. Brocchus, one of the judges of the Supreme Court, publicly insulted them in a speech he was invited to make. President Young replied to him with much warmth of feeling, vindicating their virtue and integrity, from his base insinuations. Judge Brocchus' hostile feelings, however, would not allow him to apologize, and shortly after, with the Chief Justice, L. G. Brandebury, and the Secretary, B. D. Harris, he left for the States. The Secretary took back with him 24,000 dollars which had been appropriated by Congress for the per diem and mileage of the members of the Legislature. They afterwards addressed a very malicious communication to the President of the U. States, which was published in the *N. Y. Herald* of Jan. 10, 1852, but it had little influence in official quarters, while they were derided in the public press for leaving their posts of duty. The Legislature of the Territory protested against their proceedings, setting forth the inconvenience arising from the absence of these high officials, and the funds necessary for organizing and carrying on the government. To fill the place of Secretary, the Governor appointed Willard Richards *pro tempore,* and shortly afterwards, the President of the U. States appointed other judges and a secretary. [For an excellent account of the troubles of the Mormons with the United States Government during these years see Norman F. Furniss: *The Mormon Conflict, 1850–1859* (Yale University Press, 1960).]

During the year 1852 many emigrants from Great Britain and other European countries arrived in the Territory, and before the close of it the population had increased to upwards of 30,000. Considerable advances had also been made in tanning leather, constructing machinery for making nails, and in the manufacture of iron, earthenware, woollen articles and many others of constant consumption. An indication of the growing prosperity is furnished in the fact that during the 6 months prior to October, the citizens, principally those of G. S. L. Valley, had made purchases of goods imported from St. Louis and other cities of the States, amounting to upwards of 300,000 dollars or £62,500.

Early in 1853 a block of oolitic limestone, in lieu of marble, which had not then been quarried, with the Bee-hive, beneath which was the word "Deseret," and other emblems cut upon it by Mr. Ward, was forwarded, in compliance with a resolution of the late State of Deseret, to Washington to take its place in the "Washington Monument," then being erected by the respective States and Territories of the Union.

On the 17th of July Indian hostilities recommenced by a menace on Springville. Washear and a party of the Utes had manifested a very surly disposition for nearly a year previously, which at length led them to make open warfare upon the citizens. These hostilities continued for nearly 12 months, during which time the progress of all the southern settlements was interrupted, as it was found necessary by the Governor and the Military authorities, to order the citizens into forts for protection, and to destroy their houses, to prevent the Indians from using them as points of defence. During these troubles 12 of the citizens were killed and many wounded. The esteemed Cap. Gunnison and 7 of his party were murdered also, on the 26th of Sept., about 20 m. N. of Nicollet or Sevier Lake, while exploring a route to California for the contemplated Central Pacific Railroad.

Of the Indians about the same number were supposed to have been killed. On the partial cessation of hostilities the inhabitants commenced to rebuild their cities and to wall them, a policy which had been much urged prior to the present aggressions and which seems now to be the only one, in connexion with kindness and forbearance to the native tribes, by which the valleys can be settled. The expense incurred in this 12 months' difficulties amounted to 200,000 dollars, which Congress, according to established usage, should pay on receiving the accounts, but it has merely refunded a small portion. The whole amount appropriated by the Government from 1850 to 30th June, 1855, for expense in suppressing Indian hostilities, Indian service, and for the expense of negotiating treaties with and making presents of goods and provisions to them is 95,940 dollars, 65 cents, and small as it is, when the drafts from the Superintendent of Indian affairs are presented at the Treasury, some frivolous reason is found for dishonouring them, and perpetual annoyance ensues. More economy has been observed in Utah than in Oregon or California, to which much larger appropriations have been made, where there are no more Indians to be taken care of, and a far less permanent improvement of them has been made. Again, in Utah no treaties have been held with the Indians by the Government, and no troops have been stationed in the country for the protection of the citizens, and yet the Indians are more peaceable than in either of the other places mentioned. The Indian title has not been extinguished, and it is only recently that a Surveyor-general has been appointed to Utah, enabling the settlers to obtain titles to the land, and now that such a functionary has been appointed no lands have been donated to the original settlers, although such bequests have been made to Oregon and New Mexico. This invidious treatment of Utah by the parent government, fostered by a rancorous spirit of religious persecution which unhappily still guides statesmen in their conduct toward that Territory, naturally enough causes her citizens much unpleasant feeling, but they are still struggling on with indomitable energy, relying upon their own resources, and trusting in God to defend the right.

No State or Territory ever progressed in importance and prosperity at a more uniform and healthful rate than Utah has done, or probably ever accomplished so much in the same amount of time. It cannot now be long before she will apply to be admitted into the Union as an independent State and take her place among the other constellations of the Union, when let us hope that no party feelings or religious prejudice will prevent her immediate admission.

(34) GREAT SALT LAKE CITY is the largest and most populous city in Utah. It is also the capital of G. S. L. County. At Temple Block, the latitude is 40° 45′ 44″ N.; the longitude about 112° W.; and the altitude about 4300 ft. Pop. in 1855, variously estimated from 10,000 to 15,000.

The city "lies at the western base of the Wahsatch mountains, in a curve formed by the projection westward from the main range of a lofty spur which forms its southern boundary. On the west it is washed by the waters of the Jordan; while to the southward, for 25 miles, extends a broad level plain, watered by several little streams, which, flowing down from the eastern hills, form the great element of fertility and wealth to the community. Through the city itself flows an unfailing stream of pure sweet water, which, by an ingenious mode of irrigation, is made to traverse each side of every street, whence it is led into every garden spot, spreading life, verdure, and beauty over what was heretofore a barren waste. On the east and north, the mountain descends to the plain by steps, which form broad and elevated terraces, commanding an extended view of the whole valley of the Jordan." North of Temple Block, towers up Ensign Peak, which overlooks the city, and is a prominent object in approaching it from every quarter.

G. S. L. City is laid out on a magnificent scale, being nearly 4 m. square, and having streets 132 ft. wide, with 20 ft. side walks. The streets cross each other at right angles, forming blocks 40 rods square, which are subdivided into lots of 1¼ acres each. The blocks are so surveyed that no two houses face each other, but their neighbours' gardens, giving the city quite a suburban appearance. An ordinance of the city requires the buildings to be placed 20 ft. back from the front line of the lot, leaving the intervening space for shrubbery or trees, which may be nourished by the irrigating canals flowing on each side of the street. The citizens are carrying out this design, and when the margin so appropriated is studded with noble trees or planted with flowers, the effect produced will no doubt be delightful, especially in contrast with the neighbouring country, which has no woodland scenery. Four public squares are laid off within the city, upon one of which a Temple is being built.

The accompanying view of the city was taken in 1853, about 6 years after it was laid out. The cluster of white buildings in the left, at the base of the mountains, belonged to President B. Young until recently, when he donated them, with others since erected in connection with them, to the P. E. Fund. Their present value is upwards of £5200, and they have been purchased by a gentleman in Yorkshire. The President has erected, since the view was taken, two other houses, on the opposite side of the street, to which are attached the President's Office, and the Governor's Office. The dark looking building to the right of President Young's, and in the foreground, is President H. C. Kimball's. It was then unfinished. The street crossing the centre of the engraving, lies N. and S., and is called East Temple Street. Proceeding down it, or southward, the largest building on the left is the Tithing Office and Church Store. A little lower down on the right, is the Council House, a stone building 45 ft. square and 2 stories high. It was built by the Church, and originally used by it, but has chiefly been occupied by the State and Territorial Legislatures. Immediately in front of the Council House, and running to the extreme right of the engraving is Temple Block, on which are seen the Public Works to the left and the Tabernacle to the right. The Tabernacle was built in 1851, is 126 ft. long, 64 ft. wide, arched without a pillar, and will accommodate 2500 persons. Another building of wood has since been attached to it—the Bowery, 156 ft. long and 138 ft. wide, which will hold 8000. At the present time the Temple itself is being erected. It was proposed to build it at a General Conference, Oct. 8th, 1852, and on the 14th of Feb., 1853, the ground was surveyed, consecrated by the First Presidency, and opened by President Young, in presence of the Twelve Apostles and a large concourse of the citizens. On the 6th of April following, the corner stones were laid—the S. E. by the first Presidency; the S. W. by the presiding Bishop and Council, with the Presidents of the lesser priesthood; the N. W. by the President and Council of the High Priests' Quorum, with the President and High Council of the Stake; and the N. E. by the Twelve Apostles, with the First Presidency of the Seventies, and the President and Council of the Elders' Quorum. The edifice will cover an area of 21,850 ft. The following description of it from the architect's plans is written by Elder Geo. A. Smith, the Church Historian, and quoted from the *Mill. Star*, vol. xvi. p. 635—"Foundation for the Temple—193 feet, east and west through the centre of the building, embracing footing of the walls; 125 feet, north and south through the centre of the towers, embracing footing of the walls; 105 feet, north and south through the centre of the building, embracing footing of the walls.

"The main basement 119 feet by 79, the wall on the north and south sides being 8 feet thick, intercepted with pedestals of buttresses; the windows half circle. In the centre will be the baptismal font room, 58 feet square, with offices for clerks, and appropriate dressing rooms. The whole foundation will be sixteen feet wide at the bottom, and tapering equally on each side to the basement floor to 8 feet thick, 16 feet below the surface of the earth, and 8 feet above, making the rock work from the foundation 24 feet in height.

"The first floor above the basement, 120 feet long by 80 in the clear, arched over 35 feet high in the centre of the arch, walls 7 feet thick, with two tiers of offices on north and south sides, 16 in number, in the dead work of the arch, lighted with oval windows.

"The second room above the basement, 121 feet long, 81 wide, 35 high, walls 6 feet thick, having sixteen offices in the dead work of the arch.

"The roof will have 8 feet rise to the centre, and be covered with metal.

"Each buttress at basement ceiling represents a globe, each changing its position, beginning at south east corner—sculptured of stone. Each buttress at termination of ceiling of 1st room, represents the moon in all its phases—sculptured of stone. Each buttress at termination of ceiling of 2nd floor, represents the sun in all its phases—sculptured of stone. Each buttress on the sides of the building, Saturn with his rings and satellites—sculptured of stone.

"The four corner towers will be ascended by spiral staircases around a stone column; each tower will embrace an area of 40 feet in the footing, with 4 octagon turrets on each of the 4 towers, crowned with pinnacles; the crowning of the buttresses on the towers represents clouds, with rays emanating therefrom. The west corner towers embrace the Great Bear, pointing to the polar star, or as near as can be. The towers will be crowned with pinnacles, breaking off with battlements in sections, surrounded by a spire; every stone has its moral lesson, and all point to the celestial world.

"The walls are ornamented with 9 buttresses on the north side, 9 on the south side, and 32 adorn the towers; each of the side buttresses will be 100 feet above the base of its pedestal."

Some idea of the magnitude of the edifice may be gleaned from the fact, that its foundation has swallowed up more stone than the Temple at Nauvoo contained altogether. A graded road has been made from Temple Block to the stone quarry on the E., for the conveyance of building materials.

Other public buildings erected in the city since our view was taken are the Social Hall, 73 ft. by 33 ft., built of adobies, and used for public entertainments and dramatic representations; the Territorial Arsenal, on the "Bench," N. of the city; the Endowment House, on the N. W. corner of Temple Block, used by the L. D. Saints for the purpose indicated by its name; the Penitentiary at the S. E. of the city, and the Seventies' Council Hall, 50 ft. by 30 ft. In addition to these, there are in course of erection a Court House for G. S. L. County, the cost of which it is estimated will reach 20,000 dollars; a Music Hall, by the members of Capt. Ballo's band; a Seventies' Hall; and an Office for the Church Historian and Recorder, on the S. side of South Temple Street. Private buildings, manufactories, and stores have multiplied beyond all expectation. In the year 1854 as many as 8 stores were built in East Temple Street and 6 more in other parts of the city. Several good hotels have been opened.

Such rapid improvement greatly enhances the value of city lots and of the adjoining lands. Many persons hold pre-emption rights who would not sell their city lot, consisting of an acre and a quarter, without buildings upon it, for less than 1000 dollars, nor, when their title to it is recorded in the U. States' land office, for considerably more.

In the midst of private prosperity, public improvements have had very prominent consideration. In 1849 the Jordan, which forms the western boundary of the city, was bridged at an expense of 700 dollars, and has since had a more suitable structure extended over it at a cost of not less than 6000 dollars. In 1850 the waters of one of the hot mineral springs at the N. of the city were conducted by pipes into a public Bath House, affording the citizens a great luxury and contributing largely to their health. Much work has been done upon the public roads, and the wide space allotted for side walks or foot paths will doubtless soon be paved to add further to the neatness and comfort of the city. An excellent sanitary supervision is maintained by the City Council, which extends to the minutest object that might endanger the general health of the citizens. A quarantine is established to receive such passing emigrants as may arrive with contagious sickness. Lastly, owing to the Indian difficulties elsewhere spoken of, G. S. L. City, in common with the other cities of the Territory, is being walled in as a prevention from sudden attack. The wall was commenced in 1853, is 12 ft. high, 6 ft. thick at the base, and tapers to the height of 6 ft. where it is $2\frac{1}{2}$ ft. thick, which is maintained to the top.

The manufactures of G. S. L. City, considering how recently it has been founded and its great distance from where many tools and raw materials have to be obtained, are highly praiseworthy. In addition to the manufacture of flour and lumber, the ordinary avocations of Shoe-making, Tailoring, Blacksmithing in all its branches, and Building, there are several Tanneries; Brush, Comb, Woollen, and Hat and Cap Manu-factories; Cooperages, Cabinet and Wood Turners' Shops; Chair makers, Watch makers, Jewellers, Whipmakers, &c.; a Paper Manufactory, a Carriage and Wagon Manufactory; a Pottery and a Saddlery, all doing regular business. Beside these, there are the large Sugar Works at Kanyon Creek, and the Public Machine and Work Shop on Temple Block, both owned by the Church. The former, we have previously noticed under Utah. In the latter, there is a Foundery, the fire of which is blown by heavy machinery, and which turns out excellent castings; a Blacksmith's Shop, in which 7 fires are constantly in blow; a Stone Cutting Shop; a Paint Shop; a Modeling Shop; and a Machine Shop in which flanges, wheels, cranks, gudgeons, and machinery are manufactured. Cutlery, con-sisting of Congress knives, swords, spears and pruning hooks, and saws and fine locks equal to any imported, have quite recently been produced in the same establishment, which, altogether, is said to be inferior to none in the U. States or Europe. The city abounds with excellent mechanics from many parts of the world, which, with the great self-reliance of the people, and a sturdy encouragement of home-made goods, will ere long develop the arts and manufactures in a high degree.

Education has received more attention in G. S. L. City than could reasonably be expected. Ere the inhabitants had built houses to shelter them all, schools were opened in which the elementary branches of edu-cation were taught, and as early as the winter of 1848–9, the living and dead languages were added. In 1850 the Legislature incorporated the "University of the State of Deseret," located the same at this city, and appropriated for its benefit 5000 dollars annually, to be paid out of the State treasury. The 4th sec. contemplated the establishment of branches of the parent institution throughout the State. The site selected for the buildings and grounds attached lies E. of the city, and covers a mile square. While the University is in progress, several high schools are afford-ing to the youth of the city every facility for acquiring an excellent education. There are a few good private schools of humbler pretensions, but doing much good. There are also 24 common schools, supported by a city tax. The common schools are held in buildings erected for the purpose and are generally about 30 ft. by 20 ft. The Legislature has appropriated 2500 dollars for the construction of an Academy.

Various religious, literary, scientific, and other institutions have been formed for the advancement of religion and general literature. The "Deseret Theological Institute" claims our first attention. It was organ-ized at a General Conference of the Church of J. C. of L. D. Saints on the 7th of April, 1855, and has at its head the President of the Church. During the previous February the "Universal Scientific Society" was organized, with Wilford Woodruff of the Quorum of the Twelve president. The Society announces its intention to establish in connection with it a museum, library, and reading room, and also requests the aid and guardianship of the Chancellor and Regents of the University. There is a kindred institution called the "Polysophical Society," Lorenzo Snow, of the Quorum of the Twelve, president. Lectures are periodically given by each of these societies.

Music, both vocal and instrumental, is much cultivated by the citizens, and the musical talent of the city have recently organized themselves into the "Deseret Philharmonic Society," James Smithers president. The drama, conducted on moral and elevating principles, is held in esteem. An Amateur Dramatic Association give excellent representations during the winter season in the Social Hall. The Public Library of the Territory is kept here until the State House at Fillmore shall be completed, and the inhabitants have access to it under proper restrictions. The printers of the city have formed themselves into a fraternity called the "Deseret Typographical Association," for the advancement of their art. There is one Medical Institution—the "Council of Health," which exercises a general watchful care over the health of the citizens.

In addition to these institutions, there has lately been organized in connection with the American Pomological Society a "Horticultural Society." The city is also the seat of the First Presidency of the Church of J. C. of L. D. Saints; and the Chief Tithing Office, the Church Historian and Recorder's Office, and the Head Office of the P. E. Fund Company are located here. The sessions of the Legislature also have hitherto been held in it.

Historically, G. S. L. City is to a great extent represented by the note on Utah, but there are a few other items which may be profitably named in connection with the civil and ecclesiastical government of the city. This was not only the first place of settlement in G. S. L. Valley, but in the whole Territory. On entering the valley, President Young declared that the Pioneers had reached the place of the new home of the Saints and drove his team on to what is now called Temple Block, indicating it as the spot upon which the future Temple was to be built. The site of the city was commenced to be surveyed on the 31st of July, 1847. A week previous to this the Pioneers had commenced to plough and plant the virgin soil and shortly after proceeded to build their houses. The first habitations erected were undoubtedly rude enough, but were sufficient to shield their occupants from the rigours of winter, and were placed so as to form 4 forts, including an area of about 47 acres. Fifteen months afterward, the population of the city had increased to about 5000 souls, and by the spring of 1849 the Council House, a bridge over the Jordan, 6 or 7 bridges across minor streams, and the Bath House were in course of erection, the forts were breaking up and houses were being erected on the city plots. On the 24th of July following, being the second anniversary of the arrival of the Pioneers, a magnificent celebration was made in the city, at which several thousands of the citizens "dined sumptuously on the fruits of the earth prepared by their own hands," and invited the California emigrants who were passing through the City to the feast; many aged veterans declared they had sat down at the festive board in America and Europe, but had never enjoyed themselves as they did on that day; not an oath was uttered, not a man intoxicated, nor did any disturbance occur to mar the peace or happiness of the citizens on that joyous occasion.

On the 9th of January, 1851, the city received a Charter of incorporation from the General Assembly of the State of Deseret, which is similar to those of other cities of the Territory. It embraces the usual municipal powers to levy and collect taxes for city purposes, upon all taxable property, real and personal, within the limits of the city; to establish support, and regulate common schools; to provide the city with water; to open and keep streets in repair; to establish a police; to light the city and provide night watches; to tax, restrain, prohibit and suppress public houses, dram shops, gaming houses, bawdy and other disorderly houses, &c., &c.

The city government under this Charter consists of a Mayor, Aldermen, and a board of Common Councilmen, who are also Justices of the Peace. They are elected by the free white male inhabitants of the age of 18 years and upwards, who are entitled to vote for Territorial officers, and have been actual residents of the city 60 days next preceding the election. The first Mayor of the city was Jedediah M. Grant, who still fills the office. At present there are 19 wards within the corporation, each of which elects 1 Councilman: the number of Alderman is 4.

Ecclesiastically, the city is with the L. D. Saints a Stake of Zion, having its President and two Counsellors, also a High Council, consisting of 12 High Priests. Each ward is presided over by a Bishop, assisted in his duties by two Counsellors. In cases where it can be done, the citizens have recourse to these functionaries in preference to settling their disputes (which indeed rarely occur) by an appeal to the civil courts. The first President of the Stake was Elder Daniel Spencer, who is now on a mission to England; he was succeeded by Elder David Fullmer. Being the seat of the First Presidency of the Church of Jesus Christ of Latter Day Saints, the General conferences are held here, and the Epistles of the First

Presidency are dated from thence. The first Epistle written after the reorganization of the Church with a Presidency of three, to succeed that disorganized by the martyrdom of Joseph and Hyrum Smith, emanated from this city in April, 1849.

The present appearance, wealth, refinement and prosperity of the city may readily be inferred from previous portions of this note, but we cannot refrain from quoting the remarks of the Chief Justice of the U. States Supreme Court for the Territory, John F. Kinney, made at a Legislative party on the 1st of January, 1855.—"This is to me an occasion of rejoicing—this is a time when the mind will reflect on the past history of this country. I can scarcely realize that we are here, ten or fifteen hundred miles from civilization, and yet we are in the very midst of it; not only civilization but the most perfect refinement. I am reminded of the words of Daniel Webster on the occasion of celebrating the landing of the Pilgrim Fathers. 'The same heaven,' he remarked, 'is over our heads, the same earth under our feet, but all else how changed!' The same remarks may appropriately be applied to this Territory. When we consider only seven years have gone since this people landed here without food to support them, living on herbs and roots, and behold now the splendour, the magnificence and taste that have been displayed here, we may wonder and be astonished." The same exalted functionary on another occasion declared that there was less immorality, less drunkenness, and less licentiousness there than anywhere he had ever been.

General Wilson, Navy Agent at San Francisco, who passed through the city to California, in writing to Hon. Trueman Smith, expressed himself concerning the citizens as follows—"A more orderly, honest, industrious, and civil people I have never been among than these, I have not met in a citizen, a single idler, or any person who looks like a loafer. There is a spirit and an energy in everything you see that cannot be equalled in any city of any size that I have ever been in." This was quoted in a speech made by Mr. Smith in the United States Senate in 1850. Mr. Fuller, Editor of the *New York Mirror,* who has also visited the city, writes in his paper thus—"A more industrious, honest, law-abiding community can hardly be found. The municipal regulations of Salt Lake City are admirable, and more moral (barring their open polygamy) and orderly citizens, we have never seen in any part of the world. They number very many men of intelligence and education, and a residence of several weeks among them failed to note a single vagabond in their midst. They are exceedingly hospitable to California emigrants, and furnish them supplies at reasonable rates."

Corroborating testimonies are on record in abundance, all showing that the illiberal and coarse sentiments expressed in many quarters, and by those who have nothing but hearsay to guide them, concerning that city and its people are alike untrue and unjust.

But while the public are allowing themselves to be deceived by false and uncharitable reports to so lamentable an extent, the city of the mountains is growing rapidly in population and wealth; and its inhabitants, presided over by righteous men, ruled by wise laws, and actuated by ennobling and virtuous sentiments, are acquiring every characteristic of a great and worthy people. There is not a tippling house, a gambling house, nor a house of ill-fame to be found within its precincts, indeed the City Council have repealed all licences to sell or traffic in beer or spirituous liquors, which are generally the source or cause of the other two evils. The people are devoted to the advancement of religion, the arts and the sciences, agriculture and manufactures. They find little time to waste on degenerating pursuits and have less inclination for them, while the physical and intellectual development of their race is a great subject with all. The city itself will no doubt ere many years pass away become, architecturally, the finest of the earth; while its excellent sanitary arrangements, its tasteful decoration with trees on every side walk, the cultivation of trees, shrubbery, and flowers before each dwelling or building, and the naturally salubrious climate, will render it one of the most healthy and delightful abodes which ever yet graced any country.

(35) BRIGHAM YOUNG, the subject of this memoir, was born at Whitenham, Vermont, U. S. A. on the 1st of June, 1801. He was the son of John and Nancy Young (formerly Howe), who removed from the State of Vermont to that of New York, when he was about one year old. His father, who was a native of near Boston, Mass., was a farmer and had been a soldier of the revolution. His grandfather was an officer in the revolutionary war also. Mr. Young was about 30 years old when the doctrines of the L. D. Saints were first introduced to him by Elder Samuel H. Smith, brother of the prophet Joseph, who was the first preacher of them he had heard. In the year 1832 he was baptized by Elder Eleazer Miller, at present a member of the High Council of G. S. L. City, and was shortly after ordained to the priesthood, opening up to him the distinguished and honourable career which has since characterized him and made his name famous in almost every land.

In noticing the leading events of the President's life, after his ordination, perhaps the first in interest may be considered his journey to and from Missouri, in the spring of 1834, with Joseph Smith and others, in "Zion's Camp," which went by commandment of the Lord to the relief of the Saints who were persecuted in that State. In the following year, on the 14th of February, he was chosen at Kirtland, in compliance with a previous Revelation, a member of the first Quorum of Twelve Apostles since the organization of the Church in this dispensation. He was blessed and set apart to this calling under the hands of Oliver Cowdery, David Whitmer, and Martin Harris, the three witnesses to the Book of Mormon. On the 12th of March the Twelve were appointed a mission through the Eastern States, Brigham Young being specially appointed to "open the door to the remnants of Joseph who dwell among the gentiles." At a Grand Council of the officers of the Church held at Kirtland on the 2nd of May, the appointment respecting Elder Young was extended to include Elders John P. Green, and Amos Orton, and at a Council of the Twelve held at Freedom, New York, on the 25th of May, the Council laid their hands upon each one, that he "might have their faith and prayers to fill (with humility and power) that very important mission."

He was present at, and assisted in, the dedication of the Temple at Kirtland in 1836, on which occasion, he, with many others, was blessed with spiritual gifts, and gave an address in tongues. From this period he preached much and zealously in the Eastern States, occasionally visiting Kirtland. He was ever a constant and devoted disciple of the Prophet, and supported him in the midst of the machinations and persecutions of mobbers and apostates, which were then becoming pretty numerous. This excited their evil passions against him, and on the 22nd of December, 1837, he had to fly from Kirtland for his life. He then went to Missouri and by commandment of the Lord settled there.

After the apostasy of Thomas B. Marsh, he succeeded by seniority to the Presidency of the Quorum of the Twelve. About a year later, the persecution in Missouri had reached its worst, and after having been the most energetic person there in helping the poor Saints out of the State, he was compelled a second time to fly for his life. This occurred on the 14th September, 1838. He reached Illinois in safety, transacted Church business in Quincy, with other members of his Quorum, and then returned to Far West with four of the Twelve and other Elders, where, between midnight of the 25th and dawn of the 26th of March, 1839, in compliance with a Revelation given July 8th, 1838, they held a Conference; re-laid the foundation of the Lord's House, and took farewell of the Saints prior to crossing the "Great Waters" on missions to preach the Gospel, notwithstanding the mob had declared that the Revelation should not be fulfilled, as no "Mormon" would be allowed in the State.

The Twelve having been appointed to go on a mission to England without purse or scrip, President Young left his home at Montrose, Iowa, on the 14th of Sept., 1839, for that purpose, and on the 9th of March, 1840, sailed from New York on board the *Patrick Henry*, with H. C. Kimball, P. P. Pratt, O. Pratt, Geo. A. Smith, and Elder Reuben Hedlock.

They landed at Liverpool on the 6th of April, the first day of the 11th year after the rise of the Church, having had a tedious and unpleasant passage, during the whole of which President Young was sick and confined to his berth. They landed with shouts of Hosannah, for being permitted to carry the treasures of Eternal Life to Israel, in Old England, and proceeded to No. 8, Union St., where they obtained a private room, bread and wine, and partook of the Sacrament of the Lord's Supper. At a Council of the Twelve held at Preston, on the 14th of April, he was unanimously sustained as the standing President of the Quorum.

While Brigham Young was in England, the *Latter-day Saints' Millennial Star*, P. P. Pratt, editor, was commenced at Manchester; and the first L. D. Saints' Hymn Book for Europe was compiled, of which an edition was published. The first European edition of the Book of Mormon also was printed and published. In addition to superintending this business, he travelled and preached much among the Sants, instructing them in their newly espoused faith, and organizing them with proper officers into Branches and Conferences. Before his return Peter Melling and John Albiston were ordained patriarchs to the Church in England, and Elder Amos Fielding was appointed to superintend the Emigration of the Saints to the United States. This done, the President embarked on the *"Rochester"* for New York, April 20, 1841, in company with 6 of the Twelve Apostles, and about 130 emigrating Saints, on his return to Nauvoo, which he reached on the 1st of July following.

From this period until the assassination of Joseph and Hyrum Smith he was chiefly engaged, during the winter seasons, in Nauvoo with Church business and the affairs of the city. He held the office of councillor in the municipality. Each summer was occupied in preaching through the Eastern States. At the eventful period when the Church was deprived by the Carthage tragedy of its First President and Patriarch, Brigham Young and the principal portion of his Quorum were absent, he being in Boston, Massachusetts. In their absence, Sidney Rigdon, the only remaining member of the Quorum of the First Presidency of the Church, but who had long before lost the confidence of the Saints, and the spirit of God, as is fully manifest in the Church History, called meetings in Nauvoo with an idea of being appointed successor to Joseph Smith, but his expectations failed. In the meantime President Young and the majority of the Twelve returned. On them rightly devolved the Presidency of the whole Church (after the removal of the Presidency of Three), and on the 7th of Oct., 1844, the Quorum of the Twelve Apostles was almost unanimously acknowledged by a General Conference held in the City of Nauvoo, as the "First Presidency of the Church." A disinterested commentator upon the circumstances of this eventful period of the history of the L. D. Saints has remarked as follows—"As regards the polity of the Mormons, it has been fortunate for them that in a time of peril and perplexity, they were not induced to entrust themselves to his [Rigdon's] guidance. Under Brigham Young, and his able management, they speedily assumed a high position, not simply as religionists, but as citizens of the United States. Under Sidney Rigdon, it is probable the sect would have gone to pieces altogether."

After the Presidency of the Church had devolved upon the Twelve Apostles, it may be said that the career of President Young become more largely identified with the progress of the Church generally, and in Nauvoo particularly. To build up the City of Nauvoo, gather the Saints thereto, complete the Temple, and carry out Joseph's measures and the Revelations given through him, engaged his unwearying zeal, notwithstanding the persecution which renewedly assailed the Saints in Illinois and rendered it daily more apparent that an exodus therefrom must shortly ensue to prevent their universal massacre by an armed mob too powerful to be curbed by the law of the land, or embracing too many of her rulers to meet with resistance from that quarter.

When it was decided by the Saints to evacuate Nauvoo, as related in our note on that city, Brigham Young led the way to the far distant West, being compelled by the fury of the mob to commence the journey early in February, 1846, while the Mississippi was frozen over. Prior to his departure, the Temple had been so far completed as to allow of endowments being given within its walls, and a Committee was appointed to prosecute the building to completion. Committees were also appointed to sell such of the possessions of the citizens as purchasers could be found for; and to see that the poor who were unable to commence the journey on their own resources were assisted, that all who were willing to go to the West, might go as well as those possessing the means.

While President Young was crossing the State of Iowa, his acquaintance was made by Col. T. L. Kane, the author of an eloquent lecture upon the "Mormons" delivered before the Historical Society of Philadelphia. He speaks of having found the President "sharing sorrow with the sorrowful, and poverty with the poor," and describes him as a man of rare natural endowment. He likewise had an opportunity of witnessing his patriotism in the formation of the Mormon Battalion for the Mexican war, and which the U. S. government had called upon the L. D. Saints to furnish, notwithstanding they were then flying from a persecution which the Government had failed to prevent or afterwards to punish. From this period Col. Kane became a sincere friend of Brigham Young, and it was mainly owing to his recommendation of him to President Fillmore that he was appointed in 1850 to the Governorship of Utah. It is well known that shortly after this appointment was made all kinds of political slander, as well as general invective, appeared in the public prints against Gov. Young. He was charged with being an abuser of the United States and her institutions, with leaguing with the Indians to harass the U. S. emigrants to California, &c. President Fillmore naturally enough referred to Col. Kane to refute or explain the allegations, and he furnished a satisfactory vindication of the Governor reiterating "without reserve the statement of his excellent capacity, energy, and integrity" which he had made to Mr. Fillmore prior to the appointment. It also enabled the Colonel to call Mr. Fillmore's attention to the Governor's patriotism, exhibited in the organization of the Battalion in the following eloquent passage—"It happens felicitously enough for the purpose of accusation before you, that Brigham Young was the man of all others, whose influence carried that measure through with the Church. It was his American flag that was brought out to float over those hills for the first time; his drums beat, and his brave American speeches rang through the hearts of his people. I have given no name in my pamphlet, but it was he who said there— "You shall have your Battalion at once if it has to be a class of our Elders."

Returning to the next consecutive event of importance in President Young's career after his arrival at Council Bluffs, we find him starting in the Spring of 1847, at the head of 143 picked men, embracing 8 of the Twelve Apostles, across the unexplored Indian country in search of a new home for the Saints beyond the Rocky Mountains. The Pioneer band pursued their way over sage and saleratus plains, across unbridged rivers, and through mountain defiles, until their toilsome and weary journey of upwards of 1030 m. was terminated by the discovery of G. S. L. Valley, and the choice of it for the gathering place of the Saints. [The notion that the Mormons "discovered" the Great Basin was properly corrected by Dale L. Morgan in *The Great Salt Lake*, pp. 177, 189.] They then returned to Winter Quarters, Council Bluffs, where they arrived on the 31st of October, and an Epistle was issued on the 23rd of December, by the Twelve Apostles, noticing the principal events which had befallen the Saints since the expulsion from Nauvoo and the discovery of G. S. L. Valley. It also stated that it was in contemplation to re-organize the Church, according to the original pattern, with a First Presidency and Patriarch. Accordingly, at a Conference commencing on the 24th of December, 1847, and held at the "Log Tabernacle" in Kanesville, State of Iowa, the suggestion was brought before the Saints who "hailed it as an action which the state of the work at present demanded," and "Brigham Young was nominated to be the First President of the Church, and he nominated Heber C. Kimball and Willard Richards to be his two

Counsellors, which nominations were seconded and carried without a dissentient voice." The appointment was afterwards acknowledged at a General Conference held on the 6th of April, 1848, at the same place as the Conference at which the appointment was made. In the following May, Presidents Young and Kimball set out to return to Utah, at the head of a large company of Saints, and arrived on the 20th of September. In April, 1849, the newly appointed First Presidency issued from G. S. L. Valley their First General Epistle to the Saints scattered throughout the earth, which has been followed by 12 others issued from the same place semi-annually.

It may appropriately be said that a new era had now dawned upon the L. D. Saints at head quarters. They were free from persecuting neighbours, but they were also in the midst of Indian tribes, in a new country, whose resources were yet undeveloped, and a thousand miles from the great depots of trade and commerce. To conciliate the Indians and to adapt the resources of the country to the wants of the people needed the direction of a master mind. Such an one was exhibited in all the movements of the President. He had wisely led the Saints through the wilderness to their new home in the mountains, and now all the energies of his soul were brought into exercise in establishing them in it and promoting their prosperity. Action and not speculation distinguished him, which was infused into his immediate associates, and spread through all the settlers, so that little difficulty was experienced from the aborigines, and plenty speedily abounded on every hand.

When the State of Deseret was provisionally organized, Brigham Young was elected Governor of the same, and when it merged into the Territory of Utah, he was appointed by the President of the United States its Governor for the usual term of 4 years, and until his successor should be appointed and qualified. His first term expired in 1854. Col. Edward Steptoe was appointed to succeed him, and simultaneously with the making of the appointment at Washington he was at G. S. L. City and signed a petition in connection with the Secretary of State, the U. S. Judges of the Supreme Court for the Territory, all the Territorial Officers, numbers of merchants, and the officers of the United States army who were passing through Utah with Col. Steptoe to California, praying President Pierce to reappoint Gov. Young, "as he possessed in an eminent degree, every qualification necessary for the discharge of his official duties, and unquestioned integrity and ability," and was "decidedly the most suitable person that could be selected for that office." The Colonel has not accepted the appointment in his favour, consequently Brigham Young is still the legal Governor of the Territory, in pursuance of sec. 2, of the Organic Act. Many gratifying and indeed highly complimentary gratuitous testimonies have been publicly made regarding President Young, by distinguished individuals unconnected with the L. D. Saints, but our space forbids the insertion of more than the following from the pen of the late deeply lamented Captain Stansbury—"To me President Young appeared to be a man of clear, sound sense, fully alive to the responsibilities of the station he occupies, sincerely devoted to the good name and interests of the people over which he presides, sensitively jealous of the least attempt to under value or misrepresent them, and indefatigable in devising ways and means for their moral, mental, and physical elevation."

In his ecclesiastical capacity of President of the Church of Jesus Christ of Latter-day Saints, Seer and Revelator, his name is more prominently before the world than in any other. His course has continually been upward and onward, and in tracing the history of the Church, one fails to find any record made of him, otherwise than such as points him out in almost every action as the individual to occupy his present exalted position. He has the unlimited and universal love and esteem of all Saints, and his righteous example they endeavour to follow. In addition to the important offices of President of the Church of Jesus Christ of L. D. Saints, and Governor of Utah, he is also the Trustee in Trust for the Church, President of the Perpetual Emigrating Fund Company, President of the Deseret Theological Institute, &c., &c.

(36) HEBER CHASE KIMBALL, son of Solomon F. and Ann Kimball, was born, on the 14th of June, 1801, in the town of Sheldon, Frankland Co., Vermont. In 1811, at the time of the Embargo, he moved with his father's family to West Bloomfield, Ontario Co., New York. His father was a blacksmith by trade, but carried on the farming business in connection with it to a considerable extent. In 1806, the subject of our memoir commenced to attend school, and continued to do so until he was 14 years old, when he was put to work in his father's shop to learn blacksmithing. At the age of 19, his father having lost his property in the time of the war, he was left to seek a home for himself. After spending several weeks of sorrow and trouble, being cast abroad upon the world, his brother Charles offered to teach him the business of a potter, which he accepted, and continued with his brother until he was 21 years old. While he was living with his brother they moved into the town of Mendon, Monroe County, N. Y., and there established themselves as potters.

In Nov., 1823, H. C. Kimball married Miss Vilate Murray, an amiable young lady of 17 years. Immediately after his marriage, he purchased his brother's interest in the concern, and went into business for himself, which he carried on for upwards of 12 years.

Being brought up by strictly moral parents, he frequently attended the

Baptist Church while living in Mendon, and connected himself with that body. About 3 weeks after his union with the Baptists he heard some Elders of the L. D. Saints preach in the house of Phinehas Young, in the town of Victor, Ontario Co., N. Y., and was immediately convinced that they taught the truth and believed their testimony. The spirit now showed him many things relative to the Latter-day work, and he was so anxious to hear more from the Elders, that soon after, in company with Brigham Young and Phinehas Young and their wives, he went a distance of 125 miles to Pennsylvania and spent about six days attending the meetings of the Saints. In the month of April, 1832, he was baptized by Elder Alpheus Gifford and soon after was ordained an Elder. In the month of September of the same year he went to Kirtland with Brigham and Joseph Young and saw Joseph Smith for the first time. He spent a few days there and returned. In the Fall of 1833 he moved to Kirtland with his family and in the Spring of 1834 went up to Missouri with Joseph Smith, in "Zion's Camp," from whence he returned in the following July. He then resumed his business as a potter. On the 14th of Feb., 1835, he was chosen to be a member of the first Quorum of Twelve Apostles and was ordained to that office under the hands of Oliver Cowdery, David Whitmer, and Martin Harris. In connection with his colleagues of the Quorum of the Twelve he performed the mission to the Eastern States which was assigned to them on the 12th of March, travelling as far as Maine. He then returned to Kirtland and was present at the dedication of the Temple in 1836.

Early in the summer of 1837, a mission to England was formed, being the first foreign mission of the Church, and on or about the 1st of June, Heber C. Kimball "was set apart by the spirit of prophecy and revelation, prayer and the laying on of hands of the First Presidency, to preside over" the same. In pursuance of this appointment he left Kirtland on the morning of the 13th with O. Hyde, of the Quorum of the Twelve, Elder Willard Richards, and Priest Joseph Fielding, and proceeded to New York, where they were met by Elders John Goodson and Isaac Russell, and Priest John Snyder, who also accompanied the mission. They all sailed together from New York on the Ship *Garrick,* on the 1st of July, and landed at Liverpool on the 20th. After spending until the 22nd, they were led by the holy spirit to go to Preston, where they arrived in the midst of an election. Just as the coach reached its destination a flag was unfurled right before them, having upon it the motto—"Truth will prevail," at the sight of which their hearts rejoiced, and they cried aloud "Amen. Thanks be unto God, truth will prevail." Here they were requested by the *Rev.* James Fielding, brother of Priest Joseph Fielding, to preach twice on Sunday the 23rd in his chapel, which they complied with. They also preached in it on the Wednesday evening. The result of these meetings was the close of the *Rev.* Mr. Fielding's doors against the Elders, and the baptism of nine of his members, George D. Watt, now of Gt. Salt Lake City, being the first candidate. Thus was laid the foundation of the most important foreign mission of the Church in the last days, and we regret that want of space prevents us from quoting largely from the history of Elder Kimball's labours in these lands, which is replete with incidents affording the most thrilling pleasure, and shows the great success which attended his first mission to this country.

On the 20th of April, 1838, in company with Elders Hyde and Russell, he re-embarked on the *Garrick* for New York and reached Kirtland again on the 21st of May, immediately after which he removed to Missouri, arriving at Far West on the 25th of July. Here he suffered in the persecutions of that blood guilty State. He was present at the death of the beloved and brave David Patten, who had been shot by the mob. He frequently went to see Joseph and Hyrum Smith and other brethren, while confined in prison, but many times after travelling 40 or 50 m. for that purpose, he was refused the privilege by the jailors and guards. He remained in Missouri until April 26, 1839, on the morning of which, in compliance with the Revelation of July 8, 1838, the foundation of the Lord's house was relaid, and the Twelve took farewell of the Saints on the building spot for the same, and departed on their missions across the "Great Waters" to promulgate the Gospel. On the 14th of Sept., he landed again in England in company with Brigham Young and others. Among the labours of his second mission he established the work of the Lord in London, in connection with Elders Woodruff and Geo. A. Smith. He returned to Illinois, with President Young, leaving England on the 1st of April, 1841.

After returning to Nauvoo, and until the expulsion of the Saints from that city, the career of H. C. Kimball was that of the Twelve Apostles generally—in the winter seasons he was engaged in and around the city in the business of the Church, and the affairs of the municipality; in the summer seasons he laboured in the Eastern States, preaching, and building up the Church. With them he was absent at the martyrdom of Joseph and Hyrum, and with them returned to Nauvoo, shortly after which the Quorum was acknowledged the First Presidency of the Church. At the expulsion in 1846, he left Nauvoo in the month of February for the West and was one of the 143 Pioneers to G. S. L. Valley. On his return from this journey, and when the Church was re-organized with a First Presidency of Three, he was unanimously chosen First Counsellor to President Young, which office he still holds. The appointment was made at a Conference commencing on the 24th of Dec., 1847, at the "Log Tabernacle," in Iowa. In May, 1848, he returned to G. S. L. Valley, and on the organization of the Provisional State of Deseret, he was elected by the people, Lieutenant Governor, and also Chief Justice. After the State had merged into the Territory of Utah in 1850 he became President of the Council of the Legislative Assembly. He is also a member of the Perpetual Emigrating Fund Company.

The unwavering integrity, the benevolence, and urbanity of President Kimball endear him to the hearts of the Latter-day Saints universally, while the recollection of his labours in England, which we have before adverted to, fills the bosom of every Briton emancipated from the thraldom of sin and the chains of ignorance regarding true religion with a gratitude which such only can appreciate. [Elizabeth Wells Randall Cumming, wife of Utah's first non-Mormon governor, described the colorful and controversial Heber C. Kimball in a letter to her sister-in-law, Sarah Cumming, dated June 17, 1858: "In H. Kimball's reported speeches, he is coarse, vulgar, denunciatory. In conversation he is plain, sensible, straight forward & gentlemanly—full of humor & sometimes witty but nothing coarse or disagreeable as I saw him." Quoted in William Mulder and A. Russell Mortensen: *Among the Mormons* (New York, 1958), p. 310.]

(37) JEDEDIAH MORGAN GRANT was born at Windsor, Broome Co., State of New York, on the 21st of Feb. 1816. His parents were Joshua Grant and Athalia Grant (formerly Athalia Howard) who removed, when he was about 1 year old to Naples, Ontario Co., within the same State. At the period of J. M. Grant's boyhood, the country was very thinly settled, and in common with other children, he was deprived of early opportunities for an education. His father was a farmer and brought him up to the same occupatioin. When he was about 14 years old his parents removed westward to Erie Co., Pennsylvania. Nothing of special importance marked his life until he was about 16 years old, when he heard the doctrines of the Latter-day Saints. They awakened in him for the first time serious reflections upon the subject of religion, notwithstanding he had been taught the obligations of a Christian life by pious and devoted parents, who were members of a society called "The Christian Church," which held, among other doctrines, Baptism by immersion. He became convinced of the truth of Joseph Smith's mission, and on the 2nd of March, 1832, he was baptized into the Church. His parents also were baptized.

In 1833 he went to Kirtland, and in the Spring of 1834 he accompanied Joseph Smith to Missouri in what is known as Zion's Camp. On his return to Kirtland the following winter, he was ordained a member of the first Quorum of Seventy organized since the rise of the Church in this dispensation. The next Spring he commenced preaching, in which capacity he continued to act for 11 years, his labours being chiefly confined to the Middle and Southern States of the Union. Elder Grant usually attended the Annual Conferences of the Church, at the seat of the First Presidency, and in the winter of 1845–6 was ordained into the First Presidency of the Seventies. At the expulsion from Nauvoo, he left, in Feb. 1846, with the first camp of the Saints for the mountains, and was among the earliest families that arrived in and settled G. S. L. Valley. From this place he has performed two missions to the Eastern States. He has been connected with the Provisional Government and Legislature of Utah, and at the present time is Speaker of the House of Representatives. Besides these offices he has filled that of Brigadier General in the Nauvoo Legion, in which he is now Major General, and has been Mayor of G. S. L. City from its incorporation.

At a General Conference of the Church, held at G. S. L. City, in April, 1854, Elder Grant was called to the honoured and exalted position of Second Counsellor to President B. Young, rendered vacant by the decease of President Willard Richards, and was set apart to that calling, in which he now moves with the respect and esteem of the Latter-day Saints in all the world.

(38) JOHN SMITH, eldest son of Hyrum and Jerusha Smith (formerly Jerusha Barden), was born at Kirtland, Ohio, on the 22nd of September, 1832. With his father's family he went to Missouri in 1838, and with them removed to Illinois. After remaining a little at Quincy the family removed to Commerce (since Nauvoo), from which period he has shared in the various vicissitudes through which the Church has passed. He arrived in G. S. L. Valley in 1848 and has since occupied himself in farming pursuits. On the death of the Chief Patriarch, Father John Smith, the subject of this memoir succeeded to the vacant office, and, on the 18th of February, 1855, was ordained and set apart to that calling, which he had inherited from his father Hyrum, but at his death was not old enough to officiate in. At the April Conference following his ordination he was unanimously sustained in this appointment. [The office of Chief Patriarch is the only one in the Mormon Church that is held by virtue of blood ties. All have been descendants or relatives of "Father John Smith."]

(39) JOHN SMITH, or as he was familiarly called by the L. D. Saints, Father John Smith, was born at Derryville (now Manchester), Rockingham County, New Hampshire, on the 14th July, 1781. He was the son

of Asael and Mary Smith (formerly Mary Duty), and uncle to the Prophet Joseph. In 1815 he married Clarissa Lyman, by whom he had three children—George Albert, a member of the Quorum of the Twelve Apostles, and the Church Historian; Caroline; and John Lyman, at present presiding over the Swiss and Italian missions of the Church.

The subject of Joseph Smith's mission was introduced to the late Patriarch by his brother Joseph, the Prophet's father, which resulted in his baptism on the 9th of January, 1832, at a time of sickness near to death, and when the ice had to be cut to reach the water. He was at the same time ordained an Elder, and afterwards filled various offices until he was ordained to be the Chief Patriarch of the Church of Jesus Christ of L. D. Saints. His irreproachable and valued life was brought to a close on the 23rd of May, 1854, at his residence in Great Salt Lake City, after a month's severe illness. The chief events in the life of this venerable servant of God, after his admission into the Church, are thus detailed by the *Deseret News,* from which we quote—

"In 1833, he moved to Kirtland, Ohio, and in 1838 to Far West, Caldwell County, Missouri, and thence to Adamondi-Ahman, in Davies County, where he presided over that Branch of the Church until expelled by the mob in 1839, and arrived in Illinois on the 28th of February of that year. He located at Green Plains, six miles from Warsaw, where he put in a crop of corn, split rails, and performed much hard labour unsuited to his health and years, but obliged to be done for the support of his family. In June he moved to Commerce (since Nauvoo), and on the 4th of October was appointed to preside over the Church in Iowa, and on the 12th moved to Lee County to fulfil that mission.

"October, 1843, he moved to Macedonia, Hancock County, Illinois, having been appointed to preside over the Saints in that place. In January, 1844, he was ordained a Patriarch, and in November of that year, was driven by mobbers from Macedonia to Nauvoo, where he continued to administer patriarchal blessings, to the joy of thousands, until the 9th of February, 1846, when he was compelled by the mob violence of the free and Sovereign State of Illinois, to again leave his home and cross the Mississippi with his family, in search of a peaceful location, far off amid savages and deserts, in the valleys of the mountains.

"After passing a dreary winter on the right bank of the Missouri, at a place called Winter Quarters, he again took up the weary ox train march on the 9th of June, 1847, and reached this place September 23rd, where he presided over the Church in the mountains until January 1, 1849, when he was ordained Patriarch over the Church, under the hands of Presidents Brigham Young and Heber C. Kimball.

"He moved out of the Fort on to his city lot February, 1849, and this is the only spot on which he had been privileged to cultivate a garden two years in succession for the last twenty-three years.

"In addition to a vast amount of varied and efficient aid to thousands in the way of salvation, during his long and faithful ministry, he administered 5560 Patriarchal Blessings—which are recorded in seven large and closely written books, and has closed the arduous duties of a well occupied probation, and passed to a position of rest, where his works will nobly follow and honour him, and where he will continue his able counsels for the prosperity and welfare of Zion."

Index

THE JOHN HARVARD LIBRARY

The intent of
Waldron Phoenix Belknap, Jr.,
as expressed in an early will, was for
Harvard College to use the income from a
permanent trust fund he set up, for "editing and
publishing rare, inaccessible, or hitherto unpublished
source material of interest in connection with the
history, literature, art (including minor and useful
art), commerce, customs, and manners or way of
life of the Colonial and Federal Periods of the United
States . . . In all cases the emphasis shall be on the
presentation of the basic material." A later testament
broadened this statement, but Mr. Belknap's inter-
ests remained constant until his death.

In linking the name of the first benefactor of
Harvard College with the purpose of this later,
generous-minded believer in American culture the
John Harvard Library seeks to emphasize the impor-
tance of Mr. Belknap's purpose. The John Harvard
Library of the Belknap Press of Harvard University
Press exists to make books and documents
about the American past more readily
available to scholars and the
general reader.